Praise for *My Journey*

"*My Journey* is the story of a truly remarkable life. Robert Schuller chronicles the twists and turns of the road he has traveled from his birth on a farm in Iowa to the founder of a multi-million member ministry."

> —Dr. John C. Maxwell, founder, The
> INJOY Group

"Thirty-one years ago I prayed, 'God, if you can do this through Robert Schuller, can't you at least do something through me?' I continue to be inspired now, as I was then. Read this book."

> —Bishop Charles E. Blake, pastor, West
> Angeles Cathedral

"An amazing read. A truly inspirational autobiography that shows a new side of the man who refused to give up on his dreams. *My Journey* is a remarkable testament to the power of possibility thinking."

> —Zig Ziglar, author and motivational
> teacher

"By choosing to live in the present and be optimistic about the future, Dr. Schuller has empowered millions of people with the knowledge of Christ, and serves as an extraordinary role model for others to follow."

> —Richard DeVos, co-founder, Amway
> Corp.

"This is a life that not only instructs, but inspires."

> —The Reverend Theodore M.
> Hesburgh, C.S.C, President
> Emeritus, University of Notre Dame

"Dr. Robert H. Schuller's memoir chronicles the inspiring story of his rise from humble beginnings to become one of America's and the world's most influential and admired clergymen. With his remarkable warmth, sincerity, and positive spirit, Dr. Schuller tells the story of how he applied his Christian beliefs, vision, and dedication to create an enormously successful television ministry and build the Crystal Cathedral, one of the most resplendent places of worship ever constructed. In these pages, his readers will find a celebration of the empowering values of an extraordinary man of faith."

—Coretta Scott King

"If you want to feel better about life, keep this book handy for the time when things are not going well. Or when you just want to feel good!"

—Art Linkletter

"I have known the author of this book, *My Journey*, since the beginning of his career. Robert Schuller always said when a project was proposed 'It can be done and I can do it.' He has been an inspiration to millions."

—Ruth Stafford Peale, chairman,
Guideposts

MY
JOURNEY

MY JOURNEY

From an Iowa Farm to
a Cathedral of Dreams

ROBERT H. SCHULLER

HarperSanFrancisco
A Division of HarperCollinsPublishers

HarperCollins books may be purchased for educational, business, or sales promotional use. For information please write: Special Markets Department, HarperCollins Publishers, Inc., 10 East 53rd Street, New York, NY 10022.

HarperCollins Web site: http://www.harpercollins.com
HarperCollins®, ♠®, and HarperSanFrancisco™ are trademarks of HarperCollins Publishers, Inc.

FIRST EDITION
Designed by Joseph Rutt

Library of Congress Cataloging-in-Publication Data
Schuller, Robert Harold.
My journey : from an Iowa farm to a cathedral of dreams /
Robert H. Schuller. — 1st ed.
p. cm.
Includes index.
ISBN 0–06–251603–5 (cloth: alk paper)
ISBN 0–06–251604–3 (pbk.)
ISBN 0–06–008114–7 (Crystal Cathedral edition)
1. Schuller, Robert Harold. 2. Reformed Church in America — Clergy — Biography. I. Title
BX9543.S36 A3 2001
285.7'092 — dc21

[B]   2001039202

01 02 03 04 05 ❖/RRD 10 9 8 7 6 5 4 3 2 1

To my parents, Jennie and Anthony Schuller,
who gave me life and the faith to follow
the path on my life's journey.

CONTENTS

ACKNOWLEDGMENTS

I am profoundly indebted and passionately grateful to the special people without whom this autobiography would never have come together.

First to Howard and Marjorie Kelley. For their innumerable hours of research providing dates and details of forty-plus years of the Crystal Cathedral Ministry. For their decades of encouragement and service, and finally for convincing me that this story had to be told.

For Barbara Ann Evans. For once again making sense of my scribbling and spending hours transcribing my words—all handwritten with a ballpoint pen on more than seven hundred yellow legal-size sheets of paper.

For my brothers and sisters whose "I remember" stories stimulated my memory.

For each of my children and grandchildren. For their willingness to become part of a public story.

For Arvella DeHaan Schuller. For giving me, through love and laughter, the priceless material from which this true story evolved. For once again prodding me to move ahead when I became unenthused about this project. And for retaining a keen memory for names, dates, events, and details that thread a meaning in our years together. For reading and checking, the multiplied hundreds of hours she did what she alone could do: read every word of every sentence of the entire manuscript once, twice, and a third time to make sure that no errors in fact would creep in. The book can be trusted for her honesty in my story as it appears in print.

Carol Schuller Milner. For enlightening me on the beauty of memoir-styled autobiographies and providing the creative strategy that proved liberating and life-giving to me in the telling of my story . . . and for keeping me in the "emotion and heart" of the story, adding her own poetic touch to these pages. For her numerous hours of research of my "early years" and doting over the story and its many deadlines, coordinating all aspects and parties involved. She has truly been an artistic and creative assistant in this project.

William Patrick. In over thirty of my published books, never have I had the pleasure of an editor that brought the combined skills, talents, and dedication to a book as he has done in this project. Beyond a doubt he's a marvel in skill and creative talent—a talent that led him to perfect the flow to this story. For his honesty and objective advice on content, for giving this manuscript a layer of sophistication, and for his constant commitment toward the integrity of the craft that makes me look like the writer I wish I had always been.

Lois de la Haba and John Loudon of HarperCollins Publishers. For believing my story was interesting enough for publication.

Finally to the many people who knew of this project that consumed three years of my life; who prayed for me and gave me encouragement.

And, of course, to all of the great people who did so much to lead me on *my journey.* If all of those to whom I was indebted were mentioned, then these pages would have passed the two thousand mark easily.

Thank you and God bless you all.

INTRODUCTION

When first presented with the idea of writing my autobiography, I was unenthusiastic. In fact, I resisted. I truly was not motivated to leave behind such a book.

However, my family, my friends, and some of my advisors felt that for future generations—especially those people who will come to the Crystal Cathedral in the decades and centuries ahead—there should be a reliable document detailing the development of this ministry and the life of the person who has been its primary force.

In 1955 I accepted a call from the Classis (governing board) of California of the Reformed Church in America to establish a church in central Orange County. Certainly the scope of the ministry that resulted is something no one could have predicted from its all-too-humble beginnings.

I have said many times, and have meant it sincerely and honestly, that I couldn't have done this by myself. Over and over again, God has brought the right person to me for the right job at the right time. Yet I also know that without my energy and my commitment, the ministry here more than likely would not have happened.

So where did the vision come from?

My maternal great-grandfather, Gerrit Van Amerongen, was, from what I can learn, a dreamer of great and daring dreams. He was what I call a classic "possibility thinker." His bloodline was that of those big-thinking Hollanders who conceived of building the dikes, pumping out the ocean, and using the vast bottom to expand the shores and the size of their nation. "Nothing is impossible," they believed.

Then there's my Grandpa Schuller. He was a simple, ordinary man by most standards. Yet after his arrival in America, his drive for survival allowed him to surmount the odds and become a successful farmer and respected citizen in his community.

So what am I to make of this heritage? What's the influence of the gene pool that has swirled in my bloodstream for more than seventy years?

When, at last, I made the decision to write this memoir, my wife challenged me to ask myself certain questions and to provide answers, allowing them to become the basic structure of the book:

- Who am I?

- Where did I come from?

- Why am I here?

- How did it all happen?

Taking up her challenge has awakened in me a desire for self-discovery, but I must confess that though the process has been fascinating, the results have been at times a bit obscure and murky, even daunting. Now that I'm in my seventies, remembering my early years doesn't come with ease. Thus I've relied heavily on others' accounts, and I've used storytelling techniques to bring to life certain crucial moments that my limited recollections otherwise would have left as drab accounts of colorful experiences I know to be true.

In trying to recollect my life, I've often felt like a sleuth attempting to solve a nagging mystery. At other times, the process has been like a familiar drive I make along one section of the Pacific Coast.

It's a weekly trip I take from the fast-paced life of central Orange County to a lazy Southern California stretch of coastal beauty. I travel toward Laguna Beach—south of Newport Beach, between Corona del Mar and Dana Point. As I drive the north-to-south route, the elevation drops to sea level and the haze begins to thicken.

I can predict the view. There are rolling hills dropping to touch that point where waves that have been traveling silently through the Pacific for thousands of miles touch the sandy beach of mainland America. The Pacific Coast Highway rises and dips along that ocean edge that marks the end of their journey.

I search the surface of the ocean. Catalina Island is fog-hidden in the distance, twenty-two miles off-shore. The mystery of the morning mist and the silent fog demands that I slow down. Caution takes command of my hands on the steering wheel and my foot on the gas pedal. I have surrendered leadership to this misty, mysterious fog. Even though I know the path, I must watch for the familiar landmarks and signposts. I must be careful not to get lost, off track.

So it is in the writing of this book. If I'm not careful, I might get lost in the mist and fog of questions about the mystery of heredity and lose sight of the signposts that have directed my life's journey. These landmarks are the defining moments and the guiding principles that have motivated and directed me through the years and have thus become the navigating system for this account.

As a result of my wife's prompting, and of this cautious introspection, this book has become the most honest and authentic account of my life that I'm able to provide.

Despite occasional mists and fogs, I have always stood on the edge of tomorrow, my vision always the distant horizon. This book explores the mystery of how I learned to do just that and more. I now see that I've been living on the edge of tomorrow every moment for fifty years of my professional and family life. I continue to dream big for God, "*Why not?*" My prayer is that you will be inspired to do the same.

Robert H. Schuller

I am a part of all that I have met.
Tennyson

PART I

SMALL BEGINNINGS

*There are infinite possibilities in little
beginnings if God is in it.*
—*Robert H. Schuller*

I

You can go anywhere from nowhere.

My life is witness to that.

I was born at the dead-end of a dirt road that had no name and no number—in a flood.

It's September 16, 1926, and it's raining hard enough in Sioux County, Iowa, to flood the Floyd River, that usually meanders lazily through the back pastureland of our family farm.

It's raining so hard in this northwest corner of Iowa (near the South Dakota and Minnesota borders) that just eight miles west, a father and a son drown in what would come to be known as the "Sioux County Flood of 1926."

But it isn't raining hard enough to keep Anthony Schuller (pronounced "Skuller") from his Model T Ford. In the downpour he ushers his four children—a girl age twelve, a boy age eleven, a girl age nine, and a girl age seven—out of the house and into his black automobile.

Lovingly, Tony settles his labor-intense Jennie onto the seat beside him. It's been seven years since Jennie's last childbirth, and everyone had assumed she'd passed that season of life. Jennie's four brothers and three sisters were shocked, then seriously concerned, when they learned the news. "She's too old to bear another child," the sisters would confide to one another after church services. They would meet and whisper and fear the day of delivery. These seven younger siblings had been raised in large part by Jennie, looking up to her and listening to her as a second mother. Jennie was well past the prime of youth, and everyone knew it, and everyone knew the risks.

This mile-long dirt road is the only way out, if it *is* a way out. If the road has turned to deep mud, Tony worries, will this Model T Ford make it to Jennie's mother's house in town? Then, after they drop off the children there, will it make it back to the farmhouse before Jennie delivers?

Anthony pulls away from the small, white clapboard house. The land is flat beneath a canopy of dangerous and darkened skies. Sioux County, Iowa, knows almost all the natural drama a county could know: windstorms, thunderstorms, and twisters; snowstorms, duststorms, and lightning. The farmers are often held hostage by nature's fury, but Jennie, as usual, gets her way. Even the roads must succumb to her insistence. And so they drive slipping, sliding, but not sinking in the mud, with sheets of water slamming from the dark skies down onto the metal roof of their car. They slush and plough that first long mile, then all the way to the town of Alton, Iowa, and the home of Jennie's Dutch-born "Moeder" and "Vader."

Alton was a town the census bureau could easily overlook. After all, between the years of 1920 and 1930, its population grew by a total of only four. But these Dutch, reputed for their vocal views and their staunch judgments on many of the day's moral and religious issues, were hard to ignore.

The rough ride delivers them to the front of the porch-encircled house. With open arms, Grandma and Grandpa Beltman welcome their oldest daughter's four children out of the pouring rain.

The reason for their visit is never mentioned. It's the cultural belief of that time and place that children should know nothing of human birth. If a cow were calving . . . yes, the children participated. If a litter of piglets were being birthed . . . yes. But a baby brother or sister . . . absolutely not. The boy and three girls would remain uninformed and unknowing—until morning came, when they would be surprised by a new baby. Did they not harbor suspicions about their mother's enlarging belly? Probably not, for most farm wives had bellies large enough to camouflage such a change. To innocent eyes, Jennie looked no different. Little did the children know that very soon now they would need to make room for a new arrival at their dinner table, in their bed, beside their fire, and in the affections of their mother and father.

So, shrouded in secrecy and battered by the storm, Tony and Jennie retrace the route, back through the town of Alton, across the bridge over the emboldened Floyd, down the muddy dirt road that causes the wheels and motor of their little car to moan with a labor that echoes Jennie's own cries.

They make it back to the dead-end farm with no name and no number. The downpour continues as Tony stops the car, covers his heavy wife with a raincoat, then holds her tightly to keep her from stumbling along the short, uneven path to the house.

The house is cold in an autumn chill, but at least they're dry and safe. That is, of course, provided that the doctor who's been called shows up. The question now is, Can his car make it through the mud?

Jennie gives a shrill cry, out of character for this strong farm wife.

Tony nervously clicks the tip of his finger on the white sill of the window. He isn't trying to ignore her. It's just that he's used up all of his comforting words. He can't honestly say with any conviction that Dr. Gleysteen will be coming. Could the doctor really make it through the muddy trenches? Tony can hardly see through the rain-flooded window. Still, he gazes out through the pane.

Jennie cries out again. She's beginning to sound desperate. Anthony feels desperate too. He's confident as can be helping an animal give birth, but terribly intimidated with this woman. After seven years, will he remember what to do?

He should return to her side, but he doesn't want to leave the window. He wants to bring her good news.

Then—oh, sweet relief!—he hears the doctor's car. Now he can answer. "Dr. Gleysteen's here, Jennie. He's here."

Minutes later Jennie makes a final shriek. With Dr. Gleysteen's assistance, and as Tony watches, I come into the world, in the middle of a storm and on the edge of my first tomorrow.

II

Jennie Beltman and Anthony Schuller first met in church fifteen years before the stormy night of my birth. The parishioners were a mixture of Dutch families of all classes. Where did this poor farm-boy, Anthony, ever find the courage to court this young lady from an "upper-crust" family? Jennie's father, my Grandpa John Henry Beltman, was the owner of a large farm inherited from his father. There were no corporate CEOs in Sioux County—certainly no celebrities or aristocrats. The closest thing was a landowner. If you owned enough land, you were "upper class."

To further complicate Tony's romantic matters, these lords of the land would hire poor boys, like the orphaned Tony, to do their daily dirty work. Tony was a servant, which definitely made him "low class."

Tony's father, my Grandpa Schuller, had left the Holland of his birth, taking his wife and all that they had—mostly poverty—to America. They joined their fellow immigrants in the new Dutch colony that had settled in the gently rolling plains of northwest Iowa.

Here, in Alton, Tony's poor parents had built their unlordly sod house from the skin of the virgin soil. Firmly netted together by wiry roots of native prairie grass, this tough hide could be cut and peeled like the skin of an orange, leaving the deep, rich, black soil ready to be cultivated. The sod could then be cut into firm squares and stacked square upon square, creating a home of earthen bricks. You could quite literally build "something" from "nothing," a lesson from the prairie that's been embedded in my soul for as long as I can remember.

In his sod house, my Grandpa Schuller would dream his dreams of a new life in this new land. Here he would make love to his wife, who would give birth to nine boys and one girl. Every Sunday, they would go to the church where eventually one of these nine boys, Anthony, would begin to dream of becoming a preacher. He would imagine himself standing in a long-tailed black suit reading from the great Bible and preaching a strong and stern sermon in the most prestigious building in town: the First Reformed Church of Alton.

But this young Tony Schuller's dream to become a preacher would be shattered. Both of his parents would die young, leaving the children to fend for themselves. Tony dropped out of school in the sixth grade to take the only work available as a helping hand on the nearby farms.

Farming would become Tony's life. He would never travel more than fifty miles from Alton until he would make an all-important six-hundred-mile trip to Chicago, to witness the fulfillment of a dream: his youngest son's ordination to the ministry.

But every Sunday, without fail, Tony would dress up in church clothes: suit, shirt, tie, and well-buffed black shoes. Every man, woman, and child in the Dutch colony had one set of these dress-up clothes. Every Sunday the men of the community would replace their patched and worn denim overalls, their heavy work boots tied ankle-high and crusted with mud and manure, and their blue shirt with its large red handkerchief stuffed in one of the two pockets, with that one set of "good" clothes.

Jennie was first pointed out to Tony as the eldest of the eight children of the wealthy and imposing man who often filled the preacher's shoes. As such, she was the "princess" to his "pauper."

In the Dutch culture of Iowa, the minister was called the "Dominee," a title that has the same root as the English word "dominate." And the Dutch minister was definitely the "dominant" local figure. One might disagree with the Dominee, might even dissect and debate his sermon behind his back at Sunday dinner, but anyone who came face-to-face with the Dominee treated him with respect and reverence.

When the Dominee in Alton was sick or on a mission, Jennie's father substituted in this venerable role that Tony so admired. And Jennie was this "lay preacher's" delight. Her father would spend his last healthy years in my mother's home, where he would sit in the big, expensive wooden rocker that was his private chair.

My grandfather was always proud when I visited home after going away to school. He was almost smug about the fact that the last and unplanned child of his firstborn daughter was in college and then seminary, preparing to be a formal Dominee. After all, the Dominee ranked with doctors in the highest class. John Henry had been only a "lay preacher," and Tony wasn't even that. `

If Tony had married "higher up," then that meant that my mother had married "lower down." Why?

The story goes that, as the eldest of seven children, Jennie had become the chief cook, maid, and wash-girl. Her blue-blooded mother, prosperous though the family was, still couldn't afford servants as her own mother had. She simply adapted Jennie to the house-servant role.

Jennie's mother, Jacomina Beltman, my grandma, was daughter to a Holland higher-up, said to have been a baron in the Netherlands. Jacomina was easily angered, rather spoiled, and somewhat lacking in warmth and affection. I don't remember Grandma, but many accounts depict her as a most unlikeable person—swift to pout and put down "lower-class folks" with mean words and intimidating looks and gestures.

I think it's fair to assume that my mother was anxious to get out from under this domineering and demeaning influence. Is it possible that she said yes out of desperation to the first man who pro-

posed to her? Or was the contrast between the behavior and personality of her controlling mother and this gentle, kind, soft-spoken
Tony so dramatic and compelling that she didn't hesitate to say yes
when he proposed?

Whatever the case, the marriage was a major event. The grand
wedding picture, taken at the home of my Grandpa Beltman, hangs
in my home today. As one of the top men in the county, Jennie's
father had built one of the grandest homes in that countryside. It
was not the typical farmhouse. It was equipped with rare state-of-
the-art services, such as electric lighting and running water
(pumped by a carbide gas generator), and a coal-burning furnace.
There were seven rooms downstairs and five bedrooms upstairs, as
well as a bath on each of the two floors. Wide porches curled
around the sides of both the first and second floors. All of this open,
outdoor balcony space is filled with guests for the wedding picture.
All of my mother's seven siblings, all of my father's eight brothers
and one sister, plus assorted uncles and aunts, cousins, and other
close relatives of the bride and groom—all are in the photo dressed
in their Sunday best. My mother looks slim and beautiful in her
floor-length white wedding dress, my father handsome in a black
suit with a formal white bow-tie.

Were my mother and dad really in love? I'm sure they were—
though because of their culture and time they rarely showed physical
signs of affection, like a hug or a kiss or holding hands. I never once
heard them say to each other, "I love you." I never once noticed their
eyes light up with a flirtatious glance or affectionate twinkle. On the
other hand, I never once saw or heard a sign of verbal or physical
abuse from one to the other, though my mother did inherit an intensity and passion that could have been interpreted as anger. I experienced that side of her often firsthand, but I always suspected that I'd
earned the heated reaction. I never read it as a lack of love.

She stands so elegantly regal of posture in her wedding photograph. In all of her seventy-nine years she always stood just this

ramrod-straight—shoulders back and head held high. Even when she lost her trim figure, she didn't lose that noble bearing. It was in the tradition passed down from her mother and grandmother—and yes, from her father too. He was always a pleasantly proud man, strong but sweet. He always said, "Walk up straight, Jennie. Lift your head up high!" Whether sitting in his huge wooden rocker with its upholstered back and seat of black leather, or walking around the house, he was always straight as an arrow. And he expected as much from me—his grandson—and told me so! Even as the ever-present smoke from his famous Dutch cigars swirled around his head—well covered with gray hair in his ninety-fifth year—you could always see Grandpa through the smoke, head held high.

III

It's March of 1927. Jennie walks back down the aisle of the nineteenth-century Dutch church, Tony at her side. I'm in her arms, six months old, and she's not happy.

First, the Dominee could have been more convincing in his delivery of his statement on the importance of baptism. Second, Tony could have held his head a little higher. After all, this was the holy baptism of his son. Third, her mother's gaze.

Jacomina's haughty, satisfied, approving stare declaring her victory. Jennie can't stomach the fact that she's just baptized her infant son with the Christian name that her mother chose. Jennie wanted the name Harold Robert. Her mother, the affluent Mrs. Beltman, insisted upon Robert Harold.

Tony escorts Jennie in silence from the church to the car and then to the party in their little country house. He will do all he can to avoid the coming cyclone of catty conflict. He has learned the art well during their fifteen years of marriage.

The tiny farmhouse overflows with Jennie's siblings and their spouses and children, along with Tony's. It's a good thing the place sits on such a large parcel of land.

Soon the celebration is interrupted by Grandma's ostentatious entry. As always, Grandma arrives riding in the back seat of her rich husband's new Ford. Her husband sits alone at the wheel. This is customary—not for Sioux County, but for Grandpa and Grandma Beltman. Story has it that everywhere she went, she did so in the back seat, pious and proud, with her landowning, lay-preaching, dignified husband playing the role of chauffeur at the wheel.

Jennie seems pleased with her home, most of her guests, and in particular her new son in his long, white baptismal gown, made of soft, sheer Batiste, delicately hand stitched. Its modest Netherlander embroidery frames an infant's face of fresh innocence.

Jennie is pouring coffee into cups and saucers laid systematically in rows on her kitchen table. As Jennie prepares to serve, Grandma sits like the queen in the living room off the kitchen, presiding over the gossipy chatter.

As is customary, only women are in the parlor. Jacomina's husband, John Henry, is outdoors with the other men, enjoying their cigars. Jacomina can see him in the shade of the front yard. It's an unusually pleasant and quiet day, a welcome respite in a generally windy and still-cold March.

Jacomina turns her gaze back to the slumbering child upon whom she's lavishing great expectations. With every reference to her grandson among the women, Jacomina boasts the lovely and proud name he's been given: Robert. She raises her voice slightly, with accent and injury especially designed for her daughter's ears— "Robert Harold," she touts. Jennie's nerves grow frayed, but she manages to shake off her exasperation.

Grandma goes on, "Robert Harold—I insisted on his name, you know." They know; oh yes, they know. She insists on everything.

Jennie invites her guests to come for their coffee and cake. All rise, except Grandma.

Jennie, as her familial role has always demanded, picks up one of the cups and saucers and brings it to her mother. If only they might engage in one moment of affection and common acceptance. Jennie places the cup and saucer on her mother's lap-tray, resting the china upon a large lace doily. Then Jennie sits beside her.

Grandma says again how glad she is that Jennie finally saw the necessity of giving this child the noble name of Robert. Jennie takes a deep breath, summoning the courage to set the record straight.

"His name is Robert . . . ," Jennie begins, then pauses, trembling slightly.

"But," she continues—pausing again as she clutches her hanky—"we'll call him by his middle name."

(Gulp.)

"We'll call him . . . Harold," she concludes.

Clink! Jacomina drops her cup onto the saucer.

Silence.

Still . . . silence.

Grandma rises. Jennie reaches to offer a helping hand, but Grandma shrugs away the gesture. The elder of the two approaches the kitchen with her cup and saucer, now slightly chipped. Everyone is aware that Grandma Jacomina Beltman is upset and tense, yet she keeps her head raised in pride. She reenters the living room, nods to her daughter as a final note of congratulation, glances at the sleeping "Harold" lying on the lap of his eldest sister, twelve year-old Jessamine, and walks out the door.

As Grandma steps onto the porch, John Henry enters the living room through the kitchen. He watches the feathered hat and raised linen bustle of his wife disappear from view.

Jennie looks sheepish. Grandpa comes to her side, placing a tender and understanding hand on her shoulder. John Henry stands with his firstborn daughter, Jennie, while a living room filled with

Jacomina's descendents reach chins over shoulders to catch a view of their matriarch through the parlor window. With her long skirt hoisted up in large Dutch hands, Grandma Jacomina marches alone outdoors, down the dirt road, determined, if need be, to walk all the way back to the town of Alton.

More often than not, this is how Grandma Jacomina Beltman left our farm. She arrived in the back seat of the Ford, chauffeured in grand style by her husband, and after an inevitable argument with her daughter left the house on foot.

Jacomina had heard stories of her own mother's courtship and marriage to the dashing aristocrat who lived the life of high society in the Netherlands. Given that heritage, Grandma would never be allowed to think of herself as anything but a Dutch baron's daughter, her mother a beauty from the upper crust. Sadly, Grandma expected her life to measure up to that fanciful image.

Jacomina's father was a flamboyant dreamer of great dreams. Dashing, handsome, and wealthy, Baron Gerrit Van Amerongen of the Netherlands had no ambition to spend his life in the big estate that was Amerongen Castle. His dream was to take his inheritance, sail to the New World, buy vast acreage, and start a new colony that might be his own legacy. He—as a privileged child—had grown up hearing the stories of his fellow countrymen who, two centuries before, had sailed their ships to found a Dutch colony in the far-off New World. "New Amsterdam," they had named their colony. The year was 1628. Years later, when this Dutch colony became a part of the British Empire, the name would be changed to "New York."

Gerrit Van Amerongen was also inspired by other Dutch colonists who had dared go to this New World. Albertus Van Raalte, for example—a religious leader of an earlier century—had set sail and founded a colony in what would be called western Michigan. He had named the town "Holland." And there was another Dutch colony in the middle of Iowa settled by devout Dutch Reformed believers who had named their settlement "Pella." From that out-post, Dutchmen would travel to the western edge of the state, there establishing a branch colony named after the royal house of Orange in the Netherlands—a colony that would become the county capi-tal. So Orange City, three miles from the little town of Alton, would become the seat of power in the new Dutch settlement in Sioux County, Iowa.

Baron Gerrit Van Amerongen dreamed of starting his own new colony in a vast region of this New World called Texas.

In Holland, this baron shared his dangerous dream with the aristo-cratic beauty he came to love, and she agreed to marry him. Together they would take his fortune—so the dream went—purchase six thou-sand acres in Galveston, and with the exploding wealth of Texas live as an American "baron"—the kind of life his wife deserved to live.

Everything went as planned until a hurricane hit the Texas coast without warning. The Gulf of Mexico exploded over the totally unprepared Dutch colony and wiped out my rich great-grandpa, Gerrit Van Amerongen. He retreated to the nearest Dutch colony, in Orange City, Iowa. There his beautiful but shattered wife would bear her first child, Jacomina, who would become my grand-mother. But Mrs. Gerrit Van Amerongen could never face up to their financial disaster, and the humiliating decline in her social standing that had come with it. The name Van Amerongen—she still fantasized—would be as grand and noble as the Dutch names along the East Coast of these United States. Names like Vanderbilt and Roosevelt. Or even a name like that of a local landowner, the family known as Beltman, future in-laws to her Jacomina.

So my grandmother was shaped by the elitist imagination of her disappointed mother.

"You must never forget who you are," my great-grandmother had insisted. "You are a rich baron's daughter. You will not do house-work! You will never be a maid, housekeeper, cook, laundry woman, or childkeeper, and . . . you will marry well."

Jacomina did marry well, but not well enough to fulfill the grand self-image she had been raised with. And so my mother became the house-servant that her own mother couldn't afford to hire.

"No, Jennie cannot go to high school! I need her at home. Yes, her brother Henry will go to the Academy, Hope College, and Princeton Seminary, but Jennie's place is in the washroom and kitchen."

As my mother and grandmother parted ways on that day of the baptism, they had no idea that, years later, Grandma Jacomina would regain the upper hand with respect to my name.

But when I became "Robert" instead of "Harold," it was not because of Jacomina's indomitable will. It was because of my own discovery, as a young man, of the formidable power of my own free will to create my own destiny.

IV

It's the middle of the day. I'm in the house, just shy of my toddler years. Dad is working in the toolshed, mending horse tack. My brother Henry is with him, working on other fix-it chores.

Someone knocks on the front door and my mother goes to answer. It's a stern-looking man, gray-bearded and black-suited. He has a wide-brimmed hat that shadows his eyes.

Jennie greets him, a familiar figure, as she rescues me from the hard wood floor. The man knows her parents—John Henry, the lay preacher, and his demanding wife, Jacomina. He knows of her brother, Henry Beltman, graduate of Princeton and now doing missionary work in China. Jennie hasn't done as well for herself, but no matter; she's a pious woman and he respects her. He asks kindly how she's doing, and Jennie invites him in for coffee and rhubarb bars.

It's the annual "Haus Bezoek," or "house visitation," when the Dominee calls on all members of his church individually to inquire of their spiritual condition and hear any necessary repentance of sins.

I'm on my mother's lap now. I like the rhubarb bars and lick the sweetened fruit off her large, callused finger as she talks to her Dominee. She speaks of ordinary things, interspersed with sacred musings. She sets me down and plays a hymn on the piano. She suggests that this hymn might be nice to hear the next Sunday. The Dominee nods as he exits and says he'll visit with Tony out at the toolshed before leaving.

Dad is sitting, looking down, when the Dominee enters, but he rises immediately to greet him. Henry, the eldest son of Tony and Jennie (named after John Henry and Uncle Henry, Jennie's missionary brother), is quiet like his father. He stands and mutters, "Hello, Dominee," then returns to working with his hands, something that he loves.

The Dominee says that he's come to pay Tony a house visit. Tony says that he's grateful and asks if the Dominee has stopped to visit Jennie already.

The Dominee's face sours as he stiffly nods his head. He confirms the visit with Jennie, mentioning the moment of piano music and adding that he's always grateful for her input into the order of his Sunday services. "But I didn't come to give her 'Haus Bezoek,'" the Dominee insists.

This last declaration is quite emphatic, and it's made with such a dismissive look that Tony is confused.

Then the Dominee tips his chin down and gazes up with piercing eyes from beneath his brimmed hat.

In a Dutch dialect that Henry uses still today when retelling this story, the Dominee explains, "Tony, don't you know that Jennie was 'raised at the foot of a prophet'?"

Every Dutch family knows that expression.

Jennie is "special."

She is of a "pious family."

She is of the "social elite."

She comes from "good blood."

The Dominee then delivers a vicious blow. His eyes narrow as if he's peering into Tony's soul.

"Tony, Jennie doesn't need visitation," he says. "You do."

Tony's face turns ashen. Then it turns red—the result of both embarrassment and anger. Henry thrusts his head down toward his work to avoid the conflict, and to avoid having to look upon our father's shame. The absurd view that the Dominee is projecting— that social standing ensures piety, and that somehow Tony's stand- ing means that he isn't a righteous man—makes young Henry burn. Everyone knows Tony to be a man of intense honesty and kindness, a very sincere and spiritual soul! Henry is proud to call him father. But Henry holds back. To challenge the Dominee would bring instant reproof from his father. No matter what, no one confronts the Dominee.

Tony thanks the minister, says his goodbyes, and returns to the tack. Then he and Henry resume their work, saying nothing.

The Dominee was the unquestioned core of our community. Religion was the unquestioned core of our humanity. And it was only religion that kept Tony from cursing on that tempestuous day.

The Ten Commandments formed the backbone of our moral and spiritual conscience. They were the center of our lives. "Sins" were labeled and listed. It was very clear what was allowed and what wasn't allowed around Sioux County.

Profanity was a sin. "Gosh," "darn," "golly"—these were consid- ered to be profane no-no's. Such language was considered to be even more sinful than "barn talk," which was used only to convey the words' literal meaning, never to belittle a human being and *never* around women and children!

S-H-I-T was what you stepped in while walking through the cow pasture. A B-I-T-C-H was a mother canine. And D-A-M-N-E-D is what we kids would be if Mom ever heard these words escape from our mouths!

Dancing, too, was a sin. *No Dancing!* was the eleventh commandment of the Reformed Dutch in Sioux County. As teenagers, some would sneak up to the roof of the drugstore opposite the second-story dance hall in Alton, from which outpost they could see the "Catholics" enjoying a Friday night on the town. Imagine the uproar in our church when Lawrence Welk came through for a show!

Alcohol? There was that occasional rumor of someone in town making beer in the basement in celebration of "harvest" time. But in the Schuller home, strong drink was taboo, though a tablespoon of whisky or brandy could be used for medicinal relief for what today would be called the flu.

Tobacco? Now here was a different story. Tobacco was very much a part of our culture. After all, in the Netherlands cigars and pipes were major commodities. Later, when Dutch folk came to America, cigarettes were added to the list of "acceptables." Most men smoked, though my dad never did. I never knew why, but it wasn't because it was considered a sin—at least not for a man. When my family visited the relatives around town or on a nearby farm, smoke from the men's indulgence filled the house, but if a *woman* had smoked, she would have been considered a harlot.

I was never allowed to see a movie. They were frowned upon in Alton. I didn't see one until I reached high school. On our senior class "skip day," a bunch of us went to a faraway town called Hawarden and saw whatever film was playing in the movie-house there. Though we knew it wasn't encouraged, we hadn't been told it was a "sin," so none of us felt too guilty until later, when movies were also added to the "list."

Movies with naked bodies on display just didn't exist in that world, nor did magazines with sexual content. Boys would joke about pictures showing women in their underwear in the Sears-Roebuck catalog, but that was generally the extent of "explicit" content in our world.

And sex? Never before the wedding night!

We also believed in keeping the Sabbath day holy. That meant that Sunday was only for church and family. No stores would ever be open on Sunday. No fishing—my favorite pastime—was allowed on Sunday. Tools such as scissors, hoes, hammers, saws, and the like couldn't be used on Sunday save in an emergency.

Children in Sioux County were constantly reminded of these "do's" and "don'ts" at home, around the farm, in town, in school, and every Sunday in church. The Dominee's tone would grow quite serious and stern as he reminded us young ones not to participate in these wicked temptations. The Sunday school teacher would teach us in her nasal tone to be good little children. Catechism instructors would dissect the legalities of scripture, supporting the moral codes of our culturally ingrained religion.

Church was my world, and its views were my precincts and my boundaries—never to be challenged or questioned. All towns had a church (or two or three), and most of the churches belonged to the Dutch Reformed denomination—or at least that was my impression as a boy. Alton did have a large and prosperous Saint Mary's Catholic Church (always mentioned in whispers), but there was no Catholic church in Orange City.

So many teachings of our religious community simply were never debated. Once, as we were getting into our car to participate in a funeral procession, I asked my mother why we didn't just walk to the graveyard. After all, it was only across the street and about a hundred yards down the road. We walked everywhere else—why in the world wouldn't we walk this short distance? Mother shushed me and curtly said, "Harold, the Catholics walk to cemeteries. We drive!" It was never mentioned again.

First Reformed Church in Newkirk, where my family attended, was one of the more newly constructed houses of worship. Not because of its important standing—on the contrary, Newkirk was (and still is) the most sparsely populated of all the surrounding towns—but because the original building, with its beautiful Dutch architecture, had been lost in a fire one year after my birth.

It didn't have a parking lot, even though by the time I was born cars had arrived. Horse-drawn carriages had given way to Fords and Chevrolets, but the barn, having survived the flames of 1927, still stood. Instead of holding horses, however, the barn had become the favored place for men to relieve themselves before and after services. The women would go to the outhouse, but the men used the barn walls.

Every church had a main lobby where, during the winter, coats and scarves would be hung below the hat racks. Most of the devout farmers carefully placed next to their black hats their stubbed-out cigar butts, to be lighted up again with all of the others when church let out. In their first moments of freedom, they would stand on the lawn beside the church (if they didn't need to visit the barn) and discuss, debate, argue, criticize, and occasionally even compliment the preacher's forty-five minute sermon and fifteen-minute prayer—all in a cloud of smoke.

Every family had its own pew, which they occupied every one of the fifty-two Sundays—without fail—each year. The very back row was the Schuller row—seven seats total. Here I would drop my nickel in the offering plate every Sunday.

There were two church services. The afternoon service was the "modern" one: hymns were sung, and the language was one hundred percent English (which they called "American"). The morning service was entirely in Dutch. No hymns were sung—only Psalms in Dutch. The sermons, in both Dutch and English, weren't "Bible lessons"; rather, they were lessons in "Reformed theology," based on the Heidelberg Catechism written in the sixteenth century at Heidelberg University in Germany.

As children, we were expected to attend Sunday school for one hour, then the afternoon adult service. In addition, we participated in midweek catechism classes, learning the doctrine of the Reformed Church.

Children were baptized as babies. As they grew older, their religious education was based not on the Bible, but on the catechism, which they eventually had to memorize, both questions and answers. Young people, in their own time and at their own choosing, would join the church by meeting with the elders who tested them, starting with the first catechism question: "What is your only comfort in life and death?" They would be expected to know and recite the answer to that question and each one that followed. Those who succeeded would then be voted by the elders into the church as "members in full communion."

That first question from the catechism, and its answer, would shape my whole life.

"What is your only comfort in life and death?"

"That I, with body and soul am not my own, but belong to my faithful Savior Jesus Christ."

Throughout my life and my ministry, I would be spiritually driven to focus on "human comfort."

Years later, many would criticize me for being "a preacher hung up on comforting people." Some Baptists would fault my tradition for never having altar calls. Some Bible churches would fault my tradition for teaching theology instead of teaching the Bible, verse by verse, in every Sunday sermon. And some people in my own tradition would criticize me for not drilling into people the "list of sins."

So religion—not just the heart of the matter but the law of the matter—was very evident in our community. This was a wonderful and healthy thing, for the most part. It created boundaries that were clear and safe. And when someone crossed those boundaries, there was no second-guessing it. But, as one might imagine, such strict piety could backfire. The hearts of people and the tender treatment of humanity could be forgotten at times.

My father was shattered by just such a backlash when the Dominee's criticism, based on social standing, belittled his identity long ago on that day of "Haus Bezoek."

Henry tells today of that day with conviction and moist eyes. "You have no idea how that hurt Dad," he says. I doubt that my father ever personally shared this account with anyone. My hunch is that it went with him to heaven as a secret between himself and the Dominee, shared only by accident with his eldest son.

The Sunday following the Dominee's visit, and every Sunday thereafter, Tony sat dressed in his very best, in his black Model T, waiting for Jennie and the children. The sun, still near to the east where it had risen from slumber only hours earlier, spilled across his features, reflecting a new and disillusioned sadness. But he would still worship, focused not on the Dominee but on the God he knew would one day reward him for his diligence and vindicate his good name.

V

It's late afternoon and the sky is beginning to bid farewell to the sun. A gray cloud delicately trimmed in pink catches our eyes as my sister Margaret and I walk to the hen house.

"Harold," she says, "if you see them coming"—she nods toward our private, dead-end road—"you scat, jackrabbit fast, or they'll snatch you up, kidnap you, and you'll grow up as a Gypsy kid!" I'm wide-eyed, sure that I don't want to be a Gypsy kid. My sister Violet, if she'd been along, would have reassured me: "Nah, Gypsies won't snatch you up." But Margaret would have come back even more convincingly: "Yeah, they will!"

Even though it's spring, with the sun low on the horizon it's quite cold. Wearing our heavy coats, we gingerly place the eggs in the large metal bucket that's too heavy and too cold for an almost-school-aged child like me to handle. Margaret holds it with mitten-guarded hands while I nestle the eggs in the soft, protective straw. We scatter kernels of corn on the ground to reward the clucking chickens for their eggs.

We step back outside to bring this valuable cash commodity to Mom. Our farm will be the last stop for Arie, the store peddler, who will take our eggs and, in exchange, give us sugar, flour, miscellaneous odds and ends, and—best of all—free peanuts! We're always given a fistful to divide amongst ourselves, though I don't like to share. I *love* peanuts!

Margaret places the pail of eggs beside a bush and moves toward an oil drum alongside the hen house. "Harold, let's just say that the Gypsies started coming down that road right about now and you couldn't get back to the house, jackrabbit fast as you are." (Margaret graciously overlooks my shortcomings. I'm chubby and anything but fast.) "This is what you would do: you'd climb up like this." She makes sure that I'm watching her every move. Lithe and limber, she reaches the top of the empty drum with ease. I shiver slightly beneath my coat, watching with fascination.

She demonstrates the drill. "You would choose one of these drums and just squeeze . . . in." She's grown a bit since the last time she used the oil drums during a hide-and-seek game. The clothing she's layered in gets caught, but she squirms and wiggles her way down. Then she calls from within the metal belly in a voice that echoes against the steel, "Can you see me, Harold?"

"Not at all," I assure her. It's a fine place to hide. Very smart my Margaret is.

I see her hands reach to the top edge of the drum. I wait for her to emerge, but I'm distracted by a rumbling noise. It sounds like a wagon coming down our driveway. I wonder who it could be coming into our isolated yard. Maybe—I shiver—maybe it's . . . Gypsies!

"Oh . . . my . . . *goodness*," I swear in whispers; it seems befitting at this moment, never mind if it's a sin.

"Oh, my *goodness*—Gypsies. *Gypsies!*"

I can't see the wagon because of the trees that block the driveway from my view, but I know they're coming. Everyone in our family knows the sound of approaching visitors—or in this case, strangers.

I should climb up into a drum like Margaret, but I'm frozen in place.

On the other hand, I suppose that I should try to defend my sister and myself so that Dad won't be grieved to lose us both. We don't want to be Gypsy kids, no sirree. Even though Margaret told me I should scat, jackrabbit fast, I mustn't run; I must stay and defend. I must . . . I must . . . hide behind the bush with the eggs.

Margaret calls to me from inside her drum. In my mind I tell her to be quiet; I'll protect her. I crouch behind the bush with the eggs. She won't hush up. She calls louder. Soon she's screaming. I can't get her to be quiet.

I catch a glimpse of the encroachment of these nomadic strangers as they draw closer. Their wagon makes its way down the backside of our tree-lined drive. The still-barren trees that were planted for storm protection are now Gypsy protection, drawing the battle line between them and us. The rhythm of the approach—tree, wagon, tree, wagon, tree, wagon—and the consistent grind beneath the wheels become almost hypnotic in the silent countryside.

As the wagon rounds the last obstacle and heads toward the hen house, I see its white slatted wood side. I think I see its top rail holding the valuable chattel of these bohemian visitors. But as dusk shadows the scene, details lose their definition. I'll be red-fox sly and snake quiet.

Even Margaret is silent now.

I wait and I crouch, the pail of eggs hidden behind me. I tuck my head lower so that the Gypsies remain out of my sight. Mom always tells me, when we visit a strange town, "Harold, stay near! If you can't see me, I can't see you!" So . . . if I can't see the Gypsies, the Gypsies can't see me!

I think up a plan of attack. If they come over here by Margaret and me, I can startle them with my egg ammunition. Mom won't mind donating the whole batch for the valiant cause of saving her children. While the Gypsies raise their arms to ward off the explosive poultry bombs, I'll run and cut their horses loose with my trusty pocketknife and send the team galloping. Then, the situation well in hand, I'll whistle to Henry and scream to Mom.

I wait patiently, less anxious now that I have a plan. I listen. At last the wagon grinds to a halt.

But I don't hear horses snorting. I hear nothing but the slam of a metal door. I peek around the bush to catch a glimpse of . . .

Arie Bomgaars!

He's here for the eggs!

Margaret calls me again, but my hero role is over. My survivalist self emerges, wishing to satisfy simple hunger. I can see the rounded hood of Arie's Newkirk Store Peddle Wagon, with its Ford pickup front. I see the space atop the truck where Arie has placed the egg cartons that he's gathered throughout the day. And I see the door that opens the white slatted sides to reveal the dry goods and the groceries and the peanuts. *Peanuts!*

So content am I with this once-a-week treat that I forget all about Margaret. Munching away, I'm oblivious to the fact that she's stuck in her oil-drum hideaway!

As I eat my peanuts, Mom, Violet, and our oldest sister, Jess, having overheard the screams, pull and tug and laugh as they wiggle free the stuck and frightened Margaret.

Our house sat on the northwest corner of our land, protected from the north and the west (where storms typically came from) by a perimeter grove of scraggly cottonwoods and maples, mixed with a few apple trees.

The grove rested close behind the back part of our house like a fur collar on a woman's overcoat. Our driveway followed the outer boundary of the grove. When viewing the approach of visitors from just about any angle on our property—especially from inside, perhaps from our parlor or from an upstairs bedroom—I would do my scouting through the trunks and branches and shadows of our mini-forest.

But I never saw a Gypsy. For that matter, I rarely saw any visitors. It was quite the event when we would hear a car or a truck coming down the road. That was the extent of the excitement on our lonely and often boring farm. We kids were always thrilled with one of these infrequent occasions, and if we were outside and saw the visitors first, we'd run to the house to announce the news.

If you had visited our farm sometime during these years, long about 1930, this is what you would have seen:

First, a forty-foot-tall red hay and cattle barn in the open farmyard, with white trim, hip roof, and litters of kittens keeping the mice at bay. If you opened the barn door, separated into two parts (the top always open during good weather), the kittens would scatter and hide the moment they realized that you weren't Dad and could offer them no milk.

Inside the barn was our bull, a most valuable animal, because without the bull the cows wouldn't have calves, which meant that we would have no milk to drink or sell! But Mom always warned us to be careful. "The bull is to be respected and feared," she cautioned. A sure way to get a passionate scolding from Mom was to make the bull mad.

Our riding horse, Mabel, was stabled there too. She was my best friend during these years. She would neigh to Violet and me, trying to solicit a carrot. Though we were often tempted to steal one from the garden, Mom didn't like that at all, and we weren't brave enough to risk the consequences. So Mabel received this treat only if Mom was in an especially good mood.

Dad could often be found in the barn, checking on his prized Ayrshire milking cows. They were a rare breed, delivering milk and cream that Dad deemed the sweetest and best of all.

Overhead, hay was stacked high and neat in the loft, and the smell settled down around everything with a misty dust that gleamed in the occasional shaft of light and tickled the nose. Otherwise, the barn was cool and dark, keeping it bearable in summer for both animals and farmers.

When you stepped out of the barn, the small hog house, with its matching red and white paint, would be to your right on the north side of the barn. Phew—could it smell! Especially if a thunderstorm had come through, soaking the hog yard.

In spring we could hear noisy sows with their piglets. I often had to nurse the ones that were denied a place along their mama's two rows of teats. When they got a little older, some would squeeze out through the slats of fencing, and Mom would order me to collect them and return them to the pen.

To the south side of the barn stood the hen house and the corncrib and the toolshed, where my father's saws and hammers hung from heavy, rusty nails bent out from two-by-fours in the wall. Out back of the corncrib lay our collection of out-of-use buggies and farm equipment. This was my favorite place to play.

Here it wasn't unusual to find a fox hiding under the buggy, or sneaking about in search of a stray chicken. Just as common, therefore, was seeing Henry, hunting the fox. He couldn't let it get our hens or we wouldn't have any eggs to trade for flour and sugar. And if we didn't get our sugar, we wouldn't get pie with our milk come suppertime. Go, Henry!

The vegetable garden was on the north side of the house. There you'd likely find Mom weeding, swatting at mosquitoes whenever her hands were free. They bit her more than the rest of us, so she claimed to have honey for blood.

The sheets, drying on a clothesline suspended over the small plot of grass between the garden and the house, waved to Mom as she worked in the garden. I think she enjoyed their company. Even though their wave wasn't much of a substitute for the wave of a friend, it was certainly more consistent! For me, the drying sheets served as makeshift curtains for a make-believe stage where I performed to a curious crowd of dandelions.

A mile to the east of our one-acre open farmyard, the Floyd River snaked along with the railroad tracks beside it. Just beyond the tracks was what we called the "Big-Time Road," because it was always busy with cars and trucks going from Nebraska across Iowa and into Minnesota.

Imagine standing in that farmyard.

Now imagine spinning around, slowly, a full circle. Now again . . . again . . . slowly . . . again. Can you see all that space? Land, as far as the eye can see—just vast, flat, nothingness, with acres and acres of corn, oats, and pasture. And the sky, as blue as Mom's Delft china, which Grandma Jacomina had brought from the Netherlands. And the clouds like the whipped cream we would put on the ice-cream that Dad made for our birthdays.

This was the setting for the small, white Sears-Roebuck farmhouse that my father bought from the catalog and assembled for Jennie and his growing brood. The shingled-roof frame held within its core a kitchen just large enough for a stove and a table with crowding chairs; a small living room, called a "parlor"; and three bedrooms—one for my folks, one for the two boys, and one for the three girls. There was no bathroom. We bathed in a basin in the small kitchen, privacy a constant challenge, and the toilet remained outside—with a quarter-moon carved into the door.

That facility was a tiny wood hut—frightfully cold in the winter. I would stand inside that timbered outhouse, the wind howling through the cracks in the wooden wall, the darkness playing shadow games, and I would close my eyes with my fingers resting at the top of my trousers. One, two, three—I would try to summon the courage to expose my bare skin to the frigid conditions. And toilet tissue was unheard of. We used pages torn from last year's Sears-Roebuck catalog, choosing the nonslick ones first. The temptation to curse was strong when the end of the year rolled around and only slick sheets were left.

Our home had no electricity or proper running water, though my mom had grown up with those things. Kerosene lamps and lanterns remained our only light until 1939.

I slept every night with my brother in a bedroom that was at the top of a flight of wooden stairs that squeaked when we walked them. He was eleven years older than I was—tall, thin, and handsome.

On hot nights in the summer, our single bedroom window was opened to catch the occasional breeze. Waiting for that fresh breath of air was like waiting for "Sinter Klaas," in July. The open window was shielded by a screen to fend off the buzzing mosquitoes, but they always came in anyway. I grew up perpetually covered with swollen red bites that silently screamed for relief. How those buggers found their way in dumbfounded us.

In the winter, it was our bedroom, on the northwest side, that was the coldest. The quiet of a February night was frequently interrupted by the wailing of a sudden winter wind, often driven by a subzero freeze. At those times I would reach into warm memories of summer days for comfort. My brother and I had nothing to keep us warm except huddling closer together under layer upon layer of blankets.

In the mornings the panes of our window were often covered with white frost, and the interior windowsill often cradled a fresh drift of snow that had somehow found its way in through an unseen space between the window frame and the north wall. On such mornings, the frosted pane that gave view to the cottonwood grove would take on the impressionistic look of Monet, suggestive and subtle and dreamily undefined.

On such mornings, I'd hop to the beat of chattering teeth.

I never conceived of having a heater in the winter or a fan or an air-conditioner in the summer. We weren't rich! Sleeping was seldom pleasant. In July, I'd dream of Christmas cool; in winter, July's muggy escapes.

My brother and I shared the same bed until I was sixteen, when I left home for college and he was drafted to fight in Europe in World War II. I never again shared a bed with any person until the night of my wedding. Henry's half was almost always cold by the time I awakened, for he was up long before me to milk the cows.

For me, every day began at our two-gallon white porcelain portable potty kept at bedside. Mom always emptied it in the course of the day, just as she also made our bed without fail. I never emptied a potty; I never made a bed, even when I grew older. Duties were very much divided into sex-specific roles—duties for the men, duties for the women.

Dropping my small nightgown to the floor, I would step into overalls that had been bought extra-long, so as to last me during my fast-growing months. If still fairly new, the pants would be folded up once or twice to form crude cuffs, keeping the hem from wearing out under my shoes; if I'd had them a while, they might top my ankles. Little pockets in the chest would hold my things—a dull pocket knife used more for digging than anything severe, and a bullet pencil made of plastic, advertising the business places that sold seed to farmers or markets that hoped to buy fattened hogs for butchering.

My big toes generally poked through my socks, and heavy cardboard covered the holes in the soles of my shoes.

I would head for the kitchen, down the old wooden stairway, creaking and narrow.

There I would find Henry back from milking, reading a feed store journal, drinking coffee already as a teenager. Margaret would be standing by the cookstove if it were cold outside, trying to warm herself before going back out into the still-black morning hours. She also typically had a cup of coffee. Mom might be busy baking or canning or making sausage for the noon meal, but she would pause and prepare me a saucer of coffee with cream and sugar to sip once it had cooled — her way of saying, "Good morning, Harold."

And I would get to see Dad then too, back from his early chores. But I didn't much like Dad's smell at breakfast. "Yard smell" Mom called it.

The kitchen sink had a small pump that pulled water out of a tank supplied with rainwater. During the wet season, rain flowed from the roof to gutters that ran along the roof sides, emptying their precious collection down a spout into a below-ground cistern.

When it was time to eat, Mother would offer us plates piled with "Fet en Stroop" (fat and syrup). Slices of pork were fried in a pan on the hot stove until the bottom was covered with hot melted fat. Slices of homemade bread (we couldn't afford store-bought bread) were then dropped into that fat and lifted dripping onto the plate. When the pitcher of syrup was passed and tipped, the warm, sweet liquid swamped the fat-soaked slices of bread.

Cereal? We never heard of it. Coffee? You bet — always with lots of rich fresh cream and sugar. I learned to enjoy it at an age I can't even recall because I was so young. Eggs? Seldom. They were saved for "supper," the hot evening meal when cracked eggs that couldn't be sold at market were added to fried potatoes left over from the big "dinner" at noon.

On cold days the oven door would be open during breakfast, bathing in warmth the one family member fortunate enough to sit in the single chair facing the toasty resting-place for cold feet. More often than my older sisters, brother, or parents, I sat in that privileged seat — perhaps because I was the baby, or because they were out doing chores. Or, more honestly, perhaps because I was just plain cunning and stubborn.

"Get out of that chair, Harold!" I'd hear from Violet.

"I was here first," I'd fire back. This, coupled with a nasal whine, generally assured my throne.

During the days when Jessamine was still living with us, I readily moved for her. Jess was twelve years my senior, and she left home at the age of sixteen, so my memories of her aren't extensive. But she was one of the greatest sources of joy and laughter in our home and in my life. She left at a time when we needed money badly on the farm, becoming "nanny" for a missionary family who took her to New Mexico and then the state of Washington. Upon her return, she married young. Far too soon, deteriorating hips forced her onto crutches and eventually into a wheelchair.

I also gladly moved from the chair for Henry, my hero! I would have been overjoyed to evolve during my growing years into his model of manhood, but the shape and size of my body weren't so genetically blessed. Where his belly sank in, flat and hard, mine stuck out. Where he was silent, I was vocal. Where he was a farmer, I was a dreamer. No two individuals could have been as opposite, or as fond of one another.

My other two sisters, Margaret and Violet, were born two years apart from each other. Margaret was nine years older than I; Violet, seven. Margaret was Dad and Henry's helping hand on the farm, and she shared their temperament. She knew all there was to know about the management of animals and equipment, soil conditions, weather forecasting, and . . . Gypsies. I would move for Margaret, though sometimes grudgingly.

Violet was Mom's helper around the house, and my babysitter, especially after Jess left. She was levelheaded and practical. "Gypsies? Nah!" According to Vi they were just travelers. She didn't believe all the colorful tales that Margaret believed. She preferred reading storybooks to me—our special time together. Violet was the agreeable, fun-loving, and pretty blond girl in the family.

Violet often wanted the chair so that she could sit while doing some kitchen chore—perhaps cleaning the green beans, pulling off their little skinny ends and snapping them into bite-sized pieces, ready to be cooked for the noontime dinner.

I wouldn't move for her, I suppose because she was closer in age to me and I could take her on as a challenge. I'd just cross my arms, lean back, and use my weight bulk as an anchor. I simply wouldn't budge. Eventually she'd give up. Then I'd relax and revel in my luxury. Such stubbornness and tenacity would prove valuable in the years ahead. *Tough times never last but tough people do* was a thread already surging in my young personality. And to Violet's chagrin, I would bask contentedly, almost slothfully, in its reward. Such talent, I confess, I still possess today.

VI

Violet was more like Mom and me than the others were. The three of us were very vocal when it came to everyday matters, and spoke with passion; as a young boy I was simple in my expressive conviction, but expressive just the same. We three liked company and busy days with lots of people, new and exciting and event-driven moments. Henry and Margaret were more like Dad, soft-eyed, quiet, gentle, and consistent in manner. Whenever there was a conversation, we—Mom, Violet, and I—did most of the talking. Dad, Henry, and Margaret did the listening.

Mom was large in bone and flesh, nearing six feet tall, and the dictator of the home. I heard her "preach" to Dad often, but never in a volume or intensity that caused me to fear that their marriage was in trouble. (Broken marriages and divorces were unheard of in my childhood community.) Then again, I could never prove a reliable witness, since most of her preachings were conducted in Dutch, their private "code" whenever they didn't want us kids to know what they were talking about.

Dad was tall too, about one inch closer to heaven than Mom, skinny as a cornstalk but strong as our prize bull. Like Mom, he was white-haired, already seasoned with years by the time I came along. He never responded to Mom's verbal scoldings. Mom could grow hopping mad at him, but he just took it all silently. In fact, the madder she got, the quieter he got.

Still, she was always Tony's strong support in good times and bad. "I'm going out to help Dad with the yard work, Harold," she often said to me. "Be good for Violet and stay out of my pies!"

Dad not only volunteered himself to be the quiet subject of Mom's verbal admonitions; he expected the same from us kids. Once, after I started school, I talked angrily back to her, and this drew the one and only spanking I ever had. To my shock, it was from my gentle father.

I can still feel his powerful hand on my arm. "Come with me, Harold," he said soberly. Then he led me to the two-holer outhouse and spanked my rear end with a flat board.

Was this abuse? No. I never felt uncontrolled rage directed at me. I never felt intimidation or fear or shame as a consequence of something my parents said or did. Respect? Yes. I respected Dad and Mom immensely. Fear? Never.

I never once saw or heard a sign of verbal or physical assault from one parent to the other or toward any of us kids. But my mother's eyes! What volumes those round brown pools could preach. What a strong and silent vocabulary her look could communicate. Ouch! I would live with her eyes and her strong opinions though all my years of childhood and on into adulthood.

My mother was a self-appointed authority on what made preaching great, or less than the grandness and greatness this honorable role demanded. "Study hard" were two words I would hear from her all of her life.

I would be my mother's "baby boy" until her death. And never until then would she abandon in letters or words her assumed responsibility to reprove and correct me as needed. Never would I hear the words I wanted more than anything to hear: "I'm proud of you, Bob." I'm sure that she *was* proud of her one child who became a Dominee. After all, for her this meant returning the family to its honorable roots. But affirmation and affection were emotions that she seldom expressed. After all, pride was a sin.

Even as a small child, I can't recall ever hearing from her lips the words "I love you." I can't recall ever being kissed by my mother or my father. Though she spoke her mind about practical things, the Dutch simply weren't known for affectionate display. But I do recall vividly the security I felt sitting on my mother's wide lap with her large, soft breasts tenderly pillowing my head.

What feelings moved in this woman's heart? What deep thoughts went through her mind—a mind that remained sharp and alert and wisely critical until the day she died? I remember years later riding on the plane from California to Iowa, hoping I'd reach her for one last touch and one final word. I'd have to resign the hope of ever knowing the many intimate thoughts and emotions that were never shared.

I inherited from my mother her vast capacity for intense passion and her strong sense of verbal spontaneity, which ranged from dramatic whispers to loud outbursts punctuated by bold gestures. I also inherited her shape and frame. As a matter of fact, I'd venture to say that I acquired just about everything from my mother, except her ability to play a musical instrument.

She was my piano teacher. "Practice more!" she would say. And she was right—but neither the instrument nor the instructor could motivate me.

As I rehearsed my pieces she would say, "Get the opening strong and perfect, and get the closing down just right. You can make mistakes in the middle and people will forgive and forget, *if* your start and your finish are great!" I sensed then, and still believe today, that this is a universal principle of success.

My mother was very good on both the piano and the organ, which she played in church. My most moving memories involve the imparting of her faith as she sang hymns, accompanying herself, with me at her side.

And though the piano held no future for me, it was at that instrument, my chubby body nestled close to hers on the piano bench, where we were the closest.

I wanted to be more like Henry and Margaret and my father: strong and motivated by the earth and its bounty. I begged myself to awaken before dawn, to come to consciousness during that quiet, dark time when the sky lies in wait for the sun. I don't know why my body more often insisted on sleeping, leaving Henry with the frustration of rousing me for chores once I was old enough. Or why my brain demanded reprieve from chores, drifting into its wild and fictitious adventures once he succeeded in recruiting me. Or why my fingers fumbled when I grew old enough to help Dad and Henry with the farm tools, making me a threat to any fix-it chore that they hesitantly attempted when I was near. Or why, when I grew to a supposed age of dependability, fishing would become more important to me than milking. Or why I was so lazy.

I didn't *mean* to hate the smell of the barn or the squish of a cow pie in the pasture. I didn't *choose* to be an out-of-place farmer's son. I just *was*.

After breakfast and piano practice, I had to collect corncobs from the hog yard, a dirty duty I grudgingly began at the age of five. Whether it was autumn, winter, spring, or summer, I never had a vacation from this chore until I moved from home. As I grew older, milking was added to my must-do list, in addition to walking the fields to clean the crops of wild weeds called "cockleburs," a task that bloodied my small hands. But as a child, cob-collecting was my primary responsibility, after which I'd venture into some make-believe game.

In the winter, I was bound to the house and kept from outdoor adventures. Then I daydreamed all the more. I so hated the winter, when blizzards would shake our small house like a squirrel in the mouth of a fox. The howling wind would creep in like an unwelcome intruder beneath the kitchen door, sometimes rattling Mom's china in the cabinet. I would try to find a sheltered corner in which to read a favorite storybook while keeping warm beneath a hand-crocheted blanket. The wicked winter wind and subzero temperatures made me look wonderingly at the palm trees and gaudy flowers I saw pictured in my storybooks.

Outside, the blizzards would pile snow in mounds about the house and farm and fill the roadside ditches with snow, leaving huge drifts three to four feet high that made the roads impassable. Then the only outdoor fun we had occurred at blizzard's end, when Dad would give my sisters a ride to school in the horse-drawn sleigh and I'd get to go along. Eventually, the county-owned snowploughs always reopened the roads. First the plough would clear the "Big-Time" cement road far away, then the gravel roads that ran from one small town to the next. Only when those were clear would it get to the dirt road that led to our house.

The country gravel roads, so early and easily snowbound, were what connected the elements of my world—a world made up of Hospers, Alton, Orange City, and Newkirk. Our telephone office was in Hospers, population three hundred; our post office was in Alton, population three fifty-nine; marriages, births, and deaths were recorded in the county seat, Orange City, population three thousand; and our church was in Newkirk, population fourteen.

Our congregation in Newkirk drew upon eighty families from outlying farms that averaged six children per household. (Families of seven and more weren't unusual in that day, when birth control was unheard of.)

In our religious community, all of life was sacred, a gift of creation. This went without debate! You accepted the birth of every child as a gift from God.

The only political discussion I remember hearing in our house growing up was prompted by a new law, one supported by President Franklin D. Roosevelt (for whom my father had voted). The law would, among other things, financially reward farmers who killed their newborn pigs. It was theorized that this would eliminate the overabundance of pork, which was driving down the market price.

"I will *never* accept money for killing little pigs!" my father stormed to Mom as he heard the new law announced on the radio. If I thought he'd ever swear—which I didn't—it would've been that day.

"We should respect life and control population," Dad argued, "but not by slaughter."

So he bred fewer hogs to cut down the overabundance. The same principle would apply in our religious tradition to problems of human population. Abortion was murder. It was never, ever heard of in Alton, Iowa.

Winters weren't the only extreme in Sioux County. In summers only the outdoor water pump—one that we worked by hand—brought us a touch of something cool. The long iron arm rose up with little effort on our part, but forcing it back down to bring frigid relief pouring from the pump's rusty spout was quite an effort. Some summers, water became frightfully scarce, though even the driest seasons brought noisy and angry storms. During the worst of them, Mom could be heard pleading, "*Heere bewaar! Heere bewaar! Heere bewaar!*" "The Lord protect! The Lord protect! The Lord protect!" So . . . be it summer, winter, storm, or drought, we knew the power of weather. We all looked skyward with profound respect and reverence.

Come spring and summer, my chores expanded to include helping Mom in the vegetable garden. I'd catch kittens and count them, trying to figure out which ones were missing. I knew them by color, never by name: black-and-white, multicolored, yellow-and-white, brown, tiger-striped. I'd also catch the piglets. When I grew a little older, I'd hunt gophers and trap muskrats for bounty. Trapping for pelts earned me my only spending money and savings for college. (Wildlife protection wasn't an issue in the country when I was a boy.)

The treat of all treats was when Mom ordered Violet to take lunch (our snack between meals) to my dad in the field. She always took me along. Violet would throw a western saddle onto Mabel and I'd ride behind her, my rear on Mabel's rear, my legs settled under and around the back of the saddle, my fingers grasping the saddle's back edge for support.

Mabel was beautiful to me. Dark brown, and what I suppose would be considered a dark "bay" in horseman's terms. She wouldn't have seemed large to the average adult, but in a boy's eyes she towered above the earth. I imagined myself a mounted knight riding to bring food to the warriors. (I often heard tales of such chivalry from Violet during our story times.)

Our noon meal always included hot meat, potatoes, fresh vegetables, and—with rare exceptions—homemade pie: apple, pumpkin, lemon, or butterscotch. The apple pie was always topped with a pastry; the pumpkin and butterscotch pies were uncovered, adorned with neither pastry nor ice-cream nor whipped cream; the lemon pie always had a meringue "frosting." Butterscotch, creamy and golden, was my favorite. I *loved* pie!

"Family devotions" were a mealtime tradition too. After plates were cleared, Dad would read from the well-worn, leather-bound Dutch family Bible. If anyone dared allow a snicker to escape (as sometimes happened when I mimicked for Violet the twitching of Dad's serious eyebrows with every "thou" and "shalt"), those stern paternal eyes would quickly restore reverence. I didn't mind Dad's stern eyes, though. I'd take them over Mom's any day.

We had devotions following every meal that included potatoes. These were the meals when all of us were gathered around the table. It was said in our county, in Yankee Dutch, "No aardappels, no gebeden." Translated, this meant, "No potatoes, no prayer." A snack that didn't include warm potatoes—boiled, mashed, or fried—wasn't a "serious meal" and therefore didn't require a prayer of blessing. But the three hot meals that did include prayer also and always included potatoes (with the exception of breakfast, which never included potatoes). So, three times a day, without fail Dad would read and we would try to be good.

Following dinner at noon, Dad would take his tired farmer's frame that had been up since before dawn—to the rocker for a rest. Henry would do the same. Margaret and Violet preferred to read, sitting in one of the six unmatched kitchen chairs.

Mom would typically go back into the garden or clean a chicken, plucking feathers off the dead bird. The result would be delicious fried chicken for the next day's dinner. Or she would take down freshly laundered clothes that had dried in the sweet sun and clean breeze. They smelled so fresh! The smell of sunshine.

If the weather was good, I would join her outside, though Mom encouraged me to nap, especially when I was only three or four. Short naps were common for those who had been up since dawn, but at midday it seemed that *my* day had just begun! I had things to do, places to go on that big, sprawling farm. I had adventures wait-ing—always wondering what was around the next corner, or what new territory I might explore, or what animals were digging new holes behind the chicken coop, or what wild creature was glowering at me with reflective eyes from beneath the barn. Poor Mom: in my hurry I often scattered her pile of plucked feathers, sending them floating about her lap or onto the floor or back onto the plucked and naked hen. Occasionally I even carelessly (or naughtily) dumped clean clothes from the line onto the green grass, still moist from a spring shower.

"Auch, Harold—don't do that!" Mom would scold.

I could be likened to a pesky wind that flung havoc in a flurry to break my childhood boredom.

Throughout my childhood, my quests, by and large, were expeditions that I would face alone. In many ways, because of the age gap between my siblings and me, I grew up like an only child. I would emerge, in my teen and adult years, as a natural "loner." That inclination would—I now believe—encourage me to think and act for myself. I was becoming more of an "individual" than a conditioned and manipulated member of a "community."

Memories of play with my siblings—who, being older, were expected to work when not in school—are few and far between. In later years, the neighboring Roos boys would come over and play, but not with regularity. More often than not, then, I was the solo and lead character in my childhood escapades, and daydreaming became a reprieve from my isolation.

In this environment, when I neared the age of five, something dramatic invaded this secluded existence. I was about to discover the comfort and companionship of a dream.

VII

It's the summer of 1931, and the day is already hot by early morning. The corn is growing, eagerly reaching toward the blue sky. The virgin green shoots near the top of the stalk are tight with fresh awakening, while the lower stalks spread open more confidently in the warm sun.

It's four weeks before my fifth birthday, and I'm dressing for town. Mom says we must go see the tailor, Mr. Beckman, for a final fitting of my new Sunday suit. This has been going on for weeks, because Uncle Henry is coming to visit.

Henry Beltman, Mom's younger brother, is coming all the way from China! I don't know exactly how far China is, but the way

Mom keeps talking, it must be farther than Minneapolis. Uncle Henry has been a missionary, and it's been a long time since Mom has seen him. "Eight years," she keeps saying to us, "eight years!" I assure her that I'll look my best for our first meeting.

At the tailor's I get to stand on a stage in front of a huge window and watch all the townspeople going by while Mr. Beckman examines his work. Mom attempts to smooth the course material that gathers in odd and stubborn creases about my legs. Pants never seem to hang just right on me, as they do on my brother, Henry. They pull here and there to accommodate my chubby thighs.

Mom shakes her head at Mr. Beckman. She isn't satisfied. After all, the reason she brought me to the tailor is that I'm so difficult to fit. She's spending good money and she expects good tailoring. I don't want to confirm her suspicion that Mr. Beckman really isn't at fault. I've been in the pantry sneaking pie bites all week long. But Mom is very concerned, because I was supposed to put the suit on, look sharp, and take it home. Uncle Henry is due at the farm at two this afternoon, and Mr. Beckman had said it would be done for sure.

Mom shrugs sadly and there's the beginning of a frown on her face. I don't like that frown. Mr. Beckman, after making sure my hands are clean, lets me walk down the rows and touch the bolts of cloth while Mom talks with him. I get to see the colors and feel the fabrics he has in stock—nubby, soft, silky, grainy, sleek, rough.

Quickly bored with that, I return to the window. The dance hall is just across the street, next to the *Alton Democrat* on the second floor. And down the street a little way is the Goebel Saloon, owned by the mayor. Mom won't ever let me look at this place of interest, so I stretch my neck a little for a guilty and curious glimpse while she's busy with Mr. Beckman.

Mom comes back to me and seems relieved.

"Okay, Harold. Say now, go and change back into your overalls. Your suit will be ready in two days. It won't be ready for you to wear when Uncle Henry comes today."

Disappointed, I return to my dungarees. We move quickly back outside where Dad is waiting in the Model T and hurry home. While Mom and Dad busy themselves for Uncle Henry's visit, I wash up and put on a "newer" pair of overalls.

It's nearly two o'clock now, and I'm sitting outside in the sweltering heat on a stone step waiting for our famous visitor. The small white gate in the three-foot fence—keeps the animals out, Mom says—is hinged open where I sit. He'll park his car right in front of me when he comes.

Mom has been acting funny all day. She's so nervous about Uncle Henry that I prefer the peace of the outdoors, even with its sticky, suffocating heat. The flies seem to like the smell of my hot skin. They won't leave me alone. But no matter: I won't miss this moment, heat or no heat, flies or no flies.

Though Mom is jittery now, her enthusiasm over the past weeks has been quite contagious. The stories I've been told have raised Uncle Henry into heroism alongside my brother, Henry, and my favorite radio hero, Captain Midnight. To be the first missionary building the first Christian church in Amoy, China, when he and his newlywed wife were just fresh from the altar . . . *wow!* A Princeton graduate welcomed into a land of strange tongues and customs seems as brave as Captain Midnight, with his amazing adventures. The death of Uncle Henry's infant son in that foreign land just weeks ago is the saddest story I've ever heard told. To speak about it makes my mother cry.

The air is incredibly still, though an occasional faint breeze rattles and rustles the leaves in our grove of trees. The farm animals are quiet, the sun hot and bright. I can hear Mom rushing around in the house and Violet and Margaret fussing at each other, but their voices seem more distant than normal.

I have a funny feeling in my stomach. It's a new feeling; I've never had anything like it. It feels like the day I thought the Gypsies were coming, but it's not a scary feeling. It feels kind of like the morning of my birthday when I know that Dad will be making ice-cream later, but it's a *quiet* happy feeling, not a *jumpy* happy feeling. It feels like when I go to church and they sing my favorite Sunday school song.

A rabbit stops and looks at me for a minute, then hops away. I can't help smiling a bit, but I sit still. A bird lands on a crooked branch of a box elder tree and looks my way. My smile spreads, but I sit still. I feel as though when I sit still and listen really hard, I can almost hear my heart singing to me.

This is like a wonderful daydream; but unlike all of my other daydreams, this is *real*. It's not just something I thought up. It's come all by itself, dropped out of heaven.

The corn and the fields of alfalfa move slowly with the breeze to a rhythm that makes me wonder if they sense the excitement. The still, almost-time-stopping feeling is rising up within me like mist rising slowly from dew-covered fields on a summer morning.

Then, far down that dirt road that stretches almost a mile west from our home to the top of a hill, I see a faint cloud of dust. My heart leaps and the song becomes jubilant.

I jump to my feet, and I catch a pant-cuff on the sharp edge of the step, tearing it slightly. I don't care. I run to the house.

"Mama! *Mama!* MAMA!" I call as loudly as I possibly can. Before I reach the house, I stop and turn to look once again.

The approaching car is coming steadily down the long, lonely road. It seems to pick up speed as it heads toward our little house. The trail of dust is over a half-mile long by now.

Mom comes hastily beside me, wiping her wet hands on her apron and then pulling it over her head. Her hands are shaking when she places them on my shoulders. She pinches me slightly. It almost hurts, but I can tell that this squeeze helps her feel better, so I don't say anything. She studies the approaching car, hardly aware that I'm standing beneath her with a sweat-glistened brow.

The car is moving faster now, leaving its long, unbroken trail of dust hovering on the road behind it. I move away from Mom's grasp and return to the little gate.

The car rounds the drive and stops in a small cloud of dust that swirls right in front of me. I'm speechless. Mom stares to catch the first glimpse of her favorite brother. Slowly, the car door opens and a long leg stretches its way out. A large foot with a black dress shoe steps in the still settling dust. Up rises the tallest and most handsome man I've ever seen, rising like Paul Bunyan with a righteous cause. Raven-haired, he's dressed in a white shirt and tie under his black Sunday suit.

My stomach feels funny again, but instead of sitting still I begin to jump up and down and up and down.

"Uncle Henry! Uncle Henry! Uncle Henry! Uncle Henry!"

I don't stop; I *can't* stop. I just keep calling his name and jumping and clapping my hands.

"Uncle Henry! Uncle Henry! Uncle Henry! Uncle Henry!"

A split-second later he's towering above me with his hand on my head. His open palm tousles my hair, and I stand still to feel his blessing. He smiles down at the sight of my giddy welcome.

"Uncle Henry! Uncle Henry! Uncle Henry! Uncle Henry!"

He leans down and reaches his long arms around me, hugging me tight. Then, placing both open palms on my head, he says, "So . . . you're Robert Harold."

As he speaks, the funny feeling in my stomach returns, along with a solemn stillness. I hear nothing but his voice as it echoes in my young mind, feel nothing but the slight pressure of his hands on my head. He says:

"You will be a preacher when you grow up!"

From the bottom of my feet to the top of my head, I'm captured completely by his words; they sing to me.

After supper that night, Violet and Mom start washing the dishes and Dad leaves with Henry and Margaret for the evening milking. Mom puts me in charge of entertaining our special guest.

I tell him about the gopher that Margaret and I caught the day before. "Big as our mama cat!" I say, exaggerating. I see that he's impressed.

Then I ask him something that I've been thinking about all afternoon. "Uncle Henry . . . ," I begin, then pause to gather courage. I sit down beside him awkwardly. (The sofa is off limits most days, so I feel inexperienced and unrelaxed.) I cross my legs haphazardly, trying to look years beyond my age.

"Uncle Henry," I try again, "how can I become a preacher like you?"

He takes my question very seriously. He tilts his long face and clasps his narrow chin between his thumb and first finger. He crosses his legs to match mine. I can see the scuffed bottoms of his shoes—they have no holes! I study his stately manners and his gentle and likeable ways, and I decide that I'm looking at my dream—face-to-face. I'm ready to hear his instructions.

"Well, Robert," he explains, "you'll have to go to school for a long time. Eight years in the country school, then four years in the high school in town, then four years in college, then three years in seminary. That's almost twenty years of schooling!"

He sounds as if he's expecting me to grimace at this report, but I'm not dissuaded. I wrinkle my brow and frown slightly, but only to try to look as intelligent as he is.

"When do I start?"

He chuckles. "I think I heard your Mom say that you'll start school this fall, isn't that right?"

"Um-hmm." I smile at the thought. "Will I like it?"

"I don't know, Robert. Not always, I would guess. But when you have a goal, that goal becomes more important than those days when you don't like school. So you just keep going—*if* you want to be a preacher, that is."

I nod energetically.

Uncle Henry remembers my greeting earlier in the day, when I jumped up and down with excitement at his arrival. He sees in my eyes the sparkle of my first dream, but little does he know—little does Mom or Dad know, little do *I* know—that my initial encounter with Uncle Henry, and his proclamation that I would be a preacher, would be the single most defining moment of my earthly life.

I had heard my divine call, and now I accepted without question my new marching orders. Before dropping into bed that evening, I made a commitment to my first twenty-year goal. Kneeling in my upstairs bedroom, I prayed my usual prayer—the same one I'd been praying every night since my toddlerhood:

> Now I lay me down to sleep.
> I pray Thee, Lord, my soul to keep.
> If I should die before I wake,
> I pray Thee, Lord, my soul to take.

Then, with new zeal and passion, I added this line: "And make me a preacher like Uncle Henry when I grow up! Amen."

I would pray that divine-dream-drenched prayer every night until the day of my ordination nearly twenty years later.

The following morning we gathered as a family around the kitchen table: Dad, Mom, my sisters, Henry, and me. Uncle Henry had gone to Grandpa's to sleep. (Grandma Jacomina had died a few months before, so Grandpa was alone now.)

We were all enjoying the usual hot "Fet en Stroop," eating with little conversation.

When someone said, "Please pass the syrup," I saw my opening and made my big announcement: "I'm going to be a preacher when I grow up!"

Dad stopped abruptly and shot a stunned look at me. His fork was laden with a dripping chunk of fatty, syrupy bread that stopped in mid-air, just short of his open mouth. He stared silently. It was not an angry stare. It wasn't a correcting stare. It quickly softened into an I-understand-what-you-are-saying stare as tears welled up in his eyes. Maybe he knew that I had no words to explain my decision. Maybe he knew that somehow a heavenly magic had orchestrated and given me my heart song. Maybe he knew that God didn't want me to be a farmer!

Time seemed to stop and the family conversation seemed a distant drone of noise like static on the radio when it was raining while Dad and I met in a secluded, far away, spiritual elsewhere. There we whispered without voice, speaking deeper than words—heart to heart.

"I have no words to explain how or why!" I am saying.

"You found your heart song."

"I don't mean to be different, I just am."

"God doesn't want you to be a farmer, does He?"

Even at this young age, I began to sense, in a subtle indescribable way, this type of deep knowing in my Dad. What I wouldn't know for twenty years was . . . why.

Dad and I hesitantly returned to our breakfast, but I'd caught a glimpse into the eyes of heaven. I had received a foretelling of who I was to be. I had heard the call of divinity and had accepted the heartsong meant just for me. I had been sent the new Personal Friend that God had suddenly become to me. God was now a delightedly happy feeling within me. In fact, I became convinced that this God had personally hand-delivered my heartsong to me. And for this out-of-place farmboy, this dream was worth more than a thousand words and even a hundred pies.

VIII

Grade school. First grade. I was ready for it!

I was going to be a preacher! I was going to become a missionary and build great churches as Uncle Henry had done in China. Never mind that I was the only child in all the school with such grand aspirations. I now had a confidence that no one could take from me. I was ready to do whatever I needed to do to attain my goal.

But first things first.

Grade number one.

After breakfast I would walk a mile west down the dirt road that was either dry and dusty, or wet and muddy, or snowy and slick. It led to a junction with another dirt road where there stood one lonely building—the one-room Floyd Independent School.

Actually, there were three buildings. Two small outhouses stood near the classroom, one toilet for the girls and one for the boys. There was no running water. Hands were washed in a little washroom at the front entrance of the school. The one classroom had a blackboard on the wall, a desk and a chair for the teacher, and seventeen chairs, one for each student in the first through eighth grades.

I walked to and from school every Monday through Friday. We *all* walked in from nearby farms, even the high-schoolers, who were picked up by a school bus in front of our building and taken to a country high school in Newkirk, four miles away.

I enjoyed walking alone to school. I experienced the joy of solitude that allowed me to dream my dreams.

"What do you want to be when you grow up?" my teacher asked the seven new first-graders. I raised my hand excitedly. I knew the answer. But my last name started with S, so I had to wait my turn after "Korver" and "Roos."

I was jumping in my seat by the time the teacher got to me. "Well, Harold, you seem pretty excited," she said. "What do you want to be when you grow up?"

I blurted it out: "I'm going to be a preacher like my Uncle Henry!"

It wasn't long, however, before my dream hit its first big challenge. I discovered that school was *not* fun. And recess was the worst!

On one fair-weather day, all sixteen of my classmates and I were sent outside to the lawn. The teacher then called the two oldest, tallest, slimmest, fastest boys—Eddie and LeRoy—and directed them to stand beside her. I stood with the rest, waiting to see what sort of ritual was about to commence.

"Okay, choose sides," the teacher told the chosen two. She held a softball in one hand. With the other, she tossed a coin and called out, "Heads or tails?"

"What does that mean?" I asked another first-grader. His brother was one of the two tall ones.

"It decides who gets to draw first for teams," he said. "The best player always gets picked first, then they take turns until the last one is left. The one nobody wants."

"Who's going to be the last one picked?" I asked.

"I suppose one of us first-graders," he guessed. Looking toward three girls, he pointed at Geneva Korver. "I bet she'll be the last one. Nobody'll choose her."

The choosing up of sides went fast until there were only four left standing, including Geneva—and me.

"At least I won't be last," I thought.

The next two picks were made. Only two were left standing now—Geneva and I.

It seemed forever as I watched these two athletes, tall and confident, inspect first me . . . then Geneva . . . then me . . . then Geneva. I began to chew my lip, feeling not a little bit of insecurity at the length of the critical examination. I shoved my hands into my pockets and played nervously with a smooth stone I'd picked up on the way to school. I wrinkled my nose and used my hand as a visor to shield my squinting eyes. Geez—would they please make up their minds! I shuffled my feet.

Finally, LeRoy stepped slightly forward and said, "Okay. I'll take . . . *her!*"

I couldn't believe it! I was devastated. The shame bathed over me as hot and strong as the sun. I was the last one. The unchosen!

Geneva ran to join her team, and I was left standing all alone, unwanted by either side. The tall boy, Eddie, who had lost the toss, looked unenthusiastically at me, then waved me reluctantly to his team.

"What's your name?" Eddie grunted.

"Harold Skuller," I said.

"Where do you live?" he asked.

"At the dead-end of that," I said, pointing to the dirt road that had no name and no number. As I pointed and as he looked, a line rushed into my head:

I may be last, but at least I'm not lost!

I thought defensively:

At least I know what I want to be when I grow up! I'm going somewhere . . . just you wait and see!

And suddenly I discovered something wonderful: this funny little line made me feel better! So I said it out loud to Eddie. "Hey . . . I know I may be last, but at least I'm not lost!"

Eddie laughed.

I laughed with him and discovered that I had a gift with words that could make people laugh. That made me feel better too.

But the sting wouldn't keep its distance as I had hoped.

The choosing up of sides happened again the next day. This time Eddie won the toss, so I knew that things would turn out better. He liked my jokes, after all. But it didn't matter, as it turned out. Geneva and I were the last two left standing once again.

"I'll take her." Again I heard these words, only this time from Eddie. I was crushed. I was the only one not wanted—not chosen by either team. What a humbling effect this had on a boy who had started school proudly waving his hand, eager to answer the teacher's first question.

After a few weeks of the agony of recess, with tears in my eyes and with both hands hiding in the two front pockets of my overalls, I asked my teacher, "Why doesn't anyone want me?"

"Well, Harold," she said, "You're very likeable, but you're . . . well, you're fat and slow, you know."

The description seared my mind. I knew that my clothes had been changing sizes often. I knew that I was constantly getting bigger. But I'd never been described, within my hearing, as if the descriptive word constituted who I was!

Fat!

I would never forget the sound of that word. I had discovered the power of negative self-esteem.

So recess was the hell opposite my daydreaming heaven. I would never enjoy sports. School was quickly losing its shine.

Throughout the next few years, I would often find myself tempted to leave at midday and walk back home, never to return. Then I would recall Uncle Henry's words to me:

"When you have a goal, that goal becomes more important than those days when you don't like school. So you just keep going—*if* you want to be a preacher, that is."

So instead of running, I kept reminding myself of the way Eddie had laughed at my words. In that country school, I became the "talker" and the "singer" and the "clown" and the "tease."

My walks home from school became a therapeutic element of my day. With each step drawing me nearer to home, I would feel the taunts about being fat slipping away. The first length of my hike from the schoolyard went up a slight rise. Behind it hid all six of my family's farm buildings, the only visible trace being the rooftop of the tall barn peeking proudly above the low-rising hill. But once I reached the crest of that hill, I could see our whole farmyard a mile east, shielded behind the windbreak of trees. The corncrib, the chicken coop, the toolshed, even the hog shed, and our house.

From the top of that hill all the way to our driveway there often flowed a small stream. I'd find a slender chunk of straw and launch it as a "boat" into the swirling stream. The current would immediately pick it up, and I'd watch the little thing sail away, bobbing and weaving until it was stopped by some obstruction—usually a small stone. My little boat would wait for me to nudge it free so that it could float on downstream for a longer or shorter, slower or faster cruise. Finally, when the stream reached the culvert under my driveway, my boat would disappear into the dark tunnel.

During late spring, or during the first wintry months when light snows would dam the otherwise steady flow, I'd use a longer twig to nudge my little boat along. I'd sometimes have to carve little canals an inch or two wide in the thin layer of snow to make room for my little vessel to continue its quiet passage. For the eight years I spent in the country school, and the four years I spent at Newkirk High School, I played this game daily on my walk home.

Was I learning and practicing the universal principles of success—how to set a goal and then work through and around obstructions, staying with the goal until it's reached?

My immediate "dream" would come true every day at the entrance to our dirt driveway: I was home. A feeling of immense welcome and warmth would wash over me. Here I wasn't Fatso. Here I wasn't Slowpoke or Weakling. I was . . . Harold—Harold, who had sailed the seas and brought my little vessel safely home.

Here, at home, my reward took the form of some baked delicacy—perhaps a chocolate layer cake freshly baked by Mom sometime during the course of the day. This favorite treat was generally covered with a thick white frosting. The first piece was always cut for me and waiting on a plate. I became even more addicted to high-calorie tokens of maternal affection. Only now, with every bite, I would hear the words of my teacher and the echoes of the other students: "You're fat!"

So school didn't provide the social warmth that would give me a sense of belonging. It didn't fulfill the excited expectations I had felt when talking to Uncle Henry. In fact, it would only prove to further isolate me in my dreamworld. Add to this my segregated birth order within my family, and it's no surprise that I grew up feeling out of place—a dreamer (dreams made good friends), lazy, by and large, independent and, yes, even lonely.

As my advancing years brought me into the fields with Henry and Dad, this proximity only served to further differentiate them from me. Not in terms of endearment or loyalty one to the other, but in identity. As much as I would admire them and want to be like them, I just wasn't a farmer. I was on a different course.

It was really very simple:

Dad was "farmer." Henry was "farmer." I was "not." And my heart responded accordingly.

IX

It's Saturday—a no-school, best-of-the-week day. Finally, after dragging my lazy self through my farm chores, I can go fishing in the Floyd River. I'm walking east along the path of pleasure. I'm looking down at my feet shuffling through the dusty ground, and I see my favorite shadow.

It's a bit round and distorted, but jutting up from the head is a long, thin appendage—the accompanying shadow of my makeshift fishing pole.

This skinny, bouncing stick looks to be a long, strange weapon in the hand of a determined warrior. And, in its own way, it *is* a weapon. With it, this warrior intends to overpower the biggest fish that swims the Floyd. The sharp, store-bought fish hook will hold one of the worms I dug up with a fork back home. Overturning the moist black ground beside the barn, I found plenty of them underneath the flat rocks where they always hide and placed them slippery, wiggling, and wet into an empty coffee can.

There are no trees to block the sun that projects my friendly shadow onto the ground before me. Often, as I wander the farm, I check the sky behind me for storms, looking over my shoulder for the gathering of those black clouds that come on occasion to threaten our land. Storms will ruin good fishing, because these fish bite best under a still surface. Fortunately, today there are no scattered clouds that could join forces, scheming and rising together until they grow huge and monstrous, pulsing the air with a silence that portends a storm and draping the land in a greenish hue. If I *had* seen such clouds, I would have run home quickly, looking out for the fiend of fiends—the dreaded serpentine funnel. I've never, ever seen a real tornado, but Mom always says, "Harold—watch the sky!"

I've grown up watching the sky where the sun sets. "That's west," I'm told. West—where storms come from. But west is also where our mile-long nameless, numberless dead-end dirt road opens to the rest of the world. The only way to escape a tornado is to first turn west and run that dusty mile. Unsettling as it is, on this nowhere road, if I want to escape, I can't run *from* the storm, I must run *into* the storm!

This isn't a pleasant thought for a boy who hates to run. I'm much more interested in daydreaming or eating pie or . . . fishing.

Growing at the water's edge are willows that reach their branches across the winding river, casting shadows where fresh fish wait in the cool shade—wait for insects to fall from the boughs as if the trees above were their provisioners.

Here, by the narrow, winding, and wonderful Floyd, the trees beckon me to their shaded resting-place. And as I sit, they lull me with their whispers. They don't whisper tales of dark places with gales and sinister skies. They speak only gentle words, telling me softly that I'm loved by the heavens and singing lullabies of quiet retreat. Their ancient healing sounds are carried on gentle breezes, soothing my insecurities and taming my wild thoughts.

Here, in these silent and serene shadows, I can indulge in fantasy and pretend that I'm in front of a beautiful church whose pews are filled with the old and the young and the rich and the poor. As my words to the quiet willows and the calm stream make my divine day-dreaming come alive, I imagine and visualize people in the pews being inspired by me.

Then I wander up the hilltop that rises from the banks of the Floyd, leaving my pole at the river's edge with a quiet Bobber float-ing on the smooth surface, waiting to be jiggled by a fish. There on the hilltop I raise my voice loudly as I declare: "All will be well!" I am preaching. "All will be well; all will be well! Trust in God! He's bigger than the storm!"

Silent again, I gaze at my audience of spellbound parishioners— a herd of grazing cattle that look up as I preach to them. Then I hear their response:

Moo!

And seeing the jaws of the Ayrshires as they chew their cuds fuels my imagination. I can see staunch Dutchmen outside the church, biting the ends off of new cigars while sounding praise for this fer-vent young preacher.

I descend from the grassy knoll that rises up and between the Floyd and the pasture. I lean again on the strength of a wooden trunk, beneath the shade of a friend. I wait for the floating Bobber to bop up and down to tell me that a fish is nibbling at my bait.

I'm having the only real fun I know. I'm not keen on baseball, or basketball, or football. I've never tried to ride a bike—no one in my family has. I don't even know how to swim! I fish. So here I sit, pole in hand, clouds above.

The clouds are amazing! They float, slowly shifting shape and position. One white cloud metamorphoses into the profile of George Washington in his white wig. Another cloud looks like a puff of steam from the train that chugs past a short distance away. I count its cars and give the engineer a wave. Then I count the cars and trucks that I see passing on the distant highway. I dream and I preach and I count, because this is my Saturday—my no-school, fishing, best-of-the-week day.

Fishing was a relaxation for me during childhood, but it was also a hunt and a chase. It was a sport that involved "setting goals," "making decisions," and "solving problems," all of which would become the themes of my ministry years later. In my childhood days, the never-dry rivers were shallow with warm waters between spring and winter—so warm that bullheads, catfish, and carp lived and reproduced there—and waited to be caught from fishing poles made from slim, trimmed tree branches.

Even when my father would discover me in my dreamy hideout by the Floyd, or occasionally scold me for being late for my farm duties, I would find myself encouraged. He would often model for me how to set my sights on distant discoveries, encouraging me, through example, to yearn and believe in "somewhere(s)" and "someday(s)."

Year after year, he would convey his visionary hopes as he came to find me and walk me home from my fishing spot. He would be out to gather the straggling cows, and I would be out a bit too long and running late for evening chores, and together we would walk the cows back toward the barn to be milked.

"Someday they're going to come in and take our dead-end road all the way through this pasture, across that Floyd River, clear through the cornfield, and across those railroad tracks over there."

Then he would point and make sure that my glance followed his finger. "Over there, where you see the long railroad trains," he would clarify.

"And they'll connect our dead-end road with that road that guides all those cars and trucks that you spend so much time counting when you're out here fishing. Yep—those cars and trucks movin' way off over there will someday drive right by our home. We'll be in a prime location. Our road will become a main road, paved with cement instead of dirt. And they'll give our road a name."

In his overalls, he would reach his arms toward the vast, empty plain that stretched as far as the eye could see. "Way off" meant the horizon where you could see something moving slowly. Little cars, little trucks—"little" because they were "way off." That was the main road. It was paved with cement already. It was . . . Big-Time!

"Say, Harold, did you know that many of those people traveling on that cement road out there are going all the way from Sioux City, Iowa, to Saint Paul, Minnesota? That's a mighty big trip!"

He said this with an admiration for that distant world that inspired his imagination and mine. I was awestruck by the unknown right along with him.

He would make many promises, and though he gave his utmost to fulfill any and every vow he made, this prediction of progress that would include our land would never come to pass. But his dreaming was contagious nonetheless, shaping my young mind.

I could imagine it all. Someday our dusty dirt road wouldn't be a *nowhere* road, it would be a *somewhere* road. It would no longer leave a mile-long cloud of quiet dust behind us when we came home from a visit to the country store a few miles away in Newkirk; or when we returned home after Sunday church; or when we . . . well, when we came from or went anywhere.

Someday this road would be graveled with sand and crushed stones and even hard asphalt or concrete! We wouldn't get stuck anymore in the mud on rain-soaked days.

Someday big machines would come in and make our road come alive and grow, all the way through the long, flat pasture and cropland until it crossed the river and the railroad and hit the Big-Time road where important people were riding on other paved roads coming from somewhere and going to somewhere! Someday. *Someday!*

I wanted someday to grow up and have the experience of going "somewhere." Such a place sounded awfully exciting.

I suppose my Dad believed in "somewhere(s)" and "someday(s)" because he had lived the journey. Dad had found his "somewhere." He had watched Sioux County (named after the Native American tribe who had lived here before us) grow from a sod-house-speckled land to a farming community with real farmhouses.

My father had, through hard work and frugality, moved on from being an orphaned farm servant to owning his own farmland. He had moved on from being born in a sod house, with dirt floors so hard that the women would sweep them with their homemade bristled brooms, to buying and building that Sears-Roebuck house where I had been born and where I would live until I left for college.

But it hadn't been easy for him. America in the 1920s—after World War I—went into a wild inflationary roll. Prices were out of sight. Farmland was being sold to young farmers for twice—no, quadruple—its value! The value of crops simply wouldn't be able to support the large mortgages that resulted. But the economy was going up for now. Some farmers surmised that they'd be glad they bought land at the price they did. Dad was one of those who paid too much.

And then the Great Depression hit. Once during those lean years Dad sold a fifty-dollar cow for a ten-dollar bank draft, only to find that the bank on which it was drawn had closed its doors and the draft was worthless! But he survived.

My father would be so proud when, in 1939, Sioux Electrical finally came to install tall black power poles with electrical wires running all the way down our long dirt road. Dad dug just a bit deeper into his denim dungarees to pay a photographer to take pictures of the installation. Gene Mulder and Henry Cammock, men

I've never met, hold a place among the family farm photos, still in existence today, simply because they dared to fiddle with the foreign wires that held this magical power.

Electricity would revolutionize the workload of the farm community. Pumps to draw water from deep wells would be powered by electric motors. I would no longer have to crowd around the one kerosene lamp, sharing it with Mom as she darned socks and Dad as he studied his corn and cattle prices. Instead the whole room would be lit and we each could claim our own private corner.

And the power poles, with their glass "ornaments" on top, would supply me with new daily entertainment as I walked from school. The glass jars that held the electricity becoming a perfect target with a pocketful of tiny stones for ammunition. Armed with a wooden slingshot made from a Y-shaped twig, I would discover another "sport!"

Dad knew that hard work and faith (sometimes against the greatest of odds) made dreams come true. He encouraged me to dream my dreams, to pay the price, and to never, ever give up! However, more often than not, I needed prodding, and Henry was determined to provide the motivation.

More frequently than I care to remember, our screen door would squeak open as I sat at the table furtively eating the last bite of a piece of pie left over from our big dinner that noon. My big brother would step in and admonish me. "Get out here *now* and do your chores, Harold," he would reprove.

Now old enough to do most chores on my own, I'd pick up the empty pail from the porch and head for the chicken coop, where all the chickens were sitting on the eggs they'd laid since dawn. I'd wave them off, their wings fluttering, and then carefully pick up the fresh, warm eggs and place them in the bucket. By the time I finished the job, the pail would be nearly half full. I'd carry the bucket with eggs to Mom in the house. There I'd turn the radio on and listen to the first of two exciting half-hour plays, *Jack Armstrong: The All-American Boy.*

"Okay, Harold," my brother would call out again, "it's time to milk." I would run to the barn, where all the cows were standing in their stalls with full udders waiting for the hands of my father or brother or me. I'd switch the radio on in the barn to listen to the same radio station—"WNAX, Yankton, South Dakota"—to hear the next exciting chapter of my other favorite radio play, *Captain Midnight.*

I'd grab my milk stool, a humble seat made from the twelve-inch-long end of a wooden lamppost with a flat ten-by-six-inch plank of wood nailed on top for a seat, and position myself almost under the first milk cow. Her thick teats would be swollen with milk waiting to be squeezed out in long, noisy splashes into the empty pail held between my knees.

Almost every night at least one of the three cows I had to milk would interrupt the process by switching her long tail to chase away flies. "Ouch!" I'd yell, ducking too late as the dirty tail hit my face, irritating it with the tiny, thorny cockleburs that had stuck to the tail during the course of the day's grazing. Then she would typically spread her rear legs, lift her tail, and empty her bladder, splashing urine in the gutter and sending dirty drops onto my shoes. "I'm sure glad I'm not going to be a farmer when I grow up!" I would grumble.

I thought positively even way back then . . . and was positively disgusted! I would remember that thought years later when a book I wrote made the *New York Times* bestseller list with the title *Tough Times Never Last, But Tough People Do!*

Once, when I was listening to my usual *Captain Midnight* episode as I milked, I stopped paying attention to my chore as the fast-moving plot reached an exhilarating peak. The bucket of fresh milk slipped from between my knees and overturned in the gutter. Henry jumped up from his stool, but he could do nothing to redeem the loss.

"Harold, I hope you *do* make a living talking when you grow up," he scolded me, "for sure you'll never make it as a farmer!"

Once we were done with a cow, we'd empty the fresh milk into a big separator. In this machine the milk was swirled rapidly, causing the cream in the milk to rise to the top so that it could be drained off into a large cream can. The milk and separated cream would be sold for "real money" (not just traded for other household goods) when the dairy truck came to collect.

Almost all the farmers in our region had milk cows. The cattle would graze in pastureland in those parts of the farm where swamps or creeks made the land unsuitable for plowing and planting corn or oats or beans. Cows made these infertile sections of the farm productive and brought in a daily flow of cash.

One day I was walking from the chicken coop to the house with a rich collection of eggs, feeling great about my bounty. I imagined how these eggs, added to yesterday's and tomorrow's, would be picked up by Arie or taken to the small country store where they'd be exchanged by the owner for our basic foodstuff.

In the empty yard between the chicken coop and the house stood two of our horses. Somehow they had gotten out of the barn and were standing in the open space; they were "necking," as we called it—that is, they had their long necks crossed one over the other, making it appear as if their large bodies were connected. For some reason a tiny gap between the two pairs of rear legs beckoned me. I decided to walk in between the horses and break up this little "match." Next thing I knew, two huge long legs catapulted in the air, landing one heavy hoof full force in my face. My pail of eggs went flying, and I sprawled to the ground with my chin cut open, bleeding profusely. Broken eggshells, runny egg whites, and yellow egg yokes were splattered all over.

I lay there crying until Mom came running. She patched me up, but I still carry a crease in my chin deep enough to make shaving in that old scar a time-consuming and skin-cutting ritual.

My brother witnessed the egg-splattering and chin-splitting accident, but I got no sympathy from him. If he'd had any doubts, that clinched it: farming would *not* be in my future. All I could think was that *someday* I would no longer have to milk that. *Someday* I would no longer have to collect eggs. And *someday* I would no longer have to look stupid in Henry's eyes.

We couldn't afford to purchase coal for the kitchen stove, so I was given the very important chore of gathering dirty corncobs in the hog yard for fuel, collecting them in an empty basket. The pigs would eat a cob clean and clear of its kernels, leaving the hard core to lie in the hog waste. I would try to find dry cobs that were two or three days old, but too often I had to settle for the slimy, dung-covered ones. I can still remember the stench on my fingers as I walked back to the house with my smelly bucket.

But I learned a lesson that would serve me well in my life:

Even waste products are useful for something!

The cobs made a hot fire in our cookstove — perfect for warming cold bodies, frying steak from a slaughtered cow, or roasting a chicken from our yard.

In town, where there were no pigs that left dirty cobs, boys from families struggling through the Depression often had to participate in "Lug Nacht," the night designated for a secret collection of coal. As the coal train passed through town, an older teen would jump on it and clamber up on its black gold. He would throw coal bound for Sioux City or Minneapolis into the ditch alongside the tracks, where other, younger boys would scamper and scurry to fill their bags. Should a boy be caught and escorted home by the law, his parents scolded him roundly. But when the next "Lug Nacht" rolled around, those same parents would whisk him back out the door for more fuel.

The burning cobs would heat the kitchen in the cold winter months when the temperature was often below zero. These were the days when I couldn't escape to the river with my fishing pole, so

I would often go to the horse stalls in an attempt to escape from my duties. I would talk to Mabel, her velvet muzzle warm upon my cheek. Hers was one of the most intimate touches I would ever feel as a boy.

"It's time to milk, Harold." Somehow those words always found me. I lived with that call twice a day from the age of five until, at sixteen, I left the farm to go to college. Despite blizzards in winter and thunderstorms and windstorms in summer, we were never given a single day's vacation from that chore.

During a severe drought in 1936, water was so scarce that crops withered in the hot, dry fields. The Floyd was too shallow to grant me my fishing days. Then came the duststorms that blew with fierce winds from South Dakota. Visibility was so poor that we couldn't see the barn from the house. Come milking time, we couldn't breathe as we made our way to the barn. So we each took a square of thin cloth from the house, wet it down, plastered it over our faces, and headed into the thick fog of flying dust. Skipping even one day would cause the fresh load of milk to get thick in the udder, ruining the health of a very valuable asset. No matter what the weather, the cows *had* to be milked!

I know now that I learned one of my life's most valuable lessons from this chore:

Problems are never to be turned into excuses for walking away and not performing your job.

I often wanted to walk away, but I never did. Still, I didn't understand how Henry could settle into this life so effortlessly. In fact, he seemed to love it. Dad and he understood each other and farm life on a level that was foreign to me. I was glad that Dad had taught me to believe in "somewhere(s)" and "someday(s)." Dad and Henry had found their "somewhere," and I became more and more convinced, encouraged by Dad's understanding glances, that I would find mine.

So, on those warm, stormless, no-school, fishing, best-of-the-week days, I would prepare myself for the day when I would hasten into *my* "somewhere." These became my training sessions for the years ahead, giving me courage to go beyond the known and excel at dreaming impossible dreams.

There were other training sessions as well. I remember one October, my fishing days nearing their season's end, when my teacher said, "You're going to be a preacher, aren't you?" When I nodded my assent, she said, "Then I'll give you a little poem to memorize for the Christmas play. You'll have to recite it on stage, standing alone—like a little preacher. How would you like that?"

"Oh, yes!" I exclaimed. I wondered if I'd died and gone to heaven. A real audience! A real stage! A real message! For once I couldn't wait for the winter season that I usually so dreaded.

Had the teacher, who was also my Aunt Alys, known about all the practice I'd had alone in the pasture, and just how successful my delivery would be, I think that she would have made me the master of ceremonies.

Like my faithful Saturday Ayrshire audience, the families that were gathered in the schoolhouse on the night of my debut found themselves captivated by the rhythm and passion of my delivery.

As I wrapped up that first solo oration, I knew that I'd been a real success! For the first time, I was venturing toward the unknown, greeting unfamiliarity. It was like standing at the train depot in Alton buying my very own ticket. The man in the sales booth would help me asking:

"*Destination?*"

"*Somewhere!*"

"*Where?*"

You know—Somewhere! Near "the Edge"!?!

And someday I *would go*! I would go! All aboard! To Somewhere!

X

Our small house disappears as we leave the dead-end road behind us. Dad is driving, my mother alongside him, and I sit alone in the back seat of our Model T. The dust races behind our car as if a rich purse were at stake. Driven now by a rear wind, will the dust arrive in town ahead of us? Our dusty, dirty country road always leaves its mark. Known for its bitter territorial nature, that dust owns us. We *are* farmers, and we *do* live at the end of a dead-end and dusty road, and anyone who sees us driving by, even on the blacktop, can read those facts in our telltale coating of dust.

Today, however, I pretend to be a *town* boy, for I'm going to visit a town friend Arie—Arie, Hank, John, Stan . . . seemed every family had at least one of each!—who lives in Orange City. Jess had cleaned house for his mom. Now his mom and my mom were friends. This is the first time she has taken me along for a visit.

The car slows to the side of a street lined with pretty houses and welcoming elms. I plunge from the car to race toward this enchanted place, but I feel a sudden grab on my shoulder. With that touch and a reproving gaze, my mother repositions me at her side. She nods at my father. He waits in the car parked at the curb while we ascend the steps to the front door. I gaze at the knob, waiting for it to turn. Moments later, I'm sitting at a town table, drinking town lemonade from a town glass in a town kitchen with a town friend. I may be in Iowa—but I'm experiencing heaven.

After a while, the excitement and the lemonade have me fearing for my bladder and searching for the back door. I step outside and scan the backyard. It adjoins other backyards, all unfenced, open and friendly. I see no outhouse—not even the hope of some privacy. I'm beginning to feel desperate when Arie, tagging behind, lets go of the screen door, allowing it to slam closed, and runs out to me.

"Say Harold, whatcha doin'?"

"Where's your outhouse, Arie?"

"Oh geez, Harold, come on, follow me," he says, heading back inside. *Inside?*

I hesitate. "Arie, I really have to go . . . bad!" I call out. "I can't play until I use your outhouse!"

The pressure is making my abdomen bulge. I turn back around, scanning the yard.

Arie comes out and grabs me again. "No, let's go inside, Harold."

I pull my arm free. "I've *got* to pee! I'll play in a minute!"

He grabs me again "It's *inside!*" he assures me.

Mom hears our scuffle. "Harold! What's going on out there?"

"Nothing, Mom!"

But she doesn't believe me. She comes to investigate. Once she understands the cause of my distress, she explains that Arie has a toilet inside his house, just like Grandma and Grandpa have in theirs. I don't know what she means. I've never seen one in my grandparents' house. I'm always sent to their outhouse! Can it really be that people have toilets *inside* houses? Inside *Arie's* house? And I'm supposed to *use* one?

"Inside his house is a toilet. A toilet is inside his house." No matter how I rearrange these words, they make no sense! Arie drags me along as Mom returns to more conversation with her friend. But I'm still befuddled. "Inside his house is a toilet. A toilet is inside his house!"

Who wants a toilet *inside* a house? I know what a barn smells like. I smell its stench when I wake, when I sleep, when I eat, when I clean, and yeah, when I pee. Even on the farm we keep the toilet *out* of the house and as far away as possible. But now I'm in town, and I don't know what to make of such things!

Arie takes me into their indoor outhouse. To my utter amazement, it doesn't stink! In fact, it's fresh and sparkling. It's even pretty! He ushers me to a white seat with a big hole cut out of the center and a pool of water in its depths. Pointing into the cavernous beast, he says, "Pee in there." Then he points to a chain hanging above the toilet and adds, "Then pull this down."

He leaves and shuts the door. "Inside his house is a toilet. A toilet is inside his house." I still can't believe this. I'm standing and dropping my dungarees. I'm in a house. I'm in a room. I'm not in a shack. I'm not in a mini-barn. I'm not in the outhouse.

I'm standing on a clean hardwood floor, and there's a picture on the wall of some men and women standing in front of a church. This makes me feel funny. In front of me is a mirror, so I can see myself. I have to close my eyes.

I'm standing in a field, I tell myself. But I still can't go. I just can't relax. I try another visualization tactic. I'm out at the Floyd, fishing. Finally I begin to pee, and the warm comfort of relief settles over me. My rear end isn't shivering with cold, and I don't hear the rustle of field mice at my feet.

I sigh in satisfaction. My dungarees gather at my ankles and cover every inch of my boots. I *like* this inside-the-house toilet. This is luxury. I'll stay here forever. Then Arie is knocking. "Harold?" he calls out. "Did you fall in?"

I grab my dungarees and tug them up, securing the fading straps over my shoulders. Then, with a flourish, I raise my right hand and with a sense of near-royal pride, I give the chain a yank downward.

To my dismay, there's a sudden explosion!

Skoo-pu-whoop! Poosh! Poosh! Whoo!

I jump back in horror! What *is* that?

The growl comes from the dark belly, and it doesn't end. I step even further back.

Pewsh-wha!

My heart is racing with fear. The toilet is broken and bleeding with water! What have I done?! It isn't stopping! What if it overflows the whole room? I've broken it! I just know I've broken it!

"Inside this house *was* a toilet. A toilet *was* inside this house!"

What do I do now? I don't know if I like this after all. Outhouses are familiar and safe. What will I say to Arie? What will I say to Mom? I'm frozen in shameful panic.

Then suddenly it's silent.

The growling has ceased.

I take a cautious step toward this frightful water-making machine.

Silence.

I step one more careful step toward its belly. Stretching forward, I gaze into its abyss.

The water is clean? The water is clean? The water *is* clean!

Woo-ha! It worked! It worked! Wowzy-wow!

And so Arie and I return to our play, but my mind wanders with new intrigue. What else is out there, yet to be discovered, in other worlds I don't know exist?

I would continue to visit Arie during the following years. The streets of the town would begin to change, but that house remains today identical to the day of my first visit—white, pillared, small, quaint, and for me still a very dramatic place! It stood for me as a monument to innovation.

As time delivered me upon the doorstep of my high school years, I would stop in front of that house as if it were a shrine whenever I walked the streets of Orange City. For there, in a flash, I often found myself inspired to pursue some crazy idea. And so I would feel, for a moment, akin with the dreamers and the doers who were out there in that "somewhere," trying and daring new things.

How could I transform the dull and visionless expressions worn by my stuck-in-a-rut neighbors and help them to see and yearn for a better unknown? Could they not see? Did they not know? Would they not grasp for their tomorrows with vigor and determination? Why were people always so slow and cautious to try something new and better than what they were used to?

Silently, subconsciously, these contradictions simply reinforced choice on my part. And the choice was becoming easier and easier. I would emerge as one habitually determined to move beyond limited environments. I would become addicted to exploring worlds near "the edge." And as I did, my "somewhere" just drew nearer and nearer, looking brighter with every new day.

XI

It was 1939 when I said goodbye to the familiarities of my first eight years of school. Goodbye recess. Goodbye boy's outhouse—hot and malodorous in summer and cold in winter. Goodbye Aunt Alys, who that year bragged that seven eighth-grade students graduated, a record high for that one-room country school.

Hello Newkirk High. Hello running water and indoor toilets. The times they were a-changing! I would enjoy the modern, concrete building that accommodated seventy-four students in four grades, nine through twelve. Now thirteen years old, I was a high school freshman.

The next years were busy with Mr. Ver Heul—mathematics. I barely endured it. Mrs. McCrill—general science. "What's a cyclone, Harold?" she asked one day. "A big windbag!" I joked, and my classmates roared. Mrs. McCrill was angry with what she called my "smart alec" remark, though I'm afraid that was just the first of many. Mr. Sicafoose—civics. Miss Aeilts—music, drama, and English literature. How I loved Miss Aeilts! Her classes became the highlight of my days.

I was growing tall. Nearly six feet. Still more round than lean. My voice matured into a mellow tenor. Singing became my interest; sports did not. I was likeable but friends were more like acquaintances, and my dream of somewhere was still my closest companion. My junior year started great in September, but eleven weeks later all hell broke loose.

It was Sunday, December 7, 1941. I was coming out of the barn carrying a pail of milk to the house when my mom came running out in a near panic. "Where's Dad?" she shouted.

Before I could answer, she shrieked, "Harold, we're at war! Japan bombed Pearl Harbor!"

Dad and Henry heard her and came running out of the barn. All of us, rushing back to the house, pulled the kitchen chairs around the radio to hear the strong, dignified voice of President Roosevelt. "Thousands of our brightest and happiest young boys lie dead in the waters of Pearl Harbor," he said. "This day will live in infamy."

The next morning when I boarded the big school bus everyone was buzzing with the news. None of the students were old enough to go to war, but it seemed as if most of us had brothers who would be drafted. High school would never again be quite the same.

"Why is she crying?" I asked a "friend," pointing to a senior girl I didn't really know. She'd had her handkerchief to her eyes all morning.

"Her brother left home this morning for the Army," he answered.

An unusual cloud had suddenly moved into northwest Iowa, and it would hang there for four years. I too had an older brother, and I knew that he could be drafted any day.

We all began to live from moment to moment, never knowing what the news would bring. Food rationing started early on, with every family registering for the coupons that had to be handed over to the cashier when buying sugar or gasoline. Mom had to stop baking pies and cakes, and we had to make do with Cracker Pop (soda crackers simmered in milk).

Oddly enough, studies went on as usual, though there were interruptions, to be sure. Every so often an unexpected surge of grief would explode our bubble of a world as a student or teacher received grim news of a loved one wounded or killed. Sioux County was suddenly not its own little isolated colony—a world apart from the rest. We had been initiated into the larger body of the United States of America, and all of us now were aware of a great world across the oceans! My first global consciousness. Protestants fought alongside Catholics, town and city boys alongside country farmboys.

But those of us yet to be considered men were expected to exert our energies on our studies, and we did. We were grateful for the opportunity while it lasted. We all knew that if the war kept its present pace, we would end up in uniform soon enough.

It was during this time that Miss Aeilts proved herself as my most influential instructor in these formative years. She stopped me in the hall one day, simply to make personal acquaintance. Heretofore I'd been just one of the students—a name during roll call, son of Anthony and Jennie Schuller.

She introduced herself and said, "Did I hear that you're going to be a preacher, Harold?"

I nodded.

"It's important for you to feel comfortable saying dramatic lines on stage in front of people."

I nodded again.

"We have only twelve senior students for the senior class play this year; we're one short. I know that you're only a junior, but . . . would you like the part?"

I accepted immediately, but not without a touch of apprehension. Not that I was shy by any means. And certainly I was flattered. It was just . . . well, it was the role. This was a challenging part they wanted me to do, and I wasn't sure I had it in me.

Despite my doubts, I threw myself into intense, overtime rehearsals with the cast.

As the days drew on, I found myself increasingly concerned. Nonetheless, I determined to follow through. I gradually found the determination to rise to the occasion, vowing inwardly to do no less than beguile and enchant the audience. This was my final resolve come opening night.

Waiting to go on, I am looking out at the audience and see Arie (my old town friend), which makes me think of the "watershed" moment at his house, my first encounter with indoor plumbing. I'm convinced that this night will prove equally memorable in its own way. Not too far away from Arie is Aunt Alys, my grade school teacher, sitting with Dad and Mom, and I think back to the day I recited the poem for the Christmas play, and how the audience and I enjoyed each other so much that I felt I'd found my destiny.

Speaking in public has never caused my nerves to quake; it enlivens me. It's something I do well. Throughout my years in grade school I had continued as "cleric" to the cattle by the Floyd, and as "entertainer" to the audience I was given seasonally at the country school. I was determined to prod myself. I wanted to continue to be the daring pacesetter I had been when I was brave enough to use an indoor outhouse. I was constantly looking ahead for a new growth experience that could come with any and every tomorrow, standing again on the edge. But for now that meant playing a new role—the role of a *woman!*

Standing backstage, peeking through the curtain, I am wondering again, for the umpteenth time, why in the world, when they needed a junior for this role, did they pick me—a boy—instead of a girl? Were there really no girls at all who were willing?

I look at myself in the mirror, checking my costume and my makeup one last time.

"My gosh!" I'm shocked as ever, seeing myself in a long dress with thick pads for breasts!

I flatten out the full skirt, pat my long wig, and secure the flimsy cloth hat I'm wearing—and then it's time for my entrance. I clear my throat. Tonight I'll need to project my tenor voice high-pitched and far enough to be heard by this entire audience—the largest one I've ever had.

I hear my cue and lunge from behind the curtains to a roar of laughter. The response thrills me! This is what I've been working for with Miss Aeilts all year. I bound over to join the other performers. My fake bosom shifts a bit, but I'm having such fun that I continue my skip about the stage, dress hoisted in hand. The audience is crying with laughter, thoroughly entertained as I say my first lines in a shrill falsetto voice. I suddenly think of a quick line to add, and the crowd claps with joy. The actors are a little confused by my improvisation, but when I end with the rehearsed line, they rebound and deliver their parts.

As the play ends, I bow to exhilarating applause. I think what a pleasure preaching will be if I can just remember to have fun and entertain my audience.

I was learning that good, clean fun and humor have an amazing capacity to lift people above their daily cares. I recalled the healing power of laughter I discovered as a child (I may be *last*; but not *lost!*), and my rewarding experience with the senior play surged in me the desire to deliver joy to others. During those years of World War II, laughter was gravely needed to compensate for all the heavy hearts the war had created. In a funny way I began to see such uplift as a form of ministry (though I'm sure the Dominee from my childhood would have begged to differ). Subconsciously this would motivate me in later years to become a preacher who entertained people *and* honored God as well!

It was Miss Aeilts who, as my high school English teacher, exposed me to the wonderful world of Shakespeare and Tennyson and Browning. She made us memorize classics word for word. And we were called on to recite them "with feeling and passion" in front of the whole class. I would never take courses in college or seminary that I enjoyed so thoroughly.

"Gesture! Raise your voice!" she insisted. "Slow down here. Let your voice drop to a whisper. Feel the feelings in the words! Lock eyes with your audience. Use that body language: your eyes, your face, your head. Yes! Throw your head back here; drop it there. Really get into it. I'll make a preacher out of you yet!"

She also made a singer out of me.

In her other role—music teacher—Miss Aeilts carefully chose

four boys whose voices stood out in the school chorus. "Gentlemen," she told us, "I'm forming a male quartet. Harold— you'll be first tenor."

She coached us. She worked us. She was fantastic. She made us so good that in the high school music contest for the state of Iowa, we won first place among all the male quartets, though we were one of the smallest high schools in the state. We won over Des Moines, Sioux City, Fort Dodge, Iowa City, and other huge schools!

The fun we had with our quartet got me hooked on singing. I enjoyed making music so much that I would later form a male quartet at Hope College, a move that would prove profoundly providential. But I'm convinced that this college quartet, so pivotal in my life, would never have happened without my high school experience with Miss Aeilts.

As happens to nearly every young person in high school, my small world of relationships began to evolve. Through my experiences with drama and music at Newkirk High, I began to believe in my gifts to woo a crowd, and I discovered new friends. The high school quartet "guys" became my buddies at school, but I had yet to find a "best friend" with whom I could hang out on weekends and after school. I would cut up in class, then withdraw back into my isolation. Even at our Newkirk church, where I had grown up among a close-knit group of parishioners—people I had shared every Sunday with since my birth, sitting in the back pew next to Mom once I left her arms—I hadn't acquired what so many other kids seem to discover: a best buddy.

Meanwhile, Henry was feeling an increase of the fidgets, listening every Sunday to the preacher in our country church to whom my folks had been faithful all these years. Despite the lovely and loyal spirit of my folks' pastor, this restless condition eventually led my siblings to another church—First Reformed Church in Orange City—seven miles from our house. From that pulpit a vivacious Dominee was enticing and stimulating the county's youth. Now that I was a high-schooler and enjoying some newfound independence, I tagged along with Henry in his car every Sunday for the drive to Orange City.

This house of worship was huge, seating hundreds of people. The entire balcony was often filled with teenaged boys and young men, a group that sometimes forgot proper ecclesiastical etiquette. The preacher, a famous orator named Henry Colenbrander, would often stop in his forty-five minute sermon to lift an arm like a rifle taking aim, pointing toward the balcony. There he would stand for a long moment, exposing transgressors who were whispering through his sermon or otherwise causing a disturbance. Though he would say nothing, silence would fall over the huge audience. Mothers and fathers would turn to see if it was their son—heaven help us!—who had prompted the rebuke.

It was in that balcony, in an irreverent state of "naughtiness," that I met Stephen Earl De Jong. We were the only two from Newkirk High School, so we began to chat. (Yes—during Reverend Colenbrander's sermon.) We hit it off immediately. I liked the fact that Earl was on the quiet side, which meant that I could do all the talking. It was a boon that he also liked my jokes. For his part, I think Earl liked the fact that I was outspoken and willing to take the lead in new situations and social settings. Earl was smaller than I, both width-wise and height-wise, but he was strong—a hardworking farmer like Dad and Henry.

And so Earl became my friend. And it was natural, as we grew old enough to drive ourselves (usually in Earl's car) that we would join along in the Sunday night ritual of what today would be called "cruising the boulevard."

After church the girls would promenade, either with the intention of attracting the admiration of a male passerby or with the simple purpose of going from one place to another. Which one of us males could ever have hoped to truly know the intent of these females? I *still* don't boast such intuition!

Either way, the girls walked; and while they did so, the guys drove slowly by. Sometimes a whistle erupted from a slow-moving car. Earl and I drove by, too, noticing how pretty this one or that one was, even speaking to one or two on occasion—usually at my outgoing instigation—but that's where it stayed. I don't think we knew to do much else. Even if we had, though, we wouldn't have dared. Every farm kid knew all there was to know about "reproduction," because animals had a way of being quite public about such business. But so revered was the sanctity of marriage that stealing a kiss was about as scandalous an act as we could imagine.

I learned to smoke cigarettes with Earl, a habit that my mother and father bitterly hated and that I would grow to regret. We would walk over to the Newkirk Store after school and on the way "roll our own" tobacco. Once at the store, we would pick up a pint of ice-cream for fifteen cents. If we lacked the full quota of change, we'd settle for a half-pint for seven cents. We'd sit on the front step of the store—the whole place couldn't have measured larger than thirty feet wide and ten feet deep, including the four steps—to enjoy our once-a-week treat, our newly rolled cigarettes peeking from our front shirt pockets as a symbol of wild masculinity.

I was a senior in high school the Sunday evening I sat in the church balcony and heard Reverend Colenbrander call out, "Someone in the balcony needs to come out and give his life to Jesus Christ. You will come to the elders this Wednesday night and personally accept Jesus Christ as your Lord and Savior. The elders will then accept you as a member of this church."

I was sitting in a row up there with Earl De Jong and some others. The Dominee's call engulfed me. I knew that I had to go forward and commit my life publicly, personally, and eternally to Jesus Christ. Earl and the guys were snickering about something or other among themselves, and I could tell that they were wondering why I wasn't joining in. But I wasn't thinking of anything but this one thing: I had to go before the elders. I didn't go "cruising" that night.

Earl wondered what was under my skin, but I assured him it was nothing. This was a *personal* decision, not a *social* decision.

"I'm joining the church, Mom," I announced when I got home. "The elders are meeting this Wednesday night. I'm going—all alone."

She smiled.

In the Lutheran church they went through "confirmation classes." In the Baptist church they would walk to the front of the congregation to accept Jesus Christ and get "saved." As I noted earlier, in the Reformed tradition I'd grown up in—the tradition that my new Orange City church was also a part of—young people studied the Heidelberg Catechism from first grade on, until they could recite it as high-schoolers, and then they'd "hear Christ's call" and go to the elders.

I'd studied the catechism; now it was time for a commitment. It was with a strong sense of expectation that I met with the elders that Wednesday evening. And I wasn't disappointed. "Your eternal salvation is assured forever," they confirmed. I didn't know all that they meant by that statement, but I did know what I felt inside: suddenly, out of nowhere, that "happy feeling" I'd experienced the day of Uncle Henry's proclamation swirled anew within me. In the months and years that followed, I found myself experiencing this "kiss from heaven" more and more often, and wanting it more. I rely on it even now, sixty years later. Meanwhile, I determined that I would show greater reverence during services. I was focused again not only on a "dream" but on my "call," not only as an aspiring preacher, but as a firm believer and follower of Jesus Christ.

As my graduation from high school drew near, I decided that it was time to talk to Mom and Dad about college. I couldn't imagine how they could ever afford an education for me, and yet they knew of my goals and hadn't discouraged me. I'd been studying the colleges in our area, and I'd narrowed down my search to Hope College in Holland, Michigan—a Reformed Church college. Somehow, if I wanted to be ordained into the Reformed Church of America, I had to attend one of the denomination's own schools.

Besides, Uncle Henry had gone to Hope; furthermore, it had been rated as one of the top-ten liberal arts colleges by the North American Association of Accredited Colleges and Universities. Reading through the college's catalog, I'd learned that Hope also offered summer school.

I had made my decision—set my goal. I was going to waste no time getting on to the next lap. I'd be sixteen years and nine months old by the day of my high school graduation. The war was raging in the Pacific and in Europe, and my eighteenth birthday, when I'd have to register for the draft, was only fifteen months away. I wanted as much school as possible under my belt, so that, once drafted, I could qualify to become an assistant to the military chaplain. If I went straight into college, as opposed to relaxing over the summer, I could have a full year's pre-ministerial study before I turned eighteen.

When Jess had taken the job with a missionary family at age sixteen, that had marked the end of her formal education. Henry had stopped school after eighth grade to work the farm. Violet had also been needed on the farm and had returned home after eighth grade. Margaret was my lone predecessor in a quest for higher education, and she had gone into a teaching career living away from the farm. Now it would be my turn. But I needed to communicate these intentions to Mom and Dad.

The conversation took place on a Saturday, a dreaded day that turned out also to be a blessed day, all wrapped up in one big, memorable package. We were sitting at the kitchen table on our ten o'clock lunch break, Dad and I both in from chores. Henry was still working on something he'd been fiddling with all morning in the toolshed.

Mom and Dad listened to my plans with expressions of growing concern. Then they explained that although they had planned and hoped and dreamed for me, they had failed to meet their goal of saving enough to finance my schooling; they simply couldn't afford my college tuition. The news was devastating.

It's one thing to lose one's dream because of laziness or lack of determination, but because of lack of resources? Because we didn't have the same means as another family who would send a passionless youth into his uninvited future? My heart was dashed along with my hopes. My ticket to "somewhere" shredded. It wasn't fair. It simply wasn't fair!

But I said none of this. Instead, I assured Mom and Dad that I could find a part-time job in Holland to pay for expenses. I told them that I was grateful for their faith in me and in my dreams. Then we were all silent for a long time.

Had I been able to peer into Dad's heart, would I have found him questioning his faith? Had I read Mom's silent thoughts, would I have heard her scolding Tony for not planning better?

During our long silence Margaret walked in through the back door. She had come over to visit before going into town. We quickly changed the mood and welcomed her for coffee, but not for access into the secret conversation. I rose and left to sort out my prospects.

Later that evening, after supper and chores, Dad and Mom called me to the kitchen. I wasn't yet sufficiently recovered to endure small talk or attempted reassurances. Then it came, one of those moments when suddenly I sensed that I was on the edge of a miracle.

At that wonderful little kitchen table, where eleven years earlier I had declared my intention to be a preacher like Uncle Henry, Mom and Dad told me that Hope College was a good choice. Confused, I leaned forward, trying to understand what they were saying. They had taken a second look at their finances, they said, and had decided that they could help supplement my earned income in college. They told me not to question how or why, just to apply for admission and to "trust God."

I couldn't believe my ears! What had happened in the intervening hours? How could my plan have looked so lost and dead in the morning and now be restored and resurrected?

I did as I was told, though, and I didn't question. That very night I began the application process and decided to leave for college as soon as I had my diploma in hand.

In the weeks that followed, I discovered that Margaret, on the day of her visit, had told Mom and Dad that she wanted to help out. She couldn't afford the room and board—"Harold should be able to earn that if he gets a job at school," she said—but she offered to pay my tuition from her teacher's salary. "It will be my gift to my kid brother's dream," she said. "It won't be a loan." So she became the first person to "invest" in my life's work.

The war continued to drag on. The night I graduated from high school bombs were still falling and young men were still dropping dead in pools of their own blood. But Henry remained home in our sanctuary on that no-number, no-name road. Was it possible that even the U.S. government didn't know our address?

Our senior class chose as our commencement motto a line that I'll never forget:

Tonight we launch. Where shall we anchor?

It was the summer of 1943, and I was leaving the two-story brick building of Newkirk High, central to that small rural crossroads, flanked only by the tiny store down the road and, on the other side, the small country church where I had been baptized.

"I'm glad I'm not coming back next year," I said to John DeHaan. He had sung in the male quartet with me during the past couple of years. We had finished our last performance the week before, and he had stopped by the school to pick up something he'd left with Miss Aeilts. He had joined the navy and would be leaving in the coming week.

I was on my way to the bus for my last ride home. "I won't miss anything," I remarked glibly to John. Earl, who was walking with me, nodded in agreement.

I was gravely wrong, though. I would miss meeting the incoming freshman class, which would include John's little sister, Arvella DeHaan. This young woman who would unbeknownst to me, become the most important and beloved person in my whole life.

XII

It's morning. The last morning that this young man, just shy of seventeen, will wake up in the northwest bedroom of a Sears-Roebuck farmhouse on a dead-end road that has no name and no number.

I've been excused from chores so that I can be clean and dressed for the day's travel to Holland, Michigan. I'm not sure I could have concentrated on anything anyway (as if I ever did!).

Mom and Dad have painstakingly afforded me a small new wardrobe to last me, ideally, the entire four years that I'd be away. I must be sure to stay away from sweets, or I'll find myself wardrobe-less!

Even early in the morning it's apparent that this will be a mild, warm, pleasant June day, appropriate for my new "going-away" Sunday suit.

I button my white dress shirt as I look through the pane of glass, speckled with evaporating dew. I see sunbeam sprites dancing about the cottonwoods that my father planted so long ago. I think again about that other long-range plan, the one that began the day Uncle Henry came. The proclamation he made, the goal he laid for me of the twenty-year scholastic path, the prayer I said as I knelt by my bed, the vow to my father.

"Harold!" Mom calls, and I snap back into action, quickly finishing dressing.

Mom has made a feast of a breakfast. I smell it as the stairs squeak their farewell. It's unusually quiet as we eat—Dad, Henry, Mom, and I. Then we hear the crunching of gravel, the sound that alerts us to visitors.

It's Jess and Margaret and Vi, come to see me off. Jess's little ones run around, occasionally tripping over their mother's crutches and evoking a scolding from "Grandma Jennie." Vi, her baby due very soon, asks if she can borrow the infant baptismal gown that I wore and goes upstairs to find it. Margaret is quiet.

We all finish our black coffee and speak little until we hear another vehicle coming down our lonely road. Then the chatter flares and motion abounds as Mom jumps from her chair to check, once more, the going-away items that she's lovingly baked and carefully packed.

Mom now shifts her attention back to me, hurrying me out of my seat. She whisks her large hands across my shoulders to give a final press to my black Sunday suit. She speaks in Dutch, her words coming fast. She's nervous. I can tell, because even though she tries to conceal her emotion, her voice is shaking. Dad stands, lanky and silent by the icebox, looking down at the floor, his white hair and eyebrows in handsome contrast to his leathery tan skin. His hands are hidden in his dungarees. Henry goes outside to greet the guest, Reverend William Van't Hof, come all the way from Holland, Michigan.

Mom continues her inspection of my things—the baked goods meant to last the week, my small traveling trunk—but all seems in order. She moves about in anxious Dutch chatter, speaking mostly to herself. She says how nice it was for Reverend Van't Hof to take me to school so that I wouldn't have to go on the train. With all those boys going to the service, she's sure I'd get lost if I traveled through the stations along the route all alone.

I think about other mothers and other sons, and other farewells much more burdened with worry. Earl told me the previous night that he was signing up, but I was so preoccupied with my own imminent departure that his news hardly registered. It hits me now, though, and I realize that I'm lucky to be heading for college and not the Army. (I should've given him a heartier goodbye!)

Mom continues her chattering. "He's important, too, Harold!" she says, reminding me *once again* that Reverend Van't Hof is pastor of a large church in Holland, Michigan.

Is she afraid I'll be disrespectful? For heaven's sake, I'm sixteen years old! I'm going off to college! But I let it go. She continues, "The Lord was just so good to have the Reverend here visiting his sister right when we needed him." She reminds me once more to be grateful.

Then I hear a familiar phrase, quietly spoken under her breath. Had I questioned her about it, I'm convinced that she would have denied saying it. But I heard it: "*Heere bewaar.*" "The Lord protect." She shoots a tense glance at me, embarrassed. She doesn't want to lose her composure in the sight of *anyone*, especially not her baby son. But I know that I heard those words. To my ears, her whispered prayer is her most sincere and precious goodbye.

The poignancy of the moment passes. She charges me to "beware of the cults." I know that by this she means the Methodists and the Baptists and the Catholics and the . . . well, any church *other* than the Dutch Reformed. I promise and take a mental note to be on guard.

I put my things, small and few, in the reverend's car trunk, then look up to see my family standing by that same picket gate where I sat waiting for Uncle Henry years before. I approach my family pensively to say goodbye.

First Jess. I give her a hug as she sits in a lawn chair. Her body is strong and big despite her debilitated legs.

Then comes Violet. She pokes at me with a teasing jab. "Be good, Harold!" My "fun" sister whom I love dearly. I grin and want to chuckle, but I'm determined to carry a serious air in the presence of Reverend Van't Hof.

Margaret is quiet and wet-eyed. I don't know how to tell her goodbye, much less how to express my gratitude. I just look at her soft features and smile. "Thank you, Margaret," I say. I don't tell her that I know she'll be paying my tuition each semester, but she senses my meaning. Then I remember the stories about the Gypsies, and all our times together gathering eggs, and so with glistening eyes I say it again: "Thank you, Margaret—for ... everything!" She just smiles and shakes her head, denying that she's done anything worth my gratitude.

Henry is next. He holds himself at full height and thrusts his hand into mine. "Harold!" he says commandingly, smiling with a pride I've not seen before. But that's *all* he says, as if saying only my name in such a tone says it all. I know what he's thinking, though: "Thank goodness you're not going to be a farmer!"

Mom is too nervous about the time and our need to get going to give a lengthy goodbye. A strong, abrupt hug, a heavy pat on my back, and a quick, firm kiss on the cheek. Her eyebrows have that stern look, but I know it's only that she's worrying and wondering about the time.

Dad still has his hands in his pockets. His eyes are so moist that his vision must be blurred. He bites his lip and nods slowly. It seems like an eternity passes before he clasps my hand, his head still nodding, as if to say, "Yep—it's really happening. You're doing just as you said you would do when you were a boy. I knew you would! You make me proud."

I grin triumphantly, give one final wave, and climb in.

Now, eleven years after that missionary's leg extended itself, it's my black Sunday shoe rather than Uncle Henry's that rises from the dusty, humble soil as I pursue the call that I heard right on this very spot. Mom wrinkles her face to keep the tears from coming, perhaps also remembering that earlier day. Shading her weathered brow with one hand, she waves goodbye with the other.

As the car pulls away I twist my neck for a final look at the distant horizon, at the pastureland and the friendly Floyd River from whose banks I so often watched cars and trucks going somewhere on the Big-Time Road. At last I'm going with them! And I didn't even need to buy a ticket to board a train!

I look back and see Mom saying something to Dad. It has to be: "I hope he studies hard!"

Moving down the no-name mile-long dirt road, all I can see is one big, dusty cloud. It rises like a veil between me and the farm. Now my past is becoming just that . . . my past! My future is all that I can see, my somewhere. All aboard! To Somewhere!

On that long-ago June day we rode in silence for many miles. Reverend Van't Hof finally interrupted my reverie to ask how I was doing.

"Great!" I responded, surprising both of us. My enthusiasm erupted so suddenly and passionately that we both chuckled. I smiled as we sped past the endless rows of corn. I would never again live at the end of a dead-end road.

Reverend Van't Hof smiled. "It'll be a long ride to Chicago, Harold. Relax. Take a nap." His look told me that he understood the emotions that were racing through my young blood.

Satisfied and confident, I soon fell asleep, as stalks of golden grain, basking in the sun, swayed to wave me a final goodbye.

I awoke sixty miles west of Chicago and watched the countryside go by. For the most part it was familiar-looking farmland, but the towns we passed through gave me a jolt. There were churches aplenty, which should have been reassuring but wasn't!

The first church I noticed after my nap was set off from the highway a bit. A large church, it must have held two hundred people or more. I looked at the sign that labeled its affiliation.

Methodist!

I gawked in disbelief. Methodist? Not . . . Reformed?

A little farther along I saw another large church; in fact, this one was huge. It must have been big enough to seat seven hundred!

Lutheran!!

I was dumbfounded. Lutheran? Not . . . Reformed?

Then farther yet was another huge church that surely held hundreds!

Baptist!!!

I was befuddled. Baptist? Not . . . Reformed?

And so it went: Episcopalian, Pentecostal, Catholic, on and on. I didn't see a single Reformed Church in America! How could it be that these "cults" Mom had warned me about were so much bigger than all our churches in Sioux County?

The thought nagged at me as we followed the highway into Chicago. Already I was gripped by a growing passion to build such a church. And already, just a few hours on the road to somewhere, my worldview had vastly expanded.

Chicago was so big! Cars—beautiful cars! Trucks—huge and by the hundreds! Trains zigging here and zagging there! People everywhere!

Reverend Van't Hof took me to a coffee shop. "Stay close to me," he said as we got out of the car. On the crowded sidewalk he said, "Don't be so bug-eyed that you lose me."

I was determined to heed his warning, since to this farmboy the city was a madhouse. Boys in uniform were all over the place. Men carrying satchels and briefcases strode quickly around us. Women in what looked like their Sunday best had a more leisurely pace.

We ducked into the little diner to find it pulsing with one of the musical hits of the day: "Pardon me, boys, is this the Chattanooga choo-choo?"

The words were catchy and the beat contagious. I watched the young people humming and bobbing their heads to its pace. I heard one soldier say to another, "Did you know that this song's sold a million copies?"

I couldn't believe my ears. I couldn't even begin to count that high! A million?!

We finished eating—a huge hamburger and a chocolate malt for me—then returned to the car. We'd parked under a movie theater's marquee, and though I would have loved to duck inside to catch a peek at a big-city theater, I didn't dare tell this to Reverend Van't Hof. What would he think of me? My first exposure to the modern world, and already my conscience faced a temptation!

Back on the road, we tried to get comfortable for the next long haul, heading east. It was late afternoon before we arrived in Holland, Michigan.

I'd always imagined my first day at college with the trees decked out in their autumn colors, but this was June. Nonetheless, as we rolled into Holland, I was pleased. *Very* pleased. The colors, the architecture, the smells—they all seemed familiar. It was like being back in Orange City, only many times the size. I felt a warm, homey comfort settle on me as we drove through the quainter sections of town and then onto the Hope College campus.

But then a note of disappointment settled in. The breeze blew through a campus that seemed almost deserted. With the war on, and with it now being summer, only a very few students were in sight.

Reverend Van't Hof and I walked with a quickened pace to the Student Admissions Office. After our long drive we didn't want them to close their doors on us.

As we swung open the large double doors, a friendly woman asked, "May I help you?"

Reverend Van't Hof held back, and I took my cue to assert my independence.

"Yes, I'm registered for summer school and I just arrived from Orange City, Iowa." She would never have known where Alton was, but she'd have heard of Orange City for sure!

"Oh, I have a sister there," she exclaimed. "I was just back for the Tulip Festival in the spring!"

We had a pleasant exchange about tulips, and then she smiled and said, "What's your name?"

For some reason her simple question seemed suddenly complicated. With more than a little trepidation I realized that from now
on, many of my life's decisions would be entirely up to me. This
woman wasn't looking to Reverend Van't Hof for her answer. She
wasn't looking to my mother or my grandmother. It was all up to
me. It was just a name, to be sure, but it was *my* name.

I thought longer than usual, I'm sure. She must have been curious
as to how such a youth could forget his own name! I glanced toward
Reverend Van't Hof. He'd already proven that he wasn't going to act
as sheriff for Mom, policing my ways and reporting back.

"Your name, please?" she repeated.

The words spilled out before I knew what I was saying: "Robert
Skuller."

The unfamiliar name had a pleasant ring to it, and so I raised my
shoulders a bit more proudly and confidently and said it again.

"Robert Skuller." I could now choose who I would be, and I
chose to be Robert.

"Well, let's see," she said, her finger going down the list on her
clipboard. "I have a *John* Schuler spelled with one L." She looked at
me questioningly.

I shook my head. Negative. Not me.

"I have a . . . well, here's a *Harold* Schuller, or maybe it's pronounced Skuller, from Alton, Iowa." Again she looked up.

"Yes, that's me," I said. "But Harold is my middle name. I go by
Robert."

"Okay, Robert. I apologize for the mix-up. Now do I call you
Robert or Bob?"

I hadn't thought about this complication and didn't think I was
ready to. "It's Robert," I said, though later I would come to prefer
Bob. And very soon Skuller would lose its proper pronunciation
submitting to the public's insistence that it be SHOO-LER.

"Okay then, Robert. Here's a list of your classes that a counselor
picked out for you from the limited selection we have during

summer school. You'll have a few days to get settled before classes start. This map is pretty good, and you can just ask anyone you see for help if you can't find what you need. We're like a family around here. Welcome to Hope College, Robert."

A surge of exhilaration rushed through me, from the tips of my toes to the crest of my skull. *Robert Schuller.* "Today, dear church, we will hear a sermon from a visiting young pastor, the Reverend *Robert Schuller.*"

Yes, this is who I would be. Harold was left on the farm to do the chores and be "Mama's boy." Robert would be "The Man."

Saying goodbye to Reverend Van't Hof that day, and hearing his hearty farewell—"Goodbye, *Robert,*" said with eyes twinkling—was the finest moment I'd ever known. But between you and me, I was glad that Mom wasn't there to hear it.

XIII

What would college cost Margaret?

Once at school I discovered soon enough. Seventy dollars per semester! That was a lot of money to a farmboy. I wrote Margaret a heartfelt thank-you and signed it "Robert."

Meanwhile, I had to come up with money for room and board. The nickels and dimes that I'd saved from my gopher and muskrat trapping as a boy wouldn't go very far.

Mom and Dad had sent some money with me to get through the first few months, but most of this went for a room in town. I couldn't afford to stay in the dormitory. During this time, I lived on milk, sweet rolls, and chocolate bars.

After a while I found a job as a waiter in the school's dining hall, which gave me free meals as well as a room. In time I would also be a delivery driver for a local furniture store, a clerk in Montgomery Ward, a janitor at a women's club, and a waiter at an exclusive resort. But this first job was heaven to me! Hot meals—as much as I could eat three times a day—and a room to boot! And would you believe that of all places for a cafeteria, ours was on the first floor of the *girls'* dormitory? If only Earl could see me now. Robert Schuller, on campus with a girl/boy ratio of probably twenty-to-one, spending forty percent of his time in the girls' dorm!

My laundry? Mom did that. Every week I'd send a box of dirty clothes home to Iowa. She'd launder and press, then pack the clean clothes and send them back. The first box that I received back had not only clean clothes but a spice cake. The next week there was a batch of rhubarb bars. Each and every week I received a baked treat with my freshly laundered clothing. Funny—in this regard I didn't feel any urgency to exercise my independence from Mom. I would always welcome this connection and attention.

I hadn't been at school too many weeks when I received word from the Student Affairs Office to come and retrieve an important telegram from home. I thought this strange. After all, I was due to receive my clean clothes with the weekly treat from home any day now. Why didn't Mom just slip the note in with my package? Puzzled, I took my break from the cafeteria and went to the office.

"You have a telegram for Robert Schuller?" I inquired.

"Um . . . there's one for *Harold* Schuller," the clerk responded.

Sheepishly I admitted, "Yeah, that's me."

I took the telegram outside into the August humidity and found a quiet space under a maple. I read my mother's words:

Harold:

I encourage you to look into the possibility of clerical deferment. I'm told that as a student interested in theology, the government will allow you to defer from the service. You must make up your own mind, of course, but your father and I encourage you to remember your goals. Henry leaves at week's end for the Army. The way I see it, I give one son to serve the country and my other son to serve the Lord.

Love,
Mom

So Henry had been drafted. The government knew our road and our number after all. It was a sobering moment.

I looked about me, and the few young men I'd seen hidden in the nooks and crannies of the campus seemed to have disappeared altogether. I felt very alone. I felt as if I were the only man in the whole United States of America not already wearing, or preparing to don, a uniform. A knot appeared in my stomach and settled in to stay as I returned to my work.

The next morning I awoke and the knot was still there. What would I do? I didn't know if I could sit safe and uninvolved at school while Earl and now Henry trained to go overseas.

It was early and I had to get coffee going for the breakfast hour. It was my job to lift a three-gallon pot of boiling water and pour it into the top of the commercial coffeemaker. I did this task every morning, taking the pot in hand with potholders, stepping up the stepstool in order to reach the top of the machine, high as my head, and lifting the scalding water above my shoulders.

Only this morning I slipped. The water poured over me, sizzling my flesh.

I screamed and writhed in pain. Another student who had arrived to start up the griddle rushed to get help. I remember little else except for the custodians carrying me out and putting me on a bed. These men then took the apron off me and unbuttoned my shirt, the skin sloughing off as well.

The doctor soon came. He examined me and said that the burns would heal within a few weeks but that I was sure to be in a lot of pain meanwhile. We were to administer the care he prescribed and keep an eye open for infection, but he insisted that I wasn't to be moved for quite a few days.

With time off from work, I had time to think. Would I stay at Hope? Would I apply for a draft deferment? Or would I abandon my goals for a good cause and join Earl and Henry and the countless others heading off to fight the Germans or the Japanese? As I lay in bed, I thought and I prayed and I shifted position to seek relief from the pain. I prayed more and thought more with each passing day, and eventually the pain subsided as my pink, blistered skin began to heal.

When I was ready to resume my duties, I said goodbye to the girls who had nursed me in their dorm. I would miss their attention, but it was time to get back to business. I would do as Mom and Dad had suggested and request a deferment. But I wondered if I would ever see my brother again.

A few days later I was called into the office of the president of the college. Dr. Willard Wichers welcomed me, my request for deferment on his desk, awaiting his signature.

"What are your goals, Robert?" he asked me.

I blurted out my answer with a newly sobered passion: "To be a preacher, sir. And then enlist as a chaplain wherever I'm needed."

He eyed me over the rim of the glasses perched on his nose. I squirmed a bit under the prolonged stare as he sized me up.

What was he thinking about me? No geometry? No foreign language? And only average grades in simple courses like music, drama, civics, and geography? English literature . . . good! But no hard sciences? Was this average student from one of the smallest and most underrated high schools in America actually college material?

I don't recall the give-and-take of his questions, but I was in there for a good long time.

Not long after our conversation, I learned that Dr. Wichers had signed my deferment. Only later did I discover that he'd done so against his better judgment. I had assumed it was just a matter of putting information down on some form—information that he'd gleaned during his "inquisition." I never suspected that he'd harbored serious doubts about me.

Years later, after I'd been recognized as a "successful" preacher, a friend said to me, "Bob, I saw Dr. Wichers just the other day, and do you know what he said to me about his experience with you? He said, 'I'll never again look at an incoming student and think, He's got no future!'"

Dr. Wellmers, my Greek professor, would have agreed with Dr. Wichers's unenthusiastic judgment. I got a D in his class, my first foray into a foreign language. That wasn't good news for a pre-seminary student. Greek and Hebrew would be required in divinity school—all three years! But no one had told me how to study a foreign language. In my little high school none of the farm kids took studies seriously. When final exams came, they were simple assignments from sympathetic teachers. A person could goof off all semester, then cram and catch up on the Saturday before Monday's final exam. I tried that now in Greek, and it didn't work.

Likewise, if Dr. Wichers had shared his deep misgivings with the mathematics professor, Dr. Timmer, he would have found little argument. I had started my college education with no more math than first-level algebra. From day one in math class, the professor wrote strange numbers and symbols on the board and used words I'd never heard. He assumed that everyone in his class had taken geometry. And *almost* everyone had. I was the only exception. I foolishly held my head high and bluffed an air of comprehension. "Everyone understand?" he'd ask frequently. I always hoped that someone else would confess confusion, but no one ever did. Well, *I* wasn't about to expose my ignorance.

Near the end of that year, the math prof called me in.

"Robert, you want to be a preacher, I'm told."

"Yes, sir."

"Well, fortunately you won't need to be a math expert in the pulpit."

"That's what I've been thinking all semester," I replied.

"But you need these four hours to get your bachelor's degree. You know that?"

"Yes, sir."

"Well, Robert, to be honest, you haven't passed this course. I can't give you even a D. I *should* give you an F. But here's what I can do to help you. After all, I'm an elder in the Reformed Church. We need good preachers, and I think you can be one. So I've decided to give you an I; it stands for *incomplete*. I'll give you some special assignments and tutor you through them. Then in six weeks I'll give you a private test. There'll be no grade on that one—simply *pass* or *fail*. Pass—and I'll give you a D."

I wanted to embrace him!

Six weeks later I earned my hard-won D.

But that was only one subject.

"To get your bachelor's degree you'll need eight hours of science," my enrollment counselor had told me. "Would you like chemistry, biology, or physics?"

"What are they?" I'd asked. I'd never heard these words in my kitchen. They weren't in our family's Dutch or English vocabulary.

"With only a general science and algebra course in high school," the counselor had said, "I suggest that you take a biology course. It's good for four science credit-hours, and if we add those to your four hours in mathematics, that'll do it."

I took the counselor's advice and ended up in the classroom of Dr. Ver Geer, biology prof. He passed me with a C. After all, he rationalized, I was "very focused on preaching." (Dissecting a formaldehyde-drenched frog had no future in my pulpit!)

But if Dr. Wichers had shared his dismal projection of Robert Schuller with Dr. William Schrier, head of the speech department, there he *would* have faced an argument.

I really felt at home in my speech classes, but even there I had a problem. In my first oratory class I imitated—perfectly, I might add—the tone, tempo, and delivery of my pulpit hero, Dr. Henry Colenbrander, whose mesmerizing oratory was the rage of Sioux County. It was he who had packed the huge church and drawn all the young people into the congregation. And it was his preaching that had pulled me out of the balcony to go to the elders' meeting.

When I finished my passionate impersonation, I assumed that I would win raves from the other students and an A from Dr. Schrier.

But my professor just looked at me and shook his head. "Who do you think you are, Robert?" he asked me in front of the class. "Are you trying to imitate some preacher?"

"I want to be a great preacher, sir."

"I can teach you how to speak—how to preach—but if you want to be a *great* preacher . . . well, you and you alone can make yourself great."

I swallowed hard. Another defining moment in my life.

"You have what we call a 'preacher's tone,'" he said. That was the beginning of weeks and months of his coaching, his critiquing, his rough interruptions of my speeches. "You raise your voice, then you sing out a sentence without dropping, but with the next sentence you raise the tone to a still higher note. That just won't do. You have to learn to be yourself. Talk as you do in the hallway, only with more enthusiasm!"

Years later, when I saw *My Fair Lady* with Rex Harrison battling Eliza Doolittle's Cockney accent, I saw what Dr. Schrier had gone through with Robert Schuller, and I chuckled in reminiscence.

"Now Robert, I'm putting you in debate," Dr. Schrier decided. "I think that you'll do very well there."

He was right. I discovered what I can only call a "gift"—the uncanny ability to think on my feet, to summon almost intuitively a sharp defense against my opponent.

"You'd make a really great lawyer, Bob," Dr. Schrier said after I'd won a few debate contests hands down. As a reward, I was elected into the National Honorary Forensic Fraternity—Pi Kappa Delta.

I intuitively thought—and still do—like a lawyer preparing a case and persuading the jury. I always shaped my argument to match my audience. In debate I tried to think as my opponents were thinking.

"Begin always by looking for where you and your opponent agree," Dr. Schrier instructed. "Build on that. Then proceed with the skills of 'anticipatory rebuttal.'"

And there was more to Dr. Schrier's masterful strategy: "Anticipate the argument that your opponent will unleash, and before he gets a chance to make his case, defuse it. Propose your answer before he offers the challenge."

I got top grades in speech and debate. Dr. Schrier instructed and I learned, and his wisdom has served me well all of my professional life.

Another strong influence was Dr. Hinga, my history professor. I took away more than one profound insight from him:

"Don't try to make a hit; try to make history."

"In all that you do, think *long* thoughts."

"Think not in *decades*, but in *centuries*."

The awesome lessons of history would so possess and control me that I would choose to major in this subject. Years later history would guide my thinking as I began to build churches; it would influence my choice of architects and architecture.

The single most motivational sentence that would push my dreams into proactive, make-it-happen action was something that Dr. Hinga said in one of his history classes. It started with a question. "How many of you have started your term papers?" he asked. "Let me see your hands."

Not a single hand went up. Dr. Hinga was clearly upset. But he was also the football coach, and he wasn't about to give up. He began to pace the front of the classroom as if he were in a locker room at halftime confronting a winning team that was about to throw away their lead. He raised his arms. Standing ramrod straight and drawing every person's attention, he raised his voice as well, booming:

"Beginning is half done!"

After a pause for that thought to settle, he exclaimed passionately, "I don't care if you forget everything I've tried to teach you here about world events. But don't you *ever* forget that sentence."

I never forgot it. Everything I would ever do in my life would start with the recollection of that forceful line.

Then there was psychology. I'd never heard the word. I signed up for a class in it because my counselor felt that it would be helpful to me as a pastor. Helpful? That would be the greatest understatement of my college career. The textbook for that course, titled *The Dynamics of Human Adjustment,* remains the single most influential book in the shaping of my perspective on human nature.

In the historical theology in which I was raised, there was never any explanation of negative or positive behavior. For the first time, my psychology course gave me insight into why human beings behave the way they do. I would continue the study of psychology for the rest of my life. Eventually I would benefit from the teaching and come under the influence of two of the greatest psychiatrists of the twentieth century—Dr. Karl Menninger and Dr. Viktor Frankl—and I would enjoy their friendship.

But it all began here, at Hope College, with Dr. Lars Granberg, the head of the psychology department.

It was during my first year at Hope College that I discovered I'd acquired a love of excellence. To me the mystery of my college days is how—and from whom—I caught this compulsion and passion. Somehow the seeds were planted in my heart, and somehow they were cultivated in such a way that my passion didn't become negative perfectionism.

Was this drive for excellence ego-driven?

No. I was beginning to see that God captures our imagination to accomplish and achieve goodness and greatness for His honor and glory. This is a theme that I would explore later at divinity school, poring over the teachings of John Calvin. We are to embrace our dreams—pursue them and then present them as our gifts back to God. But this was a huge leap across a major theological chasm.

Calvinist theology had long been characterized as a daily battle against the supposed "depravity" of human beings. What I would discover in my studies is that this dismal picture of human life was a product of Calvinist *followers*, not of John Calvin himself. My reinterpretation of Calvin's teachings revealed a theology of hope and joy, liberating humanity from a shaming, blaming, cowering Christianity, with its railing against the "sin" of pride, and replacing that view with a God-inspired drive for self-worth. I didn't know it then, but expounding this liberating force would become my life's work.

My first year drew to a close and it was time to go home for a visit. I was ready to see Mom and Dad again. But how strange it would be with Henry gone. I left Hope with a mixture of excitement and consternation. Things had changed—at home and in me. But when I thought of the meals ahead—all of those wonderful home-cooked meals—the hesitation magically vanished.

Little did I know what lay ahead.

I've often thought that the reason God never lets us see into our tomorrows is that if we *did* know what the future holds, we simply wouldn't go there.

XIV

I'm in the barn with Dad. He's spent the last months milking alone, and even though he doesn't say much, I can tell he enjoys my company during this late-afternoon chore. He asks me questions that encourage me to carry the conversation, giving him a crash course on all that I've learned at school. He's especially interested in my theology and psychology courses. I decide that he would have been a brilliant student had he been given the opportunity. His sixth-grade education created in him an insatiable curiosity that farm life couldn't satisfy.

I've been home a few days, and I never thought it would feel so nice. The quiet of the farm, the spicy smells of the kitchen, the voices of the people I love—all these feel comfortable and right.

Margaret is also home for a visit, now helping Mom with supper. I stopped in the kitchen earlier to get a snack before starting the milking. The warm cookstove beckoned me to reminisce at its heated belly; the little kitchen table where all my dreams were birthed and dissected and resurrected welcomed me.

When I headed back outside, even the smells in the barn, to my surprise, were pleasant.

Now Dad and I stand together to empty the milk into the separator. Bearing the milky load in a balanced way—a heavy three-gallon bucket in one hand and a matching bucket in the other—we approach the separator that stands near the front of the barn, next to the red, paint-chipped wooden door with its bottom half shut and its top half open to the outside. As I set down the milk, I suddenly sense that something is wrong. I feel a strange sense of disquiet. Stretching my head out the open half of the door, I peer out into the yard. Dad comes alongside me and gazes out appraisingly.

The sky above is hidden behind a blackening cloud that's blocked the late-afternoon sun and sent an ominous shadow over the land. An unholy calm has moved in upon the farmyard. All of nature seems to sense that something hostile is looming. Not a sparrow is chirping. Not a leaf is quivering. The chickens have stopped their running in the yard, and the roosters are stretching their necks, holding their heads high, as if to discern what sort of unfriendly spirit rides these turbulent clouds from the west, where storms come from.

"Looks like a bad one," I say to my dad. It's an attempt to mask my nerves; I'm hoping for reassurance from him. The sky grows stranger by the minute. Then I hear a steady, distant rumble like that of a faraway freight train. It's not the roll of thunder. I look at Dad. His bushy white eyebrows are drawn low in concern.

"Mmmhmm," he says. "I don't like the sound of it. I've never heard one quite like this. Let's cover the rosebushes around the house. A hailstorm would wipe them out."

Then, in words louder and faster than I've ever heard from my soft-spoken father, he issues urgent orders. "We've got to save the roses, Harold. Hurry—we've got to protect them! Grab pails from the hog house, the chicken coop, and the barn! Run! *Run!*" These bushes are Dad's pride and joy, and they've just come into bloom. We break into a run, each grabbing now-empty milk buckets, one in each hand. Then we run back to the barn for more, until there's one bucket over every full-of-buds bush.

"That should save them," Dad says, relaxing a bit.

The wind has quieted deceptively, and I begin to think that our alarm was unnecessary. Dad's snow-white hair is now blowing softly in the disarming breeze. Then suddenly that strange, distant sound recurs—louder now, ever louder. In startling resurgence it rages into view—a growing lump in the flat black sky.

The lump grows larger—quickly, ever larger!—like a pregnant belly in the middle of a foreboding body creeping toward us. "Dad," I say, but can manage nothing more. We watch together as a long, black funnel-shaped cloud drops swiftly and angrily from the swollen "lump," then slides into a twisting, weaving, slithering serpent.

We stand deathly still beside the bucket-covered rosebushes. It's strange sometimes what we try to save. Then the head of that long, slithering black snake of a cloud strikes the dry ground a mile and a half west of us. Instantly a perfectly round whirl of dust swirls in circles where the twister has struck down.

"It's a tornado, Harold!" Dad shouts, his voice raised to be heard over the roar. He runs toward the house.

The reality of the twister plunges me into panic. Mom! We have to get Mom and Margaret!

When we get to the house the funnel is heading straight for our farm. "Tornado!" Dad calls as he runs inside. "Jennie! We've got to get out of here *now!*"

Mom runs to her bedroom and grabs her jewelry box.

"Margaret!" I yell, but my sister is already bounding up the concrete steps, up from the basement to the indoor porch.

Moments later Mom and Dad join us. In her left hand Mom clutches her jewelry box, and Dad's got a firm grip on her right hand. He pulls her from other belongings that she desperately wants to save and keeps her moving. I have Margaret by the arm now, and the four of us run to the garage, Mom's dress whipping about her thighs.

We jump into Henry's car (it's newer, thus faster and safer) and wait anxiously, silently, while Dad fiddles with the keys. Mom clutches her jewelry box to her chest; Margaret and I look out the back window. Dad reverses with sudden acceleration out of the garage. Now we whip our heads forward as Dad lunges the Chevy ahead and begins a desperate race down our drive. Then he whips the car to the left and down that dead-end dirt road that heads only one way—*west!*—straight into the face of the twister. It's hardly more than a mile away now, and still coming straight toward us.

Nobody says a word as Dad speeds faster. Margaret and I clutch the back of the front seat, our knuckles white, our eyes locked onto the beast coming down the road. We all know Dad's intention: he's racing for that crossroads where my grade school sits; then he'll turn south to escape the tornado—that is, *if* we get there before it does. We all know the innate risk of the matter, but no one acknowledges it. It seems that if I even breathe, that might slow us down. All is completely silent save for the gravel sliding and tearing beneath us.

It's like a scene from a silent movie—no words, no sound, no musical score . . . no audio, only visual. And what a visual it is: the twister slithers back and forth and back and forth, all the while hulking closer to our approaching car.

We reach the school corner. Now the violent and whirling cloud of dirt and debris is no more than a quarter-mile away. The land that it has already swallowed stretches a city block wide. Everywhere the funnel touches the ground, things explode and then are mercilessly sucked up beneath it. Dirt and trees that have been drawn up are spewed out again as dust and splintered rubble.

We whip left onto the intersecting dirt road. At last we're leaving the funnel behind us instead of heading straight into its face. We head south. Margaret and I exhale a collective sigh of relief. My father is more subdued, as is his nature. Mom remains tense, clutching her treasure.

A mile down the road we stop the car and get out. Mom raises her eyes to assess the still-foreboding sky, then gets out of the car. She is trembling, so I take the jewelry box to help her. My dad comes around the car and puts his arms about her, pulling her to himself in one of the few embraces I would every witness. Together we stand and watch the strange hurling funnel—now probably two miles away—as it rips through the land.

As suddenly as it came, it retracts into the sky—a mirror image of the retracting periscope on a submarine—disappearing into total blackness. The deadly silence is still with us. Not a breeze. Not a sound. Only silence.

"It's gone, Jennie," my father says. "We can go home now." Then, looking at me, he adds, "It's time to finish the milking, Harold."

I'm trembling with excitement. I've seen—for the first time in my life—a real tornado. We raced into its face to escape, and we survived!

"Boy—Henry missed this one!" I shout, thrilled with the story that I now have to take back to college with me.

Everything is still eerily quiet and calm when we reach the school crossroads. The school is still there, undamaged. But just across the road the nine farm buildings of the Van Ess farm and the grove of trees that lined it are all either flattened or completely gone! We see no one, nothing. If we'd outrun the twister—surely they had. A ditch alongside the road is littered with telephone and power poles still tied together by their long black wires. No one comments. None of us dares say what we're all thinking. Instead, Dad drives more slowly.

When we crest the same hill over which I used to walk when I made my daily trek home from school, we don't see the top ridge of our barn roof above it.

Dad grips the steering wheel with white-knuckled fists. "The barn," he exclaims, his voice catching, "it's . . . gone!"

Then, passing over the crest, we see our farmyard. Dad stops the car, shuts the engine off. We all stare in silence. All nine buildings, including our house, have simply disappeared.

As if the car were to blame, Dad pounds his two angry fists again and again against the top of the steering wheel. "*Everything* is gone," he shouts, his voice tinged with the fury of the twister. In only a matter of minutes, all of Dad's lifelong labor has been wiped away.

We stare down the long dead-end road. We stare at the vast land, extending as far as the eye can see. The dead-end road and the land—that's all that remains. No grove of trees—just a road ending in the middle of nowhere. No barn. No hog shed. No corncrib. No toolshed. No chicken coop. No house. Just a road and empty, vast land. Tony and Jennie's "somewhere" has turned into a "nowhere."

With teeth clenched tight and jaw hard in anger, Dad again pounds on the steering wheel. Then he groans in agony as total defeat overwhelms him. Slumping over the wheel with his arms hanging limp at its side, he begins to cry. "It's all gone, Jennie," he says between sobs. He cries and he cries and keeps saying, through quivering lips, the saddest sentence I've ever heard: "It's all gone."

After what seems an eternity, Dad's sobbing stops and he rests quietly against the steering wheel, looking deceptively peaceful. A power pole lying across the road ahead of us sends up hissing sparks, as if it has received Dad's anger. Finally, he lifts his head from the steering wheel and opens the car door.

"Stay here," he says abruptly. "I'll walk home."

Mom clutches the jewelry box again, as if to protect Dad by protecting it. We cry as we watch his lonely figure walk down the road to our driveway.

I turn my head away from this formerly indestructible man of determination. I can't bear to witness such a man being beaten into the ground by life's irrevocable circumstances. I stare out of the side window, wiping away tears. Then I see, in the ditch by the road, the dead body of Mabel, our horse. She has a long two-by-four sticking through her belly like a toothpick through an olive. Mom and Margaret see her too. Margaret and I jump from the car and run to her. Margaret falls to the ground beside her, weeping harder now. I remain a few feet back, in total shock. I simply can't believe that only thirty minutes ago everything was so different . . . so healthy . . . so alive. Now everything is dead.

I pick up a small piece of wood, as I did so often on my walks home from school, when I created makeshift boats to float home in the ditch. I stare at the splintered piece. Is it a remnant of my home? I turn it over in my hands and occasionally glance back at Mom, still sitting stunned and silent in the car. She watches her husband walking alone toward the place where our house stood only a few minutes ago.

When Dad returns, he's bent-shouldered, arms swaying hopelessly and helplessly at his side. He leans against the car, as if for support.

Sighing deeply, he folds his arms across his chest, fingers tucked in his armpits and long thumbs pinching near the top of his shoulders. His soft and quiet way has returned, but I detect a slight hint of shame. He won't look me in the eye. I wish I could tell him that I think of him as the grandest and bravest man to walk the earth — tears notwithstanding — but I can't. The moment is just too somber. He looks down at the ground for a moment, then turns to Mom to give his report.

"There's nothing left, Jennie. The bull is standing dazed but alive in the middle of the yard. There's a chain hanging around his horns and down the sides of his head. I don't know where the barn went. I can't imagine how he survived and why he wasn't blown away with it."

Mom doesn't seem to be listening. She stares in dazed solitude. I wonder if she's remembering the day she stored her Dutch linens from Holland, the ones her mother had given her, in her dining-room hutch. It was a memory she shared with us whenever she withdrew those linens for use. On the day of that memory they had moved into the Sears-Roebuck house. Her mother had harshly scrutinized the little place, but it was Jennie's home — Tony and Jennie's home. She had never let us kids forget that we could be proud of what they had built with their own fortitude and hard work.

Dad continues, despite Mom's inattention: "Jennie. Some cows made it — alive in the pasture. They must have been just out of the twister's path. But the chickens, the hogs, the house, all the buildings, the family car, and the garage — they're all gone."

Dad turns and begins walking back to the farm. This time we join him. I put my arm around Mom and walk with her. When we reach what had been the windbreak grove of trees, there isn't a single sign of them. Even the roots have been sucked up out of the ground, and no trunk or branch has been left behind.

What catches our eye when we get to the farmyard — a sight I'll never forget — is a mother sow lying dead in the driveway, her six little piglets still alive, still sucking at her and squealing. There's not much else to see. Where the house stood only a half-hour before, not even a board of wood or a piece of glass remains. No comforting cookstove, no family-uniting kitchen table—*nothing;* there's no sign of any furniture in the entire farmyard. Only a deep hole with a clean cement foundation. Not even rubble.

It still strikes me, when I think back on that awful day, how *clean* the place was, as if a huge vacuum cleaner had sucked up the house and all its furnishings. It was the same with every farm building on that land. Only white concrete foundations remained. Every possession had been taken away to God only knows where.

We slept that dark night in the country house of my married sister Violet, four miles west of our place. She fed us supper and breakfast. I remember missing my toothbrush. I slept in my underwear.

"I've still got your baptism dress, Harold," Vi said the next morning. It was the only one of my childhood keepsakes that would remain, saved simply because she had borrowed it for the baptism of her daughter. "Got a few photos Mom gave me when I got married." To this day, we have only those few photos, no certificates, no tokens of any kind from those decades. Only my baptismal gown and those childhood things that Margaret and Violet had taken with them when they left home, and items belonging to grandparents and other relatives.

When Violet brought the gown to me, I buried my head in its soft, unblemished sweetness. It seemed to me a token that God had not forgotten the promise he'd made to me years before, when Mom had held me in her arms and I'd been baptized "Robert Harold Schuller."

I had already begun to wonder whether or not I would return to Hope College. My studies seemed so insignificant in light of what had happened. But the baptismal dress seemed a sign that I wasn't to question my life's calling.

We had saved Henry's car, a Chevy Coupe, that he had bought just before being drafted and sent overseas. Tony's Model T, totally flattened, as if by a wrecker, lay a half-mile away in the now-devastated cornfield. We also found our flattened, smashed house.

It had been dropped across the road a quarter of a mile away. The largest piece of anything in that flat chunk of rubble was the sounding board of our piano. We looked carefully through the surrounding area and found only five pieces of the family silverware plus a linen tablecloth, torn but still in one piece.

Then I saw something else. On our kitchen wall we'd had a porcelain decoration with the words "Keep looking to Jesus." The top half had broken off and was lying in the rubble pile. I picked it up and read, "Keep looking." We *did* keep looking but found nothing more. So we would "keep looking" for God's provision in all the tomorrows to come.

With nine farms completely destroyed (but fortunately no human death toll), the members of our community called a prayer meeting. Telephones rang with the summons to gather in the First Reformed Church in Newkirk. The church was completely filled at meeting time with farmers from miles around. As a college student headed for ministry, I was the only young person to pray. I quoted from memory the words of a famous Wesleyan hymn:

God moves in a mysterious way.
His wonders to perform.
He plants his footsteps on the sea
And rides upon the storm.

The total insurance on our buildings, farm machinery, furnishings, dead livestock, and lost crops in the field added up to only three thousand dollars. The mortgage on the farm was due to be paid in full in only two months, but unbeknownst to me, Dad had already been feeling a serious financial squeeze. He had bought the land twenty years before at the height of inflationary prices, and the price of farm products had been dropping in recent years. Even before the twister hit he'd occasionally worried about losing his life's work through a bank foreclosure. If not for the three-thousand-dollar check from the insurance company, he would have lost the only thing he now had—the land.

"Keep looking"—here was God's hidden provision. Now, though all was gone, Dad had found a glimmer of hope. With the three thousand dollars of insurance money, perhaps he could save his land.

I rode with Dad to Orange City the day he went to the bank to discuss arrangements. On our way into town, we noticed a grand old house being dismantled. One chunk—like the last piece of a three-layer cake—was still standing, open at each floor like a dollhouse. My father suspected that, dismantled, it would be large enough for us to rebuild into a small, new, house. When he stopped to check it out, he learned that the final portion hadn't yet been sold.

"You can have it for fifty dollars, Tony," he was told, "but you'll have to haul it all away." Dad bought it on the spot.

"We'll come to start taking it down tomorrow," Dad said. Then we drove on to the bank.

"Come in, Tony," the banker said. "I'm so sorry . . . *so* sorry. You lost the crop in the field too?"

"Yes, but the mortgage—that's my concern," Dad replied firmly. "I've got three thousand dollars coming in insurance. If I give you two thousand to apply to the mortgage and keep a thousand to build a house, can I keep my farm? Can you rewrite the mortgage? I'll just rent the land out to another farmer. Then I can get by without a tractor or any other farm machinery. I lost all that too, you know, but I've still got my milk cows. We can live on the cash from the milk and cream, and we can eat from the crops in the garden."

Mr. Rowenhorst, the banker, had moist eyes as Dad made this pitiful offer. He stood up and offered a warm handshake. "Okay, Tony—you're a good man. Sure, we can work it out. Go home. Rebuild the house. We'll write a new loan for you to hold on to that land. You know, with the war going on, prices are going up fast. A couple of solid years of good corn and oats and you'll make it."

Years later Dad would tell me, "If I hadn't gotten that three thousand dollars in insurance benefits to put toward my mortgage, I wouldn't have been able to save the farm. That and the sympathy of that good banker kept me from what I'm sure would have been a foreclosure sale."

"God moves in a mysterious way, His wonders to perform," I reflected.

We borrowed my brother-in-law's big flat trailer and pulled it with his tractor into town, parking by the piece of house we'd bought the day before. We climbed to the rooftop and began to take the thing apart, starting with the shingles. With claw hammers we pulled out and saved every nail, laboriously flattening the bent ones. (With all the practice we gained, I can still flatten a bent nail today!) We saved every window, every door, every floorboard. We even broke down the cinderblocks that made up the basement walls. Then we loaded everything, including the coffee cans filled with nails, onto the trailer and hauled the precious pieces home. There we designed and built our new little house board by board, nail by nail.

At some point during the building process I lost my pocketknife. When the home was finished and Dad and I stood back to admire our work, we saw a bulge in the shingled roof. My pocketknife would remain there for the life of the house—a reminder of the day that Dad and Mom lost and found their "somewhere."

The tornado had completely wiped out all three farms on that road that had no name, taking everything away with it. Of the three farmers, only Dad would rebuild, making us the only house on that mile-long dead-end road. And so finally, after all those years, the road got a name: people called it Schuller (pronounced "Skuller") Road.

My grammar school class—I am in the last row with the dark overalls

Pauper marries princess—the wedding of my parents, Anthony and Jennie Schuller—on house porch, center of photograph

The house at the end of a dead-end road with no name and no number

My one-room
schoolhouse in Iowa

In my Sunday suit—
ready for church

Ready to perform at a square-
skipping party—my first
performance

Our house the
morning after
the tornado

Above: Trapping with
Henry

Right: Henry in his
Army uniform

My girlfriend Arvella—she's special.
I'm falling in love

My photo to Arvella when we were
dating

Ordination! My first twenty-year dream comes true

Our wedding party—an amateur photographer

I'm a proud father!
Our first born, Sheila

March 1952—our family of three

Sheila has a little brother, Robert Anthony

California, here we come! Our first home in California, 1955 . . .

. . . and our first church—a drive-in.

My view on a Sunday morning. We are growing . . .

The drive-in marquee for the church service

XV

Leaving Mom and Dad to return to school after the twister's devastation was one of the most difficult moments of my life. Not only did I feel guilty for leaving Dad to reestablish his livelihood, but I had trouble accepting Margaret's continued financial assistance when the money could have gone to new machinery and the like for Dad and Mom. But they insisted, all of them. Whenever I wrestled with my decision, I would remember the baptism gown—my little sign that told me God had called me to serve him all my life, so I recommited myself to the schooling that was part of that process.

Returning to the dorm, I found that the tornado story I had once thought I would boast about had become a humbling account of God's faithfulness. I still told it often, but not with the purpose I had originally envisioned.

I now had less in the way of material goods than I'd had the year before. I returned to campus with one suit, which had been donated to me by a neighbor, and a few other meager essentials. And yet I found myself grateful for what I *did* have and refocused on my studies, motivated by the model of my father.

Then, one day following class, I returned to the house where I rented a room to find it in flames. And so I became homeless for a second time in only two months, losing the clothes that had been given to me following the twister. These personal concerns—major though they seemed at the time—were soon forgotten when startling news came at year's end.

It was 1945 when the biggest story of the twentieth century broke. It shook every student in Hope and every human being in civilization. The headlines read:

Atom Bomb Dropped on Japan!

The demise of Hitler had already ended the war in Europe; now the bomb ended the war in Japan. New headlines proclaimed:

Peace Declared!

Hope students swarmed to Grand Rapids, Michigan, jamming the streets with tens of thousands of others celebrating the end of World War II. I could now live my life without war and without storms—or so I thought.

How wrong I was.

World War II was over, but the Korean War would soon break out. Then came the "Cold War" between Russia and America, with its threat of nuclear catastrophe hanging over the world, centered on the issue of communism versus anti-communism. While the Cold War still simmered, the Vietnam War began and then dragged on, though eventually we would see the collapse of communism. From my seminary days through the last decade of the century, my ministry would be lived out under cloudy skies of wars and rumors of wars. It was a good thing we didn't know this at the time. We could believe in peace, and so that day—the day World War II well and truly ended—we all celebrated.

Not too many days after, I was working my job in the cafeteria when I saw a tall, handsome soldier step through the double doors at the other end of the room. His cap was tipped slightly to the side, and his dark mustache gave him the look of a ladies' man. Soldiers had been pouring onto the campus since the war's end, using their government education vouchers. I figured this one was registering and needed orientation. I dried my hands and went to see if I could direct him to the Student Admissions Office.

Then I recognized him. "Henry!" I whooped. My brother was home from the war! Hurrying toward each other with the broadest strides our long legs could manage, we embraced, myself admittedly, with tears of joy.

He would stay with me a few days before returning home, having hitchhiked his way to Michigan from Pennsylvania, where he had been demobilized. He planned to hitchhike the rest of the way to Iowa but wanted my company as a sort of "reentry" into civilian life. He hadn't been back on U.S. soil more than a few days. The Army understood that he was needed on the farm following Mom and Dad's loss, so they had let him depart early.

Henry was quiet a lot of the time, and sometimes when I looked into his eyes I could see that he was worlds away. Had I been able to look deeper, I don't believe I would have liked what I saw. He had been a litter-bearer at the front, running onto the fields to sort through the living and the dead, hoping to return with a soldier who might have survived his wounds. The images in his mind would have robbed me of my innocence and ignorance. I would have seen the day when he carried the front end of one stretcher while friends ran alongside with a second stretcher—both stretchers carrying wounded men. A shell went off and everyone else was killed instantly—litter-bearers and wounded alike. He would be the only one to return to camp.

But I wouldn't hear such stories until later, when the years had made their telling slightly—but *only* slightly—easier.

Henry's two-day visit was too short. When it came time for him to say goodbye and go home to Mom and Dad, I wondered how he would fare. Perhaps the farm would prove to be a healing place, distanced as it was from violence and bloodshed. Perhaps he would find peace, quiet, and security as he reconnected with what was so central to his temperament: the gentle handling of animals.

Some years later, Henry would marry and buy the farm. With his wife, Alberta, he would move into the same house that Dad and I had built after the tornado and farm the land on his own. With the cash Henry paid Dad, my parents would be able to buy a nice home in Alton, Iowa, where they could retire from working the land. Only a few years after losing everything in the tornado, Tony and Jennie would find themselves living in what, to them, was real luxury. My "rich" grandpa, John Henry Beltman, would move into the spacious new home with them, bringing his best furniture—a dining-room table with six chairs and his huge, fabulous rocker! All of which I would inherit to enjoy in my California home today.

The war behind us now, in my third year at Hope, the campus was suddenly flooded with male students. Fraternities boomed overnight. Heretofore the only fraternity on campus had been one I had started with about thirty other guys. We called it "the Arcadian Fraternity," and we gathered weekly for fun and fellowship. But now, with our expanded roster, a few of these newcomers and I started to casually sing old folksongs in four-part harmony. Known as "the Arcadian Four," we became the unofficial Hope College male quartet. We gave concerts in town, at college events, and at local churches. We were good, too, if I do say so myself!

As our reputation grew, we began receiving invitations from outside Holland. It finally dawned on me that, come summer, we should go on tour, beginning in Michigan, then heading on to any other towns that we could line up across the country, venturing all the way to California if we could swing it! I envisioned us serving as a public-relations arm of the school.

"Great idea!" said Dr. Lubbers, who had replaced Dr. Wichers as the president of the college.

So the four of us—yours truly and my fellow singers, Bill Miedema, Warren Heitbrink, and Ken Leestma—began to plan. My voice had dropped from first tenor in high school to low bass in this quartet. Since I was a "talker" by nature, I was deemed the master of ceremonies for all our concerts—in other words, I was the one who would ask for money.

We thought that we would use Ken's old Pontiac, but he got cold feet when he thought about the distance. "No way will my old car make it," he concluded. But to back out now, only two weeks before we were supposed to depart, would leave the many churches we'd lined up in the lurch, and that just wasn't acceptable. We pressed our point with Ken.

"Oh, come on, guys! I don't think it can make it. My odometer just clicked over; the old jalopy has ninety thousand miles on it! Do you want to end up hitchhiking? That's what's gonna happen," he warned.

His eyes begged for understanding, but we refused to give any. He tried again: "The tires are worn nearly bare. Do you really think my old car can make it all the way to California and back? You're nuts—all three of you!"

We kept staring at him, our heads cocked slightly and our hands on our hips.

"Ah, gee, guys," he protested. "We'll have to go across deserts and mountains and—"

I interrupted his pleas. "Have *faith*, Ken! Let's just go and see how far we can get! So what if we need to hitch a ride back?"

The other two agreed enthusiastically. Ken grimaced but didn't say much more for the rest of that evening.

We were turning our dream into a goal. We had no cash, no assurance that we wouldn't run into real problems on the road. Years later I would share this lesson:

Never let possible problems defeat your decisions!

This was quite an adventure in possibility thinking!

I no longer worked in the cafeteria. By this time I had a job waiting tables at a fine resort. I would have to quit this job at Castle Park to embark on our cross-country trip, hoping that they'd hire me back come fall. None of us had money in savings, because most of the money we earned went to school supplies, food, and lodging. We would have to sleep in homes of church members and take up offerings at every concert to pay for our gas.

"Hey, I've got an idea!" I piped up one day. "We're supposed to be promoting the college, right?"

"Yeah," they agreed, though hesitantly. It hadn't taken them very long to learn that when Bob Schuller got an idea, it generally involved the unusual—which meant risk-taking, which meant work!

"Come on, you guys," I said reassuringly. "This isn't a bad idea. Just listen: let's go to the wooden-shoe factory in town and buy a big wooden shoe."

"What in the world would we do with that?" Warren asked skeptically. He wasn't known for being a visionary.

"We'll have the factory burn the name Hope College into the shoe, and we'll bolt it to the grill of Ken's car!" (You should've seen the look on Ken's face!)

I continued, "When we enter any town, they'll know who we are right off. The shoe will become our signature!"

I was enthusiastic. They were not. Always eager to put my debating skills to use, within minutes I'd swayed my buddies to see things my way.

Finally the day arrived when the four of us piled into the car, loaded almost past capacity with our belongings, and said goodbye to Holland, Michigan.

We would start by heading to Wisconsin, where we would pick up Sam Postma, our organist for the tour. From there we would head to Iowa and Nebraska and on to Colorado. Then, if the old car held up, we'd face the Rockies and head for California. We had received enthusiastic responses from Dutch Reformed congregations all along the route.

As we drove, other drivers and pedestrians would point to our wooden shoe and giggle. We were proud: the wooden shoe was becoming our logo. I still have the shoe in my home library today, a lifelong icon to possibility thinking!

We drove all day and arrived in Vriesland, Wisconsin, at eleven o'clock at night. We parked the car downtown on Main Street. But now what?

Sam's instructions had been ludicrous. He'd told us to drive into the center of town (a town the length of probably two city blocks), park somewhere on the middle of the street, get out of our car, and call his name.

We'd been so excited about taking off that we hadn't really questioned the plan. But now that we were here, in the dark of night, with the town sleeping on either side of us, we felt like fools.

Reluctantly, we pulled ourselves out of the sedan and stood around it looking at one another. Finally I said, "Come on, Bill." He was the other outgoing one of the bunch. We nodded at one another, and then with Bill's loud voice leading us all, we bellowed out, "Sam! Sam Postma! SAM!" as the town lay sleeping and dark around us.

Ken and Warren grew sheepish and began to giggle. Just as Bill and I drew in breath for another call, a window right above our heads was thrown open and a body leaned out.

"Hey, guys! Come on up!"

Sam, who lived above his family's shop, had thought it would be a kick to see just how we would execute his instructions. He was delighted that we'd carried them out to the letter. We all five began to whoop and holler and laugh, forgetting momentarily about the sleeping residents. Then, as lights began to pop on down the street, we hushed and ran to meet Sam.

That experience provided the meat of my first mini-sermon for our first church concert. I told the story of hollering in the dark and applied it as a good lesson in faith, hoping that it would incite our audience to give generously to these penniless but optimistic boys. I referenced a Bible verse in the thirty-third chapter of the book of Jeremiah—verse 3, which reads, "Call to Me, and I will answer you and show you great and mighty things which you do not know."

I was grateful that day (as I've often been since) that preaching is a one-way conversation, for if that first audience had asked about specific "great and mighty things," my evidence would have been weak indeed. After all, our trip had just begun. But when I later delivered the same sermon following our return to school, I had ample testimony of wonder upon wonder.

We had a grand time at that first concert stop. The music was a hit, and we began our trek from Wisconsin to my home territory to sing for the First Reformed Church in Orange City, where I had made my public confession four years earlier.

Mom and Dad were very proud that night when they saw their son singing before a capacity crowd; though unspoken, I could see it in their beaming faces. Not too far away from them sat a young Newkirk High School student, a beauty, the sister to my buddy John DeHaan. When I saw her from the stage, I made a mental note to ask John about her. But it would have to wait. We would stay the night with family and leave early the next morning. We had places to go; commitments to fulfill.

The concert in Orange City was followed by one the next night in a small country church in Holland, Nebraska, forty miles south of Lincoln. The road to Holland would take us along the edge of Macy, Nebraska, near a Sioux Indian reservation where I had spent the previous summer interning as a pre-seminary student at the Native American mission. During that internship I had dated a beautiful girl, the daughter of one of the missionaries.

"Could we swing by for a short stop?" I begged the guys as we neared town. It was well past noon, and we had another couple of hours to go before reaching Holland. I felt that a short reunion with my not too serious girlfriend would still allow us time to make it to Holland, change into our dress suits, rehearse, and get to the church by seven. Warren, always the practical one of the bunch, argued, "But it's already two o'clock!"

I mentally reviewed the itinerary and still thought we had plenty of time, so I pressed the issue further. "Hey, I lived here, remember? I'm telling you: Holland isn't that far down the road. We have *plenty* of time. Come on."

We headed twenty miles east to my girlfriend's house. Amazingly, she was home, and her family treated us to cookies and lemonade. I was having a great time, feeling relaxed and romantic, but Warren was anxious. "Come on, you guys. We've got to get going!" I gave my girlfriend a quick hug, and we were off.

As we retraced the last twenty miles of our route, Warren grew increasingly agitated. The dirt road that led back to the main highway seemed rougher than it had been on our way in. "The concert starts in only four hours!" he said urgently. No sooner had he said this than—BANG!—our tire blew.

I slumped low in my seat and threw my hands over my face. I couldn't believe it! I just couldn't believe it! We sat frozen for some moments until Warren exploded into action.

Following his lead, we tore into the trunk of the car, throwing almost everything out to get at the spare. It didn't look too good, but it was all we had. We grabbed the jack and hoisted up the car, switching tires in record time. But we were a good ten miles from the reservation and ten miles from the main highway—a lot of rugged road in either direction. Our faces betrayed what we were all thinking but no one dared to say: *No way. We'll never make it.*

"Come on. Let's go!" Bill shouted. We threw the stuff back into the trunk and took off.

Ken tried to calm us down as the car bumped through the ruts. "Don't worry, guys. We'll make it. I'll step on the gas. My car can handle it!"

Well, *that* sure was a surprise—optimism from Ken?! Then he betrayed his true concern: "I just hope we don't blow *this* one." I stared sheepishly out of the side window in an intense and prayerful vigil. "I hope we don't blow the motor either," he added.

Despite our fears, we made it to the main highway just fine on that spare. A little more confident now, we pressed on to Lincoln and found ourselves doing pretty well for time. We were going to make it after all! Then the Pontiac began to cough. Sputter, putt-putt, sputter. Providentially, we were just passing an auto-repair place.

"Pull in there!" four voices hollered at Ken in unison.

He swung into the garage, and a slow moving mechanic saun-tered to the car and eased open the hood.

"Shut if off!" he called, and then made a cursory examination. A few minutes later he approached the driver's window, wiping his greasy hands on a dirty green towel. "Looks like you need new spark-plugs. Won't take long." Good news. But Warren was looking at his watch.

Warren glared at me, then announced with a bite, "It's a quarter past six." The venue in Holland was still miles down the road.

Bill said, "We'd better get dressed. Let's change here while the sparkplugs are being replaced." We all grabbed our suits and shirts from the trunk. Bill hollered to the mechanic, "Hey, where can we change?"

"Over there," he offered, pointing to an enclosed space used for painting cars.

Within minutes, five men dressed elegantly in black suits, white shirts, and black bow-ties poured out of that paint shop. All of the mechanics and pump attendants turned and stared.

"Step on the starter!" the mechanic ordered. The car ran beauti-fully!

In minutes we were out of town, racing to cover the forty-mile stretch in our forty remaining minutes. We had a chance, but a slim one. At least we were already changed; we could jump straight from the Pontiac into the church.

Adrenaline ran high in that little car. Then . . . BANG!

What was that? No! No—this can't be happening!

We skidded to the side of the road. A second blowout. All five of us simply collapsed in our seats. No one said a word. We'd been blown away by a blowout! All hope of making it to the concert was completely gone. Even Warren was too defeated to be angry. Now we had to figure out how we could get word to the church. There was going to be a packed crowd for our no-show performance.

Then we heard a car bearing down on us fast and saw a flashing red light. A cop! The officer pulled swiftly beside us and listened to our tale of woe.

"Come on," he said, "get in. I'll get you there on time!"

We abandoned the Pontiac, climbed into the back of the black-and-white Nebraska State Highway Patrol car, and off we sped toward the horizon. Ken stretched forward to look at the speedometer. "Ninety miles per hour!" he told us later.

At two minutes to seven—the scheduled start-time of the concert—most of the crowd was milling about outside, bewildered that we were still absent. Their bewilderment increased when they heard the screaming siren and saw the red light flashing as we raced down the country road.

The officer pulled up in front of the church with a flourish and we opened our doors. The crowd applauded as we calmly, casually stepped out, well dressed and smiling. (Years later, when I saw news clips of the Beatles making their grand arrivals, I would always chuckle, remembering this moment.) We felt like *somebody* as we emerged from the patrol car in our black suits and bow-ties. This was by far our most dramatic entrance of the trip.

I grinned at Warren with triumph and said, "See—we made it. I told you so."

Well, that concert brought in the biggest offering on the whole tour. We were offered beds in church members' houses, as usual, but in addition a local gas station provided two good used tires at low cost. Despite being the cause of our near fiasco, I got the credit for getting Ken two almost new tires. We had four working tires again by the time we left town, and a new spare to boot. We would laugh about our Holland, Nebraska, adventure all the way to the West Coast.

With each concert we raised enough money to get us through to the next stop, but rarely did we have any extra. When we did, it typically went for those few nights when we had to fork out money for a motel. One night we faced a dilemma: we had enough money for one room only, but the owner of the motel refused to allow more than two guests per room.

"No, you *cannot* sleep on the floor," he insisted, in response to our plead. "There's one double bed that two of you can sleep in—and no more! I'll call the cops if you pull a fast one!" The grumpy innkeeper might just as well have said, "There's no room in the inn unless you fork over more money"—which we didn't have.

We drew names to see who would sleep in the car. Bill wound up in back, and Sam and I slept in the front with feet twisted and tangled until we finally opened the windows. What a sight we must have been—my feet hanging out one side of the car, Sam and Bill's hanging out the other.

When we arrived in Denver, a college buddy welcomed us to his church. We'd arrived early and he'd made plans to show us around and introduce us to some people. That sounded good to us: into our third week of being together full-time, we needed a break from our own company! Our friend introduced us to some girls, and we made plans to go out following the concert to get a soda. Our singing was especially good that evening, probably because we knew that the girls were in the crowd. I gave a great speech at the end, and we wrapped up the program confident that we had won their affections.

We had just finished changing into our casual clothes when the pastor of the church sought us out. "Boys," he said, "that was wonderful! We're so grateful that you put us on your tour! It's been ages since we heard such fantastic music!"

Our chests puffed up a bit as we received the accolades.

He continued, "My elders and I got together . . ."

Here it comes, I thought. *They took up a big offering because they were so impressed! We won them over—maybe I did it with my speech! All right: now we can buy the girls a soda and maybe have a few extra dollars left over for California!*

"Boys . . . my elders and I decided that we simply had to treat you to a good home-cooked meal. It must have been quite a few days since you had some good cooking. So now you boys just come right along with us and we're going to my house, where the women are already preparing a meal. Tonight you'll eat well. You deserve it!"

"But . . . but . . ." We began our panicked protest as we saw our friend with the girls approaching. Soon they stood waiting at the door.

"No, boys—now it's no trouble at all. You just come right along. Here, Warren, let me give you directions."

Bill and I peeked out the window and sadly watched as our friend and the girls got into his car and drove away—without us.

We left town that night. We'd been offered rooms to sleep at the homes of our hosts and hostesses, but we were all anxious now to get out of there fast. And we were on our way to California, legendary California! None of us could sleep, so we drove on into the night.

We were off to a good start. Hours later somewhere along the Rockies we watched the rising sun hit peaks, huge and towering! The road stretched on toward Flagstaff; a one-mile hill with a steep grade lay before us. If our tired old Pontiac could make this, it would be downhill the rest of the way.

But it was simply too much for Ken's poor old car. We'd just begun to climb the steep incline when the Pontiac sputtered and stopped, the engine steaming. We had some drinking water in the car, which we poured into the radiator. After allowing the engine to cool a bit, we decided to try it again—but this time with only three of us in the car. Bill and I volunteered to hitchhike to the top of the pass. Meanwhile, Sam, Warren, and Ken motored on. By the time Bill and I crested the summit, they had been sitting at the top for over an hour, laughing at us.

We were deeply worried now that Ken's car wasn't up to getting us to the coast, let alone to the coast *and back!* Occasionally one of us would ask Warren, who was acting as treasurer, just how much money we had left in the collection. Did we have enough to buy a bus ticket back to Michigan? How about *five* bus tickets? The answer was always a cold, crisp no.

Nevertheless, I at least had no regrets. The road from the Rockies to the Pacific had presented an awesome image to the eyes of this eighteen-year-old. Mountain peaks that disappeared into the heavens, jagged and celestial; mesas that, when struck by sunlight, were festooned in the southwestern colors of bronze and gold and purple. Our American landscape indulged me with visual delicacies, magical and miraculous.

The sun was intense as we drove through the desert. We were awestruck by something we'd never seen—a forest of cacti. The tallest of these prickly, strange-looking plants were like trees without branches; they stood, bare and bleak, like stunted and swollen elms or cottonwoods, with plump fingers groping into a cloudless sky.

Then gradually the scenery began to change from barren to green, and palm trees replaced the cacti. As we drew closer to the coast we began to see orange groves, and the smell of orange blossoms blew in through our open windows. We were charmed by the heavenly scent. We pulled over next to an unfenced grove, and each of us picked an orange and peeled it, devouring the sweet fruit. Then, thanks to long summer days and a new time zone, we were at the ocean by sunset!

Wow! That was all I could think. *Wow!* The sun was shimmering on the blue waves, causing it to look as if liquid silver had been poured into the churning sea. The breeze moved across our faces in cool intoxication. And the salty sea smell—I didn't know where it came from. It was a fragrance I'd never encountered before, so different from the smell of farmland.

We slipped our shoes off to walk barefoot on the sandy beach. The waves rolled lazily, leaving their wetness on our cuffed-up britches, but we didn't care. The mild weather, unlike the hot and humid summers of home, beckoned us to stay . . . and stay . . . and stay. And then I felt it—a tug on my heart to *really* stay!

Not now, I responded silently to this strange new passion. *Not now, but someday this is where I'll spend my life as a preacher.* And I meant every word. Everything about this place spoke the word "home." Everything about it made me lighthearted and confident. I could feel it: this was it. I found it! I made it! I'm here! Though this was just a visit, one day I vowed for good, I'd return.

The concert tour concluded the following week, and *oh* how I had grown through it. I had learned that you can go anywhere from nowhere with no money, as long as you have a burning desire and a God-inspired dream. I had also learned that, no matter what, dreams never leave you where they find you.

XVI

In 1947 I became a college graduate; my life's first goal—that nearly twenty-year goal—was progressing on schedule. Grade school: finished. High school: behind me. College degree: fresh in my pocket. Now only three years to go and the dream that I had embraced at the age of five would come true.

I was twenty-one years old when I entered Western Theological Seminary, one of two Reformed Church seminaries in the United States. The other was New Brunswick in New Jersey. Western served primarily the Reformed Church in the Midwest and West. New Brunswick served the eastern Reformed Church. Both seminaries were fully accredited by the American Association of Theological Seminaries.

What degree would graduation from this three-year seminary award me? Ph.D? No. Th.D? No. D.D.? No. It would offer *no degree whatsoever!* Even though seminarians were required to be proficient in two foreign languages, Greek and Hebrew, before graduation, I would receive only a "professorial certificate" unless I chose to do a thesis or an approved faculty work project. By so doing, I could upgrade my certificate to a bachelor of divinity degree.

I knew that I needed that degree, so I chose to do a thesis. I had found that I was increasingly interested in the French lawyer Jean Chauvin—John Calvin—and his four-volume flagship work, *Institutes of the Christian Religion.* Such reading wasn't easy; the four volumes were heavy and long. But my love for debate sparked my desire to delve into the mind of this lawyer turned theologian. My brain was challenged as never before by the deep and awesome logic of Calvin's writing.

John Calvin had founded the Reformed Church while Martin Luther was building his Protestant Lutheran Church. Because John Calvin was a lawyer, he always posed his argument and made his case in a precise, logical manner, so that when he finished, the reader said, "Now *that* makes sense!"

Over the course of my seminary study, I would eat and breathe Calvin's profound arguments, reading and rereading his volumes, captivated. Under my theological faculty's supervision, I would write the first topical and scriptural index of his four-volume flagship, qualifying me for the B.D. thesis. This project was enthusiastically accepted by my professor of systematic theology, John Mulder.

For the next three years I would tackle that project, but I had no idea what I was in for. I had made a decision to achieve a great possibility before I knew the price that such a possibility would demand. But providentially, this project would become my first introduction to theological negativism versus theological positivism. Later I would come to see this distinction very clearly in the contrast between the teachings of Saint Paul and the teachings of Jesus Christ Himself. Paul railed against sin, but if you read your New Testament as I did, you'll see that Christ never called anyone a sinner. His ministry was the teaching of peace, love, and joy.

My first memorable conflict with the negative versus positive interpretations of theological doctrine came when I was confronted by the long-standing concept of "total depravity." It was from this excerpt of Calvin's teachings that negative extremists were dangerously misinterpreted, over the years, producing generations of preachers who fed their parishioners a strong, guilt-generating, humiliating consciousness of "sin." Any sermon that made every person feel guilty as hell was a great sermon. The preacher had succeeded in "generating conviction in the human conscience." It seemed to me, though, that such a perspective said, "There's no good at all in unsaved humans."

In the course of our many discussions, I was given an alternative interpretation of sin by Dr. Mulder. He began by saying, "There's much good in many if not all humans." That may sound ridiculously simple to many people, but it had a tremendously positive impact on me. He continued, "Every human just needs help in dealing with life's negative realities. Sin, evil, selfishness, injustice—these are life's realities. So man isn't totally depraved, but he's totally incapable of saving himself from these realities! Every person needs the divine forgiveness and grace that only God can offer—and that He generously offers to all."

My thesis would eventually conclude with my own interpretation—formulated from what Dr. Mulder had said to me—of Calvin's theology of sin. I would come to define sin as primarily a *condition* rather than an *action* (though that condition is often revealed in action); an inborn *absence of faith* more than a *turning from faith*.

As a result of these conclusions, I deduced that if I focused not on generating guilt, but on generating trust and positive hope, I would be preaching against sin via a creative, redemptive approach. Then I would really be preaching "Good News" (which is what the word "gospel" means).

Needless to say, these were significantly defining conclusions for me. Eventually they would lead me to emphasize that we're "saved" not just to avoid "hell" (whatever that means and wherever that is), but to become positive thinkers inspired to seek God's will for our lives and dream the divine dreams that God has planned for us. We are "saved" so that we can go on to do good works and thus truly learn to live our lives for the glory of God. This to me was an exciting, proactive approach to the problem of sin—and it became the basis for my possibility thinking message that would eventually become my signature call.

Though I was receiving what I would in hindsight call "a taste of the positive" under Dr. Mulder's theological instruction, the Reformed Church was divided in its theological perspectives. On the extreme right were fundamentalists who adhered to the letter of the law and scriptures. On the left were liberals who offered shallow interpretations of the sinful condition infecting humanity. Both sides had forceful theologians promoting their opposing views. I saw a destructiveness escalating on both sides because of these arguments.

This conflict would set up my subconscious for the "flavor" of ministry that I would adhere to and promote for the rest of my life: choosing to focus on the positive rather than the negative. And it would eventually influence me to choose Isaiah 58:12 as my lifetime biblical north star:

"You shall be called a repairer of the breach, and a restorer of paths to dwell in."

Dr. Mulder was my primary mentor at the seminary. He was positive, distinguished, and intelligent—perhaps brilliant and certainly very dignified. If I'd been forced to choose a single member of the faculty to emulate, it probably would have been Dr. Mulder. He evoked in me my love for refinement. I admired the way he carried himself and the way he presented his theological profundities. Certainly I wanted to be like him—a theologian upon whom decades of clerical understudies could hang their hopes. Did I want to be a professor? No. But I wanted to distinguish myself intellectually and deliver a store of weighty, higher thought that the world would hear—thought that, if accepted, would lift people above the dullness of their days.

Another teacher I held in high regard was the seminary's full-time professor of preaching, Dr. Simon Blocker. He was ebullient, very spontaneous, very emotional in contrast to Dr. Mulder's cognitive presentation. Efferent enthusiasm was the core of Blocker's personality. He made preaching fun.

Though I'd been dreaming big since Uncle Henry made his proclamation that I'd be a preacher, it was these teachers in particular, and my careful reading of Calvin and other theologians, that helped me to shape my dream about the nature of my future ministry.

Dr. Raymond S. Lindquist was also a catalyst who influenced my ministerial design. I'd first been influenced three years earlier by him, when he spoke at Hope College Chapel on how to live a truly fulfilled life. In his sermon, he'd advised the following:

- Don't luxuriate.

- Don't vegetate.

- Don't procrastinate.

- But *do* dedicate!

In all of my dreams, for the next fifty years, this sermon would stay alive in me to drive me through the dreaming process.

When Dr. Lindquist came to speak to us at seminary, I had a chance to become more familiar with his thinking. One day I cornered him in the hall with a question: "How long—how many years—should a minister plan to spend in a church before he moves on?"

His answer burned through me. "*Never* go to a church," he answered, "without planning to spend your whole life there."

Wow! In the Reformed Church it was assumed that preachers would move on to a new pastorate every five years—ten years at the most!

Soon after that conversation, my professor of homiletics (preaching), Dr. Blocker, happened accidentally (no—*providentially*) to assign our class a paper. He handed out a list of the names of twenty ministers in America whom he called "great preachers." We were instructed to choose one, research the person, and prepare a term paper. Weeks later—and not long before the due date—he asked me who I'd chosen. The truth was I'd neglected to choose. Unable to come up with my usual quick comeback, I hemmed and hawed and then confessed my procrastination. He wasn't happy. "Then you'll take George Truett," he ordered.

I had no choice and no argument, nor did I have the foggiest idea how defining this assignment would become in my life. I sat up many consecutive late nights researching Truett in the library, and I was inspired by what I read!

Truett was a young Baptist minister who had been called to the small congregation of the First Baptist Church in Dallas. He accepted his assignment there with what I decided to call a "Ray Lindquist attitude"—he went intending to spend his life at this church. Forty years later he'd turned the First Baptist Church into the largest and most acclaimed one in the world! Wow!

Lindquist and George Truett inspired me with a grand dream that would solve a massive problem that was growing in my heart. I was now a "middler"—a second-year student in seminary, and I had become consumed by a desire for greatness. This desire had come uninvited into my secret soul, and while it filled me with immense excitement and enthusiasm, it also filled me with fear. For I saw us graduating seniors all wanting a "*big* church"; I could feel that we were competing, and I sensed the jealousy raging among us. I had to come to terms with this potentially dangerous ambition or it would sink me.

This desire to excel, to be a truly great preacher in a "trophy church," frightened me. I knew that if I gave in to the dream of landing the top job in the biggest church, that decision would force me to play my cards carefully, jealously, politically, opportunistically. In short, this negative ambition could lead me into an unthinkable and poisonous career.

I found the answer in the message and example of Lindquist and Truett; they inspired within me a *new* dream. Instead of seeking a large church, I'd look for a small church in a big city—a venue where there'd be lots of folk who needed divine forgiveness and assistance in dealing with "life's realities" in a positive-thinking way. What's more, I would spend my life there! I would compete only against myself. And I'd channel my ambition over the next forty years, leaving behind at my retirement a church as big and as great as God willed it! I still wanted to be a Mulder—but I'd do it in a Truett way.

Reflections such as these occupied much of my day, but there was still plenty of time left over for outside activities. Take girls, for example.

There were fifteen of us guys who had started Western together as freshmen, and with one exception we'd remain classmates until graduation. (Chun Young Chang would have to drop out four months before the end of his final year to return home in a Korean wartime emergency.) Two of these fifteen guys were married. The rest of us single guys kept an eye open for the right girlfriend. There wasn't a female to be found in our theological seminary, but since Western was just across the street from Hope, we were privileged to know quite a few college girls.

I actually already had what everyone called "a girl." But that just meant that when we went out as a group, I'd sit by her and not someone else, and occasionally I'd buy her a soda or a burger. I liked her, but any time I thought about having a serious relationship with her (or anyone else), I'd remember some advice I'd gotten while still in college—advice that I know was divinely directed.

Back when I worked at Castle Park Resort as a waiter, I dressed in a long-tailed tuxedo and served the richest of the rich. I'd just finished my shift one day when a beautiful brunette, dreamy and fragile, passed by. Within minutes we were carrying on a conversation. The topic was of little interest to me, but I was captivated—absolutely entranced—by her eyes. An hour later, we were on an outside dance floor, under a canopy of stars on the quiet shoreline of Lake Michigan. The whole scene was like a Hollywood fantasy, sensual in all respects. I heard water stirred by a gentle breeze. I smelled a mixture of sweet fragrances from the flowers that edged the dance floor and the girl's perfume. I touched her slender waist, and her silky hair came close to my cheek. I saw stars and linen and lace and pretty people, and my head was swimming in romance! As soon as we parted from that dance floor, I wanted to see her again.

As I stepped out of psych class a few days later, Dr. Granberg nailed me in the hall with an uninvited comment. "Bob," he said, "I just want to say—when you get ready to be serious about a girl, start with your head and your heart will follow.

What provoked that? I wondered suspiciously. *Had he heard me tell the guys about my big romantic moment?*

His pronouncement clashed with the memory of Castle Park. "Start with your head and your heart will follow." Did I respect that girl? No, not particularly. Our conversation had been nothing special. Did I trust that girl? No, how could I? Even as we held hands, I didn't know anything about her; and the truth was that I felt no tremendous interest in attempting to get to know her. The entire evening had been nothing but infatuation.

Dr. Granberg's words echoed in my head every time I thought about my new acquaintance. "Don't allow yourself to get carried away, sacrificing your career goals in a mood filled with romance and sensuality." In the end, I heeded those words. I never called the phone number she'd scribbled on a stolen linen napkin.

From that incident on, every time I wanted to measure the weight of my intentions regarding a girl, I'd ask myself, "Do I respect her? Do I trust her?"

Actually, from time to time I seriously considered remaining single. After all, I could travel much more easily without a family. I could become a global cleric, a missionary of some sort (like my Uncle Henry), if I didn't have to worry about being tied down. Many of my heroes from the clergy had never married. Phillips Brooks, for example, who wrote "O Little Town of Bethlehem" and was a powerful author and theologian. And Clarence McCartney, then the most famous Presbyterian pastor in America.

I was nearing the end of another school year at Western, and the seminary had assigned me to an internship in Preston, Minnesota. I was to help start a new church in a beautiful but abandoned Presbyterian house of worship. So I packed up my battered suitcase, tied it with my belt to keep the broken latches from giving way, and went home. Home—where I could turn off both my heart and my head. Where I could hook up with Earl and fish the Floyd. Where I could satiate my appetite with Mom's cooking. This was just what I needed at the close of another year in seminary. I'd head for Iowa for seven days and then be off on my summer assignment to be an unofficial preacher-in-residence. I had no idea that this would be the summer I would meet the girl God had prepared for me.

XVII

"So you'll be home for a Sunday, Robert?" an elder of the First Reformed Church in Newkirk asks me only a day after I return to Alton. "Will you preach for us?" This sounds pretty exciting to me—my first public, formal sermon ... and in my childhood church! I agree, of course, and of course Dad and Mom are proud. Dad even has a glint of a tear in his eye when he hears the news.

I find that home is a great place to study, so preparing my sermon is fun and easy. Henry is working our land again with Dad, but he no longer hounds me about the chores. He recognizes that my life's work is destined for a different direction, and he respects this.

The days flow quickly by. It's now early Sunday morning, and I go over my notes one more time as I eat a farm-style breakfast of hot "Fet en Stroop" and bacon. Giving Mom a smile and a wave as she scurries to her bedroom to dress for church, I don an air of professionalism and head for the door.

Visions of Dr. Mulder inspire me, and I accelerate my pace to Dad's car (not new, but replaced after the tornado) that I'll use to get to the church. My eagerness causes me to drive a little more quickly than this countryside is accustomed to.

When I arrive at the church, I'm so early that no one else is around. I decide to pass the time alone in my car, taking a moment for meditation on this pleasant morning.

The trees are green with foliage. Their limbs sway in the slight breeze, shifting the gentle shadows that they cast across the stained-glass windows—green and purple and blue and gold set ablaze, even from outside, by penetrating rays of morning sun. The bell-tower, white and stout as a Dutchman, rises twenty feet above the roofline, one lonely church bell hanging in the tall square-shaped spire.

I glance across the street to my high school, dark and vacant on a sleepy Sunday. Today my dream is within my grasp. Today I'm grown up. *Today I'm a preacher!* Everything at this moment seems so right with my world. I sit back and bask in the joy of it.

I set aside my reverie and resume rehearsing my message. Soon another car drives into the parking lot, stopping at the far end. A girl springs out of the car with an energy that seems to awaken the morning from its slumber. So fresh and exuberant is the bounce in her step that I flinch unexpectedly. I lean forward a bit to study her. Do I know her?

She has long, auburn hair now catching a bit of the playful sun. She's slender and graceful as she moves, and I find myself drawn to her radiant energy.

Why is she here, all alone?

She heads for the back door of the church. I see now that she carries sheet music in her left hand. Finally I put the pieces together. She must be the organist, I conclude. Boy, they didn't make them like that when I was a kid!

I pull myself from the car and enter the church. I step through the back door and walk up six steps to the side room. I'm quivering slightly as I open the door, and there she stands. Alone. Striking. Confident. Radiating an aura of friendly intelligence.

"Hi, Harold. I'm Arvella DeHaan. I'm your organist today. What hymns have you chosen?"

I'm dumbstruck by her sense of command. She's so in control of her world! And her eyes are so green!

I remain silent so long that she looks at me rather suspiciously.

Quickly I regain my composure and we do business, lining up the order of the service. She's very helpful, and I thank her profusely.

With a quick check of her watch she says, "Time for the prelude. See you later."

She disappears through the door that leads to the organ loft, and then her music begins to fill the sanctuary. I open the door slightly to watch her from this private room. Her brow is furrowed in concentration, and her lips are pursed. Her curls hang softly on the gray, white-trimmed suitcoat that shapes her beautiful figure.

Worshipers have been trickling in for some time, and when I make my entrance into the sanctuary, I see that it's now full from front to back! I take my seat in the pulpit chair, facing out toward the parishioners, who sit quietly enjoying the organ music.

The ensuing hour seems to be simultaneously the heaviest and the lightest moment of my life. As I deliver my best Mulder imitation, trying to appear intelligent and convincing, I can't help but focus on that auburn-haired, green-eyed organist.

She fidgets under my gaze, looking around to see if others are noticing the odd mannerisms and unsolicited attentions of this visiting minister. After my message draws to a close, I watch her return to her place at the organ for the closing hymn.

Why had my hearty thank-you when we spoke before the service caused her to look so nervous? Every preacher thanks the musicians! Was she onto me? I never was good at hiding my thoughts. I wonder about this self-consciously as she leads the congregation in the closing hymn.

When the service is over, the congregation swarms to greet me. Each member wants to share his or her individual "I remember when . . ." memory, but I'm looking for Arvella. Soon just a few women are left, their men standing outside smoking. By the time I politely withdraw, Arvella is gone. And so is my heart. Only this time, it's run off *with my head in tow!*

I climb into my car, feeling clumsy and frustrated as I attempt to assess what happened to me on this surprising morning. As I drive home, I summon my head back to reclaim my heart and do my little self-test. Do I respect her? At this I let out an audible chuckle. I was *so* impressed! *Definitely* I do.

Then comes the more serious question: Do I *trust* her? I just met her. How could I trust her?

Do I trust her? Do I *trust* her? *Do I trust her?* And then a deep sense of indescribable peace and—yes, trust—wells up within me. I'm stunned. I *do* trust her! How? Why? I don't know. But I *do!* A rush of thrilled amazement shoots through me. In sudden acceleration, I whip my car around and head to Earl De Jong's house. Earl has to know who this girl is, and I'm going to find out.

Talking into late afternoon, Earl and I spent hours catching up. How life had changed for the two of us! He was now responsible for the family farm. I was a preacher. But both of us *were* still single! And by the time I got home that evening, I had Arvella DeHaan and her whereabouts nailed down. She was the little sister of my old high school singing buddy, John DeHaan. She lived not more than a quarter mile from Earl. He had pointed out the farm to me as I followed him around as he did his chores. Then, after I had supper with his family, he told me what he knew about her, which wasn't much. Nevertheless it was *something*.

"Comes from a good family," he told me. "A big one. Lot's of brothers and sisters . . . well, you knew John, so . . . there you go. Basketball player . . . a darn good one, Harold. She's pretty, but I guess you know that. But did you know that lots of guys think so?"

"I suppose," I told him.

"Good luck, Harold—lots of competition!"

It was late by the time I got home. Creeping into the kitchen, I tried desperately to be quiet. Mom and Dad were already in bed, and there, on the kitchen table, was a note so typical of Mom. There was no word of praise about the sermon, no expression of maternal pride. The note read simply:

Harold:
   School called. Your professor says,
   "You'll have to wait a week before going to Preston. They aren't ready for you yet. Enjoy another seven days of vacation."
   For some reason, he called you by the name of "Bob." Explain this to me in the morning.
   I love you, Harold.
                            Mom

The next night I drove the four miles to Arvella's farm. Their driveway stretched a quarter-mile long—a narrow, rutted, single lane through the cornfields leading to a farmyard with a white house, small and old. I stopped momentarily partway down the drive, planning my strategy. I decided that I could make an excuse for my visit by telling them I'd come to see John. That settled, I drove on down the long, narrow strip, my insides bouncing wildly.

There were seven children in that family, from the ages of ten on up, and a bunch of them spotted me long before I had a chance to step out of the car. They seemed to pour from the nooks and crannies of the surrounding farm buildings. A visitor was an exciting moment in these parts, as it had been when I was younger. The kids had all clustered into the kitchen by the time I got to the door, and they ushered me in to join them. For a moment I felt like a mini-celebrity, the student who had preached in their church the day before. Stella DeHaan, mother of the brood, was also in the kitchen, as was father Lou DeHaan, sitting white-haired in his rocker. Three of Arvella's brothers and two sisters surrounded me in light chatter.

"Where's Johnny?" I asked, when I had the chance. "I'd hoped to see him."

"You know, he was in the South Pacific with the Navy for four years," Mrs. DeHaan answered. "He's studying his music now at Drake University in Des Moines." Then she inquired about Henry, my brother, who had survived the terrible fighting in France and Germany, and she bemoaned the war and its ill-effects on the community. As she spoke I could hear steps coming down from upstairs, and my heart picked up a few extra beats. Into the room she stepped—Arvella!—but she headed unwaveringly for the door.

"Hi!" she said, passing through. "Sorry, but I've got to get to church. Good sermon yesterday!" And she was gone.

"I've got to go too," I told Mrs. DeHaan. "Sorry Johnny wasn't here. Please give him my greeting next time you write."

I practically sprinted out the door, trying to catch Arvella, but all I saw was the dust from her car rising down the dry dirt driveway.

I jumped into my car and followed. She drove a fast two miles into Newkirk, then pulled hard and swift in front of the lonely Newkirk Store. I was right behind her and parked my car next to hers. The two of us threw open our car doors at the same time.

I wasn't going to allow procrastination to rob me of my goal. "I'm going to be around a week," I said. "I'm preaching next Sunday night in Sheldon. Want to go along?"

She seemed a little taken aback, but I thought I could sense—or was it just hope?—that the attraction was mutual.

"Sure," she said. "Sounds nice."

"You know," I confessed, "I really went to your house to ask you that, but I never had a chance!" We both laughed. Her face was beautiful. I felt energy in the air when we were together.

My family gathered at the church in Sheldon to hear me preach. Afterward, Arvella rode with me back to our home, where we had a family gathering.

"Why did you choose to preach that particular sermon tonight?" she asked.

"I was assigned that text in seminary," I answered, a little defensively. "I got an A on the sermon I wrote then—so I felt okay with it." (The subject of the sermon had been the five wise and five foolish virgins.)

Arvella gave me a weird look and said, "Now that's one sermon that's out of left field. I don't think you'll want to preach it again."

Little did I know that she would become my finest critic throughout all the many years ahead.

After our family gathering I took her home. At the door I asked, "How about going to a movie tomorrow night in Sioux City? I'm leaving Tuesday."

"Sure, let's do it," she answered.

The date was fun, relaxed but energizing nonetheless. The walk in the dark to her door found us holding hands. This was our second date, two nights in a row, and we kissed. Once. Politely.

"May I write you, Arvella?" I asked

She nodded affirmation, and I drove home listening to my heart singing. I tried to use my head, too, though. "We both love church work," I said to myself. "We both come from the same kind of Dutch

Christian farm family, and we're both relaxed and comfortable in our conversations. She's the kind of girl I should marry."

The next morning I got up and reached for a tablet to write to my fraternity brother and quartet singing buddy, Bill Miedema. Overpowered by a spirit I know was the Eternal God Himself, I wrote these words: "Dear Bill—I've met the girl I'm going to marry."

Arvella today insists that I began to make this marital intention known to her over the next few days, but that she didn't know me well enough to accept. But I stand by my account that I didn't ask her to marry me for almost another twelve months, when she enthusiastically said yes and we became formally "engaged." But whether I immediately verbalized my intentions or not, my mind—and my heart—had been made up. I knew she would be my wife.

For the next two years we courted mostly by letter. In school, and away from Arvella, I had difficulty focusing at times on my studies. She would invade my thoughts incessantly. But my education continued to mold me and shape me despite my distractions.

Looking back, I realize that there were two Robert Schullers during this time, and I refused to allow them to converge. The passionate, emotional, artistic, poetic part of me was released in my letters to Arvella, and I could be dramatic in my social outings with friends, adding much of the humor in our circle. But I never allowed this first part of me to invade the theologian and preacher. In that realm I donned the dignified air that I so admired in Dr. Mulder. I would stand before my audience in controlled form, arms at my side, voice predictable, my conclusions intelligent, my hearers treated as studious lovers of theological dissection. I know now that, while my words were intelligent and thoughtful, to everyday people they were boring.

But about this time my friends and I were instructed by our professors to go on a field trip. We were to go and listen to a very successful preacher who served the oldest church in our denomination—the Marble Collegiate Church in New York City. He was also a part-time professor of preaching at the New Brunswick seminary. The name of this pastor was Norman Vincent Peale.

Founded by fifty-four Dutch colonists in 1628, Dr. Peale's church was most prestigious. It was also (and still is) the oldest church with an unbroken ministry in the United States.

Though our professors were eager to send us on this trip, they didn't think much of Dr. Peale. He was widely criticized in the circle in which I found myself; we were being sent not to admire but to dissect and critique him and his delivery. "Paul is appealing and Peale is appalling" was the popular, though crude and unfair, criticism heard in the theological halls of Western.

Obediently, but with little enthusiasm, I piled into a car loaded with classmates and headed for Grand Rapids, Michigan, where this preacher would deliver a secular speech in the city auditorium.

The crowd was huge, maybe three thousand people. I was curious about this preacher we'd heard so much about. The applause was warm as Dr. Peale took the stage, and my anticipation grew. When he opened his mouth, however, my anticipation deflated. The vocabulary that spilled out was ordinary and everyday, and he employed a melodramatic style—replete with undignified, wild gestures—that completely turned me off. Faithful to the seminary's mindset, we students knew that to exude emotion in this way clearly demonstrated a lack of intellectual rigor. Furthermore, Peale conveyed no theological profundity. He used simple words, simple stories, and basic emotions to carry his points.

I was unmoved by the presentation, but the audience loved him! They clung to his every word. They cried; they roared with laughter; they *listened*. I left utterly disillusioned.

On the drive back to school, my classmates and I agreed, "Peale is terribly shallow. Where's all the intelligence he's supposed to possess? He didn't say anything that we haven't heard before!" Thinking back on what I'd heard, I was sure that I didn't want to be a preacher like him.

I spent the next days mimicking and mocking Peale. I would throw up my arms, wide as a windmill. I would modulate my voice in wild exaggeration. As I pranced up and down the dormitory halls giving my Peale impersonation, I had no idea that years later I would identify with and even embrace his calling to abandon a contrived dignity on behalf of delivering a heart-moving message. At this time, I had yet to appreciate such humble heroism. Mulder was my kind of a preacher and therefore remained my hero. But Peale was my future.

Vacations gave Arvella and me short times together—times that we treasured. At Christmas it was so good to see her that I gave her my fraternity pin. I learned that this was a wise move. She told me that many boys had been asking for dates, and she'd been responding simply, "I'm not dating anymore." One infatuated farmboy hadn't been willing to accept that answer. He'd said, with derisive incredulity, "You're not waiting for *Skuller*, are you?!" She came back with, "Maybe I am. I don't know, but one thing's for sure: I'm not going out with you!" Accepting my pin put all of this to rest. It showed a real commitment by both of us.

A year after our first kiss I carried home in my pocket a diamond ring that I'd bought for one hundred and eighty dollars in a jewelry store in Holland, Michigan. It took me six months to pay for it out of my Saturday job as a clerk at Montgomery Ward.

The night was dark as Arvella and I sat in the front seat of my Chevy in the yard by her house. The smell of field and cattle was pungent and the night was clear, lit by a billion stars, as I asked her, "Will you marry me, Arvella?" And she answered, "Yes."

I reached in my pocket, pulled out the ring, and held it up. It was barely visible in the yard light that glowed from the top of a tall pole. She smiled the smile that she's shared with me for over half a century. Without a word she reached out her left hand, fingers spread apart, and I slipped on the ring. We hugged. We kissed. We laughed.

She wouldn't take that diamond ring off until eight years later, when its diamond solitaire fell out, never to be found.

That summer Arvella joined me in Michigan to attend Hope College. Her education had been interrupted after high school by the illness of her mother, whom she had cared for, so she was one year behind her classmates. But now, at last, she was able to study her beloved music and to take courses in theology and psychology, preparing herself to become a pastor's wife. But her time at school was short. As we studied our finances and looked ahead, she decided to return home the next fall to work and earn money for our future. Her sacrifice was great, and she would remain torn over this decision for years. Any man who has been the recipient of such generosity knows that words are not enough to express the anguish I felt over this necessity, and the gratitude I felt for her choice.

How I passed my courses with an A average during that time away from her still befuddles me, except that my passion for my dream would surge afresh, blending beautifully with my passion for Arvella.

The threat of war returned to the land and once again hit close to home. We listened to reports of the North Koreans pushing MacArthur's forces to the edge of the ocean at the very tip of South Korea. Four months from graduation, my classmate Chun Young Chang asked permission to leave seminary to go home to Korea. "If the freedom-fighters are driven to the ocean, I'll need to be there with my family," he said. We were all stunned that he would walk away from his three-year, hard-earned postgraduate degree. We grieved that he had to make such a horrendous choice—fulfill the dream, or be loyal to family.

The day came when we were to say our goodbyes. A farewell prayer service was held for Chun, and it was there that we all heard a surprise announcement. Dr. John R. Mulder, then president of the seminary, called Chun up before us. As tears shimmered on many cheeks, he handed Chun his diploma! Then he said, "This fully credentials you, Chun, to be an ordained minister in any major denomination in the world. Now go with God!"

Chun left, and the rest of our class finished the last months of our three-year study. In Korea, MacArthur fought back to the thirty-ninth parallel, and the war ended there without a peace treaty.

But we heard no more from Chun Young Chang.

Not until many years later, that is, when I was on a U.S. Air Force mission tour of Asia. We were in Korea, being entertained by an orphans' choir, on Thanksgiving morning. I mentioned the name Chun Young Chang to the choir director, and his face brightened. "Oh, yes!" he said, "I know him. He's a school teacher." He described a location five hours away over terribly rough roads. Knowing that our schedule didn't include ten hours for a Jeep trek there and back, I merely said, "Tell him that Robert Schuller sends his love."

Later that night, who should appear at the Air Force base but my old classmate. He had gotten the word, and Air Force officials had been kind enough to let him visit me inside the compound. We talked long into the night, and I asked him, "Chun, what are your dreams?"

"To build a high school," he told me. "The need is so great."

So when I went back to California, I helped him raise the money. Keo Chang High School was the result. It was the first building in Chun's district of Korea to have forced-air heat, running water, and toilets. Some years later I visited him there and received a warm welcome. And though our departure was scheduled for four-thirty in the morning, all one thousand students lined up in the glow of truck headlamps to sing for us in grateful farewell.

Ready for my graduation, I accepted a call to a church near Chicago—a tiny, thirty-five-member church in the suburb of Ivanhoe. It was as small as Truett's church in Dallas, Texas, had been when he first took it on. Ray Beckering, a denominational representative introduced to me by Dr. Mulder, advised, "There are enough unchurched people in Chicago to keep you busy all your life." I accepted the challenge gladly. I admired Dr. Beckering and was pleased to be welcomed into his region of Illinois. He would prove to be a valuable mentor and lifelong friend.

I would be ordained and installed in only three short weeks.

"Chicago—here I come!"

But in the meantime, I was going home to Iowa to marry that girl on whose finger I had placed an engagement ring the year before. We had waited long enough.

I graduated with the highest honor in my class for preaching. The award was printed in the announcement bulletin for Western's commencement, a service that Arvella was able to come up for with my parents.

God had answered my single most passionate prayer: "God make me a preacher when I grow up!" And now Arvella would drive with me back to Iowa, with a stop in Ivanhoe, Illinois, for a glimpse into our very near future. We would get to see the parsonage in which we would live, as well as purchase a few pieces of furniture with the money Arvella had earned over the past months, and Arvella could meet Dr. Beckering.

Our wedding date had been changed three times due to the wild scheduling of events: graduation, wedding, ordination, and installation—all within a three-week period. Whew! Arvella would discover that marriage to a Schuller was not boring. As for myself, I had only one thing on my mind now . . .

"Arvella—here I come!"

XVIII

"I'll never forget the date of my wedding anniversary," I said to my classmate Warren Heitbrink. I'm getting married in the middle of the month in the middle of the year in the middle of the century— June 15, 1950!"

"Well, I'm ahead of you by a few days," he responded. "I'll expect you to stand up with me at my wedding."

All of us students were heading home after four years of close friendship in Hope College and three years of closer friendship at Western Theological Seminary.

Arvella and I, after being home from Illinois for only a day, drove from northwest Iowa across the South Dakota state line to the little country church where Warren would be getting married.

The ceremony went splendidly at first, but something deep and disquieting happened to me as I thought about the ramifications of marriage. I stood in the center of the ceremonial circle that enclosed the bride and groom and the attendants at the front of the church and pondered the bond that was being affirmed there. When the soloist began singing the words of a country hymn, "I Surrender All," my heart was gripped with anxiety. Did getting married mean that I would surrender *all* my freedom and personhood for the rest of my life?

Arvella, I could tell when I glanced at her out of the corner of my eye, was thoroughly enjoying the whole event. But I was not.

During the reception that followed in the church basement, I grew more ill at ease as I sized up Warren. *You have surrendered all, old friend,* I thought. For me there were more misgivings and anxiety than joy as the family and friends enjoyed chicken sandwiches, coffee, and wedding cake. But Arvella was having a ball, talking and laughing with some guy I didn't know. I found out later that he was the fiancé of the maid of honor I was escorting for the evening. But at the time I was jealous and disquieted all at the same time, and these negative emotions began to drive a wedge between Arvella and me.

The long, dark drive home to northwest Iowa was unlike any other night we had shared, or would ever share again.

"Just think," Arvella said, jubilant in the fresh afterglow of this wedding experience. "Only a few days and it will be *our* night!"

She squeezed my arm affectionately as I drove through the countryside, but I couldn't respond with the enthusiasm I knew she expected. My mood was too dark. I kept my grave thoughts to myself, though. I said nothing of the unnerving emotions that had entered my heart, uninvited and unwelcome, only a few hours before.

It was past midnight when we reached her farmhouse. I stepped out of the car, politely opened her door, and reached out with my left hand to help her out of the car. The yard light was on, and it reflected color from the small diamond ring I had placed on her left hand a year before.

She walked so close that our bodies touched from shoulders to hips. She snuggled warm and close, her left arm hugging my back till we reached the door. Then she turned to face me, hugged me with both arms, lifted her head (eyes closed), and pressed her lips firmly and passionately on mine.

"I love you, Bob," she said, and I knew she meant it.

"I love you, Arvella."

After we said our goodbyes, she turned and went inside with a wave. Alone and troubled, I returned to the car and drove the four haunting, dark, and silent country miles to my home.

In only seven days I was scheduled to marry Arvella DeHaan. My original plan—off and on, anyway—had been to remain a bachelor. So how did I get onto this wedding track? In high school I'd been so young that I didn't have a single date. In college, after I'd danced with that one girl on that one romantic evening, I'd determined to "start with my head." So where was my head now? *This wasn't the plan. How did I get here?* Arvella was wearing my ring, and I was due to "surrender all" in one short week. What on earth had I done?

I dragged my sorry self into the house and into bed and had a troubled night of restless sleep.

"How was Warren's wedding?" Mom asked me at the breakfast table the next morning. I didn't answer. I wanted to forget about the whole thing.

"Well?" she asked.

Whenever I wasn't chatting away with my usual enthusiasm, my mother knew that something was up.

"Mom," I blurted out, "I'm not sure that I should get married."

She looked concerned.

"What are you saying?" she asked. She seemed genuinely confused and definitely disapproving.

"I'm just not sure that I should get married, Mom." I tried to leave it at that. I didn't want to explain. How could I?

Then she laughed. "And you're going to be ordained as a minister in two weeks? You're going to be telling people to live 'by faith'?"

My face burned with embarrassment, but at least I had the sense to listen to my mother's wisdom.

"Let me tell you something," she continued, her voice animated as usual. "I don't have a college education, but believe me, I know that any time you're about to make a big decision, you can expect to have last-minute questions. This is where your faith has to take over!"

That lesson has stayed with me ever since. In fact, it would later become a sermon I would preach as I presented (with credit to Mom) the five phases of faith. I would offer these phases with conviction, though at that solemn moment in the kitchen I was only beginning to learn them—the hard way:

1. *The Nesting Phase* Here an idea is dropped like a fertile egg in the womb of your imagination, as in the moment I first met that pretty organist.

2. *The Testing Phase* Here you ask the right questions and see how the dream fits in with your values and your life's mission statement. This is the wisdom of "Start with your head and your heart will follow." I had done this.

3. *The Investing Phase* Here you make a commitment. You propose. You become engaged. You slip a ring on her finger. You write poetry and passionate letters.

4. *The Arresting Phase* Here you pause to make a final check, as I did that morning at the kitchen table. "Is this your final answer?" You remember the old tailor's line: "Measure three times, but cut only once." And be darn sure that you don't abandon your first three steps out of fear!

5. *The Cresting Phase* You'll reach your mountaintop, as I did when I pressed through to reach the day of my wedding.

The night before the ceremony, I slipped this verse into Arvella's hand:

Rise up, my love, my fair one,
And come away.
For lo, the winter is past,
The rain is over and gone.
The flowers appear on the earth;
The time of the singing of the birds has come
And the voice of the turtledove
Is heard in our land.
                    Song of Solomon 2:10–12
                    Love, Bob

Now I stand waiting alongside my best man, Henry Schuller, in the country church where both Arvella and I were baptized, where I sat every Sunday morning of my childhood life until I transferred to Reverend Colenbrander's church in Orange City. First Reformed Church of Newkirk, Iowa, feels like home.

The organ begins to play the classic wedding march, "Here Comes the Bride," as Arvella glides down the candlelit aisle. Her hair, its ringlets edged in copper, falls about her slender shoulders. She wears a floor-length wedding dress that she made herself, its whiteness the symbol of her virginity, which she will give to me tonight, so innocently, so trustingly, so willingly. For days and

weeks she's fitted, cut, and sewed, and now—here, bathed in candles glow—only twenty years old, she's a radiant bride. Fun flashes
from her flirtatious glance as our eyes make contact. How could I
have been so foolish as to question this miracle?

"Do you, Robert Harold Schuller, take this woman, Arvella
DeHaan, to be your wedded wife?"

Unhesitatingly, with heartfelt conviction, I answer firmly, "I do!"

No sooner had I said my vows at that ceremony (over a half-century
ago) than I became overwhelmed by a consuming spiritual consciousness that this would be the most right thing I would ever do in
my whole life! I wondered, at that moment, whether I was experiencing the presence of God. Today I answer my own question with
a resounding yes! God had come to witness that day. *Our* day. For it
was holy.

We celebrated our joy and love with a traditional reception in the
church basement—chicken sandwiches, punch, coffee, and cake.
Then a quick change from Arvella's bridal gown to a "going away
outfit" and we were in the car. But "going away" to where? I really
hadn't thought about where we'd go!

In the madness of our schedules, I had completely forgotten to
plan a honeymoon!

But I didn't let on to Arvella. I *couldn't*.

I helped her into the car in a gentlemanly fashion; then I started
the engine and headed for the main road that I'd watched so often
as a boy from my perch by the Floyd. After all, it did run all the way
from Sioux City, Iowa, to Minneapolis, Minnesota. Surely it would
take me *somewhere*.

I prayed, "Lord, please don't let Arvella ask me where!"

Maintaining an appearance of calm, I headed north.

"Well, where are we going?" she asked, eyes dancing. "Where did
you make reservations?" So much for the power of prayer this day!

I tried desperately to come up with a fib that would rescue me without stretching the truth *too* far, but I couldn't think quickly enough. Her innocent and trusting look forced me into a confession.

"Nowhere. I didn't make any."

"You're kidding, right?"

Oh, those eyes! Those beautiful eyes, now aghast.

"You've *got* to be joking!" she said.

"Well," I sighed, flustered with embarrassment, "there's Sheldon, Iowa. And if *they* don't have a hotel . . ."

"Sheldon!? They *don't* have a hotel—or a motel. Only a town park. And for sure we're not spending our first night together on a park bench!"

"Then . . . um . . . there's Worthington, Minnesota, only a short drive, just across the Iowa/Minnesota border. How does that sound?"

Amazingly, she was content with that. And right away we resumed the fun, chattering excitedly about the wedding, the guests, and the attendants.

There was only one long main street in Worthington. It was late at night when we arrived, and we seemed to be the only car on the road. Straight ahead I saw the word I was looking for. Five large red letters spelled HOTEL. We pulled up, parked, then entered the tiny lobby, each carrying our own suitcase. Arvella waited while I went to the registration desk.

"I'm on my honeymoon," I said. "Do you have a room for my wife and me?" It sounded so good to hear the words "my wife" coming from my lips.

The man gave a broad smile, and I knew we were home. "We've got a *good* one for you. Congratulations . . . uh—what's your name?"

I carried both suitcases up the steps to the second floor, down the hall, and to our assigned room. I unlocked it and Arvella stepped in. I followed, then closed the door behind us. Standing tall, with both arms wide open, I threw my head back and shouted, "I'm free! Free! Free at last!"

"What are you saying?" She looked at her new husband as if he'd lost his mind.

"Honey, I'm *married*! And I'm free at last from my mom! And I'm free from four years of college! And I'm free from three years of term papers and final exams! I'm free to live the rest of my life with you!"

I grabbed her in my arms. "We've got three days here. We'll make love. We'll go up to Lake Okaboji and Spirit Lake and fish. Okay? And then we'll move to Chicago to be ordained and start our ministry, and together we'll build a great church and a wonderful life!"

I held her close, feeling an exhilaration like nothing I'd ever experienced before. It was the most perfect moment of my life.

"I have a wedding gift for you, honey," Arvella said. "It's a gift I can give only once to one man. I've saved it for my husband, to give it to him on my wedding night."

"And I have the same gift for you," I said, smiling.

First we knelt and prayed for God's blessing on our lives. Then, free of any restraint, embarrassment, guilt, or fear of exposure, we made love for the first time. The explosion of true joy and unalloyed affection was our reward for having waited to offer our virginity, each to the other!

XIX

Arvella and I have been in Ivanhoe for two days now, married for one week. My sister Violet and her husband, Heinie, have made the drive from Iowa to help us unpack our few belongings into the Parsonage, the home that the Church owned. But we had to furnish it. The new table and chairs and the new bedroom set we purchased when we passed through before have all been set in place. The church saw to it that the delivery men placed everything in the proper room with care. We have no refrigerator, but the basement is cool enough to keep our butter and a few other items from spoiling. Still, the milk and meat will need to be purchased daily.

But now the day of my ordination has arrived, and so I'm having a moment alone for meditation and prayer. My eyes are closed, my head lifted to heaven in silence. Suddenly, sharply, into my mind pops a Bible verse I know well. It's from the book of Isaiah — chapter 58, verse 12: "You shall be called the repairer of the breach and the restorer of paths to dwell in."

My body tingles with the excitement of God's presence. This moment confirms my most ardent hope, that He will be with me on this special day. He has given me a biblical north star, filling me with faith about my future. I feel a smile break across my face as the tears begin to fall.

As this moment of "visitation" from God passes, I get up and go into the kitchen to find my lovely wife. She croons, "I'm so proud of you, honey. So proud!" Her eyes sparkle with affection. I draw her close and bury my face in her hair. Then I leave to shower and walk to the church alone.

Today's ceremony could be likened to a wedding between me and the church and the Lord. It's a sober day of making vows in the presence of those who will guide me and those who will come under my care.

Unfortunately, my parents won't be able to attend. Farmers can't easily get away from their land and livestock; and since they came to my graduation so recently, I can't expect them to travel again.

Ray Beckering, whom I have asked to officiate as the senior pastor at my ordination, meets me inside the back door of the church. He's wearing the traditional clerical robe of gray and black with two bands of purple extending down the robe's length. For now, I'm dressed in my black Sunday suit, white shirt, and black tie.

I hear bustling activity from down in the basement, where women from the church are preparing the ordination reception. The smell of coffee wafts up as we stand on the cold tile floor.

Ray embraces me with a fatherly hug. It's God who put Ray Beckering into my life, of this I'm convinced. I learned early that when God's will is being done, He always puts the right people in the right spot at the right time. People with the right spirit or skill or position of power and influence, or people with the right insight, connections, or financial resources.

Ray grips me by the shoulder with his large hand. "Bob, I know from personal experience that this is, along with marriage, the most significant day in the life of a man who's called to serve God and the church of Jesus Christ.

"I know that your parents' presence will be missed today, but I want you to know something, Robert. I'll be committed to you with the loyalty of a father. I'll be available to you at all hours, in any circumstance you find yourself. I'll help to watch out for you and Arvella, and when children come I'll watch over them as well. And I'm honored to do what I do today."

The small church is filled now. Ray and I file in to take our places, and I join my wife in the front pew. She clasps her two warm hands about mine. My mind blurs, overwhelmed with emotion.

The congregation rises for the hymns, and their voices, led by piano, fill the tiny sanctuary.

I can't hear the words to any of the songs. I'm too intent on my own individual communion with heaven.

Ray Beckering rises from his chair, stands behind the pulpit, and booms:

"WHAT IS RIGHT WITH THE CHURCH?"

Bang! He gets my attention! I'm jolted by his tone of conviction. His question hits me like a ton of bricks.

"What's right with the church?" he repeats, this time in a more subdued and probing fashion. Then he drives home his message: "Everyone is always talking about what's *wrong* with the church. But what's *right* with the church?

"Number one: the church has a great *mission!* Our mission is to find the lost and save them. Find the troubled and help them. Lead them to Jesus Christ.

"Number two: the church has a great *message!* It affirms the value and worth of any and all persons. The message of the church is to convince people not how bad they are, but how beautiful they can become!

"Number three: the church has a great *method!* Our method, when we are true to the gospel, isn't judgmental assessment but nonjudgmental love. People want to change. They want to be better than they are. They must be nurtured to dream beautiful dreams, and they *will* dream beautiful dreams *when they experience real love, agape, grace*. Remember that grace is God's love in action for people who haven't earned it! Introduce others to Christ—and let them experience His perfect love!

"Number four: the church has a great *Master!* The church, at its best, is called to bring health and harmony to a world divided and diseased by prejudice and parochialism, and the church has a great Master who modeled how to do this. And this Master has the final word, and this final word is the Word—not *a* word on a piece of paper but *the* Word: a person. His name is Jesus Christ. Let Christ be Lord over the church. Let Him be our Master, and His beautiful, loving spirit will empower the church with success.

"So what's right with the church? I'll *tell* you what's right with the church: it has a great *mission*, it has a great *message*, it has a great *method*, and it has a great *Master!*"

Now Ray looks me straight in the eye—serious and sober. I return the intensity of focus as he lets out his final challenge:

"Robert Schuller! Go—and build a great church!"

Dr. Beckering then gives the formal ceremonial words: "Will Robert Schuller rise, come forward, and stand before the pastors present and the congregation to make his sacred vows?"

I let my hand slip from Arvella's tender grasp. Feeling as if I'm in a dream, I rise from my front-row seat and slowly walk to stand before the altar. The pews behind me are full of well-wishers who share this moment with me. Although I sense the support of the gathered congregation, I can't know that quietly, at the back of the church, an elderly man and a younger woman have slipped in. There are no seats left, so the two stand at the back. His white hair is brushed to the side of his tan brow, framing a radiant face now wet with tears. He can't wipe his face or brush aside the tears as he leans on his cane, so they spill upon his large farmer's hands, callused with years of labor.

Dr. Beckering continues: "Do you, Robert Schuller, feel in your heart that God has called you to the holy ministry? Do you accept the Bible as God's Word? Do you promise faithfully, to the best of your ability, to live out the faith of Jesus Christ as a pastor to God's people?"

I stand erect, inspired by my calling. Without pause or hesitation I answer, "Yes, truly with all my heart."

Dr. Beckering gestures and says, "You may kneel, and all visiting pastors from the Reformed Church of America may come forward for the laying on of hands."

I kneel and bow my head as one by one the ministers come. I feel one hand touch the top of my head, then two, then three—then many hands. They become heavy with a holy weight, and my heart pounds with a quickened pace that's driven by indescribable spiritual joy! At this very moment, my nearly twenty-year-old prayer is being answered.

Everyone and everything seems suddenly far away. The only sense I have is kneeling at the foot of my bed in the northwest bedroom of a tiny white Sears-Roebuck farmhouse at the end of a dead-end road that has no name and no number. I hear a young voice say, "O God, make me a preacher when I grow up!"

Then my reverie fades and I hear Ray's voice again: "Robert Harold Schuller—you may rise, a minister of the gospel of Jesus Christ, ordained to do His works and bring His word to the world."

I rise to receive warm and earnest handshakes from the seven ministers present. I'm surprised that I'm not crying.

Then I turn to catch the elated expression of my wife. I lift my face to smile at the congregation, and then I see him. The old man leaning on his cane captures my entire awareness. Smiling and crying, my father waits his turn to bless me.

I practically run down the aisle, though I try to maintain some shred of dignity as I embrace my father. Wracked with painful rheumatism and arthritis, he's crying so hard that he can barely get out his words. His cane falls to the ground and I clutch him.

"Do you remember, Harold?" he blubbers. "Do you remember when Uncle Henry came and you told us the next morning that you were going to be a preacher? You knew . . . I knew . . . I couldn't tell you why. But now I can." He looks at me with an expression I had seen sometime before. I support him with my strength as people swarm from the pews greeting one another and respecting this moment between father and son.

"Harold . . . I wanted to be a minister when I was a boy. I couldn't have been older than you were when you told me that morning— you were still so little. Remember? When my parents died, I had to quit school, but I never forgot my dream." I help Dad to an empty pew, but he can't wait to finish his tale. He is still speaking as I help lower him next to Jess. I am stunned by what he is disclosing so I sit beside him, weak with emotion. "I started praying, 'God, give me a son to be what I could never be.' Your brother Henry, he never liked school. Then your three sisters . . . then that long stretch. I was sure that God hadn't heard. Then you . . . I was just so surprised, Harold!"

He takes a deep breath, as I hold on to his arm. I can't believe what he's saying! Or can I? He's known all along? Of course he has! I recall that boyhood morning at the breakfast table.

"Harold, I prayed . . . and prayed . . . never told anyone . . . didn't want you just to please your dad . . . wanted you to know you were really called by God. Then that day when Uncle Henry came—oh, Harold, I just *knew*."

Dad and I hug, and he sinks into me. I'm his sole support now as he'd been for me for all these years. Then . . . I cry.

Later that evening, back in the parsonage, Dad explained how he had finally told Mom the whole story of his dream for me. He shared with Arvella and me how grieved she had been that she couldn't be at the ordination with us. (She wasn't doing well in her battle with high blood pressure, and the doctor had forbidden her to travel.)

Then he detailed for Arvella and me the harrowing events of his day. He and Jessamine, my oldest sister—who walked with the aid of a walker—had arrived by train in this huge and foreign town. They'd had no idea that Chicago was so gigantic. They'd thought rather simply that they need only catch a taxi and all would be fine. But their driver had had no idea where in the world Ivanhoe sat— south, north, east, or west. Neither did Dad or Jess. It had taken them over an hour to get here from the train station.

Now it was time for bed. I walked with Dad, his gait slow and painful, down the hall to the spare bedroom. Our faces were so close that I could read his love in every wrinkle. His eyes were shining, his face glowing. In that beloved countenance I read the words, "I love you, Harold! I'm proud of you." And I realized that, despite Mom and Dad's reticence, I'd heard that same message from their hearts all my life. And I knew that if Mom had been able to attend, she would have echoed Dad's expression, conveying, if not saying, "I love you, Harold. I'm proud of you."

I was a preacher. I was loved. And the door to my future stood wide open, promising boundless possibilities. I fell asleep that night with the greatest joy I'd ever known.

PART II

THE WONDER YEARS

Today's impossibilities are tomorrow's miracles.
—Robert H. Schuller

XX

On the far south side of the Windy City, Ivanhoe Reformed Church of Dolton, Illinois, sat literally on the border between two suburban towns, giving us the name of Ivanhoe but the address of Dolton.

Little did I know how emblematic this division would be when I arrived at this small, poor, and struggling church of thirty-five quarreling members.

"Eighteen against seventeen? Are you sure of that?" I asked Bain Fisher, the vice-chairman of the church board.

"Well, maybe it's seventeen against seventeen," he conceded, grinning, "and I'm in the middle. I've been trying to hold this bickering congregation together for months now."

My zeal, and perhaps my natural optimism, had blinded me to what I was stepping into.

"Our first pastor was loved," Bain explained, "or not loved (depending on whom you ask), but he just couldn't get the church to unite under him. Now that he's gone, there's a lot of hurt here."

Then Bain dropped another bomb. "You know, Bob, there's the reality of our finances. If either side pulls out, we'll be bankrupt."

Welcome, Schuller! Wow! And I'd been here only seven days!

"What's your advice?" I asked.

"Well, first off, don't take sides," he advised. "Focus people's attention on Jesus Christ, and just be a pastor to all of them in His name. Given a little time, they'll refocus on their new pastor if he points them forward. Eventually I think the church will be able to heal."

"Meanwhile, I can go out and win new people who won't be a part of the congregation's history. All I have to do is win another thirty-six members, and the new ones will outnumber the old ones."

Bain seemed undaunted by my grand ambitions. "You could do that in twelve months," he calculated.

Obviously, like me, Bain Fisher was a positive thinker. We had an instant bond that would make us friends for life.

The situation at Ivanhoe drew me back to my north-star scripture, Isaiah 58:12:

> **You shall be called a repairer of the breach and**
> **the restorer of paths to dwell in.**

This passage had already become a solid source of hope for me. What if my professor of preaching hadn't assigned it to me? What would I have had to fall back on? Already I could see the value of my seminary education.

John 3:16 was another Bible verse I would cling to throughout my ministry. It was the core of my theology:

> **For God so loved the world that He gave His only Son,**
> **that whoever believes in Him shall not perish but**
> **have eternal life.**

Whenever I needed a boost, Philippians 1:6 was the verse I turned to. It reinforced a strong, sustaining, and safe self-confidence:

> **. . . being confident of this very thing, that God who**
> **has begun a good work in you will complete it**
> **until the day of Jesus Christ.**

Romans 8:28 became my lifelong frame of reference, inspiring me to put a powerful and positive spin on all negative experiences:

**All things work together for good to those who
love God and keep His commandments.**

And Mark 16:15 would forever fashion the scale, the scope, and the sharpened purpose of my life's work:

**Go into all the world and share the
Good News with all people.**

And I went right to it. Every afternoon I called on people in the surrounding neighborhoods. I walked from door to door, from business to business, introducing myself with self-confidence and enthusiasm. To my delight, visitors began to appear at the church on Sunday; but to my dismay, most came only once and that was it. After a month or so of this I became very discouraged.

For the first time in many years I was living without the security of expert help from professors. I didn't have a grade or a test score to tell me where I was succeeding and where I was failing. For this feedback I had to rely on the audience. If the congregation grew, I was succeeding. If it didn't grow—or, God forbid, if it went down in numbers—then I was failing.

To ensure my success, I spent every Saturday night as if it were the night before a major college test. Every Sunday morning my message had to "score." I'd write the whole sermon out in three points. Point one was my Thursday morning job. Point two I'd write on Friday morning. Point three, with the conclusion, would be constructed and written out on Saturday. The message was always loaded with theology and scripture.

"John Calvin would give me an A," I'd assured myself for the past several weeks. And yet our numbers stayed the same. I just couldn't figure out what was wrong.

One Thursday morning, too depressed to study, I decided to join lovely, young Arvella for a cup of coffee to make me feel better! First, to surprise her, I ran to the bakery and returned with a fresh batch of warm sweetrolls.

Arvella and I sat together in our little kitchen nook; she was cute as a button in her new bathrobe (a wedding shower gift) sipping her coffee and and watching me munch the comfort food. She listened to my complaint for a moment, her green eyes so soothing, then said, "Who are you trying to impress?"

I was taken aback by her abruptness and honesty. I was also a little hurt: Where was the sympathy? The nurturing? But after a moment of reflection I realized that what she'd said was not a putdown but a very wise critique.

I thought about her question, and I just couldn't give a logical answer. John Calvin might have been impressed by my erudition, but my small audience certainly wasn't. I was missing the mark, and I knew it.

"You know, Bob, your professors aren't the ones who need your message," she said.

I knew she was right again. I just didn't know what to do about it. My sermons simply weren't working, but I'd just graduated with first prize in preaching in my seminary class, and I didn't know how to deliver a sermon any other way! If I couldn't apply what I'd learned so well, what was I supposed to say?

As I struggled with this question, and with the unnerving insecurity it prompted, my work continued. Thursdays through Saturdays: study and writing. Tuesdays and Wednesdays: canvassing door to door, overseeing administration, and trying to pastor my still-bickering congregation.

But Monday was my day off, the one day Arvella and I had set aside to enjoy our relationship. Despite all the rigors of this introduction to the real world, my marriage was more than I'd ever dreamed it could be. Arvella and I were delighted with each other and with our new life together.

During those first few months we spent hours outfitting the two-story brick parsonage, our first home. Use of the house itself was part of the minister's compensation, but we were responsible for furnishings.

The first thing we bought was a Kimball piano. We still didn't own a refrigerator or a washer, mind you, but music was Arvella's life. Her childhood home—as well as mine—had always had a piano at its center. And I'd been told, "If you don't buy a piano first—before anything else—you'll never be able to afford one."

So, out of a salary of two hundred dollars a month, the first twenty dollars was our tithe—five dollars a week in the church offering, nonnegotiable—and the next fifty dollars a month covered the payment on our elegant new piano.

In the meantime, we continued to store longer-lasting perishables such as butter in the cool basement, and I continued to make morning trips to the market, returning with fresh milk and a bag of fresh pastries from the bakery. Arvella would go to the market later in the day to buy food for our evening meal.

Much to our delight, two months later an elder gave us his old refrigerator and washing machine. Talk about the lap of luxury!

The first floor of our manse gave us a small living room, a nook for a dining table and chairs, and a small kitchen. The second floor held the bathroom and three small bedrooms. The largest was ours, just big enough for a small double bed and a chest of drawers. Another was my study. The third little bedroom served as guest quarters for visitors, including the denominational higher-ups who occasionally dropped in unexpectedly to see how we were faring.

After paying our tithe and our piano payment, we were left with about one hundred and thirty dollars a month to live on. That's the real reason that my 1953 Chevy coupe kept running out of gas. I could never put in more than one dollar's worth at a time. Only rich people could pull up to a gas station and say, "Fill 'er up!"

In the basement was a coal-burning furnace. I'd never seen one and had no idea how to light it, but I knew I'd better figure it out quickly, because we were only a few months away from our first Chicago winter.

"Reverend Schuller," my head elder said one day, "you'll need to order coal soon. I'd suggest that you go to the lumber and coal store and order it early to avoid the rush of people coming in when the first freeze hits."

He pulled a piece of scrap paper out of his pocket and scanned it. "I did some calculating to help you out," he said, "and I figure that you'll need five tons of coal to get you through the winter. At fifteen dollars a ton, that's seventy-five dollars."

Seventy-five dollars! I didn't have that kind of money, and I had no idea how I would get it!

I asked the coal-yard manager if he'd sell and deliver the coal and charge it to me.

"Yes, I'll deliver the coal to you," he said. "But no, I won't charge it."

I was stunned. I tried my persuasive powers on him, honed by years of training, but nothing worked.

He said, "Don't be offended, Reverend. We *never* charge coal. You'll have to borrow money from the bank."

So I went to the only bank in town. "Will you lend me money to buy the coal I need for this winter at the parsonage?" I asked.

"Of *course* not," the banker said, as if I should have known better.

Had I said something wrong?

"We *never* lend money for coal, Reverend Schuller."

My puzzled look must have told him that he was dealing with a twenty-three-year-old kid who was new to all of this. He sat me down for a word of wisdom.

"Whenever we make a loan," he explained, "the item for which the loan is made—a house, a car—becomes collateral, or security. That means if the borrower defaults, we can take the item back and sell it. If there's any money left after the loan is paid, you get it. That's your equity."

I was beginning to get the point.

"But," he went on, "we never lend money for gasoline or coal, because those things are perishable—as are utilities, food, and tires. We never loan money for coal, because all that's left in the end is ashes! My advice to you is never borrow money for coal!"

"I understand," I said, wiser now for my mistake.

Then he surprised me further. "But I tell you what: I'll lend you the money this time, because I believe you *do* understand, and I can tell you need help. I'll sign the note and cover for you with my signature as the collateral. I'll do it this once, but never again."

I would never forget that banker's kindness, or the fundamental lesson in finances. Through the years of my ministry, we've often borrowed money for our church, but never for "coal" (salaries, utilities, interest on loans, television broadcast time, and so on). No matter how desperately, cash alone would have to be used for them.

By summer's end, our house was stocked with enough coal to keep us warm through the coming winter, and I found myself proud and deeply satisfied. I now lived in a house that had a number, on a street that had a name, in a suburb of a world-class city! And even though I'd hit a few bumps in the road with regard to the church and my preaching, I knew that I was on my way *"somewhere."*

Since our arrival in Chicago, I hadn't thought once about California and my exciting visit to the West Coast with the quartet. As far as I was concerned, I could spend forty years here building the Ivanhoe Reformed Church of Dolton. I could be another George Truett here. And even after forty years, I would still be only sixty-three years old! Chicago was a lot bigger than Dallas, after all, and with my extra years there would be no limits!

It was at this time that I began to notice a change in Arvella. She was more sensitive than usual. Small things I said often caused her to burst into tears. One Sunday morning, an hour before the service, I suggested a hymn different from the one she had chosen to play, and she ran out of the empty sanctuary in tears.

One evening I returned home later than usual, bushed after a day packed with one-on-one pastoral counseling with my parishioners. I walked in the door and saw an Arvella who had been transformed. The beautiful copper tresses that I'd loved to twist about my fingers were gone! She stood before me with a look that said, "Well, what do you think? How do you like my short hair?" A looked that hoped I'd say "Gorgeous!"

I couldn't believe it! All our romantic moments were linked in my mind with those auburn locks. I was so hurt, so grieved, that I said something really, really stupid. I don't even want to tell you what I said, it was so stupid—but I guess I should. At first I was at a loss for words. When the right comment failed to materialize, I fell back on my speech training, which said, When all else fails, construct a comparative. And so I compared her new hairstyle to a cluttered table after dinner.

Arvella was absolutely crushed.

She hardly spoke all evening. I felt horrible about our first disagreement, and I had caused it.

At other times during this period, Arvella would beam with more radiance than I'd ever seen on her lovely face. And sometimes she would run to the bathroom, unable to hold down her breakfast.

In time the explanation came from the doctor: Arvella was pregnant. We were both ecstatic, but we were also terrified. Would we know how to handle this new challenge?

In the meantime, though, I had to figure out how to deal with my bickering parishioners. I had to learn how to build respect, trust, and affection with the nonreligious people in my community. I had to learn how to deal with those same values from the pulpit and preach to build friendships between pulpit and pew. And most of all, to survive, I had to recruit new members.

Growing up in my country church in Iowa had given me an undisputed mindset that the preacher, the "Dominee," was to be respected at all times. But it wasn't long before I discovered the shocking truth that Chicago wasn't like Sioux County or Holland, Michigan. I was amazed to learn that most cities didn't align their loyalties with the religious community, nor did they feel the need to show even the slightest respect. But how can you influence someone when you don't have that person's respect?

Even in seminary I'd never been taught any principles relating to how to win the respect of people who aren't at all religious. Theological arguments had been seen as the mark of intelligence, so ninety-nine percent of our class time had been spent in fierce debate over controversy in scripture.

My professors hadn't faced the challenge of getting people to listen. After all, we students had been a captive audience. We'd *had* to listen! Our mentors had "preached"; they hadn't tried to "communicate."

Year after year, then, graduating seminarians left to become preachers in search of the ego fulfillment they hoped would come from posing strong arguments from the pulpit and deducing grand and pious "do's" and "don'ts." How to build happy relationships in a community was never given a thought. So what worked in the classroom failed miserably in the pulpit.

While I'd still been in seminary, a bestselling book called *How to Win Friends and Influence People* had hit the market. Students at Western had talked about it with disdain—me included, though I hadn't read it—and professional religious educators had scoffed and sneered. Academic arrogance in the centers of the great universities all over the country had snobbishly put down this book by

Dale Carnegie, as it would *The Power of Positive Thinking* by Norman Vincent Peale a few years later. But within these two books I would find the practical advice that I so desperately needed if I was to become not a pontifical preacher but a respected communicator.

One day, when I was sharing my struggle with Dr. Beckering, he directed me to Carnegie's book. Humbled by my respected mentor's accolades, I set aside my seminary prejudices and began to read. From its pages I began to learn how to treat people beautifully even if they didn't agree with my views. "Don't argue—just share honestly, humbly, and politely," Carnegie instructed. I did my best to put this advice into practice, and I found that it improved my interactions with unchurched people.

Meanwhile, somehow I had been put on Norman Vincent Peale's mailing list. When a flyer appeared in my mailbox, I decided to try again with a little reluctance to discount the naysayers—my own self included—and give this "Peale" a try. I desperately needed help, and the flyer suggested that he might have the answer. I took a chance and bought his new book, *The Power of Positive Thinking*.

The effect of Peale's and Carnegie's theories on my theology and methodology of church work would prove nothing short of amazing! What these books presented was as different as night and day from the academic world I'd been living in. What a contrast between the professors and Peale! Peale's words were therapy; professorial words were arguments. Peale's style, spirit, and substance were humble and helpful; classroom lectures were full of facts and theories, but they weren't inspirational or motivational. No wonder I was losing my audience!

I began to read about how to "preach positive," and I decided to put Peale's practice to the test. I would stop preaching heavy sermons. I would listen to Peale's advice, and to what my wife had been telling me since day one. As I began reading the gospels of Jesus Christ with my new approach in mind, I discovered that Jesus Himself had also favored a positive style. Who better to follow?

In the pulpit I began to witness to the power of positive believing. I began to tell inspiring true stories that the people could relate to and learn from. To my amazement, the "storyteller" from my boyhood days—the outgoing, entertaining youngster who had painted detailed pictures of dramatic scenarios for my siblings and my friends, who had wooed the audiences at plays, and who had learned under the tutelage of Miss Aeilts—began to reemerge. I came alive "on stage." And miraculously, lives in our tiny church began to transform. The congregation began to grow, because people could hear and see what I was trying to communicate. They connected with my new style of real and comprehensible communication.

I absorbed these new concepts like an eager student. With the help of my two new "professors," and using their books as my scholastic resources, I embarked on my own customized, personal course—one that I secretly called Civility 101. Whether I stood in the pulpit or in a store, I assumed that every person I met had a need to be treated with respect. I made it my mission to show that respect. The emotional infrastructure was being laid in my subconscious for the building of a "self-esteem theology."

During this time, my genuinely dramatic persona continued to converge more and more with the clerical persona I had acquired. As I recognized the positive effects of that convergence, a freedom began to come over me in the pulpit. I certainly wasn't willing to become like Peale—flailing my arms and the like; I needed to retain at least some element of dignity. But the storytelling he advocated sparked a familiar, old love, and I came alive. People laughed. People cried. People *listened!*

It was during this time that I boomed one Sunday morning:

"Find a need and fill it!"

This sentence, which I had read or heard somewhere, jumped out of me, boomeranged about the sanctuary, then shot back and hit me in the chest like a bolt of lightning. *Wow!* That was it! The secret of success is to . . . find a need and fill it, find a hurt and heal it! I realized that every sermon I preached (whether formally from the pulpit or casually at a coffee shop) should be designed not to "teach" or "convert" people, but rather to encourage them, to give them a lift. I decided to adopt the spirit, style, strategy, and substance of a "therapist" in the pulpit.

A few days later, I was at the drugstore picking up a prescription. The proprietor was a gruff and grumbling businessman, so applying the lessons of Civility 101 was a challenge. This man wasn't only anti-church; he was also anti-spiritual and anti-religious. I wanted to fill his need, which was pretty visible, but I didn't know yet how to reach him. All I could do was focus on being a friend. I spent some extra minutes getting his advice about the prescription and chatting about life, and I left thinking that God's work had progressed a little in that drugstore.

My encounter with the pharmacist prompted me to think more about how to reach the community. I decided to build a mailing list of all the people in the surrounding neighborhoods who didn't belong to any church. I'd then send them a special card once a week inviting them to "this coming Sunday's exciting service."

My first task was to find out who should be on that mailing list. Simple. When I went from door to door, I would ask people whether they were active members of any church. If they said no, I would ask them further questions to get a feel for whether or not they might be prospects. Unless people were downright hostile, I'd write their name and address on some blank forms I'd have printed. Then I'd rank the encounter as follows:

A = *Very good*: really good prospect, said they'd come to church

B = *Good*: no promises, but they were very friendly

C = *Fair*: they were polite, but no real interest

D = *Not good*: but keep them on the mailing list anyway

Late one afternoon, as I was making calls, I walked past a manicured lawn with a pretty flowerbed toward a pleasant little house. The dinner hour was approaching, so this would be my last call. "This will be an easy one," I thought, reacting to the well-kept and homey feel of the place. I rang the doorbell.

When a woman came to the door, I said cheerily, "Hi! I'm the new pastor in town. My name is Robert Schuller. What's yours?"

"Doss," she answered. "I'm Helen." Then, pointing to a man sitting in the half-darkened room, she said, "That's my husband, Ray."

As I wrote the names on my card, the man called out, "Who's there?"

"The new preacher in that church," his wife said.

"Tell him to come in. I've got a thing or two to tell him."

So in I went. Empty beer cans littered the floor by his chair. He gripped yet another can and raised it to his mouth. In the other hand he held a cigarette that burned ominously in the half-light.

"So you're the new preacher?" he asked.

I nodded and stepped farther into the room. The man's face was indistinct, his features blurred by the semidarkness and the alcohol.

I didn't know quite what to say, but that didn't slow *him* down. He launched right into his attack: "I've got no use for religion, Reverend," he said derisively. "You're all a bunch of hypocrites."

My ears burned in embarrassment for both of us. I realized once again that I wasn't in Iowa anymore, or in Holland, Michigan.

"I don't believe in God," he went on. "That religion stuff is all superstition. And for *sure* I don't believe in the Bible or in heaven. And hell? You get that right here on earth."

I was truly stunned. Flabbergasted. Speechless. I'd never before heard such irreverence and disrespect for spiritual faith: not in my childhood, not during high school, and not in college or seminary—surely not in all my life.

I was convinced from the outset that this was a hopeless case, but nonetheless I grew frustrated at my inability to think of the right response, and angry at the verbal abuse. Ray continued to rant and rave as if he had ammunition to last all night. After a while I'd had it. I didn't deserve this treatment. Certainly the *church* didn't deserve this treatment. To my horror, I heard myself say—no, *shout*—"Well . . . then . . . you can *go to hell!*"

The words ricocheted through my whole being as I turned and walked out and that was that!

I couldn't believe that such angry words had come from my own mouth. But I *had* said them! Where had such horrible behavior come from? My mother would have been appalled, had she seen me. My wife *would be* appalled when she heard what had happened. *I* was appalled! I couldn't believe that such a phrase could come from the lips of any minister, let alone *my* lips! But they had.

As I retreated down the walk, sudden shame and grief poured over me. I was mortified. *I don't think that this is "finding a need and filling it," Reverend Schuller!* I scolded myself. I pulled out the card I'd started for the Doss household. Beneath the name Ray Doss I looked at my choices: A, B, C, and D. I wrote, "F!!! DON'T PUT ON THE MAILING LIST!"

Despite my utter failure at the Doss residence, Civility 101 was in general a success. Attendance began to pick up. And now that my preaching was less theological and more applicable to the average person, visitors who came once began to return, coming back the next Sunday and the next and the next.

Meanwhile, Arvella's tummy had grown round and full and lovely. Then, on April 7, 1951, our first daughter, Sheila, was born.

The weeks and months passed, and I came to love the tender moments I shared with the two of them when I came home to have coffee with Arvella. Sheila, now beginning to respond to the approach of her daddy, was pure delight. Her hair coming in as a golden fuzz. Such porcelain skin! Such tiny and trusting hands! Such innocence about the world around her! Sheila's childlike optimism could quickly melt away any unwanted effects of the day. I was a happy, happy man.

Meanwhile, our congregation had begun to outgrow the small two-story brick building, which had been designed to seat one hundred and fifty people. Sunday school had become so crowded that we launched a building program to double the size of the chapel. We also set out to build a new parsonage across the street, planning to use the basement as a multipurpose room for Sunday school.

The increase in the synergy of our congregation was thrilling to everyone! Well, almost everyone. Along with our exciting growth, we began to encounter a new challenge from some of our members of longer standing.

My least favorite part of being a pastor was leading the monthly consistory meeting. As the installed minister, I was chairman of this governing board of the church. As part of our training for the ministry, all Dutch Reformed seminarians were educated as "church lawyers," so that we could understand, interpret and defend the church codes and procedures. These had become very refined and sophisticated, as might be expected in such an old denomination. I had received an A+ in my church law course, so it wasn't that I lacked confidence. I just disliked meetings with an agenda, of so much insignificance especially among this group. My elders and deacons had been chosen by a grumbling congregation at the height of discord—some chosen for their unifying skills, others for their skills at divisiveness—so these meetings weren't exactly a walk in the park. Most of the deacons were the salt of the earth and I thought the world of them. Three, however, were neither gifted, experienced nor emotionally qualified to be positive managers.

During my first year as chairman of the consistory I'd observed the negative power of impossibility thinking in these men. Their deep insecurities worked overtime, generating defensive, ego-driven manipulations. But nonetheless I thought we had come through our initial struggles pretty well and had become more unified.

Things were on the upswing, I felt, and I dared to hope that a trans-formation in the more negative elders was in the works. Given that optimism, I was utterly unprepared for the rough and rude experi-ence awaiting me.

The three naysayers had as their spokesman an elder who had never before sat on any board, committee, or decision-making body. Having been appointed to the consistory just before my arrival, he had become increasingly verbal in his criticism of me and my work. Other board members had confided to me that his negative attitude and criticisms were beginning to undermine the church, even among some of the newcomers.

Monday night came and I kissed Arvella and three-month-old Sheila goodbye, then crossed the street to the church. It was a muggy July night. The sky above a dusky gray. The smell of the humid air was pleasant as it mixed with the fragrance of a rosebush planted near the sidewalk. No need for a coat or hat, I walked in through the side door of the church a little early and found myself interrupting a huddle centered around the most negative elder. At my entrance, a guilty and timid hush fell upon the quickly dispers-ing group. But something was up, and I didn't like the feel of it. I turned my back disguising my intimidation with pre-meeting prepa-rations. Even my summer cotton dress shirt clung to me as if I had something cool to offer.

Others began to arrive and my sense of security returned with their warm greetings.

As the evening progressed, the negative three began to hint that the board ought to reconsider my ability to lead. It was all I could do to contain my emotions as their ill-will became apparent. The meeting dragged on for a two full hours as the dissentious group tried to win the others to their side.

When I returned home that evening, I was emotionally ex-hausted. Arvella looked at me slumped on the sofa and said, "Honey, what's wrong? What happened?"

I jumped back up, ready for battle. "Enough is enough!" I shouted. "After all, church law says that I'm the chairman of the board and president of the corporation!"

Arvella tried to hush me, fearing that I'd wake little Sheila. Her shocked expression confirmed this was the first time she'd seen me so upset.

"I'll call together an emergency board meeting this Thursday night," I decided. "I'll have it out with him!"

Arvella knew immediately who I was talking about. She listened quietly and then, after I'd calmed down a bit, gave me the greatest advice I've ever been offered on how to deal with people who oppose my leadership.

She looked at me kindly, her dainty hand on my forearm, and said, "No, Bob. Don't confront him. You'll simply come across as angry. You don't need to defend yourself. The other elders and deacons are already defending you. That's their job. Let them do it. You can remain above the fray and preserve your God-assigned role as pastor and friend to all."

Once again I was struck by the wisdom of my wife's intuition. Her advice would shape my attitude toward unenlightened criticism and unfair attacks for the rest of my life. And it worked!

The positive members defended me and silenced the naysayers, and I was free to refocus my attention on the members who were happy to be in our church and to continue my outreach into the community around us.

As the leaves began to take on their first hint of autumn color, I had one of the most rewarding moments of my life. One Sunday, who should I see in church, sitting somberly and rather stiffly, but Ray Doss, the man I'd told to "go to hell." He was with his wife, in the last pew, and I just couldn't believe my eyes. What I didn't know was that a volunteer secretary had somehow missed my note giving them an F as prospects, so they'd received an invitation card every week for a whole year!

The sermon came to a close, and as was my ritual, I stood at the back of the church to shake hands with members of the congregation as they filed out.

"Good sermon, Reverend," Ray said with an extended hand. I was so shocked that my mind draws a blank to this day, and I can't recall what words came out of my mouth. But I know that I took his hand and shook it warmly.

Ray and Helen came back again, and then again and again. And finally the morning came when Ray made his declaration of faith. It was at the close of the service. He'd made sure he was the last in line to shake my hand so that he wouldn't be rushed by others behind him. With tears in his dark eyes he asked, "Reverend, may I join the church?"

Over the following weeks he took private instruction from me, and then, on an appointed and wonderful Sunday, he knelt at the front of the church to be baptized.

He shared his testimony with all, telling how I'd told him to "go to hell"—I couldn't help feeling a bit embarrassed whenever I overheard that part—and how he'd realized that he was already *in* hell on this earth. No hope. No joy. No love. No faith. "That's hell," he would attest. "And I wanted out! I went to church and was introduced to Jesus Christ. I really was born again!" Never was he able to say these words with dry eyes.

Two years later Ray Doss was licensed as a fully credentialed lay preacher by the Reformed Church in America.

Ten years later the phone would ring in my California home, and Ray Doss would be on the other end. "Need a full-time volunteer in your church?" he would ask. "I'd love to help out." Ray would move to California with Helen and work as one of my most effective assistants until his death.

God had taught me a lesson:

Never give any person an F in his or her spiritual life.

From then on I would give struggling seekers the grade I'd gotten in math at Hope College, when I'd really earned an F: an I for *incomplete*.

Arvella and I had now been in Ivanhoe for two years. Sheila was a one-year-old bundle of joy, and our lives were busy with parenting our precious girl and pastoring a growing church.

Our need for a new sanctuary and extra space for Sunday school was a primary concern, which brought Ray Beckering to me with some advice. "I know an architect you should hire," he said one evening in our living room. "His name is Benjamin Franklin Olson. He's one of America's great architects. Specializes in colonial architecture. He's right here, in Chicago."

Illinois had been home to the great architecture of Charles Sullivan and Mies van der Rohe, who taught everyone the secret of artistic excellence with his line, "God is in the details." It was also home now to Benjamin Franklin Olson, about whom Ray Beckering was right. Olson was about to give me a priceless education of an entirely different sort than that to which I was accustomed.

But where would the money come from for an architect of that stature? I had just worked long and hard to raise a few hundred dollars to make the down payment on a small electric organ. I'd raised the cash over the summer by returning home to northwest Iowa and calling on the well-to-do members of my church in Orange City. I'd raised three hundred dollars, mostly in twenty-five-dollar donations. Honesty and humility had worked, reinforcing in me an understanding of the power of asking for help.

But we would need tens of thousands of dollars to build the type of exciting new church addition that someone like Olson would design!

"Never compromise on the fine details in design," Mr. Olson hammered home to me when we met. "Art—not money—must have the last word," he added.

"But what if you don't *have* the money?" I argued.

"Broaden your financial base. Raise more money."

Sure. Simple.

I'd seen advertisements for professional fundraisers and decided that we should take a risk with a firm run by H. P. Demand, which I thought was quite a name for someone seeking money! He would be compensated not with up-front cash—which we had precious little of—but with a percentage of the money raised.

Demand's efforts were remarkably successful. He left behind at his departure the funds for a beautiful addition. He gave me a warm handshake of congratulations before leaving, and then handed me a little gift. It was a book entitled *Ride the Wild Horses*, by a Methodist minister in Florida named J. Wallace Hamilton. Each chapter was a sermon that turned a negative emotion into a positive energy force.

Dr. Hamilton was the pastor of what was called a "drive-in church" in Saint Petersburg, Florida. A drive-in church? Was this a real *church*, or just services held in a drive-in theater? I was fascinated! I'd experienced a drive-in service while at Spirit Lake, Iowa, on our honeymoon. A Lutheran pastor had preached from a snack-bar rooftop to listeners gathered in a dozen cars. We two honeymooners had been in that tiny audience. I'm sure the pastor hadn't felt very successful, but he'd certainly inspired this young minister.

Now, a little over two years later, I was reading about Dr. Hamilton, who had an honest-to-God drive-in *church* with a pulpit, pews, and even a pipe organ—plus loudspeakers on trees in his Florida church parking lot, where people could come as they were and stay in their cars to hear the sermon and music.

As far as I was concerned, I was still going to spend my life in Chicago. I had no need to apply the model of a drive-in church here, nor did I have any intention of doing so. After all, people would freeze half the months of the year and roast the other half! But Hamilton's ingenuity fascinated me. His willingness to go to the

edge both inspired me and awakened within me an old longing to
do the same—to somehow push the envelope with this thing called
"faith." I was totally unaware that these influences were preparing
me for a new kind of ministry in California.

Meanwhile, Civility 101 was paying off. One Sunday, after years of
praying (and smiling!), who should appear at our church door but the
pharmacist, coming into a morning service, quietly and reverently
after it had already started. He found an empty seat in the back row
and was the first one out—but not before he had to shake the hand of
the preacher at the door. I could swear I saw a mist in his eyes! It
seemed that the spiritual hunger I had sensed in him was doing its
own work. But he would come only a few times. I seldom saw him
aside from our pharmacy formalities. I would continue practicing
Civility 101 in his store, however, and I would keep praying for him.

One day I spoke with an elder I knew I could trust. "John," I said,
"I've been here now nearly four and a half years, during which time
the church has grown to over four hundred members. We've completed our new sanctuary. But now my wife is pregnant again, and
we're still on the two-hundred-dollar-a-month salary I started out
with. Some weeks I've had money for milk only because my mom
sends me a five-dollar bill in her letters. Would it be inappropriate
for me to ask for a raise?"

"Not at all, Bob," he told me. "I'll be presenting the new budget
in November, and I'll recommend a good raise. You've earned it."

I brought the good news home to my wife, who was beaming and
very pregnant. Sheila, now three and a half, gave me a hug, and I
burrowed in her golden locks.

"Daddy, I want a little sister," she said, her sweet words enough to
melt a father's heart.

I held her up high. "This is the kind of wish we can't make,
honey. Only God knows what we need."

As I hugged her closer, she wrapped her legs about me and held
my face in her hands. "Maybe a little brother would be just as much

fun," she conceded reluctantly. "But Daddy, can I still play dress-up with a brother? Can I put him in a dress and can we pretend to be sisters?"

"Um. I don't think so, honey. But I tell you what: when I buy a new suit with the raise I'm getting, I'll save my old suit, and if you have a little brother he can play dress-up in that. He can pretend to be the daddy, okay?"

"Okay!"

It wasn't too many nights following this precious exchange that Arvella awakened me with some urgency. It was two o'clock in the morning. Her pains were regular—four minutes apart. Her little suitcase had been packed early in preparation.

"I'd better get to the hospital . . . now!" she said. "Go get Sheila. We'll take her with us and you can babysit her while I'm in labor."

We hurried to the car, parked at the curb; I slipped the key in and stepped on the starter. Arvella, huge and in agony, groaned with another heavy contraction.

"Hurry, Bob!" she exclaimed, trying not to wake Sheila, asleep in the back seat. I stepped on the starter again. It turned over so slowly, but only once.

"Battery's dead," I said, barely able to contain my panic.

Then, up that totally dark and empty street at two-fifteen in the morning, came a police car. The patrolman sensed that something was amiss and stopped.

He sized up the situation at the same time he recognized me. "Jump in my car, Reverend. I'll take you all to the hospital."

Now Sheila was wide awake, fascinated with the patrol car's flashing red light. She would happily have ridden around town all night.

Fortunately, we arrived at our destination in more than enough time. I waited an eternity—and waited some more—until finally Dr. Showalter stepped into the private "fathers' waiting room," dropped his protective face mask, and uttered five prophetic words: "Reverend! You have your son!" It was the way he said the word "your" that struck me. It had such an air of fulfillment and finality to it.

It was October 7, 1954. I now had a daughter, Sheila, three and a half years old, and a newborn son, Robert Anthony. We were pleased as could be, but I worried that my income, despite the promise of a raise, might still be woefully inadequate.

When Mom and Dad came to Chicago to see their grandchildren, I saw in my mother's eyes that she was proud of her youngest son—now a full-time Dominee. It was a nice visit, though Arvella, I'm sure, was ready to have her own home back under her authority again when it came time for their departure.

Jennie could be quite overbearing, and Arvella always remembered her mother-in-law's comment on the day we left Alton, fresh from the altar: "Arvella—you dress appropriate now! You're a pastor's wife. Do you hear?" That comment, a serious admonishment from this pious Dutch woman (who'd been "raised at the foot of a prophet?") had hurt Arvella deeply. She had tried so hard to uphold the high standards of her new role: THE PASTOR'S WIFE! (She doesn't think I'm good enough for her own son!)

Now Arvella felt the disapproving gaze once more. Her hair was shorter than it had been when Jennie had last seen her. She wondered if Jennie condemned her for trying to follow the Chicago fashion, which was generally thought wickedly secular back in Iowa.

But Mom and Arvella enjoyed each other as well, and Arvella took pleasure in hearing news of home over shared coffee.

After a ten-day visit, Mom and Dad said goodbye, and we were left to face the annual congregational meeting. This was when the next year's budget would be discussed, and when the parishioners would reassess my salary. All members were invited and given equal and unlimited floor time to ask questions or pose arguments.

The church was nearly full that Monday night. The gathering had been underway for some time when my elder friend stood up and said, "Ladies and gentlemen—I feel that we've all been richly blessed by Reverend Schuller, and now he has a second child. I suggest that we give him a raise in his well-earned salary." My friend paused, studied the large crowd, and said, "I recommend that we give him a raise of twenty dollars a month."

My breath was knocked out of me. Only twenty dollars!? I was stunned.

The motion passed unanimously, but only because I couldn't vote on it. I felt that I couldn't even complain, though clearly I'd been expecting a much larger increase. I felt dreadfully let down. The deep bond that I had felt for this parish, the bond that had connected me with passion and enthusiasm to this church, suddenly and completely unraveled. I left the building that night deeply disappointed.

I tried not to let this negative response consume me over the following days, but it did. I prayed that God would take it away, but He didn't. I tried talking to Arvella, but she struggled with it too. The issue wasn't so much the money as it was our perceived value. What nagged at us so mercilessly was that our selfless labors had been assigned such a low pricetag. What I couldn't see until later was how God had used this disappointment to make me receptive to yet another calling.

Just a few days later I was sitting behind my desk in my study when the phone rang. The familiar voice belonged to Dr. Ray Beckering, my closest friend in those days. "I've got good news for you," he said conspiratorially. He was calling from California, where he had moved a year earlier.

"Bob, the regional district of Reformed Churches here in Los Angeles met and decided to start a new church in Orange County. And they voted to call you to come and start the church. I made the motion, and Ken Leestma supported it. It was unanimous: we think you can build a church from scratch."

"But Ray," I said, "California's so far away!"

I'd forgotten that I'd shared my love of the place with him while I was still in seminary. "Get a little experience under your belt,

Bob," he had wisely suggested. "Start out here in Chicago. You've got more to learn. California will still be there when you're ready." Then he negotiated my call to my first assignment in Ivanhoe.

He chuckled now. "It's not far at all, Bob. I'm standing right here, looking at it. You've got to come out here and look the situation over. We have no church in Orange County. The area is small in terms of population, but its future is ripe. New houses are going up by the hundreds. A guy down here by the name of Walt Disney is building a new theme park just a few miles away. We're convinced that it has real opportunity!"

He began sending me letters that would enlarge upon the California mystique. One in particular I'll never forget. It read:

Bob:

We're confident that you'll love it here from the moment you arrive. It's raining cats and dogs today, but that's not snow!

Until you come, think of us sipping orange juice while taking our daily sun bath, picking roses, and eating chicken dinner at Knott's Berry Farm—in your own backyard! All this and heaven too!

Ray

But California? It *was* far away, no matter what Ray said. Far from our parents and families, our friends, our college, my seminary—everyone and everything we had ever known!

Furthermore, we now had two children—our daughter, Sheila, who was turning four, and Robert, our two-month-old son. A move to California would mean taking them away from our solid mid-western family roots to an area of the country that had a reputation for glitz and glamour rather than for the solid moral, ethical, and spiritual values into which Arvella and I had been born, by which we had lived, and to which we were committed.

"Bob, get on a train, come out here, and look the territory over," Ray insisted.

Bain Fisher, by now my closest friend in the Ivanhoe church, worked for the Santa Fe Railroad. When I finally took him into my confidence for advice, he responded, "I'll give you a roundtrip ticket, Bob. You have to go out there and check this call out."

It was January when I boarded the train. When I disembarked in Los Angeles, I saw that stunning California beauty all over again. Mountains. Deserts. Palm trees. Orange groves. The Pacific Ocean. White sandy beaches. Sunshine. Green grass—in January! Flowers blooming outdoors—in winter! Chicago was black and white in winter. This part of California was full of color—greens of many hues, reds, oranges, yellows, blues!

Ray met me at the depot in Los Angeles.

"There are no Reformed Church families in Garden Grove," he said. "It will be all up to you and God and Arvella to find members and start a new church."

But that didn't trouble me. I'd already learned that when you have God as your partner, you can build something from nothing. With God you can go anywhere from nowhere.

After several days looking over the situation in Garden Grove, I was back on the train to Chicago. In the middle of the night the train jerked to a stop high in the mountains.

I'd been dozing, and now in a semi-wakeful state I looked out the window. Seemingly from nowhere, a large buck with huge antlers ran toward the train, coming to a sudden stop just outside my window. He paused for a moment, then turned and raced back in the direction from which he'd come, his footprints leaving dark holes in the otherwise pristine blanket of snow.

Suddenly, this thought came into my mind: *The greatest churches in the world have yet to be organized!* Right then, I knew I had my answer.

Arvella was waiting for me when I got off the train in Chicago.

After we embraced, she looked at me for only a second before saying, "Bob, I can tell by the expression on your face and the look in your eyes that we're moving to California!"

Bain Fisher was the only elder I dared to confide in at first. I called him to the house on Saturday to share peanut butter and jelly sandwiches.

I was blunt. I had to be; it was easier. "I'm going, Bain," I said. We both fought back our emotion. We loved each other deeply and dearly, as if we were blood brothers.

I brushed aside a rogue tear. "Thanks for the railroad tickets," I said. "Without your offer, I might have declined and waited for something bigger and better to come along. If it goes well, you'll be remembered as the one God used to get me to leave. There are so many beautiful people here. Arvella and I love them so much. I don't think I could've left without that divine prodding you offered."

"What does Arvella say about it?" Bain asked.

I couldn't give him a simple answer. She was supportive of the decision, certainly, but I knew that she had her apprehensions. Every now and then the reality would sink in and she'd have trouble holding her anxiety at bay. "Oh, Bob—California?" she'd exclaim out of the blue. "It's so far away!" And then she'd get quiet again.

I knew that Arvella would miss the women in the church, who'd taken her under their wing when she became pregnant with Sheila. She had spent some lonely days during the first year of our residence in Ivanhoe; I suppose the people of the church had decided not to bother the "honeymooners." But once she began the childbearing and childrearing process, the women had huddled about her like mother hens.

And she had a good friend in Sheila Muir, a Scottish war bride. She and Arvella had grown quite close, Sheila singing solos in church to Arvella's accompaniment.

Yes, Arvella had moments of grief over the people she would have to say goodbye to. When she did, I painted beautiful mind pictures for her of the palm trees and the orange trees and the blooming hibiscus. Those images would reassure her (or did they only distract her?), and she would return to her silence, keeping further misgivings to herself. She looked forward to a stop in Alton on our way out west and gladly wrote the news to her mother, alerting her to our visit.

As we spread the news, Reformed Church ministers in the Midwest began warning me against the hazards of the West Coast. In their minds California was indeed "nowhere." To them there was "nothing" there. One of my best friends, Herman Ridder, who later would become my executive pastor at the Crystal Cathedral, predicted, "Bob, you'll never be heard from again if you move to California."

Deep inside, though, I knew that I was doing the right thing.

As the day of our departure drew nearer, I took a moment one day to assess all of the invaluable lessons I had learned at Ivanhoe Reformed Church:

1. I had learned how to bridge a divided congregation by surrounding them with unbiased, "unpolluted," and fresh recruits! Thank you, Bain Fisher and Arvella Schuller.

2. I had learned how to win the respect of nonreligious people. Thank you, Mr. Dale Carnegie.

3. I had learned how to deliver messages that would witness, not preach. Thank you, Dr. Peale and Dr. Hamilton.

4. I had learned how to conceive and be creative in sponsoring architecture that was on a world-class level. Thank you, Mr. Benjamin Olson.

5. I had learned how to raise money to achieve the highest level of artistic excellence without compromising for the sake of the bottom line. Thank you, Mr. H. P. Demand.

6. And now I would learn how to go to the edge, even when others thought it foolish! Thank you, Ray Beckering, Ken Leestma, and above all God.

After we had accepted the call, Ray Beckering wrote a warm, supportive congratulatory letter to Arvella and me. In it he said, "We had the feeling Bob sensed that he was God's man for this Garden Grove job. You were honest in facing the challenge, and God will never let you down. Our prayers are with you in this transition."

XXI

California—here we come!

Plans for our move west fell rapidly into place.

First, only five days after stepping off that train from California, it was time to make my announcement before a crowded church.

On Sunday morning I watched from the new parsonage we'd built across the street as the first cars arrived early. I reflected on the reality of all that was happening. I was twenty-eight years old, and in my mind I was an experienced and mature adult. Though in hindsight I was still just a kid, there's no denying that I had grown immensely in experience since coming to Ivanhoe fresh from my graduation, honeymoon, and ordination.

Soon the cars were lined up at the curb all down the block.

Arvella stood at the door to my study. "Time to go, Bob. Get your robe on," she said.

After a brief prayer I got up from the desk where only a few weeks before I'd received the call from Ray. I opened my closet door and drew out my clerical robe, then slipped it on and adjusted the folds. When I turned around, Arvella was back—this time with tears in her eyes, our eight-week-old baby boy, Bobby, in her arms, and Sheila at her side. "Let's go, dear," she said.

As a family, we crossed that street lined with trees bare in winter's grip—branches stark, dramatic, and frozen. I held Bobby in one arm, and Arvella clung to the other, while Sheila walked cautiously already learning that slipping on a patch of ice could ruin anyone's day. I didn't know whether Arvella's tight grip was to keep herself from slipping or from weeping.

I knew that there were whispered guesses about my response to the California invitation. Word had gotten out about my call once I'd decided to take a scouting trip out by train. Bain was the only one I'd talked to about it since our return, though.

"It'll be hard to tell them goodbye tomorrow," I'd said to Bain on Saturday. "There are widows here whose husbands I've buried. There are young couples I've married. There are lost souls I've seen saved here. Most of all, I'll miss you, Bain, and that wonderful wife of yours. We've seen the church grow from thirty-five to nearly five hundred! You've always believed in me, and I can't tell you what that means. Tomorrow will be hard. Pray for me."

Once the children were settled into Sunday school and the nursery, Arvella—donning her unwavering professionalism—played the opening hymn. The organ's notes sounded rich and powerful! She always played more dramatically when her emotions were stirred; it's as if the keys became her voice. But when the notes came to an end, her lip quivered as she fought back tears.

I stood in the pulpit of the beautiful chapel I'd helped build. Behind me was a stained-glass window of Christ—arms open to welcome all who came. There was an uneasy silence in the jammed sanctuary. I watched my lovely wife, looked at my faithful and caring parishioners, and for a moment I wondered, I just wondered . . .

Was I . . . ?

Perhaps I . . . ?

And then, as it had before, an assurance settled over me. *No, I* thought with confidence. *Just because change is hard doesn't mean it isn't right. We must go.*

Now, standing tall before the hushed crowd of nearly five hundred people, I took a deep breath and began:

"Today I must bring you a special announcement," I said. "As you know, I've been honored to receive opportunities to move to other churches over the years, but our love for you has kept us here. Then last month I received a call to go to California as a missionary to start a new church. There will be no core of denominational members waiting for me. The Southern California Council of Churches has asked our denomination to start an ecumenical mission in Garden Grove. The Classis of California has accepted the challenge and has called me to come and begin that new mission.

"I've prayed over this decision, and I feel certain that I'm being called by God. And so I've accepted."

Now the silence was broken by the soft sounds of murmuring, sniffling, and handkerchief-rustling. A knot of grief twisted in my gut, and I clutched the wooden stand in front of me for support. Looking down at it, I saw my black leather Bible, which Arvella had given to me on the day of my ordination, right here in the little church we'd outgrown. On the inside of the cover she had inscribed:

God loves you, and so do I!

This was the end of an era in my life. I felt a sting come to my eyes and they were wet. Then I raised my gaze again to see reddened eyes and pleading, probing expressions.

"I love you people," I said sincerely (and with more feeling than I'd ever expressed to an audience). "You're a strong and a good church." And one by one they offered me their smiles, perhaps recognizing my need for support at that moment.

"Please pray for me," I requested. "I won't have a group of people to welcome me there as I did here. Not one person like Bain Fisher, who was here for me when I came, fresh and young out of school, with my bride. There won't be a Ray Doss to stand in beautiful testimony. There won't be a Bill and Lillian Bruin, or a Sheila Muir, or a . . ." — and I proceeded to name almost every person in that congregation. As I did, a hope sparked in me. I could see confidence fill person after person, readying them for the next step. And I also saw, for a flickering moment, a future when there would be a fellowship of good people like this surrounding me in California.

Then I explained the practicalities of our situation as a family:

"I won't have a congregation to salary me, so I'll draw a missionary's salary established by the Reformed Church. The National Missions Board in New York, headed by Ruth Peale, the wife of Dr. Norman Vincent Peale, will pay half, and the other half will come from the California Reformed Church Mission Board. For one year we'll be taken care of in that way. After twelve months we'll have a small congregation, if God blesses the mission, and we can look to new financial arrangements then. We're in good hands so you don't need to worry, but do pray for us."

The goodbyes threatened to undo both Arvella and me. Though the crowd was large, almost everyone waited in line to shake my hand at the door and to wish us well. Barely recovered from that emotional scene, we faced individual goodbyes from special people over the weeks that followed.

I didn't attend the special meeting called by the consistory due to my resignation. I'd officially resigned and was therefore no longer chairman. This made the break clean and final — and besides, Arvella needed my help packing.

It was a wintry Monday night and the lights across the street evidenced that it was a lengthy Board discussion. After the meeting, the elders crossed the street and knocked on the door of the parsonage.

"Now Bob," their spokesman said, "we know we've said our formal goodbyes. But we have one more thing to say."

And then they handed me an envelope.

"This is from the church — it's for you and your family."

I opened the envelope and saw four hundred dollars in twenty-dollar bills—the largest gift we'd ever received from anyone in our lives! Arvella clutched me. Our grateful smiles were taut as we tried not to cry.

The next day the moving van pulled up and workers loaded all of our furniture. It would go ahead of us to California. My denominational overseer in that state, Al Van Dyke, and my close friend Ken Leestma would watch over the process of moving our possessions into the small house that had been purchased for us by the Classis of California.

The cold was bitter that next morning as we climbed into our '53 Chevy. Arvella and the other women of the church had already packed our most important clothes and personal things in the car, arranging them with loving care. Now, having slept our last night in the house filled with happy memories, we were ready for our new adventure.

The sun was just dawning in the east as we prepared to head west. We stopped in front of the church, now silhouetted against the orange and purple sky. A frosted sparkle glinted at the sun's beckoning, and the scene looked like Currier & Ives. We wouldn't see *this* in California.

With a shiver—part cold and part anticipation—I grinned and drew Arvella closer to me. "It was a good church," I said.

She nodded, barely controlling her emotions. "It was a good *town*," she agreed.

I looked back across the street at the parsonage. "In fact," I amended, "it was a good time altogether."

Arvella snuggled even closer. She lifted her face to me and smiled, ready to go. She kissed me, her nose cold against my cheek. Then with finality I declared, "But I won't miss the cold."

We both chuckled as we left Ivanhoe, Illinois, our excitement outweighing our sadness at departure. Sheila and Bobby slept, their heads resting side by side on the back seat.

The last thing I remember about Ivanhoe was seeing the drugstore where my pharmacist friend worked. I felt a twinge of sadness. Though he'd crossed our church's threshold a few times, once again I would earn an I—*incomplete*—with this one receptive soul. Unbeknownst to me at the time, years later he would call me, asking to come to California to be baptized.

But I said a last little prayer for him, and then Arvella, Sheila, Bobby, and I drove into a new tomorrow filled with hopes and dreams and grand expectations.

As we passed through Chicago the streets were covered with six inches of snow—not pristine virgin snow but snow rutted with tire tracks and streaked with the black of oil and grease. Before long we would be driving on dry cement roads that cut through orange groves. Arvella would see, for the first time, the orchards that spread across the land—the trees loaded with brightly colored fruit that hung like Christmas ornaments.

I grinned at the thought of the delightful contrast, then said, "California—here we come!"

There were two farewell family reunions planned for us during our brief stop in Iowa. My wife's family would gather in the country house where her mom and dad still lived and worked the farm. All of her six siblings would be there except for her brother, Johnnie, now in New York studying voice. His powerful baritone filled the great Riverside Church every Sunday, a solo performance accompanied by the greatest organist in the world, Virgil Fox.

Arvella, who had resumed the role of "oldest" after her brothers were drafted to war, had taken care of her younger siblings for years while her mother helped work the farm, as well as during the time of her mother's illness. Together again, the girls laughed just like old times. Winifred with her contagious guffaw; Margene—the brunette darling, now a teen; and Arvella, pretty, pretty Arvella— farmgirl turned sophisticate. The three of them huddled close, laughing with joy but often close to tears as they spent their last moments together. The three brothers also enjoyed having Arvella among them again. Hank, the tease; Frank, another tease, now married and somewhat more subdued; and Stan, the quiet and pensive one who loved the land and the animals. All of them were local farmers. Arvella's father, like mine, was a sensitive man, often having to wipe away tears as he thought of the distance that would soon separate Arvella from the rest. Arvella's mother was as stoic in her goodbye as she had been in her biddings to her war-bound sons years before. But Arvella knew she had her spaces and her times when tears would flow.

During our stay we ate, talked, laughed, prayed, and said our goodbyes to these loved ones. Then we drove down the long driveway, where I'd been stuck repeatedly in summer mud and winter snowdrifts after fond and heart-pounding encounters—the same drive that I'd chased Arvella down to ask her for that first date.

The next night we gathered in my family's country farmhouse. It still looked freshly painted after being rebuilt following the tornado's wave of destruction.

Around the home was a new grove of trees. I hadn't noticed them on any of my previous visits—so young and small I guess—so as Dad and I took a walk, moving slowly because of his arthritic legs, I asked, "What are those trees, Dad?" Pointed to an isolated grouping.

"Apple," he told me.

"But they're so small. Do you really think you'll live to eat the fruit? If you're not going to be around, why plant them?"

Dad answered as if he were the spiritual teacher and I were the farmer. "We don't plant trees just for ourselves," he said, "but for those who come after us."

So many of my father's values had been implanted deep within me. Now this powerful lesson also took root. I would carry his example with me to California. I would build a church, erect structures, and plant trees with my father in mind, creating a place of enduring beauty for future generations to enjoy.

My sisters were all back at the house—Jessamine, Margaret, and Violet—as well as Henry. As at Arvella's, we visited, talked, laughed, and ate good food. I even got to have a piece of my favorite butterscotch pie—well, maybe two or three. Then we had a circle of prayer.

After they said their goodbyes and returned to their own homes, Arvella and I tucked four-year-old Sheila in on the living-room couch and bedded down in the second little bedroom, three-month-old Bobby sleeping between us.

The next morning, Mom and Dad stood at the small gate and watched as we piled into our car for the nearly two-thousand-mile drive. I held Sheila's hand and took her to the back seat. Arvella carried the baby. Car doors opened and closed. I was the last to climb in, pausing for a final wave and a long look at the house we'd built.

Once again I noticed the bump under the shingles and remembered Dad saying, ten years ago now, "Check your pockets."

Taking the southern route through Kansas and New Mexico, we'd approach California through Arizona and enter the "Golden State" from the warmer southern desert.

"But first we have to stop at Duven's Music Store in Sioux City," I reminded Arvella. Howard Duven, my old friend from school, sold electronic organs. "I don't mind starting a church from scratch," I said. "And I don't care whatever empty hall we find. But I *do* want an organ at our first church service—wherever it is."

In Sioux City I told Howard, "I have four hundred dollars to my name. It's a farewell gift from our Chicago church."

"Well, I think we can work with that," he said. "Check this one. It's a two-manual electronic made by Conn—a good company. Put your four hundred dollars down, and you can pay the balance of thirteen hundred dollars over the next thirty-six months. That'll be only about forty-some dollars a month."

I was being paid four hundred dollars a month by my denominational missions board. A tithe—or ten percent—would cover the monthly payment. "Good deal, Howard!" I said, gladly passing over the four hundred dollars from our Ivanhoe congregation.

I decided that it was time to make my first financial sheet for the new parish. It read:

Assets: $1,700—organ

Liabilities: $1,300—organ mortgage

Net worth—$400

Accounts receivable—$0

Accounts payable—$0

At least we were starting off to California with a positive net worth! I would diligently keep my eye on that bottom line, building it safely and surely and never letting it be chipped away. "Never borrow money to buy coal!" I remembered.

My own excitement was boosted as I anticipated Arvella's. In the next three days, she would see for the very first time in her life mountains, then deserts with their grand cacti, then palm trees, then orange trees filled with fruit!

Arvella kept the maps at her seat next to me. We planned to cover four hundred miles a day, soaking up the scenery and staying in motels at night.

We had a glorious time together as a family, but by our second day on the road, we were already focused on what we might encounter when we reached our new home.

Driving down a desert stretch of Route 66 I asked Arvella, "You have the letter from Al Van Dyke, don't you? Read it aloud to me again."

I kept my eyes on the sun-baked road ahead. As the "Regional Missionary of the Reformed Church," Al Van Dyke would be my "bishop," overseeing my work.

She read, "The moving van will arrive before you do. Ken Leestma and I will meet it and have all the furniture in place, but we'll leave the dishes in their traveling crates for you to supervise. And we'll have milk and fresh fruit in the refrigerator, with bread and cereal on the shelf. Stop and call me or Ken when you're a couple of hours away. We'll give you directions to your new house then, and we'll be there waiting for you with the keys."

Then she read the sentence that had gotten me so worked up when I first read it that I hadn't yet recovered: "And Bob, to respond to your suggestion that I locate an empty hall where you can hold your first services, I have to tell you: I checked the whole town of Garden Grove, and it's *impossible* to find an empty hall."

Impossible!

That word had seared my mind as if with an emotional tattoo. Even now, a week after I'd first read the offending sentence, I couldn't focus on the rest of the letter. I just kept hearing the single word as if it were an obscenity.

Impossible! Impossible! Impossible!

I cringed. Then I shook my reaction off and asked Arvella to read the end of the letter one more time.

"It's *impossible* to find an empty hall," she read, glancing over to see how I'd react this time. "You'll just have to spend the first year building a structure on two acres of ground that we found for a church site."

I was incensed by the ludicrous word "*impossible.*" Never before in my life had I heard that word the way I heard it here and now as I was roaring along at sixty-five miles an hour across the desert. It sounded so totally, absolutely, and completely *wrong!* There had to be some empty hall somewhere in that town of Garden Grove. Someplace that was vacant on a Sunday morning.

"Bob! You're not paying attention to the road. Be careful!" Arvella had a good idea what mental gymnastics were bouncing around in my brain. Figuring that a break would be good for me, she said, "There's Albuquerque straight ahead. Let's stop and get something to eat."

We spotted what seemed like a clean and inexpensive café and pulled over to the curb. I took Sheila, with her long blonde ponytail rumpled from the drive, by the hand while Arvella carried Bobby. We found a table and looked at menus, but I was still completely withdrawn and distracted, absorbed in an internal argument with that incredible word—that totally unacceptable word—that completely unintelligible word:

Impossible!

No possible place to preach?! Wait a whole year doing nothing but building a building?! I didn't come to spend my time building buildings; I came to preach the Good News, to comfort a hurting world! The thought of spending the first twelve months erecting walls from two-by-fours was totally unacceptable!

As we waited for our waitress, Arvella reread her favorite part of the letter: "Stop and call me when you're a couple of hours away. We'll give you directions to your new house then, and we'll be there waiting for you with the keys."

I heard Arvella reading, and I heard the chatter as she and Sheila talked about menu options, but it was as if I were in another room, another world. I grabbed a paper napkin and feverishly scrawled the numbers 1 to 10 down the side. Off the top of my head I began to write ten *possible* solutions to our problem of where to hold services, challenging Al Van Dyke's negative assumption boldly and impertinently. Here was my list:

1. Rent a school building

2. Rent a Masonic hall

3. Rent an empty warehouse

4. Rent a mortuary chapel

5. Rent an Elk's Lodge hall

6. Rent a theater

7. Rent the Seventh Day Adventist church (they'd be closed on Sundays)

8. Rent a Jewish synagogue (they'd be empty on Sundays too)

9. Rent a drive-in theater (shades of the Sunday morning church service on our honeymoon)

10. Rent an empty piece of ground—put up a tent like Oral Roberts does

After I'd finished the list I held it in front of me. Studying it, I muttered, "Don't tell me it's *impossible* to find a place where I can preach."

"What did you say, Daddy?" Sheila asked. Arvella glanced over as if I'd lost my mind.

I smiled at Sheila and pulled her close to me on the restaurant's vinyl bench. Then I looked at Arvella. "I'm simply not going to sit around for fifty-two weeks doing the work of a contractor—building a church building! That's ridiculous! It's absolutely ludicrous!"

I went over the list with Arvella, and there, in that little café, we held our first planning meeting for the new church.

In less than sixty seconds I had come up with ten possible locations where I could begin preaching. Certainly we should be able to line something up before Easter, which was only a few weeks away. The awesome power of my passion to preach immediately—even that next Sunday—ignited my imagination and shook up that reckless, destructive word "*impossible*."

I became absorbed in my thoughts once again. I hardly noticed ordering or eating my hamburger, though there was now an empty plate in front of me. I frowned at the remaining crumbs and wondered what I'd eaten. "Bob," Arvella scolded in a tone that I had come to know well. She had begun to use it in Ivanhoe, lovingly making sure that I didn't lose touch with those around me or let an unguarded facial expression dishearten a parishioner.

"Bob—smile! You're not a crotchety old man—not yet. The waitress will think you're mad at her. We'll have to leave her a big tip."

Then Arvella put her hand on mine. "Bob—you're going to build a great church. I just know it."

I paid the bill and carefully pocketed the napkin with the list of ten challenges to "impossibility."

I was excited again, inspired by my list and by Arvella's contagious confidence. My dream to become a great preacher was back in high gear as we returned to our car and headed down the road to Arizona.

I was on my way to a great future. I knew it. I felt it. That awesome birth of possibility thinking overwhelmed me with confidence, vision, courage, faith, hope, enthusiasm, optimism, and energy!

And this is the message I would bring to this burgeoning, untamed, and very secular new land of California. I might be a "nobody," but perhaps—just perhaps—I could tell a whole lot of people that there was a Somebody who knew the address of every "nobody," and that this divine, all powerful Somebody could take us all from our nowhere to a somewhere far beyond our imaginings.

This would be my mission. This would be my voice.

XXII

We followed old Route 66 out of the desert and over the Cajon Pass, descending at last onto the flat coastal plain that would be our new home. We had seen so much beauty, so much open space, along these western highways. We were tired, but we were brimming with enthusiasm for the possibilities a land like this afforded.

Like any young husband following a dream, I felt a bit of pressure, wanting my descriptions of orange groves and palm trees and blue ocean to measure up. I wanted everything to be just right for Arvella. I wanted her to love the area at first sight just as much as I had all those years ago.

"Here, Bob!" she said, seeing the street we'd been told to look for.

We turned down an unfinished road that wound through a hundred and fifty look-alike, brand-new houses waiting to be painted. There were no orange trees, not even green lawns. Only bare dirt and bare stucco-framed structures.

I glanced over at Arvella and saw the disappointment in her face. To her credit, she didn't say, "Where's the California paradise you've been raving about?" That wasn't her style.

We'd called Ken Leestma from a pay phone at a gas station a couple hours earlier, and he was there to greet us. We stepped into our new house and discovered that the walls inside were as bare as those outside. The floors throughout were dark-brown . . . linoleum squares called "asphalt flooring"—a look of unfinished blah! The truck had made it with our furniture from Chicago, but now we faced the challenge of unpacking and arranging everything in the small space. As for the furniture matching the flooring? We won't go there!

Ken helped me fit my office into a tiny bedroom off the kitchen, while Arvella and Ken's wife, Bette, unpacked dishes and hung bedsheets across the windows for privacy.

Despite the drabness of the unfinished house in the unfinished neighborhood, the kitchen table was loaded with food and fresh fruit—a grocery shower from the California churches.

I picked up a large "pear," took a bite—and spit it out! "That's *awful!*" I said.

"Of course," Arvella agreed. "It's still green."

That was my first introduction to an avocado—a fruit we Iowans had never seen, tasted, or even heard of! California was going to have its pleasures. They would just take some getting used to.

As I sorted through papers in my office, I pulled out an envelope I'd received just days before leaving Ivanhoe. Inside was a letter of introduction from the most powerful Protestant voice in America, Norman Vincent Peale.

I was proud of that letter. I had yet to meet Dr. Peale, though his wife, Ruth, was the head of the National Missions Board that had offered me the salary here in California. Since Peale's book had rescued me from my dismally ponderous sermons those first months in Ivanhoe. And since he'd become a "celebrity" in this land of celebrities, he could open doors. After all, I was a nobody from nowhere. He was a somebody from somewhere. I put the letter in a spare frame and hung it in my new office.

Adjusting to California came easy to me as I anticipated the winter months to come. No more shoveling snow from the driveway. Here it was, late February, and I could walk outside in shorts. For Arvella the California weather meant that a trip to the grocery store didn't require bundling the children from head to toe, only to find that when they were all suited up and ready to walk out the door, Sheila would have to go potty or Bobby would need his diaper changed.

But the absence of green lawn and trees in this veritable construction zone left Sheila with no place to play. And Arvella missed the close friends she'd made in Ivanhoe. She also had some fears about her new role.

She often said to me, "I'm trained in music, but I don't know what's expected of a pastor's wife in a situation like this." She had been so loved and beautifully accepted in Ivanhoe; now she became insecure again, and very, very lonely. She missed her mother and sisters more than ever. "When we were in Chicago, we were still in the Midwest, near our relatives. Now it seems as if we're on a different continent."

Meanwhile, I had to launch my battle against that word "impossible." I began my search for a venue four days after our arrival. I'd held on to the list I'd scratched on that paper napkin in Albuquerque as my one and only ticket to the future! But only a few days after attacking the problem, the results looked like this:

1. Rent a school building. *It's against state law for schools to rent to "religion."*

2. Rent a Masonic hall. *There is none.*

3. Rent an empty warehouse. *I strike out.*

4. Rent a mortuary chapel. *Taken by the Baptists!*

5. Rent an Elks Lodge hall. *There isn't one in town.*

6. Rent a theater. *None in town.*

7. Rent the Seventh Day Adventist church. *Already taken by the Presbyterians.*

8. Rent a Jewish synagogue. *No synagogue in Garden Grove.*

9. Rent a drive-in theater. *There is one!*

10. Rent an empty piece of ground and put up a tent. *This might work.*

Of my original ten possibilities, only the last two remained, and neither one was very attractive.

It was while I was looking into the possibility of using the Seventh Day Adventist building that I had an unexpected insight. I met the founding pastor of the new Presbyterian congregation in Garden Grove, who was already renting this space—a young minister named Tom Gillespie.

He welcomed me with energy. "Garden Grove is a great place to start a church," he said. "It's like shaking fruit off a loaded tree! We just organized with one hundred and fifty members!"

"How many of them are transfers from other Presbyterian churches?" I asked.

"Oh, all of them, I think," he answered.

That's when it occurred to me: there were millions of Presbyterians in the United States, but only two hundred thousand Dutch Reformed.

I'll be lucky if I can find six people from my denomination living here, I thought.

The pastor of the oldest church in town—First Methodist Church—was Bob Washer. I made a point of meeting him soon after we arrived, and found him warm in his welcome. He shared the same spirit as Tom Gillespie. "We just took in one hundred and fifty members," he said.

"How many were Methodists?" I asked.

"All of them!"

Then I had my "revelation," which would be a revolution in new-church development: *Bob, this town doesn't need a Reformed Church. What it needs is a positive-thinking mission that will meet the needs of the people here who don't go to any church!*

But I still needed a place.

One day I joined Arvella for a midmorning coffee break. After she'd nursed our hungry little Bobby I said, "Remember that Lutheran church service in that drive-in theater at Spirit Lake?"

"Uh-huh," she answered vaguely, rocking Bobby back and forth in the vinyl-covered kitchen chair. I wasn't convinced I had her full attention.

I tried again. "You know, honey, that drive-in service in Iowa, when we were on our honeymoon?"

Now she looked up. "Yes, honey, I remember."

"Well, what do you think? I mean, what do you think about start-ing the church in a drive-in theater? There *is* one here."

"Well," she said, and then lost her thought as she played with Bobby.

"Arvella, *please:* I need your attention," I pleaded, knowing that I sounded as desperate as I felt.

"I'm sorry, Bob," she said, looking up again. "I do remember the service. It was beautiful. There was something very special about worshiping God outdoors. It reminded me of the fields back home. I always felt nearest to God when I was bringing lunch to Dad out on the tractor or helping with the chores. The weather is so great here, and summer isn't too far away. I think it's a great idea! A lot better than a tent."

Suddenly it seemed like a rather good idea to me too. Who wouldn't want to be outdoors with the scent of orange blossoms in the air?

The only drive-in theater in Orange County was in the city of Orange, three miles east of our new California home. I went to the manager and asked permission to rent it for Sunday morning services.

I'm sure that the manager, Norman Miner, was surprised by my peculiar request, but he listened curiously and politely. I could see the questions etched in his face: Weren't churches supposed to have steeples? And pews? And walls? And ceilings?

He said he'd need time to think about it.

That was a long week while I waited for his response. Then he telephoned and said, "It's yours for ten dollars a Sunday. That's what I have to pay the union sound technician."

I was ecstatic. "Thank you! *Thank you!* I'll take it," I said. And I prayed, "Thank You, Lord!"

We went on to discuss the details of the agreement, and then Mr. Miner asked, "By the way, Reverend Schuller, how many people do you have to start this new church of yours?"

"Including you?" I replied.

He laughed and, to my surprise, said, "Yes, including me."

"Two!" I said.

Now he really laughed, and we became instant friends. Norman Miner and his family not only joined our church, but he also became a valued Bible teacher and a dedicated volunteer.

"Possibility thinking" had worked.

But now there was much to do. Our newly purchased organ had arrived and was stored in our one-car garage. I needed to buy a trailer to pull it each week to the drive-in theater. I read want-ads in the "Used—For Sale" section and saw listed "One good trailer—only $20!"

"I made it," the seller told me when I went to check it out. "It's customized!" He kicked the back wheel and said, "That's solid!"

I handed him a twenty-dollar bill.

My neighbor, curious about having a preacher next door, came over.

"Look at my great buy for only twenty dollars," I said proudly. "Well built, huh?"

He nodded. Then, kicking one of the tires, he replied, "Just hope you never get a flat. The wheel's welded to the axle!"

I would pull that trailer behind my car for nearly six years—and I never did have a flat tire! Then I eventually sold it for . . . twenty dollars!

With the issue of transporting the organ settled, I put a notice in the paper right away:

On Sunday morning, March 27, 1955, Orange County's newest and most inspiring Protestant church will hold its first service at 11:00 A.M. in the Orange Drive-in Theater, at the intersection of the Highway 5 and Chapman Avenue.

I added a tagline, which was to become our slogan for years to come:

Come as you are in the family car!

The largest newspaper in the area saw a story there and gave us our first positive press. "Religion, along with banks and restaurants and movies, takes to the drive-in," the story read.

But then came the inevitable backlash.

On Saturday, March 19, eight days before we were scheduled to have our first service, one of my denomination's ministers visited me and proceeded to lambaste me for daring to have church in what he called a "passion pit."

To myself I allowed that he might know more about passion pits than I. But to him I said, "Saint Paul preached on Mars Hill in Athens. Not exactly the ancient world's most sinless location!"

But he wouldn't be persuaded. And I was devastated, because as I was about to discover, "impossibility thinking" is contagious. And I could catch it from this self-appointed critic. Was he right? Was this a bad place to start a church?

The next morning was Sunday, March 20, and I had a very restless night. In one week we were scheduled to hold our first service. On this, my last free Sunday, I said to Arvella, "Let's go to Hollywood Presbyterian to hear Dr. Lindquist."

This was the same Raymond Lindquist who had helped me sort things out while I was in seminary. When all of us students had talked of wanting the "biggest and best" church, he'd said, "Fellows, stop coveting what somebody else has. Go out and start your own churches—and stay there for the rest of your life!"

I had no idea what Dr. Lindquist would preach about that Sunday, but I admired him so much that I knew whatever he had to say would help me. So we piled into our car, made the one-hour drive to Hollywood, and got the children settled into the nursery just in time for the second service.

As Arvella and I took our seats in the rear of the beautiful Gothic sanctuary, I perused the printed bulletin. The title of the sermon was like a bolt from heaven: "God's Formula for Your Self-Confidence."

If there was anything I needed after yesterday's encounter with negative thinking, it was a strong shot of self-confidence!

Soon Dr. Lindquist's strong voice read the text on which his message was based, Philippians 1:6:

"Being confident in this ONE THING—" he boomed.

He paused, and then the next passage rolled like a mighty wave over my insecurity.

"—that God who has begun a good work in you WILL COMPLETE IT!"

The wave washed on by, leaving me buoyed with a calm self-assurance.

"You can depend on the God who gave you life," he went on. "He will *never* quit on you. He has already started with you! He has given you gifts and dreams.

"Everyone needs self-confidence," he said. "But how do you build it, and on what foundation?" His message went on to answer that question:

1. Not on might—not on your own power.

2. Not on money.

3. Not on magic.

4. But on the mercy of God!

Dr. Lindquist concluded, "You may quit on Him, but He will *never* quit on *you!* You can trust Him!"

I walked out of that church feeling ten feet tall, a spiritually empowered possibility thinker. Self-confidence? You bet! I would never forget that message.

On Monday morning I drove to the Plains Lumber Company in town. I explained to the owner that I needed to build a religious background on the rooftop of the drive-in's snackbar—a background that would consist of an altar and a cross. I sketched out the altar—actually, only a four-foot by four-foot by six-foot box made out of plywood—and the owner helped me pick out materials. Then I sketched a ten-foot-high cross that would be bolted to the back of the altar. The owner directed me to the appropriate boards and also helped me pick out some molding with which to decorate the cross. I bought the lumber, nails, and other materials for a little less than one hundred dollars out of denominational funds and had all of it delivered to my house.

After a few hours with a hammer and a saw, I felt as if I had single-handedly built my first church!

But soon my fresh confidence would be challenged again.

While our mission had operating funds, money was extremely tight for Arvella and me personally. Everything in California was far more expensive than it had been in the Midwest, and every penny seemed to simply vanish.

Arvella had just settled Bobby down for a late-morning nap when she came into my bedroom office. "Bob, I need cash to get some milk from the store," she said.

Cash? I had none.

Arvella looked fresh and pretty at that moment, and somehow that made my feeling of failure more acute. I had let her down. I couldn't even meet the needs of my family. But I never kept secrets from her, so I had to tell her the truth.

"Arvella, we don't have any money right now," I said. "Can it wait?"

Her pretty hazel eyes grew concerned. She'd never asked for frills or luxuries. She was a strong woman who had seen hard financial times and had learned to be ingenious. She didn't have to answer my foolish question; I knew the answer.

"Arvella," I said, "I'll get you some milk. Don't worry."

I began digging through our dresser drawers looking for loose change. I checked beneath the sofa cushions in the living room.

Finally I checked my desk drawer. Nothing, except . . . some postage stamps.

"I'll get a refund," I told myself, encouraged. I took my stamps to the post office, chipper as I waited in line, pleased with my creativity. But guess what I learned that day? The post office doesn't give refunds.

I dragged my discouraged self home to tell Arvella and to try to figure out what to do. Growing up on farms we never had to worry about milk. This was new to the both of us. I slumped on the couch as the full realization settled over me: I simply wasn't going to be able to provide for my family. Not even the basics. For *sure* I'd never be able to provide a college education for Sheila and Bobby. I needed extra income. Somehow, someway. Maybe I could write a book as Dr. Peale had done. That would really solve my money problems. Or maybe we should just go back to Iowa and abandon our dreams. Reverend Lindquist's promise that God wouldn't let us down seemed very far away.

Arvella, hearing the postman, picked up our mail and began sorting through it. A letter had come from my mom, and she passed it over to me. I opened it slowly, thinking that the last thing I needed was another letter telling me to "study hard."

I read my mother's words: "I know there's no special occasion, Harold—no birthday or anniversary. But I've been thinking about you and praying for you, and I thought you could use this."

There, in the envelope was a five-dollar bill!

I jumped up and exclaimed, "Thank You, God! Thank you, Mom!"

Arvella smiled serenely, unsurprised by God's benevolence.

"I'll be home in a few minutes," I told Arvella as I headed out the door. "I'm going to the grocery store."

God, through my mom, would not, did not, and could not let us down!

"God will *never* quit on you!" Raymond Lindquist had said.

I clung to those words six days later as I held my first service in the drive-in theater.

My biggest worry was the weather. What if it rained? I'd be drenched even under an umbrella! And Arvella, at the organ—what would she do? Again I was challenged to believe the message that Reverend Lindquist had preached. I couldn't shake my fears, though, and so finally I prayed. Then this message came through loud and clear—a message, I'm convinced, from God Almighty: "Bob, don't worry about the weather. That's my department. Never worry about something that's not your responsibility. Just focus on your sermon and make it great!"

So on March 27, 1955, with my beloved Arvella sitting at the organ, we got our first service underway.

I had arranged with another Dutch Reformed congregation in Los Angeles to "borrow" their choir. But fearing a low attendance that first week out, I had asked the choir director a favor: "Could you ask each of your choristers to drive separately? If there are fifty of you, then we can count on at least fifty cars being in the lot. We'll look successful from day one!"

"Sure, Reverend Schuller," he agreed. "That's no problem."

So on our first Sunday more than one hundred people—including my "borrowed" choir—showed up for our eleven o'clock service.

The topic of my message was "Power for Successful Living." It was based on a statement of Jesus: "If you have faith as a grain of mustard seed, you can say to your mountain, move. And nothing shall be impossible to you" (Matthew 17:28).

The printed bulletin for that day included this notice:

Welcome to the first service of worship in the Orange Drive-in Theater. Remove the speaker and place it in your car, adjusting the volume as needed. Pray that God may bless the hour you spend here. Participate in your car. During prayer, bow your head; during the singing of hymns, join in the singing;

during the sermon, listen and apply the vital truths to your own life. Return next week with your friends and relatives. Thank you kindly.

Following the benediction, we made this announcement: "Caution! Be sure that the speaker is returned to the rack before you drive away from the park stand."

Our blessings were many: it hadn't rained; the choir, which in the end had showed up in twenty cars, had sung beautifully; and about thirty additional cars had come from nowhere—and some of them would be back.

That afternoon my wife and I sat at the dinner table in our small home counting the first offering. It totaled eighty-three dollars and seventy-five cents.

I said to Arvella, "Well, we're on our way, honey; we're on our way!"

But my severest critic, the Reformed Church minister who eight days earlier had accused me of starting my church in a "passion pit," had yet to be silenced. He called me Monday morning.

"So, Schuller, how did your 'passion pit' service go yesterday?"

"It went great, thank you. We had about a hundred people come—more than fifty cars in all."

"Is that all?" he said dismissively. "Humph!" Then he declared, "Well, what can you expect in a drive-in theater?"

"Hey, how can you knock that?" I protested. "It's a one hundred percent increase over last week's attendance!" Then I challenged him, "What was *your* increase?"

Silence. Now it was my turn to say, "Humph!" But I restrained myself and waited for his reply.

Finally he admitted, "Actually, my attendance was down a bit yesterday."

After his call I sat down at my desk to work. I looked out my window and noticed how beautiful the weather was that end-of-March day. Suddenly everything seemed right with my world. Even his comments about my being a "passion pit preacher" began to amuse me, because I knew beyond a doubt that this was the beginning of what would become a truly great church.

I decided to prepare a press release telling of the success of the day before:

> Southern California's first drive-in church got off the ground yesterday with an estimated attendance of one hundred people in fifty cars. The people who came were told that they are fortunate to be part of an exciting church that God is planning for Orange County and Southern California.

There was no squelching my enthusiasm, though it wouldn't take me long to discover that my sense of California's *"perfect weather"* was something of an idealization.

Late spring in Orange County, though generally cool and seldom visited by wind or rain, has a trademark phenomenon the locals call "June gloom." This phenomenon is characterized by a marine layer that covers the area until late morning. Then the sun comes out and truly beautiful skies prevail for the rest of the day. But some Sunday mornings that are forecast to be sunny and colorful turn out to be overcast and dull.

California summers, compared to the midwest, are much more comfortable, due primarily to the absence of humidity. It also helps that there's a gentle ocean breeze that begins to blow every afternoon around four, cooling things off for the evening. But August and September are often beastly hot, and on those days the last place a person wants to be is in a car!

And yet the congregation came. Some Sundays the heat was so intense on the roof of the snackbar that I could hardly pull my feet free from the sticky tarpaper.

During the fall months, this part of the world is beset by "Santa Ana winds" often blowing at fifty miles an hour and gusting up to seventy or more. They blow down from the northeast through the canyons of Southern California—especially the Santa Ana Canyon. When one of these Santa Ana winds hits, carrying sand from the desert, the last place a person wants to be is outside on a rooftop!

And yet there I was, on many a Santa Ana windy Sunday, perched atop the snackbar. It was all I could do, during one of these winds, to hang on and try to keep my robe from ballooning and lifting me into the air.

Arvella's simplest challenge on windy days was to keep her music from blowing away. One Sunday the wind was so fierce that it toppled our trailer over backward. Arvella hung on to the bolted-on organ, and she and the equipment landed safely. But on those blowy Sundays, I was tempted to wonder whether God really meant to have a church here at all!

Fall could be fire season in the dry canyons of Southern California, meaning that we sometimes had smoke to contend with as well.

We Midwesterners were delighted to learn that the winter months could produce snow in the high Santa Ana Mountains just east of us. One Sunday, however, Arvella and I were surprised by snow at the drive-in. The thin white blanket was a beautiful sight, but Arvella's hands were so cold, and the keys so slippery, that it was all she could do to continue. I felt the cold all through me as I preached, and that night we both came down sick.

Winter in our coastal region also produces rain—sometimes in deluge. I often had to cover us with umbrellas—the pulpit, my Bible, my notes, and Arvella's music and keyboard. I had a large beach umbrella anchored in a stand next to me. When wind combined with rain, I must have looked like a circus act, fighting the lashing raindrops and struggling to hold down whatever was threatening to blow away.

On one particularly rainy, nasty Sunday, I almost canceled our service. But just as I was ready to send the cars home—nearly two hundred in number that day—something came to me: *Schuller,* I sensed God challenging me, *you're not in management, but in sales. Management is in my hands! You just get out there like you're supposed to and sell your product!*

We pressed on in that spirit, Sunday after Sunday, and within six months we had a membership large enough to qualify as an official church.

The date was September 27, 1955. We officially presented our California State Charter in the name of Garden Grove Community Church, the name I'd been using since I opened our first bank account. I'd selected that name because I didn't think "First Reformed Church of Garden Grove" would sound inviting to the unchurched people we were trying to reach. Now the name was official.

One hundred and fifty-four charter members declared themselves that day, only six of whom were from the Reformed Church and most of whom had no church affiliation whatsoever. We were on our way to becoming a missionary church!

But as I've often said, with every fulfillment of a new dream comes a new challenge.

Our small home had become the center of everything—office matters, Bible studies, meetings, counseling, choir practice (now with our own choir)—everything except the Sunday service.

This was stressful for everyone in the family, but particularly for Arvella, because she had to keep the children and the house clean and ready at all times for visitors and unexpected events.

When I was counseling, other family members had to be quiet and out of sight. And often the children had to be put to bed earlier than usual to accommodate a meeting of some type or another.

Tension grew in the home as our privacy vanished. The children were expected to act like adults, and we were at the beck and call of the community. For the first few months, we were the only home in the neighborhood that had a phone! We had been given this priority because I was clergy, and clergy were expected to be on call at all times. Consequently, our home became the message center for the entire neighborhood. In addition, our telephone number was distributed in the Garden Grove telephone book and in our Sunday bulletins as the official church number. Many nights we were awakened by calls from strangers who'd had too much to drink (some who persisted in calling back every fifteen minutes!).

It was during this time that we faced our first tragedy in the church. A young mother, Louise, began attending Sunday services as well as our women's Bible study. Arvella suspected that this young woman was deeply troubled, but Louise wouldn't open up about her problems with anyone. She often telephoned for one thing or another, and Arvella could hear the desperation in her voice.

One evening during dinner the phone rang. It was Louise, and though her slurred speech was barely discernible, Arvella was able to make out a plea: "Come and get my children." I was out of town attending a church conference, so Arvella put Bobby and Sheila in the car and raced to Louise's home. The young woman was lying on her bed, limp and unconscious. When Arvella saw an empty pill bottle beside the bed, she pulled Louise into the car, crowded Louise's two young boys in with our children, and raced to the hospital.

Louise survived her attempted suicide and returned home with her children, still refusing to share what it was that troubled her so. Two weeks later, Arvella received a second call. This time we called the police, who took Louise to the hospital. She survived once again and resumed her usual routine, still unwilling to get the help she needed.

But then one night when we were all out for the evening, our phone rang and rang, unanswered. Unable to reach us, and having no one else to turn to, Louise died. We were stunned. We felt that we'd failed. Arvella took it especially hard. I would attempt to console her, "What more could we have done?"

Louise's suicide was a painful seed that would eventually give rise to a great ministry. We would organize and train volunteer members to staff America's first church-related twenty-four-hour phone-based suicide-prevention center. As I write these words, four hundred and twenty-seven suicides have been prevented in the past twelve months.

But this kind of drama and bustling activity centered in a tiny twelve-hundred-square-foot home was just too much for a family of four. It was time to take our "possibility" to the next level of reality.

XXIII

At the outset of our ministry, the denomination had purchased two acres of ground as a possible church site. The land was about three miles west of the drive-in theater, at the corner of Chapman Street and Sea Crest Avenue.

But where could I find a world-class architect? And how would we be able to afford that class of professional? I approached the denominational committee to whom I was accountable with these questions.

"An architect?" they shot back. "They're too expensive. We've never spent money for such a frivolous thing as fancy architecture, and we're not about to start now! We have a dairy farmer on our committee who builds cattle barns. He can be your architect—for free!"

I was appalled. All I could think of was the advice of my architect friend from Chicago, Benjamin Franklin Olson.

"Never compromise on the fine details in design," he'd advised me. "Art—not money—must have the last word! If you don't have the money, then you're not ready. Broaden your financial base. Raise more money."

I loved the cathedrals of Europe that I'd seen pictured in books. I loved the less imposing but still beautiful church buildings of our own country that showed a commitment to and a love for fine design that honored God. I decided that somehow, someway, I'd find a good architect and pay him myself! After all, I'd come here to build a "great church," not a glorified "milk barn"!

I shared my feelings with one of the ministers on the committee, Bernard Brunsting, and he suggested that I go talk to a man he knew who was a member of the American Institute of Architects.

So, at his recommendation, I called up Richard Shelley of Long Beach and said, "You don't know me; my name is Robert Schuller. I'm a minister. I'm twenty-eight years old and I'm going to construct a church in Garden Grove.

"I don't have any money," I went on, "but it's very important to me that the building be designed by a good architect. If you'll draw the plans, I promise you'll be paid during my lifetime."

Amazingly, he took up the challenge and prepared a contract!

In six months the plans for a 250-person chapel were finished. The structure we envisioned would be surrounded by beautiful stained-glass windows on three sides, with a large cross as the focus in the chancel. A separate wing would contain Sunday school rooms to take care of the children who, up to this point, had been taught around tables in the drive-in parking lot.

When Richard Shelley sent us his bill, my growing church responded—generously—and paid in full. And then my local bank (which would still be our bank forty-five years later) agreed to loan us the construction money.

So now a building was rising, and as the work continued our church continued to grow. At Ivanhoe Reformed Church I had learned that people respond to face-to-face invitations. As we canvassed the neighborhood here in Garden Grove, ringing doorbells and getting to know the people in our community, my future congregation began to emerge from behind their closed draperies and shut doors.

In my first year in California I personally rang more than thirty-five hundred doorbells! I went door to door not only in Garden Grove, but also in the adjacent communities of Orange, Anaheim, and Santa Ana. When a person first greeted me, I always asked, "Are you an active member of a local church?" If the answer was yes, I encouraged him or her to stay with that church, expressed my thanks, and left. I didn't want to take people away from their churches. Proselytizing of that sort was against my ethics as a member of the ministerial association. My goal was to reach people who had no church relationship.

If the answer to my question was no, I asked, "What will you be looking for in any church that you might decide to attend?" Depending on the person's response, I typically went on to ask two more questions to refine my understanding: "What would attract you to a church?" and "What might your spouse, your children, and other members of your family want to find in a church?"

I carried a yellow legal pad with me and wrote down every response. It was this information that guided me in developing programs as I ministered to our new and growing congregation.

Many times people would ask me questions: "Do you have a singles ministry?" "Do you have something for high-schoolers?" "What's your music program? Does it include a bell choir?" "What about senior citizens—do you have programs for them?"

If I couldn't say yes, my response was often, "No, but someday we will."

Some homeowners were less courteous than others, stopping me after the first question. I had doors slammed on me on many occasions; I had dogs chase me down the street; I had people chew me out for the folly of my faith. God certainly knew how to keep me humble!

But every Sunday morning, as I stood atop the snackbar roof, I saw more cars coming that I hadn't seen before. I had to have been one of the few preachers who recognized his parishioners not by their faces but by the make and model of their cars. There was the blue Chevrolet, the brown Ford, a red Chrysler—that one was new!—and, always in the back row, the old green Buick. This car, which had been coming since the very first Sunday, was a mystery to me, because every week, without fail, it quietly drove out just as I gave my benediction. By the time I stood at the exit to greet the departing cars, the green Buick was gone. I wondered if there was some grave secret—perhaps some hideous sin—that made its passengers not want to stay to greet me after all those months of Sundays.

I not only greeted my parishioners as they exited the drive-in, but I called on them in their homes, visited some in the hospital as the need arose, and conducted weddings and funerals. But never was there any contact with the occupants of the green Buick. Sunday after Sunday I watched it drive away early, and it began to haunt me. Who were they? Where did they live? What was going on in their lives?

A few days later I dragged myself home after a long day of going door to door. I was pooped, but just as I took off my coat, the phone rang.

Bobby, now a young toddler, was tugging on my leg, begging to be held. I picked him up in one arm and grabbed the phone with the other.

I emphasized my weary tone as I said, "Hello?" hoping that the listener (and potential petitioner) would have second thoughts before asking me to do whatever he or she was about to ask of me.

"Hello, Reverend Schuller?"

Back on duty. I sighed deeply and responded as warmly as I could. "Yes?"

"Reverend Schuller, you don't know me. My name's Warren Gray. My wife and I have been coming to your church since that first Sunday at the drive-in." I wondered how this could be. After all, I greeted every person, every week. How could I not know someone who had been coming since the first Sunday—unless . . .

"We have a green Buick and park in the back, so you probably haven't noticed us before," the man explained.

The green Buick! Now he had my attention. But Bobby was pulling at the phone, making it difficult for me to hear.

"Excuse me just a moment, Mr. Gray." Setting down the phone, I went to the kitchen and handed Bobby to Arvella. Then I nearly ran back to the waiting mystery man.

"Yes, Mr. Gray. As a matter of fact, I *have* noticed you, and I've missed having the opportunity to meet you. Why do you leave early every week?"

"I'll explain that. But Rosie, my wife, and I wanted to know if you'd come to visit us."

I was both intrigued and thrilled. I took down the directions to their house, then gave a warm goodbye.

The next morning, brimming with curiosity, I made the twenty-one-mile trip to their home.

Warren was waiting on the porch. "Thanks for coming, Reverend Schuller," he seemed nervous but was obviously glad that I'd come. In time he told me their story.

"Rosie had a stroke some years back. She can't walk or talk. We stopped going to church because she's so uncomfortable in her wheelchair. This drive-in church of yours was like a gift from heaven sent special delivery just for us. We've been going ever since that first Sunday. Never missed. We just have to leave a little early so that Rosie won't get too tired."

I followed him into the house.

"Reverend Schuller, this is Rosie," he said, presenting his wife.

She sat in an armchair, her head limp and unresponsive to my hello, her gray hair pulled back neatly from her face. Someone—Warren it seeemed—was taking tender care of her. Warren leaned lovingly down and kissed her cheek.

I said, "Hello, Rosie. I'm Reverend Schuller. Warren tells me that you want to join the church."

Her lips moved slightly, her eyes lifted to meet mine, and tears slid down her cheeks. Her attempt at words never got beyond a sustained mumble. But the love of God shining from her face made her intention clear.

Two weeks later I baptized Warren and Rosie Gray in their green Buick, and they were received into the Garden Grove Community Church, members number 201 and 202.

Not long after, our first real church with offices and chapel was ready for dedication. Goodbye drive-in theater!

We held a board meeting in our home to plan our first indoor service. We went round and round with exciting ideas and hopes until one of the elders, a kind and sensitive man, asked the question I'm ashamed to say I hadn't thought of:

"What are we going to do about Rosie Gray?"

Every Sunday, Warren carried Rosie from their house to the front seat of their Buick, carefully arranging her so that she'd be comfortable and positioning her head so as to allow for good viewing of the service.

It was a stunning question—both because it hadn't been asked previously and also because of its huge implications.

But now the answer was obvious: for as long as Rosie Gray lived, which we thought couldn't be more than a few months, we would hold two Sunday morning services. The first would begin at nine-thirty in our new chapel. Then we'd transport everyone—me, Arvella and the organ, the choir—to the drive-in for the second service at eleven. There was just no getting around it; this had to be done.

So on September 23, 1956, just eighteen months after our first service in the Orange Drive-in Theater, we dedicated our Richard Shelley stained-glass chapel.

Then, each Sunday after our chapel service, we got into our cars and rushed to the Orange Drive-in Theater, three miles away, for Rosie Gray's service.

Not only did the congregation at the chapel continue to grow, but so did the congregation at the drive-in!

Meanwhile, our family was growing too. On April 2, 1957, Arvella presented me with a precious little brunette girl we named Jeanne Anne. Baby Jeanne (named after my mother, Jennie—with a twist) was delightful and happy, full of personality. She looked a lot like her dark-haired brother. Sheila, on the other hand, now had cascading long blond curls, and on Sundays all three were doted on by parishioners. Sheila in turn doted on Jeanne, poking at the baby's poor little head with bristly brushes, trying to make the hair grow and the ribbons stay put. Our tiny house became tinier with the five of us now crowding inside.

I had a lapful when I read bedtime stories to the children. Bobby always begged for *Jack and the Beanstalk*, "with those three magical beans," he would say, the beans that produced a stalk that grew so rapidly it became a ladder high into the clouds—"even up to heaven," as Sheila described it.

One night, as I read that favorite tale, it occurred to me that our ministry was growing just like Jack's beanstalk! I now had two churches growing simultaneously within two years of moving to Garden Grove. Each was expanding, and I couldn't turn my back on either.

I needed the chapel and all the facilities that came with it, and yet, as it became more and more apparent, the drive-in served a genuine human need. There were many people who, like Rosie, couldn't come into a church building because of a disability. And there were others who simply didn't want to be thrown into contact with lots of people; they were more comfortable staying in their cars. But all of these worshipers took me quite literally at my word when I invited, "Come as you are in the family car."

Though we now had a solid base of parishioners, I continued on my rounds, canvassing homes in neighborhoods that we hadn't yet approached. I never knew what I'd discover behind each door.

One day a young wife and mother greeted me. When I asked, "Are you an active member of a local church?" her response was, "No. My father is Jewish, and my mother is Catholic. They told me to pick my own religion."

Thinking that I might relate to her Jewish side, I said, "Well, as you know, in the Old Testament . . ."

"What's that?" she asked.

It turned out that she was a graduate of Stanford University, and yet she didn't know that the Bible is made up of two books, the Old Testament and the New Testament. Patiently I tried to explain.

She interrupted again. "Your religion has two Bibles?"

"No. Forget what I just said," I replied. "Just come to church, and if you like it and it helps you . . . come back."

I saw her in the chapel service a week later!

I knew then that God was sending me a clear message: *These unchurched Orange Countians don't know the Bible; and furthermore, they aren't (and won't be) impressed with a lot of biblical quotations.* I would have to learn to simplify my message.

But could I? *Should* I? Was it really okay to do this? I had already shifted a bit while yet in Ivanhoe, but when does a "shift" become a "compromise"? I had always been willing to go to the edge, but I wasn't willing to cheapen my faith! An internal conflict raged between my desire for theological substance and my desire to connect with these people. Average people who really needed the blessings of faith didn't come to church to take a seminary course. They just wanted relief from their pain; they just needed inspiration to make it through the week.

I faced a choice: I could impress my colleagues and myself with astounding theological deductions, or I could love the people around me enough to bring them a simple and positive message so that they could grasp the faith they so desperately needed. That truly would be extending the invitation to "come as you are."

Meanwhile, Norman Vincent Peale's book *The Power of Positive Thinking,* which I'd read and benefited from back in Ivanhoe, was taking the country by storm. This practical application of traditional Christian theology brought down to earth for the average person turned up on coffee tables all around Garden Grove—even in many of the unchurched homes in which I called. Everyone seemed to have read it, and everyone seemed to have found it useful and inspiring.

When I had read Peale's book in Ivanhoe, its blurring of the boundary between the religious and the secular had revolutionized my preaching. Now, seeing the book in so many area homes, I had a brainstorm: if Norman Vincent Peale was able to have such a positive impact on the people who were my targeted mission, then in person he would make a sensational guest preacher! What better way to attract the unchurched to join us in our fellowship?

So, in an impetuos moment, I wrote Dr. Peale a letter. I glowingly described the attractions of our outdoor sanctuary. I pointed out that everybody had a comfortable seat by an open window, as well as his or her own speaker! I mentioned our easy access off the Highway 5 and noted that we could park nearly two thousand cars. I described how the mountains were visible from our sanctuary and how the orange blossoms provided a beguiling fragrance to enhance our worship experience. In fact, I said, we had the largest, most beautiful church in California!

I invited him to come and preach for us on a Sunday morning in June of 1957. Did I think he would accept? Absolutely! And did he? Of course. Even though I had no money to pay him or even to cover his expenses.

On the way to California, I had played the possibility-thinking game in terms of finding a location for my new church. I had based my entire life and faith on the assurance that "with God all things are possible" (Matthew 19:26). There was no turning back now.

I sent Dr. Peale a confirmation letter in which I was a little more explicit. "Just so you'll know," I wrote, "our sanctuary is a drive-in theater." This didn't bother Dr. Peale at all. True to the spirit of his books, he said he was honored by our positive-thinking approach and would be there on June 30, 1957.

We sent postcards and letters to members and friends, inviting them to hear and greet our distinguished guest. We made telephone calls as well as announcements in our church services, Sunday school classes, and group meetings. I advertised, of course, in the Orange County and the Los Angeles papers, and I used the same words that I'd used when I'd first written to Dr. Peale: "Everyone will have a comfortable seat by an open window, with your own speaker!"

The morning of June 30 the sunlight is golden above the orange groves, the air is sweet and fresh, and all along Highway 5 cars snake along in one of the biggest traffic jams the area has ever seen. Everyone is heading for the Orange Drive-in Theater!

The parking lot is full a half-hour before the service is to start. Now cars are jamming into spaces that weren't meant to hold vehicles. *How will they hear the service without a speaker?* I wonder. I can't believe my eyes! An elder reports that we're over the parking capacity. We surpassed the legal limit of fifteen hundred cars twenty minutes ago, and they're still pulling in. The elder asks if he should close the gates. I tell him no.

I use the sound system to ask people who have space in their car to turn on their headlights, thinking that we can fit more people in that way. Sure enough, people are so excited at the tremendous turnout and energy in that moment that many gladly welcome strangers into the intimate space of their vehicle.

It's now eleven o'clock and time to begin. The elder reports to me again: cars are turning away now because they can't find a spot; two thousand cars holding an average of two persons per car gives us an estimated audience of four thousand people!

Four thousand people?!

I can't believe it. I walk up onto the roof of the snackbar to see for myself and to get things underway. Arvella, already playing the prelude, looks at me with amazement. Neither of us can believe that this is happening!

Dr. Peale, beside me on the roof, chuckles as he calls my attention to the drive-in's "marquee" for the week. In huge type the sign calls attention to both the new blockbuster show starring Audie Murphy and Dr. Peale's appearance. Visible to all travelers on the interstate freeway, it reads:

To Hell and Back
With Audie Murphy
And
Norman Vincent Peale
In Person!

I'm chuckling now at this mishap. Were this many people really interested in taking a trip to hell and back with Audie Murphy and Dr. Peale? If so, then we'd have some really good potential converts!

It's now time to introduce our guest. As I walk to the podium I see the small-statured, gray-haired master of positive thinking from the corner of my eye. Before I know what I'm saying, I hear these words come from my mouth:

"We have with us today the greatest positive thinker who has ever lived. His words have been heard and read by millions of people all over the world. He has changed more lives than can be counted.

The greatest positive thinker who ever lived is here—with us—today! In person! His name is . . . Jesus Christ! And here to tell us all about Him is Dr. Norman Vincent Peale."

Dr. Peale is surprised, I can see. He rises from his chair and passes on his way to the microphone, leaning toward me and whispering, "Pray for me!"

Now it's my turn to be surprised. It would never occur to me that a man of such greatness, a man of such confident carriage and bearing, would ever feel so uncertain as to ask for the prayers of a subordinate. And yet Dr. Peale has just done that very thing. With this knowledge comes the realization that I'm not alone on those days when I honestly feel that I can't do what's expected of me. We *all* need support and encouragement—even Dr. Peale.

He stands before the crowd now. All the people I want to reach are ready to listen. This is my mission. Before me, right before me, is my "somewhere"—the edge of my tomorrow. I see it clear, I see it strong—and I like it.

Dr. Peale's voice booms so loud and strong that I'm guessing it probably could reach every inch of the drive-in parking lot without amplification. And I notice that the dramatic intensity that once turned me off carries all the way out to the most distant cars! He's so tiny on stage that I now see why he flails his arms and exaggerates his physical mannerisms.

With his arms moving in sync, Peale booms out, "If Jesus Christ were here today, would He tell you what a lost sinner you are?"

I nod my head yes.

He continues, "Would He tell you how bad you are, how you've failed?"

Again I nod in agreement.

Then he shocks me by shouting, "I don't think so! Deep down in your heart you already know that; you already know just what your most grievous sins are!"

Then he peers out across this great multitude, making the most of a dramatic pause. "Jesus Christ never told *anyone* he was a sinner."

Dr. Peale's words resound across the parking lot, and they continue to reverberate in my mind throughout the rest of his sermon. Because I'm sure that he's wrong.

At home later that day, the rush of the morning and the euphoria of success having subsided, I retrieved my red-letter edition of the Bible. I read and I searched. I searched and I read some more. And what did I find?

I found that Dr. Peale had been right! What I didn't find was a single place where Jesus had called any person a sinner!

My preaching underwent a metamorphosis that day. Even though I'd thought I'd converted to "positive preaching" in Ivanhoe, I now realized that my underlying message hadn't changed. I'd been telling stories, but I'd continued to couple that approach with expository preaching that maintained a strong emphasis on every person's sinful nature. I was preaching more like Saint Paul than Jesus Christ.

Never again!

As I reread the words of Jesus, I discovered that He focused not on people's weaknesses but on their strengths, not on their shortcomings but on their possibilities, not on their failures but on their successes! I remembered, too, how labels can damage the psyche. In my own childhood, the other kids had called me "fat," as if that was who I was. Could I really be reduced to that one trait? Likewise, can any person truly be reduced to the label "sinner"?

I read again about the woman who had been caught in the act of adultery. Jesus said to her accusers, "Anybody here who is without sin, let that person be the first to cast a stone." Slowly those who had accused her and had been ready to stone her to death began to walk away. "Where are those who accused you?" he said. "They've all gone away," she answered. Then he said, "I'm not going to condemn you, either. Go away; and sin no more" (John 8:1–11). He was addressing sin as an action—not a label!

I reread the familiar story about Zacchaeus that I had learned as a young child (Luke 19:1–10). Zacchaeus was a tax-gatherer and a terrible cheat, yet when Jesus came to Jericho, where Zacchaeus lived, there was Zacchaeus, perched in a tree to catch a glimpse of him. Jesus said, "Zacchaeus, I want to have lunch with you. Come down." The Bible doesn't tell us what else was said, but it does offer the result: Zacchaeus returned fourfold what he had stolen from others, and everything else he gave to the poor.

Every word that Dr. Peale had spoken that morning was a word of encouragement and hope. And his approach seemed so similar to what I was reading now in the afternoon about how Jesus talked to unchurched people.

Dr. Peale had said, "There is something greater in you than you have discovered and demonstrated." He had declared, "Any human being can be anything he wants to be through the power Jesus Christ brings into his life!"

Wow! That rang a bell for me. It touched me at the deepest level of my being. Actually, the seed of this belief system had been within me all along. It had lain dormant, but now it was vibrant again! It had been fertilized and was being watered by the power of the Holy Spirit.

I became convinced that this was the message of Jesus Christ for the twentieth century—and for *every* century. It could and would reach unchurched men and women as criticism never would or could.

Then I remembered that young, well-educated mother I had met on one of my house visits—the woman who hadn't known what the Old Testament was. I concluded that I'd have to present Bible truths in simple words and simple messages as Jesus had done. No heavy theology. No intimidation. No judgment. Just inspiring ideas that might bring people from doubt to faith.

Just as our church name had been carefully chosen to be as inclusive and inviting as possible, my preaching would have to reflect the same objective. I realized that I was like a doctor in the emergency room of a hospital. Or like the Good Samaritan ministering to the injured man on the roadside. My task was to take care of the most glaring hurts and pains that people brought with them. The doctor in the emergency room doesn't try to lecture or scold the wounded. He simply tries to stop the bleeding and bind the wounds.

On Sundays, in that drive-in, I had people's attention for just a few minutes, and I had to be gentle and caring, bringing them hope.

I was revitalized as I thought about this new focus. I knew that growth was to be ours as a result of the past "Peale" Sunday, and I knew that I, like Peale, had a vital message. Now I knew better how to deliver that message.

But what about Peale's body language? I decided that it too had a purpose. I recalled my instructions from Miss Aeilts in high school:

"Harold, remember: when you're on stage, you're not the tall young man you are right now as you stand in front of me. Distance shrinks you. To the person in the last row of your audience, you're a small creature. How can you convince that distant observer that your words are important and should be listened to? *How?*

"Through body language! Throw your arms up and out; make your steps grand and dramatic! Instead of nodding your head, dip toward the ground! You may feel silly, but to that person far away from you, your movements will convey what, at that distance, your facial expressions can't."

This would be a defining moment in my preaching style. I'd exchange the dignified and reserved body language of Dr. Mulder for the dramatic body language of Dr. Peale. I had no idea how these improved techniques would increase the growth of our church. Soon our little two-hundred-fifty-seat chapel was bursting at the seams. And we had more than two hundred coming to the drive-in. We had grown to nearly the same number that we'd had in Ivanhoe, but in less than half the time! Could it be that we had already outgrown the chapel we'd built only a year before?

Meanwhile, Rosie Gray continued to live. And we continued traversing back and forth from chapel to drive-in. A year passed, and every Sunday it was the same: a service from nine-thirty to ten-thirty for over two hundred people in the chapel; then a mad dash in the car, pulling a trailer with the organ, to the drive-in theater, where another two hundred or more people were waiting for the eleven o'clock service. The trip had begun to take its toll on me, our choir, and our people.

What should I do? Should I resign from the chapel and remain as the drive-in preacher? Where would that lead? Should I resign from the drive-in but continue with the chapel? Or should I suggest to the denomination that I tender my resignation entirely so that they could solve this problem objectively? One thing was certain: I was going to have to find a better answer to the challenges before us.

Then, like a thunderbolt, came the message God was trying to get into my thick Dutch head through Rosie: *Schuller, why not build a walk-in/drive-in church to accommodate both those who can walk and those who can't?*

That bold idea grabbed all of my imagination. I began sketching a sanctuary that would accommodate people in pews but would also have a sliding window at the pulpit, allowing me to see and be seen by persons in the parking lot. I knew that it could work, but we'd have to buy more land—ten acres, I imagined. That meant that we'd have to sell the new chapel and relocate in order to merge the two drive-in and walk-in congregations into one.

I had no idea what lay ahead. Arvella and I had seen the beanstalk grow from a tiny seed into a robust vine reaching up into the heavens. I had zealously raced up that beanstalk filled with grand and glorious hopes, but I didn't know that I was heading into a very trying season of my young ministry.

I was about to realize that both ministry and beanstalks sometimes lead as far away from heaven as one can get.

XXIV

Arvella and I desperately needed a vacation, and finally we got one.
We loaded up a camper, loaned to us by a generous parishioner,
and headed to Yosemite National Park with seven-year-old Sheila,
four-year-old Bobby, and one-year-old Jeanne Anne. I had arranged
with my denominational supervisor, Al Van Dyke, to handle emergencies and to fill in for me on Sundays as guest pastor.

We had never "camped" before, nor had we ever seen Yosemite.
But I think that Sheila and Bobby were just as excited about having
their father's full attention as they were about any of the sights we
saw. We left Garden Grove singing and telling stories, and as I
watched the miles of central California speed by, thoughts of the
church grew distant.

When we got to the mountains and the giant redwoods, the awe-
someness of God's creation put all our work concerns into perspective. Once we'd picked out our campsite, Sheila and Bobby became
my pals looking for bears, while Arvella kept up with little Jeanne
and organized the food.

The quiet grandeur of the forests and streams was just what I
needed. With no telephone or radio or schedule to interrupt our
intimate conversations, Arvella and I spent long hours just talking
quietly and playing with the children.

We returned from vacation on a mild summer evening. I was tired
from the drive but refreshed and rejuvenated. I hardly slept that first
night at home as my head swirled with new ideas. I couldn't wait to
get back to my office and catch up on everything I'd missed.

But what I found waiting for me was a shock.

While I'd been away, a young seminary graduate had come into our area selling Fuller Brushes door to door. One of the doorbells he'd rung was at the home of an elder in my church.

The elder had engaged the young man in conversation. When he'd found out about the young man's background, he'd asked why someone trained for the ministry was selling instead of preaching and ministering.

The young seminary graduate had explained that he hadn't been able to secure an appointment and needed to make ends meet somehow. The elder, thinking he was helping me by easing some of my workload, had hired him on the spot.

Now here I was, face-to-face with an associate minister I'd never met. I discovered immediately that he knew nothing about the Reformed Church, and to make matters worse, he declared, with an air of authority, that he was a "fundamentalist." He was certainly not on my wavelength! Nevertheless, I tried to share my new ideas with him, since I was eager to start making some changes. He didn't respond with any enthusiasm, and in fact he seemed perturbed and even resistant.

By late morning I felt my blood pressure rising and my whole body bristling with tension. Under my breath I muttered the Bible verse, "With God all things are possible."

Could I turn this negative "fundamentalist" into a positive possibility thinker? That seemed less and less likely as the days and weeks and months wore on. Try as I might, conflicts between us arose continually. Suddenly factions appeared within the church. Secret meetings were held. People who'd been my friends and supporters began to complain about me, but not *to* me. I would hear in a roundabout way that So-and-So had said, "I'm not getting fed." Then I'd hear that another So-and-So felt hurt and was complaining, "I'm not being paid attention to."

Some of the words I heard were bitter and deeply hurtful. A person very dear to me said, "Schuller's ideas are too grandiose." I felt misunderstood and increasingly alone.

All the while, my new associate, busy consoling the dissenters, would barely speak with me. One day, more communicative than usual, he suggested that I limit my pastoring to the drive-in ministry, leaving the Chapman Avenue chapel to him. When I reminded him that I had started both, and in Reformed Church tradition was the president of the corporation and chairman of the board, he threatened to challenge my tenure in those positions. Now he was aiming to take over *both* congregations! I was appalled!

I plummeted into depression and became suspicious of nearly everyone. I needed a friend desperately, so Arvella and I took the children and drove to Pomona, forty-five miles away, to visit Ken and Bette Leestma. There, in that safe place, I sat with Ken at his kitchen table, my head in my hands.

Within the next six months, the associate had pressed charges within my denomination, asserting that I wasn't preaching the gospel. I was put on "trial" and examined by my colleagues. Several of my own peers—Gradus Vander Linden, the stated clerk of the Southern California churches, Raymond Beckering, and Ken Leestma—defended and exonerated me.

About that time, *Life* magazine carried an article on the high incidence of psychological and spiritual breakdown that was occurring among Protestant clergy. I wondered if I might be in the group affected in that way.

During that same frightful period, I experienced a physical condition that was not a little trauma for me. An old condition with my nose—the very condition that had brought me into contact with the Ivanhoe pharmacist—inflamed into what was called "rhino-phyma." I would be conducting a wedding or a funeral, or my regular Sunday service, and suddenly my nose would begin to bleed. It was horribly embarrassing and threatened to take away what was left of my self-esteem.

I turned to surgery for help, but the operation left me with very noticeable scars. One night, shortly after the procedure, I sat in front of my bathroom mirror and went into an unrealistic, exaggerated, negative-thinking tailspin. I imagined that the people I had loved and served hated me. I was absolutely *convinced* of it. The colleagues whose approval of my theological skills I so desperately wanted were examining my basic worthiness for the ministry. Now even my wife and children, I was convinced, would see me as ugly.

Then suddenly, like rain from heaven, came this thought:

Schuller—turn your scars into stars!

I had also been experiencing night terrors, awakening suddenly to find myself in a sweat-soaked bed. I'd begun to pray, "God, take me out gracefully, please. A fatal heart attack will do just fine. *Please*. Amen."

I have no idea how many times I prayed that prayer.

Then came the night when I decided to try praying a different prayer. I cried, "Jesus, if You're really alive, heal me before it's too late. Remove this obsession. Deliver me from my negative thinking. Amen."

At that instant, an amazing thing happened—something that had never happened before and hasn't happened since. I felt, out of nowhere, the genuine, physical sensation of a finger pressing through my skull and into my brain. I could feel the bones and flesh yield as that finger pushed deeper. It went in as far as it could. Then it began to pull out, to move back in the direction from which it had come, and it dragged something with it. Then it passed completely out of my brain. It was gone, suddenly, and so were the anxiety, the fear, the depression, the darkness!

Then, I remembered that sermon Raymond Lindquist had preached on the Sunday before my first service at the drive-in: "God's Formula for Your Self-Confidence." His text had been "Being confident of this one thing, that God who has begun a good work in you will complete it" (Philippians 1:6). His conclusion: "Lean on the mercy of God."

I crawled out of bed, deep in the night, and began to compose what I would call "The Possibility Thinker's Creed," thereafter the mantra of my life:

When faced with a mountain,
I WILL NOT QUIT!
I will keep on striving until I climb over,
Find a pass through,
Tunnel underneath,
Or simply stay
And turn the mountain into a gold mine,
With God's help!

The next morning, after a peaceful and profound sleep, I awoke to a new world—a new life! I dressed and walked out of the front door, shocked at the beautiful blossoms on the rosebush. I stopped to savor their fragrance. Then I turned back to the house and called to my wife, "Arvella, the roses are blooming!"

"I know," she said, "they've been blossoming for over a month, honey!"

I had found the joy in living once more. With the depression and anxiety gone, I regained my confidence in preaching and praying. I was back on the search to locate property to expand our ministry.

I knew that a church meeting to present my proposal would be attended by both dissenters and supporters, but I called one anyway. I announced, "I cannot, I *will* not, continue to pastor two congregations in two different locations. I came here to build one church, not two. In my opinion, we have before us three options:

"First, we could drop the drive-in ministry.

"Second, we could separate into two churches, each having its own pastoral board. I could resign and allow each to choose its own pastor.

"Third, we could—and I believe we *should*—merge the two churches into what we can call a 'walk-in/drive-in church.'"

I had been wrestling with these options for months, but only after that significant encounter with Christ did I feel the confidence to make them known. I called for a congregational meeting of committed charter members, asking them to vote on the three options. I shared with the members the drawing I had sketched of a walk-in/drive-in church, all glass, with a sliding wall that would open to visually accommodate the drive-in worshipers.

Immediately the question arose, "But where will we get the money to buy property and build such a building? This congregation can't afford what you're proposing."

My response was clear: "I'm not concerned about money. There's never a money problem; there's only an idea problem. Our job is to create an expanding vision and have a dream that's great enough for God to work a miracle. God's job is to create that miracle—including whatever is needed to make it become a reality!"

All of this raised a ruckus, to say the least. The debate was heated and stormy. Tempers flared. Passions ran high. Words and feelings were tempestuous. Finally, to bring things back to order, Dr. Wilfred Landrus, an elder in the church and a professor at nearby Chapman College, read the motion he had written on a small piece of paper:

"I move that this congregation, under God, go on record as favoring integration; and that we authorize the consistory to conduct further study toward acquiring property for this purpose."

I looked at Arvella; she looked back and smiled. Then I prayed. The motion was seconded—and then carried fifty-five to forty-eight!

As Arvella and I prepared to go home that evening, I noticed a crumpled piece of paper on the floor. I can't stand clutter, so I picked it up. It turned out to be Dr. Landrus's motion. I slipped it into my pocket and have kept it to this day.

My future direction had now been approved by a slim congregational majority vote.

With the help of a real estate agent, I located ten acres of ground near downtown Garden Grove. It wasn't for sale, but I knew that with God all things are possible, and I felt that the owner, a widow, could be persuaded to let it go.

One Sunday afternoon, wearing my best suit, with my Bible in hand, I walked the site and claimed it for God. (Somewhere in my religious circles I had heard that this worked.) I knelt down in the dirt, opened my Bible, and put my finger on Matthew 21:22: "Whatever you ask in prayer, believing, you will receive."

So I prayed, "God, you brought us here to do a great thing in Your name. This property will allow us to do that, so please touch the owner's heart and head and move her to sell it to us. Amen."

Negotiations with my board, who couldn't believe that I was already considering another move, and further negotiations with the seller brought us to an agreement to purchase the land at a particular price.

The appointment to sign the documents of sale was at ten o'clock on a given morning. The real estate agent and I arrived a few minutes ahead of time. We exchanged pleasantries with the seller and together reviewed the terms of sale. When the seller picked up her pen to sign the documents, she held that pen above the signature line for what seemed like an hour, and then—I couldn't believe it!—she put the pen down and said, "I can't do it. I can't sell this property. I don't think that my husband would want me to!"

Her statement was like a blow to my midsection. She had been open and ready to sell when we first contacted her. Negotiations had gone without a hitch. We had been cordially received when we arrived at her home that morning to close the deal.

Now this! No amount of pleading or discussion would sway her. The agent and I walked away in disbelief. I found my faith in the Bible, my faith in prayer, my faith in people, shaken to its roots. And my faith in God was tested again. Was I supposed to simply be content with what we had as a church? Should I allow the walls of a building to hamper the proclamation of the message? I knew that this was exactly what *would* happen: if people couldn't find a seat, they would leave and perhaps never hear the words they needed to hear.

Meanwhile, I still hadn't resolved the issue of my unwanted associate pastor. Month after month after month he continued to stir up dissension, and I was troubled by the negative feelings he was spreading.

Then one morning, seated at my desk, I heard the words of Jesus Christ. His message overpowered my consciousness:

"I will build My church!"

It was then I realized that I had been trying to build *Schuller's* church, not *Christ's* church. I also realized that Jesus Christ and I weren't *partners!* He was *Master* and I was *servant!* So I jumped out from behind the desk and pointed to the empty chair.

"All right, Jesus Christ," I said. "*You* sit there! *You* are in charge now! *You* do it! I'll step aside. You are the leader of this church. I'll be Your follower." Immediately, a tremendous load was lifted from my shoulders.

The first thing I asked my new "Boss" was, "Do you mind if I take a short vacation?" And I did! We went back up to Yosemite, to Hume Lake. When I got home, I learned that, miracle of miracles, in my short absence my associate pastor had been called to another church. The leader of the opposition was gone!

After almost two years of grueling negativity, now at long last there was peace! Energy and renewal of vision and purpose surged through my being. At our next board meeting, the chairman's chair—always reserved for me—was left unoccupied. I left it open symbolically for the *real* President of the congregation and Chairman of the board—Jesus Christ! That symbolic gesture was a breakthrough for us as a church.

One of our church members, a real estate agent, called to tell me about a ten-acre orange grove only three miles east of our chapel. "But," he warned, "it's out in the sticks." Then he mentioned the selling price: sixty-six thousand dollars.

I couldn't believe it! That was half the price of the ten acres on which I'd knelt and prayed. Not only would we save sixty-six thousand dollars, but with the passing of years we would find ourselves not in downtown Garden Grove but in downtown Orange County!

Of course, sixty-six thousand dollars was still a huge amount of money! It might as well have been a million. Then I remembered the gist of the words that had come to me earlier: "There's no money problem, only an idea problem. Our job is to have the ideas, the dreams, the vision; God's job is to show us how to achieve them."

"I will build My church!" Jesus had promised. What brilliant leadership I was seeing under His direction.

So I took the proposal to our board and then to the church as a whole, and after another noisy congregational meeting, and another narrow vote, we agreed to purchase these ten acres on Chapman Avenue at Lewis Street, about one mile west of the drive-in theater and three miles east of our stained-glass chapel.

Sale of that existing property required denominational approval. Representatives of the classis, our regional authority, met with our local leaders. There were still some voices opposing the sale, but a motion was made, seconded, and passed that this transaction be authorized. Then another shock hit.

When I got to my office the next morning, I found at the door a stack of books and envelopes. The books were the treasurer's and the clerk's records; the envelopes contained resignations from the vice-president of the congregation, the clerk, the treasurer, and my personal secretary.

I was stunned with grief. I had believed that most of the parishioners—and certainly these key people—had supported me. Then matters got worse: it turned out that there were others who questioned my motives. Altogether, more than forty people left the congregation—people who felt that they couldn't be a part of Schuller's crazy idea of a "walk-in/drive-in church." With each departure, I saw our church slipping away. I felt that I had won the battle but lost the war.

Again, those old foes—loneliness and depression—came to threaten me. I became insecure in my relationships even with my closest friends and colleagues, suspecting that they too were secretly suspicious of my motives, perhaps even ridiculing me behind my back for my "grandiose" dreams. I began to avoid small-group gatherings and one-on-one conversations. My family was my truest comfort.

But again and again God came to me with his precious reminders. I heard Dr. Lindquist's words: "You may quit on God, but God will *never* quit on you!"

I also remembered that confident promise that I had heard only weeks before: "I will build My church!"

I even reread my own words from "The Possibility Thinker's Creed":

When faced with a mountain,
I WILL NOT QUIT!
I will keep on striving until I climb over,
Find a pass through,
Tunnel underneath,
Or simply stay
And turn the mountain into a gold mine,
With God's help!

I repeated over and over a Bible verse I had learned as a child: "No one, having put his hand to the plough, and looking back, is fit for the Kingdom of God" (Luke 9:62).

I thought of Dad rebuilding after the twister when everything had seemed destroyed. Like him, I would refuse to relinquish my dreams to self-destructive negativity. I would refuse to be beaten by my own insecurities and fear. I typed up this verse from Luke, slipped the paper under the glass top on my desk, and read it a dozen times every day. It gave me faith with holding power!

The people who had continued to support me now caught the vision, and others who had been on the negative side moved beyond the friction. A couple of new members, Ralph and Lois Wendell, stepped forward to encourage me and offer their help. Lois became my faithful and beloved secretary until cancer took her life seventeen years later. People gave generously, some sacrificially, because they too knew that if we were to be a truly great church for God, we had to have more property, people, programs, and pastors! From this time onward we had a dedicated church focused on mission.

With the authorization of my denominational supervisor, I withdrew the eleven hundred dollars that was in the bank account and opened escrow to buy the ten acres. I was given one hundred and twenty days to raise the additional eighteen thousand dollars for the down payment on this piece of property that many were calling a ridiculously foolish purchase—property deep in the sticks and worthless for sure.

Then a news story broke: the Santa Ana Freeway was going to be built replacing Highway 5. And its new path would take it just east of us. Suddenly prices were doubling in the area. The owner hoped to heaven we wouldn't be able to close our purchase! He had sold at far too low a price.

Arvella and I cashed in our insurance policies and depleted all our other resources. At noon on the day of the deadline for the down payment—the day by which, at four o'clock, we had to pay eighteen thousand dollars to a man hoping beyond hope that we'd fail so that he could rescind the contract—we were still three thousand dollars short!

I went home for lunch, emotionally exhausted. Arvella was holding Jeanne Anne, now two years old, her soft little body against her own, walking back and forth in the kitchen. Bobby was seated at the table eating a peanut butter and jelly sandwich. Sheila was at school.

No one said anything for a while. Then I sighed dramatically and said, "It's over. We didn't make it!"

Arvella stopped her pacing, looked at me long and intently, and in her sweet but firm manner said, "Bob, I think you need to talk to Warren Gray. I know he's not well. But we have nothing else we can do. God brought us this far, and He won't abandon us. I know that, and so do you. You also know that Warren would be crushed if we didn't ask for his help. You *have* to call him!"

Warren and Rosie Gray, who had given us the original seed money, were both old and infirm now. In fact, Warren had just been released from the hospital; he had cancer and the doctors felt that he didn't have much longer to live.

I didn't want to make that telephone call, but Arvella insisted that I must. I rose slowly and reluctantly from my chair, went to the telephone, and prayed for guidance. Then, with trembling hands, I dialed the number.

When Warren answered I didn't know quite what to say, but then I was already saying it. "Warren—I have good news for you. I can return the two thousand dollars you gave for the land. Escrow closes today at four o'clock, and we're short three thousand dollars. We're going to lose the property, so you'll get your money back."

My friend cleared his throat and said, "Bob, we can't allow that to happen. I've got to do more for the church. Meet me in two hours at the Bank of America on Main Street in Santa Ana, and I'll withdraw the money from my account and give it to you."

If there was anybody in the world who believed in what we were doing more than I did, and had a greater commitment to it, it was Warren Gray. It was all I could do to keep my composure as I said, "Thank you, Warren; I'll be there!"

I put the phone back in its cradle and went to Arvella. I enfolded her and Jeanne Anne in my arms and let myself go. In broken tones I cried, "Thank you, God! Thank you, Arvella! And thank you, Warren!"

I thought about the verse that I had quoted back in Newkirk as the community gathered in church to find strength after the tornado:

God moves in a mysterious way.
His wonders to perform.
He plants his footsteps on the sea
And rides upon the storm.

We were seeing a break in the storm clouds—finally!

I went into the bathroom and washed my face. Then I went back to Arvella, Bobby, and Jeanne Anne, giving each of them a big kiss, and repeated the same Bible verse I'd used on the day of our first service in the drive-in: "If you have faith as a mustard seed, you will say to this mountain, 'move!' . . . and it will move; And nothing will be impossible for you" (Matthew 17:20).

With a light heart I said, "Honey, this time we're on our way! I *know* we're on our way!"

I got to the bank a few minutes before Warren. I saw him park and slowly, painfully remove his body from his old green Buick. I ran over to him and took his arm, and we walked side by side into the bank.

Warren ordered a cashier's check for three thousand dollars, made against his savings account. He handed me the check and said, "I'm doing this because Rosie needs that drive-in."

We walked out of the bank. Warren got into his car and drove the twenty miles back home. I walked one block south of the bank to the title company, stepping into the lobby just one hour before the four o'clock deadline.

I went to the counter and laid eighteen thousand dollars before the escrow officer.

The words, "I will build My church!" came back to me with full force. God was taking title to His ten acres!

But now that we had contracted to purchase that property, we were obligated for an additional four hundred dollars a month on our mortgage. The few critics still with us in the small congregation grumbled, "Where does Schuller think he'll get the money to make the mortgage payments?"

I had no idea, of course. But God did.

The next Sunday morning a check for one hundred dollars was dropped into our offering. None of us recognized the names on the draft—Vern and Lavon Dragt—but I wrote an appreciation letter to the donors. The next week a check in the same amount was in the offering from the same people, and the following week the same. Over the course of the first four Sundays after the property was purchased, the hundred-dollar checks from the Dragts provided the four hundred dollars we needed for that month's payment on the land!

By that time, everyone was paying attention. I decided I needed to know who these people were, where they had come from so unexpectedly and providentially, and what their interests and intentions were.

So I called on them in the new home they had just moved into in Orange County. I found a handicapped husband, his wife, and three children.

Back when I was preaching from the tarpaper rooftop of the Orange Drive-in Theater four years earlier, Vern Dragt was employed slapping wet plaster on new houses in El Monte, twenty-five miles away.

One night he came home from work complaining to his wife of a headache. The pain became more intense, and Lavon was concerned. Vern was a prize-winning athlete, exceptionally strong and able-bodied, and he "never got headaches."

She called a doctor, and several hours later received the shock of her life. Her husband had polio. He was placed in an iron lung for treatment. Days, weeks, and months passed as he lingered between life and death. Finally, with their meager savings drained by medical expenses, Lavon had announced to her family, "I'm getting a job."

This wasn't easy for a young mother of three children—a woman with no professional skills, no special training, no college degree. Then she ran across an opportunity to sell a product called Tupperware. "All I've got to do is talk," she said, "and I have lots of experience doing that!"

She responded to the opportunity, and she gave a tithe of ten percent of her first check to her little church. She expanded her business and soon had others working for her. She continued to give her tithe every Sunday. Debts were gradually paid off, and Vern recovered enough to get out of the iron lung.

But since there were no muscles to speak of left in his arms, he would never be able to go back to plastering. Instead, he took over the "back office" of his wife's Tupperware business.

Together, they were on their way to a huge success. In the years to come, they would develop the largest single sales organization in the history of the Tupperware Company, building the business to more than six hundred associates. The size of those weekly tithe checks grew accordingly, and they continued for the next fifteen years to help pay off our entire mortgage.

As our plans for the new church continued, we sold the beautiful little chapel designed by Richard Shelley for a hundred and ten thousand dollars—forty thousand more than it had cost us—to a Baptist congregation that's still in it. Our profit on that sale confirmed my belief that good architecture is always a good investment.

As for the land, the site we had chosen "out in the sticks" sat directly in what would become the hub of three freeways, now called the "Orange Crush," the crossroads for all the surrounding cities! We also would find ourselves located only a mile below

Disneyland! God was answering my heart's prayer with a much better location than I could have dreamed of or foreseen.

We were living once again on the edge of tomorrow!

XXV

"Richard Shelley? This is Bob Schuller calling. I have another job for you. Our new "walk-in/drive-in church"!

There was silence. Even though we'd worked together before and he knew the nature of my enthusiasm, he seemed taken aback. "A walk-in/drive-in church?" he said questioningly. "Never heard of such a thing!"

"I have a sketch," I explained. "Let me show it to you."

At his office, Shelley looked over my little drawing, then scratched his head.

"You need a bigger and better architect than I am," he said. He handed me a copy of *Time* magazine. On the cover was a photograph of Los Angeles architect Richard Neutra.

"For what you have in mind, you need Richard Neutra," he said confidently.

I drove up to Los Angeles to meet this esteemed architect Neutra and to show him our plans. But then, instead of asking Neutra to work for us, I asked an impertinent question: "Why should I hire you to do this job?"

Neutra's response was immediate. "Because if you hire me, your buildings will never go out of style." Now, nearly a half-century later, I have to say that he was correct in his assessment.

Neutra didn't speak of a personal faith in God the same way that I did. But he held that God had given the human being a built-in tranquilizing system that's triggered by a response to nature.

He said that the "green pastures and still waters" of Psalm 23, and the fact that God had first placed man and woman in a garden, were the foundation of his architectural philosophy. He also pointed to the renewal of spirit and energy that people feel after spending time in the mountains, by a lake or a stream, or at the seashore.

"Architecture should be realistic," Neutra taught me, "in being shaped by the biology of the creature who will live in the structure. The structure you need must be tranquil. Some plants are dramatic such as cacti. In my designing, I use tranquil trees and shrubs, with quiet water."

This perspective resonated within me. Ever since, I've been adamant that all permanent structures on our campus be true to Neutra's philosophy of "biorealism."

"Creative communication doesn't happen in an environment of tension, but in an environment of peace," he went on to explain. "Human beings are creatures designed to be creative communicators, so the eye and the ear should feed peace thoughts to the mind."

My own memories of sky, water, clouds, and trees confirmed Neutra's philosophy, and I knew that it would resonate with others as well. I had learned, in my more than thirty-five hundred calls on people in Orange County during my first two years in California, that one of the things people wanted most was a place of peace. They weren't able to get away every weekend, so they needed a church that would be a refuge from the stresses and strains of urban life.

Richard Neutra and I worked together to develop this kind of an environment. There were those who believed—and still are those who believe—that fountains, waterfalls, magnificent flower gardens, and sweeping lawns were extravagant, a waste of money.

But money isn't the issue. It never is. The issue is the well-being of the human psyche and the human soul. Nature is a beautiful gift of God. My Uncle Henry once said to one of my critics on this matter, "Ah, but the eye needs feeding too."

But then Neutra said to me something that really went against all I'd ever known—and would require me to once again go to the edge. "There will be no stained glass in any of my building designs," he ordered. "Nothing should be allowed to come between the eye and the sky, the clouds, the trees, the flowers, the fountains, and the tranquilizing pools of water. At least one entire wall of each building that I design will be glass, so that the interiors will be flooded with the light and beauty of the exterior."

Do away with the stained glass? But stained-glass windows, treasures of the churches of old, were practically holy relics! In the Middle Ages they'd told the story of Christ to the illiterate. I was a storyteller, and to me stained glass was like a treasured antique book! Nonetheless something drew me to what Neutra was saying. I remembered vividly sitting by the Floyd River and preaching at its edge. I thought about how much I loved preaching outdoors in the drive-in. And I remembered what Arvella had said to me that day when we first entertained the thought of trying to use a drive-in theater: "There's something very special about worshiping God outdoors."

These Neutra-inspired insights would dominate my next forty years of architectural development. What I had learned from him was this, in a nutshell: structure and space shouldn't compete for attention; structure and space should have mutually respectful emotional intercourse!

In September 1959 about one hundred cars unloaded nearly three hundred curious people onto the empty ten acres on Lewis Street south of Chapman.

Long ribbons flying from stakes marked the outline of the building. Ceremonially, members of the consistory and I turned over the first spadeful of dirt for what would become a multipurpose building containing a fellowship hall, offices, and Sunday school rooms, the first of four Neutra buildings on our ten-acre garden campus. It was a perfect solution for our immediate needs, and the first of many architectural pieces of art to be built in the next four decades.

By the end of the fifth year we were all together in one location. This new fellowship hall could accommodate nearly two hundred

Sunday morning worshipers. During the week, it also functioned as a place for all kinds of small groups and potluck suppers.

We then also built a temporary open-air platform where I could stand—as I'd done for five years on the snackbar rooftop of the drive-in theater. From this platform I could deliver my message to those who would come for an eleven o'clock "drive-in" worship service. At our new site we were able to accommodate seven hundred cars.

All of this would be built largely with volunteer labor, men from the church and I spending all day each Saturday at the task, our wives bringing over food for the noon and evening meals.

Even my aging, arthritic Dad came to help, and he and I together would hammer nails as we'd done when we'd rebuilt the farmhouse all those years before.

On Easter Sunday 1960, we gather to dedicate our new multipurpose building—fellowship hall, worship center, Sunday school venue, and office facility—uniting the congregation.

I'm standing in the pulpit and I can see my audience of drive-in parishioners in their own "home." Everything feels so right. Our move has been a tremendous success. I'm looking out over the sea of cars that I've seen every week for the past five years: the old blue Chevrolet, the brown Ford, the not-so-new-anymore Chrysler. But in the back row one car is missing—the old green Buick. My tears begin to fall as the service begins.

Just two days before the groundbreaking for her "walk-in/drive-in church"—the one she and her husband had done so much to build—Rosie Gray died. Her life had served a high and holy purpose.

XXVI

The nation was about to enter what would be a searing and scarring decade—one that would threaten to tear the nation apart, inflaming animosities between young and old, black and white, liberal and conservative.

But those same conflicts had simmered throughout the nation's history. And throughout the twentieth century the tensions would rage between proponents of "left-wing" politics and those favoring "right-wing" politics, between those describing themselves primarily as "progressive" and those characterizing themselves primarily as "patriotic."

At the end of World War II we had shifted our national energy from fighting an extreme "right-wing" foe, Nazi Germany, to fighting an extreme "left-wing" foe, Soviet communism. At that time, in the late forties and early fifties, Joseph McCarthy, a Wisconsin senator, led a series of congressional investigations into communist infiltration of the Washington power structure.

Whatever the motivation of those who began the process, there's no doubt that the hearings got out of hand and turned into a "witch hunt." Lives were ruined. Books were banned. A "blacklist" was created by Hollywood to prevent anyone associated with "left-wing" causes from being involved in movies, television, or radio. Many innocent people who simply refused to testify against friends found themselves unemployable.

But there was blame to be shared on both sides. Many people in "progressive" circles simply didn't want to believe that Stalin, the Soviet leader, was a monster. The more the "right wing" railed that there was a communist lurking under every bed, and in every progressive cause, the more the "left wing" refused to accept valid evidence of Soviet labor camps, political murders, theft of nuclear secrets, and infiltration into American society.

This atmosphere of distrust and these exaggerated accusations continued throughout the fifties, which is when I made my own naive excursion into politics.

One day a long-time member of our church called me with a proposition: "Reverend Schuller, I'd like to pay for you to go hear the lectures of a famous Australian psychiatrist, Dr. Fred Schwarz. He's giving a three-day seminar in Anaheim, lecturing on the psychology behind communism."

Being a student of human behavior, I was fascinated by the concept and enthusiastically accepted her gift.

On Thursday, the first day of the seminar, I walked into the meeting hall to a sea of faces that were serious and intense. I felt intellectually stimulated from the environment alone. Then Dr. Schwarz took the podium.

His lecture was like a survey course in twentieth-century world history. He went back to the ravages of World War I, which had led to the Russian Revolution. He told how that uprising had been hijacked by a group of zealots called Bolsheviks, and how their leader, Vladimir Lenin, had been determined to turn Russia, overnight, into the very model of a new "scientific" state built on the principles of Karl Marx. To protect that revolution, he had also determined to overthrow capitalism everywhere else on the planet.

The Western powers, of course, had been just as determined to stamp out this "virus" of Bolshevism—or communism, as it became known—before it reached their shores. The first "Red Scare" was born in America, with deportations and raids on any organization that was out of the mainstream, including labor unions and even veterans seeking a bonus for wartime service.

I listened, relishing the history lesson, but I still wasn't sure what this lecture had to do with the psychology of communism. Then, bringing us into the present, Dr. Schwarz made a statement that caught me completely off guard: "There are religious leaders fronting for communism in America."

No way! I couldn't possibly accept that! What was the evidence?

But then he went on: "There are also corporate leaders in America, posing as capitalists, who are really part of the communist conspiracy!"

He spoke of "friends of Russia," and I knew who he meant. I had read of Dr. Armand Hammer of Los Angeles, the head of Occidental Petroleum. He was always in the news in connection with his trade deals with Russia. I would later discover that this man Hammer was the son of a Jewish exile from Russia who had been one of the six founding members of the Communist Party in the United States!

I had never been able to make all the various pieces of the Hammer story add up, and maybe this dark interpretation was the answer. Maybe he really was part of the "worldwide communist conspiracy" that politicians like McCarthy always spoke of.

But . . . religious leaders? No way.

I drove home in a swirl of confusion. I knew that a great many wild and exaggerated accusations had been made during the various Red Scares. And I knew for certain that not *every* leader trying to improve the lives of working people or black people was a closet communist. Capitalism wasn't always kind, and our democracy was far from perfect. Good people from many different points of view were trying to improve society. On the other hand, I thought about Dr. Schwarz's review of history, which had included the story of dupes and "fellow travelers"—well-meaning people, motivated by genuine hopes for a better world, who had been used and manipulated by Soviet agents.

Within days following this seminar, I received a call from another parishioner, Clyde Doyle, a very respected U.S. congressman, who invited me to go deep-sea fishing with him and his family.

Now *this* was a breath of fresh air.

I had loved to fish as a boy, and fishing far offshore in the blue Pacific would be quite a charge! I certainly would have bigger fish to fry than those I'd caught from the lazy Floyd. It began as a delightful day lazing around on Doyle's boat.

But then politics reared its ugly head.

Doyle started telling me about communism's growing influence in the States. And he was a liberal Democrat! He was no right-wing extremist.

He served on a House committee that had been encouraged by Franklin Roosevelt, the ultimate liberal Democrat, to investigate "communist infiltration" in the dock-workers' union. *Man, I thought, if Roosevelt, the friend of the working man, called a "class traitor" by the rich, would go to such lengths, there really must be something going on!* My concern grew.

Shortly after our fishing trip, Congressman Doyle attended meetings in San Francisco looking into communist activities on the waterfront there. The press exploded, accusing the committee of "right-wing" extremism. Clyde became a pariah to liberals.

On the congressman's next visit home to Southern California, I probed him: "How can you handle these terrible things that they say about you?"

He answered, "You think that *our* press is bad—you should read what the Soviet press in Moscow is saying about us! I'll send you copies of *Pravda*."

A week later his letter from Washington was on my desk, with clippings from the Soviet newspaper. *Pravda* had attacked the House committee, labeling its members as vicious "fascists."

Three weeks later, with this information fresh in my mind, I received a pamphlet printed by the National Council of the Churches of Christ. I had just set down a cup of coffee on the side table next to an easy chair where my parishioners normally sat. It had been a long morning of counseling, and I was glad to have a small break when I could finally take some time to read. *What would the National Council of Churches have to report this month,* I wondered. I had always supported the council, and I was one of their chief promoters in California.

Then, as I drew the newsletter out of the envelope, I was struck by a headline that made my heart stop! I jumped from my chair and rushed to my desk. I dug through the week's papers until I found the clippings from *Pravda*.

I couldn't believe what I was seeing!

I laid the two documents—the *Pravda* clipping and the pamphlet from the National Council of the Churches of Christ—side by side on my desk. Almost word for word, the identical diatribe appeared in each document!

It really was true then. The higher-ups of the entire Protestant church were echoing communist accusations! They were being duped!

Then it dawned on me. For a long time there had been only two camps: communists and anti-communists. Now what I saw happening was the council trying to lead an "*anti*-anti-communist" movement in America's mainline churches!

I fell back into my chair, stunned. But what should I do about it?

What I didn't recognize that day was that a shadow was beginning to rise up and out of this politically charged atmosphere, a shadow that would loom as a threat to the very emergence of my young mission and my still-evolving message. I didn't see its advance. But for a time it would hover over me, darkening my focus, dimming my vision, and distracting my God-ordained direction.

Bewildered, disillusioned—those words described me well! I decided that Fred Schwarz had to be on to something. I became convinced that he was seeing the dangers and the hidden agendas that none of the rest of us were seeing. I went to my pulpit and preached a sermon about anti-communist politics, and I disassociated myself from the National Council of Churches.

The morning after my first political sermon, the daily newspaper in Garden Grove ran the following headline on page one: "Schuller Blasts Judas in the National Council."

What had I done? Politics wasn't my mission. That wasn't how the world should see me. My church! Would it survive this? I didn't know what to do. Was I right? Was I wrong? The whole thing was one big mess!

Then the phone rang. It was Dr. Bob Shuler from First Methodist Church in Santa Ana. "*You're* the Judas!" he screamed. Then he really let me have it: "Someday the name Ichabod will be carried over your church!" (In the Old Testament that name stood for "the glory has departed.")

I was targeted for abuse by ministers from all the mainline Protestant denominations—Methodists, Presbyterians, and Episcopalians among them. And included in these protesters were some of my closest friends, pastors who had been in my pastoral support circle, deriding me angrily from their public pulpits. Ostracized by the religious community on all sides, I was dismayed and crushed. It seemed that you could question the Bible and be accepted as a scholar, but if you criticized the National Council of Churches, you were seen as the heretic of heretics.

Even my denomination, which was a member of the National Council of Churches, suddenly suspected that, because I'd befriended some conservatives, I'd become an extreme anti-communist. I was falsely accused of belonging to the John Birch Society, the private organization that had become a self-appointed CIA, banning books, making wild claims against everything from the United Nations to fluoridation in our water, and trying to find "communist infiltrators" anywhere and everywhere.

Then the next pamphlet from the National Council arrived. Pastors were warned about the dangers of anti-communism. In short, it carried pontifical orders along these lines: "All preachers in all churches that belong to the National Council are to go to the pulpit and preach against the John Birch Society. It must be stopped and its members disowned! They are all inflicted with paranoia."

All the local pastors in the mainline churches obeyed the order—except for Robert Schuller. I couldn't, and I wouldn't, because I sincerely believed that many of the *anti*-anti-communists were guilty of the very things for which they were attacking the anti-communists—most notably paranoia, looking for the worst in humans!

I wrestled for many months with the negative environment that hung over the community, the church, and me. Secretly, I began to entertain the thought of resigning from the ministry in order to join with Dr. Schwarz in promoting his message. I was drawing dangerously close to committing professional and spiritual suicide.

It was then that my wife gave me, once again, her timely and wise counsel: "Step aside from your anti-communist rhetoric, Bob. Stay out of politics and focus on Jesus Christ and positive thinking."

I listened. I agonized. I prayed. I tried to close the door on politics and focus on helping people with their private hurts. People filled with love don't focus on hate. People who are emotionally healthy don't spend their energy concocting suspicions and wild conspiracy theories.

I went to my pulpit and launched a positive series of sermons that I hoped would hit the taproot of the paranoia. The first message was entitled "Believe the Best About People."

Henceforth I would stay neutral; that was my plan. Based on the priority and call of my north-star Bible verse, I returned to my innate and passionate charge of being a "bridge-builder." I wouldn't allow myself to be positioned on either side.

This would prove to be one of the best decisions I ever made, and I knew even as I made it that I was doing the right thing. However, the consequences from this whole debacle had left me, once again, feeling the loneliness of life on the edge. I found myself isolated, a lonely minister in neutral territory, during this sad, sad time of my life.

Meanwhile, for many of the clergy around me, politics and religion would continue to swirl and twirl in a dangerous and macabre dance that seemed to grow more and more divisive as the sixties came along. The political issues would shift, but they would be unrelenting in their assault. The church would continue to feel pressure as its leaders and congregants tried to make religious sense out of political issues.

Even the most respected men of the cloth weren't agile enough to escape the decade's political tensions, as Dr. Norman Vincent Peale would painfully discover.

The 1960 presidential campaign brought before the United States the possibility of the first Roman Catholic head of state, John F. Kennedy. The issue erupted into heated debate. A meeting of Protestant ministers on the East Coast drafted a statement warning against a Catholic in the Oval Office. I was puzzled as to why Dr. Peale chose to be their spokesperson, given that he had always been ecumenical. But, ill-advised, caught in that same whirlpool of political mayhem, Dr. Peale fell victim to imprudence and delivered the statement.

Understandably, the reaction against Dr. Peale was huge! I watched, grieving and aghast, as gross and unfair accusations were heaped on my friend, tarnishing his well-deserved image of wisdom and fairness. In despair he resigned his position at Marble Collegiate Church. The nation rejected Peale's advice and elected Kennedy over Nixon. Then, fortunately, Dr. Peale listened to his father's wise advice and withdrew his resignation from the church. But my continued friendship with him raised some eyebrows.

As I watched what began to happen across the continent as social activism replaced the political furor of the fifties, I agonized and I prayed. The clergy were sincere in embracing protest and political action, but politics had divided many churches and even destroyed some ministries. I didn't follow that call, tempting as it may have been at times. Instead I held to my mission from Isaiah 58:12: "You shall be called the repairer of the breach and the restorer of paths to dwell in."

XXVII

The decade was indeed searing, it was indeed scarring, but I would also find the 1960s soaring for my ministry, beginning with the tenth anniversary of my seminary graduation, my marriage, and my ordination.

We now had three children—Sheila, Robert, and Jeanne Anne—and the church, which I loved like another child.

And my how they *all* had grown! After five years, the Garden Grove Community Church was now seven hundred people strong. We had added to our full-time staff a custodian, a gardener, and a minister of education. We had created the programs that people had said they wanted when I was making all those house calls years before. God was building His church, and I found myself standing at the threshold of something incredible.

Religious giants began to rise up in the land, making their positive voices heard. They would be responsible for putting strong wings back onto the faith: Fulton Sheen, Norman Vincent Peale, Billy Graham, and Martin Luther King, Jr. (the only one of these whom, to my regret, I would never meet).

In 1960, Fulton Sheen was one of the biggest names in religious leadership, and he was the first television preacher in history. As the new decade dawned, his televised program, *Life Is Worth Living*, was being seen by an estimated thirty million people a week, generating, on average, eight thousand letters a day.

His brilliant mind blended the truths of psychology, philosophy, and theology (my kind of man!) with more creativity and innovation than any person had done to date. In the years to come, Billy Graham would praise Fulton Sheen as "the greatest communicator of the twentieth century." And no one could dispute that claim.

One evening after dinner I withdrew to the tiny living room where we had our small black-and-white television. I pulled the POWER knob, and there he was, his kind and dramatic face lit with a holy energy. He cut a commanding figure in his bishop's robe as he paced back and forth, slowly, pensively. Then he halted and looked at me; it looked for all the world as if he were peering through the screen and right into my living room.

"Is Christ the Super . . . Star?" he asked. "No! He's the Super . . . Scar!" Fulton Sheen's voice and declaration pierced me, my weekly inspirational shot in the arm. I'd never thought of Christ in that way! Leaning forward on the sofa, clean lined and taut, I listened intently, sensing this man's impact but having no idea how powerfully he was about to influence my life's work.

"How did he ever come to preach on television anyway?" I said aloud. A new curiosity peaked in me. I pushed my black framed glasses up on the bridge of my nose in concentration. Then I settled back.

"Who knows," Arvella said, "I'm just glad he did! Keeps you out of trouble!" She teased as she settled in beside me.

It never crossed my mind that television might be for me as well. I was too busy building a church, which is why I needed such inspiration from a spiritual leader like Sheen.

By 1961 Neutra had completed the architectural drawings for the main sanctuary of our walk-in/drive-in church. It would be the world's first structure designed to combine two congregations at the same time and in the same place. The scheme was simple. The pulpit would be built just on the inside of a wall one hundred and sixty feet long, facing the drive-in church parking lot (which would accommodate seven hundred cars). There I would have eye contact with both the walk-in and drive-in parishioners. But I had yet to raise the funds.

The ten acres we had purchased for sixty-six thousand dollars was, of course, an incredible deal. But it was only one-fourth of a forty-acre orange and walnut grove. I watched sadly as most of the rest of the thirty acres was divided up and sold to others: ten acres for a proposed shopping-center site to the Kaiser Corporation, two acres to the county for a flood control site, another six acres for a condominium development, and ten acres for thirty-eight private homes. I was wishing we could have bought all forty acres, but we didn't have even enough money to build our sanctuary on the ten acres we already owned!

Both congregations—walk-in and drive-in—were now uniting to raise the money. Our bank, Farmers & Merchants, wouldn't be in a position to loan the half million dollars needed to build this building. We would have to raise it from private investors.

We made a bold decision: we would proceed with construction of this large sanctuary alongside our new multipurpose building as fast—or as slowly—as promissory note money came in from readers answering our fundraising ads in the *Reformed Church Herald*. Meanwhile, we did have ten thousand dollars cash in our building fund, which we used to dig the trenches for the foundation. Then, as soon as another ten thousand dollars came in, we poured the cement footings.

Now we were standing, living, and building on the edge.

"We'll need another thirty thousand dollars next week to order the steel beams, or we'll have to halt construction," the foreman told me one Friday. "By Monday we need the cash."

All the money raised had been coming to us in amounts between five hundred and one thousand dollars. I calculated that, at this rate, it would take an entire month to raise the thirty thousand dollars to keep construction going, but I had only three days!

I was prepared on Monday to order a halt to the project. I woke on that day to a miracle. In the morning mail came a letter from a New York family who had been heretofore unknown by and unaffiliated with our ministry. In that one letter was a single check for thirty thousand dollars! This family wanted to buy one promissory note to mature in twenty years!

The steel beams were ordered without delay. Cash continued to come in, and the now-famous Neutra building went up on schedule. By November of 1961 all of the five hundred thousand dollars had been raised, and the dedication was set for the first Sunday of that month.

Dr. Norman Vincent Peale seemed a natural choice to preach at our first service in the new sanctuary. Our people still talked about the stirring message he had given at our drive-in church four years before.

I asked and he accepted.

All Saturday night the technicians worked to complete the sound system, while carpet-layers worked frantically to cover the floor. At nine o'clock Sunday morning, with people lined up by the hundreds for the first service, *the work was still going on!*

When the workers put away their tools and we were at last able to open the doors, the sanctuary crowded with a thousand persons seated inside and another thousand people sitting in five hundred cars in the drive-in. As the organ erupted in a triumphant call to worship, Dr. Peale and I led the procession. It was a beautiful sunny Sunday—November 6, 1961. He whispered to me, "What a feeling of peace is in this place."

It worked! Biorealism in architecture had had its desired effect!

The half-block-long glass walls allowed all of nature to flow in. The sky of blue with soft white clouds decorated the sanctuary. Twelve gentle fountains tumbled with tranquillity from a long pool of water outside the east wall of the large sanctuary evoking memories of preaching on the banks of the Floyd. The outside came in. And the mood of tranquillity worked a miracle. Worshipers relaxed—intuitively and instantly. The peace of sky, clouds, and water put the hearts and spirits of worshipers in a mood receptive to the ideas that would be communicated. Everyone sensed an atmosphere of prayer that generated peace through the reflection of nature.

Gone were the walls that might have been a barrier to newcomers. I had taken a big risk on the theory that a "natural" atmosphere would be less obstructive to unchurched visitors, many of whom might be nervous around the intensely religious symbolism of traditional church architecture. The risk proved to be a huge success. We had created a place where spiritual communication could be freely experienced by all!

The senses were being intentionally and effectively uplifted toward the spirit through architecture! A Bible verse came alive for me that day:

"The heavens declare the glory of God!"

I had fallen in love with God's nature as a child, and now, after almost six years of preaching under the sky at the drive-in, I felt at home. If only the sanctuary ceiling had been glass too—that would have been perfect!

When Dr. Peale and I reached the pulpit that dedication morning, the choir sang its triumphant opening anthem, "Holy, Holy, Holy!" I pushed a button at the pulpit and two giant sections of the glass wall beside the pulpit slid back slowly, majestically, silently, creating an opening in the wall twenty-four feet high and twenty-four feet wide! It seemed as if the heavens were rolling in. And I was able to step onto an outside balcony to see, and smile at, the drive-in worshipers before me.

As a warm breeze poured in, I smelled the scent of gardenia carried on the wings of the breeze. I heard the bells ring from the five bell-frames that rose ninety feet above the church roof. I felt a surge of satisfaction and exhilaration—that same happy feeling that I'd experienced years before as a boy. I'd arrived at my "somewhere," and I had no plans to leave—not ever!

We were now a church. We even had sunny overflow seating: another thousand chairs could be set up on the large green lawn directly below my open-air pulpit. We'd need them many a Sunday in the years to come.

Attendance would soar in the sixties to over two thousand people each week, making this the second largest Reformed Church in America—second only to Marble Collegiate in New York, where Dr. Peale routinely spoke to two overflowing services with a total attendance of four thousand. And the Neutra design began to win numerous architectural awards.

But while I was having this soaring experience, the rest of America remained scorched and scarred from political turmoil, especially regarding the nation's policy in Vietnam.

After President Kennedy was assassinated in 1963, President Johnson massively increased the ground and air war in Vietnam. Members of my church would die in this losing effort. Protests and peace marches became a familiar sight on university campuses and on the nightly news. Once again clergy would find themselves in the midst of a political struggle to discern their role and their message.

Martin Luther King, Jr., who had moved to Atlanta to pastor his father's Ebenezer Baptist Church, launched the civil rights movement. The flames of that movement quickly spread, ignited by a national passion. But in white Anglo-Saxon Protestant Garden Grove, California, the civil rights movement seemed far away.

One night, though, as I was driving home from a church meeting, I saw a group of neighbors gathered on the front lawn of one of the tract houses. I stopped to see if something was wrong.

"Has there been an accident?" I asked one of the bystanders.

"No," he said. "A colored family just moved in."

Here, I realized, was one of those moments in which fate hangs in the balance, both positive thinking and negative thinking capable of tipping the scale. Something "unusual" happens, so the first person stops to observe. Because of this person standing around watching, others stop, and in time a crowd builds up. And crowds are subject to manipulation, their passions easily excited. A demagogue fueled by hatred or even suspicion can engage the energy of the crowd and incite all manner of trouble. On the other hand, someone of goodwill can take that negative energy and dissipate it.

"But why the crowd?" I asked him. It was a simple question, but one worth asking. What's so unusual about a black family trying to enjoy the same pleasures in life as any of the rest of us?

He didn't have an answer for me. He just shrugged, stuck his hands in his pockets, and walked away. And in time, everyone else did the same. It was a non-event.

Not long after that I read an article in the local paper in which a new black resident was interviewed about his experiences in coming to the area. I was delighted by his witty response. He said, "Here they see only one color . . . orange."

As the protests throughout the nation grew in number and fervor, I was concerned and confused. At Hope College, we had been taught never to raise our voices in the street, but had our teachers been naive and complacent in their small-town comforts? "Too easily protests lead to violence. Use the courts and Congress," we had been taught. But now Dr. King's marches were succeeding, educating America to the sin of racism.

As the sixties continued, I focused on my studies in the science of human behavior. I followed and was impressed by Dr. Victor Frankl's teachings on the basic differences in the evolution of psychiatry in our century. He explained that there existed two contradictory models in human thinking—collectivism and individualism. Such contradictions, Frankl said, often remain unspoken, but they permeate philosophy, psychology, psychiatry, theology, sociology, economics, and politics.

In one of our conversations, Frankl said, "Freud could never and was never accepted in Russia or any communist state because Freudianism was finally and ultimately and basically . . . individualism—and that, in its core, is unavoidably and irreconcilably on a philosophical collision course with collectivism."

Much of the twentieth century could be understood as the clash between these two mindsets. My own personal history leaned toward individualism. Collectivism, in my mind, was laudable if it generated a sharing spirit within a community. But as a philosophy, in my perspective, it all too often leads to paternalism, which doesn't motivate or encourage the individual to dream, nor does it engage a person's abilities to surmount the injustices in society.

Collectivism was in fact the polar opposite of my message! But I felt called to pastor people on both sides of these ideologies! I couldn't allow myself to drift toward one side or the other.

But it hadn't always been so. I had come from Calvinism, with its strong collectivist perspective, a legacy of its mother faith, Roman Catholicism. The personal salvation of one's eternal soul was largely, if not totally, dependent on "belonging to the church," being "a member of the right religious club." If you were a fully accredited, "card-carrying" member of the right holy club, you would be admitted through the sacred security gate when your soul transitioned from time to eternity—from earth to heaven.

So the collectivist mindset would create and conceive of a collectivist strategy for personal redemption. Infants would be put in a favorable position in the club by a sacrament called baptism. But admission to "full membership" in the saving club would focus on the collective more than on the individual model. Confirmation classes prepared and presumably qualified a person to be accepted into and approved by the institution that could guarantee full and eternal privileges for that solitary soul now "saved" into the faith through "membership" in the community. That's the stance that Reformed theology took.

The biblical basis was found in Old Testament "covenant theology." This theology focused on the fact that God had called together a "chosen race" in Israel and had promised a blessing to Abraham and to his "seed after him." Because of that ancient covenant babies were born into the holy club. It wasn't a personal decision.

The founders of Protestant Christianity—Martin Luther and John Calvin—made no effort to reform the heavily collective model operating in the theology of salvation. God had His chosen community, and admission was weighted in favor of the collectivist perspective. The "family birth" was very important in this covenant theology, and church leaders controlled the collectivist community of believers. When Livingston launched a mission to Africa in the nineteenth century, the whole concept was controversial. "They aren't part of our 'family,'" was the prevailing attitude in Anglican England.

Meanwhile, evangelism aimed at a private individual's personal decision forced a subconscious conflict with the unspoken collectivist worldview of the church. I was shocked when I first witnessed a call to personal salvation at an evangelical service during my years at Hope College. Billy Graham, then a minister of a little church in Illinois, had come to preach in my college chapel. Our male quartet had provided the "special music." At the end of his sermon Billy had invited "individuals," not groups or classes of people, to "come forward and accept Jesus Christ as their personal Savior."

In a similar way, my own theology now focused on individual responsibility. And so I would stick to my strategy: plant seeds of a positive faith, water those seeds, and encourage the resulting faith to grow healthy and strong, eventually pushing out the negative.

The flowering of that strategy carried me through this tumultuous period. Three years after our Neutra sanctuary had been completed, we had more than doubled our attendance. Now another temptation came my way—an opportunity that would prove flattering and exciting.

Norman Vincent Peale, despite the flap raised by his warnings in 1960 about electing a Catholic president, had managed to remain the number-one motivational minister, still riding the crest of his monumental bestseller, *The Power of Positive Thinking.* Unbeknownst to me, he had been watching my career with interest. In fact, he sent me a copy of this memo:

May 14, 1964

Memorandum to the Elders and Deacons

From: Norman Vincent Peale

As officers and ministers of this church, we are charged with the responsibility of announcing the work of Christ in our area of His Kingdom.

We must realize that the institution that does not go forward faces inevitable decline, and we do not want to decline. And the forces of decline are very great. We are in probably the era of greatest apathy to Christianity. A whole new generation has arisen which challenges Christian morals and ideals as not in two hundred years. The only answer is to hit the situation, and hit it hard.

Required to do this are

1. Complete dedication
2. Boldness to advance, regardless of cost
3. Better organization
4. Christian evangelism in real depth

To implement this program I recommend the following:

1. The employment of Rev. Robert Schuller of the Garden Grove Reformed Church of Garden Grove, California, to be Minister of Administration and to employ his great talents and proven experience in reshaping the program and directing staff personnel; also to be the Sunday evening preacher and director of program.

"I will build my Church"—the Neutra
Sanctuary in July 1961

Left: 1961—Reverend Robert H.
Schuller—pastor of the first walk-
in/drive-in church!

Mom & Dad and the Peales with me for the dedication of the Neutra Sanctuary

Left: We're growing again! The lawn is full, the sanctuary is full, the drive-in is full. What will we do come winter?

Below: 1963—my family becomes my haven.

My father—my inspiration, my "St. Francis of Assisi" on his last visit.

Sheila's gone to college—times are changing.

Television? Me?

With Billy Graham

Pope John Paul II, at my first audience gives a special blessing to my Crystal Cathedral dream

Above: "Dig a hole!" — groundbreaking for the Crystal Cathedral

Left: The cathedral rises . . .

The cathedral is complete! It's awesome! Inside and outside.

The cathedral by sunset

In Syria with Shaykh Ahmad Kuftaro, The Grand Mufti of
Syria, before I speak at the Friday Prayer at his mosque

The Visitor's Center—International Center of Possibility Thinking

I love being a grandpa!

Our family celebrating
our 50th wedding
anniversary, June 2000

The Netherlands honors Arvella and
I each with an official tulip named
for us. (Mine is orange,
Arvella's is pink)

2. The employment of Rev. Alastair Hair of Bellevue,
Ontario, to be Minister of Evangelism, his function being to
expand spiritual call strategy within the whole church, to
organize and direct classes in spiritual study and growth, and
to have charge of the young adult program, which currently
includes over four hundred active young persons.

This proposal will cost money. But we have the money,
and I am persuaded that the stimulation of growth it will
cause will gradually absorb the extra costs. But whether it
will or not, the Lord Jesus wants us to go forward
adventurously and in faith.

The above program came to me after earnest prayer, and
to my mind it represents God's guidance. I therefore
recommend its adoption and implementation for the fall.

I recalled the day back in seminary when I had delivered a sermon to my classmates and Professor Mulder had commended me
by saying, "Bob, that message was good enough for the Marble
Collegiate Church!"

Now here it was—an invitation to make my career in New York!

I was so excited that day that I immediately called Arvella, who
didn't share my enthusiasm.

"Bob!" she exclaimed, appalled. "Raise our children in New York
City?! No way!"

But I couldn't silence the invitation's tug. For days I struggled
with my decision. Then one day the phone rang in the church
office, and Lois Wendell, my secretary, answered.

"It's Dr. Peale," she said as she peeked into my office. I picked up
the receiver and greeted my friend.

We exchanged pleasantries, and then Dr. Peale came to the
point: "How many people do you now have attending your drive-in/
walk-in church?" he asked.

"About two thousand every Sunday morning," I answered with pride, sure that this would seal the deal.

"Then stay where you are," he replied resolutely.

I was stunned! What was he saying? Don't mess with success? I wrestled with my disappointment, but only for a moment. Almost immediately, I felt relief and gratitude flood through me. I realized that God had seen the struggle inside me and was assisting me in my decision. What I really wanted was to build my own church—large or small, famous or isolated and unnoticed in far-off California.

I was content with the vote of confidence implied by Dr. Peale's invitation. And then he added, "But I'll have you come and preach from my pulpit."

On three separate summer Sundays I did—and I felt that I had truly "arrived": I had been recognized as a preacher without having to relinquish my own mission.

It was during this same period that I was able to welcome my father and mother for a visit to California. I met them at the train and was excited to show them all that we had accomplished here on the West Coast—my "somewhere."

"Dad, what do you think?" I asked. Since he had hammered nails with me during an early construction phase, I was curious to see what he thought of the finished product. He smiled and nodded his approval.

We walked slowly through the Neutra sanctuary—the fountains leaping and playing a welcome. His arthritis made it difficult for him to climb, but he did, up into the pulpit. I took him to where I stood when I preached, and I opened the doors for a dramatic presentation. I pointed out across the empty, black parking lot of the drive-in, much as Dad had done years before when he had pointed out the "big-time road."

"Dad," I said, "Sunday mornings this whole parking lot is filled with cars. Inside those cars are people who hustle and bustle around all week, and then they come here on Sunday for a boost to get them through the week to come. What you see out there, and what you see in here," I gestured to the empty sanctuary, "this is my church, Dad."

Tears cradled gently at the edge of his eyelids, and a slight grin curled at the edges of his wrinkled cheeks. "It's beautiful, Son," he said. "Just beautiful." My mom nodded her agreement.

I showed him my robe, and he ran his fingers down the trim. Then the tears spilled over those lids and dropped onto the velvet.

Only weeks later, back home, Dad went outside to garden in the early midwestern spring. Dressed too lightly, he caught a cold that would turn to pneumonia. I received the call that he was dying and flew home to say my last goodbye.

"Dad?" I'm looking at the now-frail figure of my father, lying on his bed. "Dad? It's Harold." He opens his eyes now, but only slightly.

"Dad?" He turns to me and opens them fully. I say what I came to say: "I want to thank you, Dad. Your prayers—to have a son who would be a preacher—you can know that they've been answered."

Dad's brow wrinkles and he's crying. I hold him and feel his wet cheek next to mine—skin touching skin. We stay like that for a long time.

"But there's more, Dad," I say. "Arvella is pregnant again. If it's a boy, I want to name him Anthony—after you."

He nods weakly, but this time he doesn't cry. He's too tired. Quietly and peacefully, he closes his eyes for the last time.

XXVIII

With the population swelling in Orange County, and with the public acclaim for the beauty of our sanctuary by Richard Neutra, I began to envision other buildings—Sunday school classrooms, church offices, a counseling center where we could help troubled families and marriages, as well as a chapel for weddings, funerals, and quiet retreats.

I would also need room for a new dream that had been inspired by Dr. Alan Walker of Sydney, Australia. Dr. Walker had founded and was operating the world's first and only twenty-four-hour live telephone counseling center, focusing on suicide prevention and crisis intervention. It was staffed by specially trained volunteers who had been taught how to prevent the panic and self-destructive behavior that can so easily result from depression and desperation.

As we thought back to the suicide of Arvella's friend Louise during the early days of our church, this community service struck a deep chord in both of us. More and more requests had been coming to us for counseling of all kinds. If we could start a hotline, then we could be a responsive ear twenty-four hours a day.

All the buildings needed for all the functions we dreamed of would require an acre or more of additional ground space, but we didn't have it. We had only a small inner courtyard left, since parking spaces occupied so much of our ten acres.

There was room for one high-rise tower in that space, though, and it could be large enough to house offices, classrooms, counseling facilities, a chapel, and yes, the twenty-four-hour hotline. There was a lot we could still accomplish.

It came to me in a flash: we could name the tower the Tower of Hope, and the twenty-four-hour hotline could be called New Hope. Yes—now was the time to build this tower! We could place a twelve-foot cross at the top, and the entire tower would be an imposing church steeple calling to the community, "There's a church for you! There's hope for you!"

Concerned for our future growth, one day I posed my idea to Neutra. "Do you think we could go high-rise?" I asked, handing him my sketch.

Sitting at his drafting table, he looked over my plan for a twenty-five-story bell-tower with a chapel on the top floor, and offices and Sunday school rooms coming down to the main lobby. "Could this be our gathering place? Could one high-rise skyscraper with a small footprint using very little ground space accommodate all of the facilities we need?"

He pursed his lips, studying the drawings carefully, but offered no comment.

In case he needed persuading, I added, "This will be the most creative church tower ever built!"

He picked up his fine professional pencil and drew in a few lines and numbers.

I went on enthusiastically, "This won't just be a church tower; it will be a Tower of Hope! Just think, Mr. Neutra—all the tall cathedral towers in the world are only monuments. This will be a monument that serves as an instrument for dispensing hope!"

He took off his glasses and set them on his drafting table. He leaned back in his chair, crossed his arms, and looked up. The suspense was killing me. Then he nodded his head slowly up and down. I had him! He liked it; I could tell!

I said, "Draw me a picture—make it stunning—and we'll get the finances we need."

Two weeks later he submitted his architectural rendering. The tower was twenty-five stories tall, as I'd proposed, and two hundred and fifty feet high—taller than the City Hall of Los Angeles, taller by a hundred feet than the "Matterhorn" at Disneyland! In fact, it would be the tallest structure in Orange County.

The picture attracted the press, and we had all the publicity we could want. But still we had no purse.

Desperately seeking cash, I negotiated a book contract for six thousand dollars, with which I opened a Tower of Hope building fund.

The following Sunday morning I made an announcement to my congregation:

"You have to see the picture," I told them; "you have to read the story of the most exciting church tower ever built. They estimate that it will cost a million dollars. I have news for you. We have just received, this week, an anonymous gift of six thousand dollars to launch the fund; so the building *will* be built! Even if we don't get another dollar, that six thousand dollars is earning interest today, and compounded, this fund will grow into one million dollars in just over a century!" Everybody laughed.

Soon the press carried another story, this one emphasizing the height of our proposed addition. Then came a call from Neutra's office. "Bad news, Bob. I've checked into the regulations, and we can't build a twenty-five-story structure," he explained. "California earthquake laws limit the height of a high-rise building to one hundred and sixty feet! That gives you only twelve floors, with twenty feet above for a chapel."

"But I'm quoted in the press as saying that the building will reach two hundred and fifty feet!" I said. "I can't be accused of not telling the truth."

Not wanting to have promised more than I could deliver, I tried a different approach. "How about if you design a tower one hundred and sixty feet tall and put a ninety-foot cross on the top? It would then top out at two hundred and fifty feet. Would regulations allow that?"

"No problem, Bob," he reassured me, "as long as any added structure above one hundred and sixty feet isn't occupied by humans."

Then Neutra called back again. "The cross can't be built ninety feet high," he reported, "or it might start vibrating in the wind, and that could crack the structure. We *could* do it—but only with four permanent cables from the arms of the cross down to the four corners of the top of the tower."

I cringed. "No way," I said. "Go back to engineering to find another solution."

He called back two days later. "If we build the base of the cross four feet wide and gradually taper it to two feet, that would eliminate any possible vibration."

"Do it!" I said with conviction.

Now the church board made a bold decision to "speed up the raising of one million dollars from one hundred years to ten years." The motion passed. We prayed for a lead-off gift of one-tenth of the total cost—one hundred thousand dollars.

I called Vern and Lavon Dragt, whose surprise tithe had been paying the monthly mortgage on our ten acres of ground. "We like the idea of that chapel at the top of the tower," they said. Then they added, "Nothing is impossible; it just takes a while sometimes! We'll give ten thousand dollars every year for ten years. That's one hundred thousand dollars. Will that be acceptable?" Was it *acceptable?* You bet! I was overwhelmed with their generosity. I later rephrased their optimistic answer into a line that I'd preach on for years to come:

Great dreams never fail; they just take longer!

The campaign was off and running. Plans had been drawn. More promissory notes were sold for construction.

On December 4, 1964—the night following a big fundraising dinner for the Tower of Hope—our fourth child was born. "Well," I observed, "her name won't be Anthony."

As I held her tiny, warm body against my chest, my eyes grew moist with the wonder of it all. I drew her soft cheek to my own and crooned to her as Christmas carols filled the hospital halls with their seasonal melodies—all songs of joy. And so we named our fourth daughter Carol Lynn.

When we brought Carol home to our four-bedroom house in Santa Ana, waiting to welcome her were Sheila, thirteen; Bob, ten; and Jeanne, seven.

With all the attention that Carol received from all of us and from the many church members and close friends who doted on her, we became convinced that by the time she was grown, she would surely be spoiled. She needed a younger sibling, so we planned one more child; and two years and two months following the birth of Carol— on February 14, 1967—Gretchen Joy arrived. Our last.

I was lecturing that night in Indiana when the phone rang in my hotel room. It was Sheila, my oldest, telling me that Arvella had gone into delivery two weeks ahead of schedule. "Dad, you have another daughter," she said proudly.

Bobby came on the line with a note of disappointment in his voice. "Dad—it's a girl again!"

"But Bobby," I answered, "it's February 14. You wouldn't want a brother born on Valentine's Day! This day is for the girls!" We both laughed.

I felt so far from home that night, wishing that I could hold my new little valentine in my arms. I cried tears of love, joy, and gratitude.

For the tenth anniversary of our church, the congregation surprised Arvella and me with a trip to the Holy Land. They also wanted to honor Arvella for her ten years of volunteer service as pastor's wife, organist, and worship director. This outpouring of affection and appreciation moved us deeply, because it demonstrated conclusively that we now had a church united in love and mission. The vacation would also be a wonderfully romantic escape in celebration of our fifteenth wedding anniversary.

Our visit to the land where Jesus walked moved us spiritually and emotionally. Then, as an added bonus, on the way back we had the opportunity to visit Napoleon's summer home at Lake Como, in northern Italy. There I saw the most impressive line of Italian cypress trees standing nearly one hundred and fifty feet tall—elegant, firm-bodied, but so slender that they swayed gently from their broad bases to their rising, slimming tops. Wow! Suddenly I could visualize this curtain of elegant trees surrounding our open-air drive-in church! That would be incredible! But . . . impossible? After all, these trees at Lake Como were nearly two hundred years old!

Then I remembered Dad planting his apple trees after the tornado. "Harold, we don't plant trees just for ourselves," he'd said, "but for those who come after us!" His words rang through me as I looked upon the wonder of these giants.

To my dismay, when I returned home the church's board of directors didn't share my vision. They put an immediate halt to my cypress plans, voting instead to use the long, narrow space that I had wanted to devote to that gallant row of trees for additional parking. So the ground was poured over in asphalt. Black. Dead.

But I couldn't forget my dream of a glorious, lofty green curtain encircling the drive-in church. I just *knew* that someday it should become reality. So I bided my time. Then, in reviewing the minutes of the board meeting I discovered that each elder and deacon's term of office was for a certain number of years. I realized that in four years a slim majority would all see their terms expire at the same time. One week later they would be replaced in a general election. There would be a period of six days without a quorum on the board. In that time, I—as president and chairman—would have the power to act!

I began to plan for that six-day window of opportunity four years hence. I would have bulldozers waiting to rip out the asphalt covering. Then trucks could deliver my order of three-foot-tall Italian cypress. By the week's close, all could be planted! The Dragts were right:

Great dreams never fail; they just take longer!

Our momentous groundbreaking for the Tower of Hope brought
the return of Norman Vincent Peale, along with many others asking
what in the world I was up to now—building a skyscraper in the
middle of a church setting?! Members of my congregation found
themselves once again on "Schuller's Wild Ride"! Who needed
Disneyland?

Then I got another call from Neutra. "Bob, the cross is finished,"
he said. "It's made of steel plates that will take on a brown color with
natural rusting. It's lying on the factory floor in east Los Angeles.
You'd better come with me to check it out."

When I entered the vast room, my mouth must have literally
dropped open. The cross was huge! It had to be the tallest cross ever
planned for the roof of any building in the world! It was ninety-two
feet long! The four-foot base was so large that I got down on my
hands and knees and crept inside! I came out and said, "How in the
world are we going to get it to the top?"

"No problem, Bob," Neutra said. "We'll just cut it in half. We'll
raise the bottom up first with a three-hundred-foot crane. Then
we'll raise the top half and weld the two pieces in place!"

I was speechless.

During the summer of 1967, while the plans for the Tower of
Hope moved forward, I decided to attend the World Psychiatric
Congress in Madrid, Spain. I was writing my first flagship book on
possibility thinking and needed to hear what the world's leading psychiatrists were teaching. When I registered, little did I know that I
would be taking on a sharp new focus that would affect my entire
ministry for the rest of my life.

It was the closing session, made up of three lectures, that partic-
ularly impacted me. The topic for the day was "Human Values in
Psychotherapy." The first lecturer, Dr. Rome from the United
States, spoke for thirty minutes on faith. The second lecturer, Dr.

J. W. Janz from Germany, spoke on hope. The third lecturer, Dr. Segvin from Peru, spoke on love.

I couldn't believe it: this was the teaching of the Holy Bible! The last verse of the thirteenth chapter of First Corinthians reads, "And now abide faith, hope, and love . . ." Saint Paul had elevated these values two thousand years ago, and now four thousand secular psychiatrists in this esteemed gathering were being lectured to build mental health by focusing on those same values. This was a secular, not a religious, convention. And yet these were more spiritually based conclusions than many that were drawn in America's politically saturated pulpits!

Dr. Janz, with his lecture on hope, moved me dramatically though he hadn't been the first to embrace this "blend." He quoted Dr. Karl Menninger, founder of the Menninger Clinic in Topeka, Kansas, a psychiatrist I respected tremendously. I had met Menninger a few years before in the United States when, for the first time, a secular professional had braved this "dangerous" subject. Most of the profession avoided it because it blurred the boundary between psychology and "religion." Today I have in my library a personally autographed copy of Menninger's historic lecture—a gift from Menninger himself, a token of the message of hope that I now preach.

I came home from the congress in Madrid with Dr. Menninger's lecture on hope affirmed. He had risked so much to communicate this truth—that hope is vital to the survival of the human spirit. His risk-taking had surely paid great dividends. I was convinced that psychiatry and religion were merging and blending and that I could do my part to bridge the two and become truly impacting to the entire secular world! Could my preaching become a form of therapy for both the secular and the religious in my community?

Meanwhile, back in America, mainline Protestantism was in a state of near panic, trying to discover how to be relevant. The only energy seemed to come from the political call to "march in the streets" and "fight social injustice."

With the central focus on legitimate and timely opposition to racism and war and the selfish excesses of capitalism, the mental, emotional, and spiritual hurts of the average person were being totally ignored. As a result, millions of spiritually hungry souls were leaving their churches.

I returned home and launched both an alternative message and an alternative strategy for turning a declining American church around. I had survived politics. I had survived the lures of ambition. My message was now ringing clear inside of me: I was called to be a preacher, and I was called to preach hope. Nothing more and nothing less.

The skeletal structure of the lofty Tower of Hope was "topped out" in November of 1967. The successful raising of the cross chastened my pessimism. Yes! The top of the ninety-two-foot cross was two hundred and fifty-two feet above the ground! The whole county gathered in the glare of media attention as a crane lifted the huge metal pieces thirteen stories up and into place. And just as I had demanded, neon light tubes had been installed on either side.

Just before the lighting ceremony we held a banquet in the Anaheim Convention Center, across the street from Disneyland and one mile west of the church.

Then, to the two thousand people who had come to join in the celebration in person, I said, "Let's all go outdoors and light up the cross!" We walked to the convention center's parking lot, where a flatbed truck awaited us. On the truck was a table, and on the table was a telephone. Everyone in the crowd was instructed to lay his or her hands on the shoulders of the person ahead, connecting us all as one long chain of caring individuals, a symbol that together we could bring hope to others.

I picked up the phone, and we counted down as everybody reached out. In a giant wave of humanity, four thousand hands were lifted onto the shoulders in front of them. The last hand reached out and came down on my left shoulder. Not a sound was made; not a word spoken. I dialed the telephone, which was connected directly to the light switch. Suddenly in the eastern sky over the flat land of Orange County a huge white cross leaped to life in the night sky! The crowd gasped—all two thousand—never to forget this holy moment.

"The lights are on!" I pronounced to the group. "Let this be a message to the world that there is a church where the lights will *never* go out!"

As we stood in awe, still linked together in that dark night, I called out to the crowd, "We need three hundred volunteers to answer telephones. Will you volunteer to be trained?" The crowd applauded their affirmation.

In ten months the tower beneath the cross would be finished, and we would open America's first and only twenty-four-hour live, phone-based counseling center sponsored by a religious organization.

As I headed home on that night of exuberance, I wondered how we'd find a telephone number anyone could remember. Then, as suddenly as I'd recognized the problem, I thought of the solution: N-E-W H-O-P-E.

Perfect! I called the telephone company the following morning to reserve the number. "That combination is technically impossible in the city of Garden Grove," I was told. "Sorry, Dr. Schuller."

I challenged and I argued, explaining that "impossible" was a word I refused to recognize. The best the phone company could do was to say that in Anaheim it would be possible—but not in Garden Grove.

I hung up and called the telephone office in Anaheim. "I'm here at our church in Garden Grove," I explained. "We're just two blocks south of the Anaheim city limits. Could I order a telephone line from you in Anaheim to serve us here in Garden Grove?"

Silence. "Well, yes," she said. "There's no law against it—but why? No one ever does that. It doesn't make sense!"

"If I did it, could I get the telephone number N-E-W H-O-P-E?"

"Let me check. I'll call you back."

The phone rang a few minutes later. "Yes, you *can* get a private line across city boundaries. And yes, you *can* have the number N-E-W H-O-P-E," she said. Well, *that* was good news. "But it would be expensive," she added. "The monthly rate would be the same in Garden Grove, but we'd have to bring the line in just for you!"

"How much would that cost?" I asked.

"Let me call you back again," she said.

Her research didn't take long. "Are you sitting down?" she asked when she called back.

"I am. Let me have the numbers."

She dropped the figure. I couldn't believe it! "Are you sure that's all it would cost? Only six hundred dollars? I'll take it!" I hung up and let out a whoop of joy!

Finally, Arvella was going to be relieved of the awesome responsibility of being constantly available. From now on a ringing phone would always be heard and always be answered, providing "new hope" from a volunteer trained to handle the crisis.

When we dedicated the Tower of Hope on September 18, 1968, the lines started ringing 24/7/365.

Twenty-four hours a day.

Seven days a week.

Three hundred and sixty-five days a year!

Let this lighted cross forever be a silent message to the world that in this Tower of Hope there will always be an ear that is never shut, a mind that is always open, and a heart that never grows cold. To God be the glory.

The Tower of Hope was the last of the four buildings that Richard Neutra would build for us. Years later, more growth would demand more buildings to house the Hour of Power operations and other satellite ministries, and they would be built by other architects. But

Richard Neutra's Tower of Hope would forever be the centerpiece of the campus.

XXIX

The day we dedicated the Tower of Hope, Norman Vincent Peale came to preach again. It was my first morning in my new office on the twelfth floor, right beneath the two-story Chapel in the Sky.

I walked to the window and watched excitedly as the cars came down the streets from the east and the west. Then, from my lofty perspective, I saw a problem that no one else could see: the seven hundred parking spaces were all full! What I couldn't know at the time was that the next car to drive in would cost me one million dollars.

I watched as that car drove up and down the lanes of the parking area, searching for (but not finding) a place to park. I watched as that car drove out via the exit and sped up—and away.

Who was in that car? Would they ever come back? Were they desperately hurting souls?

Now, with the completion of the Tower of Hope, we felt that we were finally finished building our church. We had the Chapel in the Sky, the minister's offices, a counseling center, our New Hope hotline, and ample Sunday school space—all in this glorious tower. The ninety-foot cross that crowned it—the largest cross on any church in the world—signaled constantly our promise of hope to our community.

I had a sick feeling as I realized that we weren't finished after all. We had let down those people in that car, and who knows how many others. Perhaps we had only just begun. After all, I couldn't beam a public invitation by way of that lighted cross and then fail to give people a place to park once they came! That was like inviting someone to a dinner party and not providing him or her with a place setting.

There was simply no getting around it: we needed a much larger parking lot. I walked to a window on the other side of my office, and from there I looked over the ten acres of walnut and orange groves that flanked our property on the north side. Now I knew that we had to buy it as well!

The owner of these ten acres was Bill Everett. The year after we'd bought our ten acres for sixty-six thousand dollars, I had made him an offer of one hundred thousand dollars for his land. He rejected it. Later we offered him two hundred and fifty thousand dollars! He refused. Now we were ready to offer him five hundred thousand dollars!

"Sorry, Reverend," he said, shaking his head. "I signed a deal with Edgar Kaiser. They're planning a shopping center. You'll have to talk to them. They've acquired another hundred and sixty acres across the street for a huge commercial development."

I went to the Kaiser office and met the president, Chuck Cobb.

"Sorry, Schuller. We're holding on to that ten acres. We have a deal signed with Bill Everett, and we're not interested in selling our position. Impossible."

I walked back to my office and prayed. Into my mind—stimulated, I'm sure, by God—came the recollection of an article I'd read in *Reader's Digest* back when I was in college. All I could recall was the fine print at the bottom of the first page: "This article by Henry J. Kaiser is a digest of a layman's sermon delivered by Henry Kaiser in the pulpit of the Marble Collegiate Church in New York City."

The Marble Collegiate Church? Wow! Could it really be the same family?

I telephoned Norman Vincent Peale, since it was his pulpit that had been named. "Yes, I know Edgar Kaiser very well," he said. "He's Henry's son."

I explained our situation. "We need that ten acres, Norman," I concluded, "or our growth will be choked."

"Well, do this, Bob," Norman offered. "Write a letter over my

name to Edgar. Send it to me. I'll have the freedom to add to it or
edit it, and then I'll send it off and we'll see what happens." I did.
One week later I received a copy of the signed letter, with the addition of only an opening paragraph.

December 5, 1968

Mr. Edgar F. Kaiser
300 Lakeside Drive
Oakland, CA 94604

Dear Edgar:

I often think of you, and regret that so much time has
passed since we last had a visit. I've always felt a close bond
with you and your family, and remember your mother and
father most affectionately.

You may not be aware of it, but you and I have two big
projects going next door to each other.

You are doing a fantastic job in the development of The
City, Inc., in Orange, California. In addition to your nearly
160-acre development, you hold a lease-option on a ten-acre
surplus parcel contiguous to a great church I have been
building on the West Coast, with the help of Robert
Schuller, who is my handpicked pastor. I've been working
hard with Rev. Schuller to develop what I believe is going to
be the greatest church on the Pacific Coast. In fact, it is that,
in my judgment, today.

Now we have completed our church development, a
fifteen-story Tower of Hope. What we urgently need is
additional acreage to accommodate additional parking. At the
same time, we have to enlarge the drive-in wing of the church.

It means that we simply must have the additional ten
acres. We have tried to negotiate with the managers of The

City, but they replied that it was not "in their interest to let this property go at this time." What I would like to do is ask you to personally look at the situation and tell us that you would be willing to sell this property. And simply tell us the price you would have to have in order to let it go to our church.

Don't think that because we are a church we can't meet the price you think you would have to get for the land.

And your influence in making this dream a reality by agreeing to release the property, at whatever price you suggest, would be an enormous contribution to the building of a greater nation.

Gratefully,
Norman Vincent Peale

Only a few days later I got a call from the corporation's president, Chuck Cobb. "Schuller? Chuck Cobb here. I just got a call from Mr. Kaiser telling me to work out a deal with you to take over our position on the ten acres."

I checked my calendar. "Tomorrow morning at ten?" I offered.

"See you then!" he replied.

With Norman's help we had just turned one more "impossibility" into a "possibility."

The next day I strutted confidently in to Mr. Cobb's office.

"Here's the deal," Chuck started off. "We have a legal option to buy the ten acres from Bill Everett for a fixed price of five hundred thousand dollars. We now value this ten acres at one million three hundred and fifty thousand dollars. That will be the cost to you."

I almost fainted!

He further explained, "We could put up a whole bunch of stores there that would justify this price."

"I'll get back to you," I answered, feeling discouraged.

After I prayed, I called him again. "Mr. Cobb, you have a problem," I said.

"Me?" he exclaimed. "What do you mean?"

"Mr. Cobb, if I tell my congregation the price you're asking, Mr. Kaiser will be viewed as being greedy. If you'll drop the price to one million, I think I can get my people to see that as an amount that can be justified—but a million and a third? Ouch!"

Now it was his turn to say, "I'll get back to you."

He was back on the phone the next day. "Kaiser will sell the land for one million," he said. "Here's the new deal. You pay us half a million cash in thirty days, and you'll have our legal position to buy it for half a million from Bill Everett. Escrow has to open tomorrow, and it will close in thirty days."

Raise five hundred thousand dollars in thirty days?! I wanted to shout that same old profanity out loud:

Impossible!

But the next thought overpowered that first negative impulse:

The only way I can truly fail is . . . if I don't even try!

So I agreed to the offer. "We'll go for it, Mr. Cobb," I said, and then I hung up the phone.

When I made the startling announcement to my church on Sunday, a visiting banker heard about it and called me in. He said, "That's a wise move. I'll help you: I'll loan you two hundred and fifty thousands dollars if you can raise the balance in thirty days."

I prayed. I preached. I appealed. In the next twenty-nine days we raised one hundred thousand dollars in cash from our congregation, leaving us still one hundred and fifty thousand dollars short.

That morning Chuck Cobb called. "One of the officers whose signature is required to close escrow is in Europe and can't be reached," he said apologetically. "We'll have to extend the escrow another week. Can you go along with that?"

"Just a minute, Mr. Cobb. Let me check." I lifted the receiver into the air above my head and whispered, "Thank you, Lord," then came back on the line. "That'll be okay, Mr. Cobb—we're in no hurry!"

Suddenly I had another seven days to find the missing piece of our financial puzzle—one hundred and fifty thousand dollars.

Then I remembered that my best buddy, Bill Miedema, was working on developing a new church. They'd been raising cash, but they weren't planning to build for a year at least. I called to explain my predicament.

"Bob, we've got one hundred and fifty thousand dollars in our savings account, but we won't need it for a year. We'll loan it to you for twelve months." What an offer!

"Woo-ha!" I hollered, and Bill laughed. Once again, "impossibility" had bitten the dust.

Seven days later we closed escrow with the necessary total of five hundred thousand dollars. The legal document gave us undisputed right to buy the land from Bill Everett for an additional five hundred thousand dollars. We would have ten years to exercise that option. And whenever we did choose to buy it, Bill Everett would have to finance it at six percent with a ten-year amortization schedule. Wow! Fantastic!

Now, with our ten-acre site climbing to twenty acres, my imagination went wild. What a great church we could build (though even I never dreamed that we'd need this space for a Crystal Cathedral)! Then I realized how very close I had come to walking away from the chance to buy the ten acres.

It occurred to me then that I probably wasn't alone. There had to be plenty of ministers in America making the same mistake I'd almost made. I had received the best education that a minister could have, but I'd never been taught how to be a successful *leader*—let alone how to challenge impossibilities. Leadership principles simply weren't a part of the ministerial curriculum.

I had a story to share with struggling pastors, I realized. But I had no platform from which to share it. Seminaries weren't interested in having me lecture. I was too "radical"! They pretty much left me alone—ignored—in this faraway "desert" of California. They relied on pastors who were in more "civilized" territory. So I decided to start my own "school."

In 1969 I launched the Robert Schuller Institute for Successful Church Leadership. In November I placed a small ad in the *Los Angeles Times*. Seventy-eight ministers enrolled for our first church-growth seminar—the first such meeting in America. Denominational seminaries and headquarters might snub our success—but frustrated pastors didn't!

I delivered five basic lectures during the seminar that challenged the thinking of the reigning religious leaders, who declared that new churches should be built in the mushrooming suburbs but that these churches should be small.

"No more than five hundred members." This was what all church "planters" were being told. "Two acres should be the most property needed. Tuck these new churches into the heart of the suburbs."

In my work in Garden Grove, I'd already violated—quite instinctively—all of these basic ground rules.

I said to my seminar participants, "A small church is great if your mission is to serve only the indoctrinated members of your sectarian denomination—Lutheran, Dutch Reformed, Presbyterian, Episcopalian, or whatever. But if you want to win unchurched people, drop the label from your name. Call it a community church. And program your church services and your sermons and your activities to appeal to the spiritual needs of the unchurched.

"You've got to be willing to shift priorities from building denominationalism to building a mission focused on generating faith, hope, and love. Be a mission station first—and a church will follow!

"Mission theology doesn't begin with 'good' believers teaching 'bad' unbelievers how sinful they are! Deep down in their hearts, all unchurched 'sinners' (like all churched 'sinners') know that they need help. What they need to learn from us is that *we can and will help them*, by introducing them to Jesus Christ. He will then lead them in becoming persons of positive-thinking faith, hope, and love!"

Sitting in that first tiny class was a young black preacher from a tiny, troubled church in Los Angeles. He had fewer than a hundred members, no money—but he had a dream. After the last lecture in the Chapel in the Sky, high on the top floor of the Tower of Hope, he asked me if he could remain behind to pray. I left him alone. Later he told me how, looking out to the sky, thirteen stories above the ground, he had prayed through tears, "Oh, God—can you do something great with me as You did with Dr. Schuller?"

He went home, alive with a new dream, and set tremendous goals! At the thirtieth anniversary of the institute, he returned to tell two thousand delegates how God had answered his prayer. That pastor's name is Bishop Charles Blake, and his church now numbers more than eighteen thousand members, including such celebrities as Magic Johnson and Denzel Washington!

In the next few years young preachers would come with only a handful of members and they would go home dreamers of great dreams! Moreover, they would come back year after year. Bill Hybels and Rick Warren would build two of the largest and most successful churches in America—Willow Creek Community Church in Illinois and Saddleback Community Church in California. These students outran their teacher.

One young student from Korea was studying at Fuller Seminary. This young man, Sundo Kim, not only listened; he took photographs. When he went home to Seoul, South Korea, he rented a tent and started from scratch, keeping the pictures of our Tower of Hope and the sanctuary to inspire him. He would return twenty-five years later to share his experience. He was—and still is—pastor of the largest Methodist church in the world, with over fifty thousand members.

We had launched what came to be called the "mega-church movement," which Peter Drucker would later say was the most significant movement in the twentieth-century church.

As a corollary to that movement, the late sixties saw the publication of my flagship book, *Move Ahead with Possibility Thinking*. My new career as an author was launched. Thirty more books would follow in the next thirty years, expounding the same simple message of faith, hope, and love.

But my message would find another medium far beyond even *my* imagination.

XXX

I remembered Billy Graham from my college days. He was my senior by almost ten years, and I looked up to him immensely. His crusades had been gaining momentum, so I was terribly excited when he announced that he was coming to us in Orange County.

I served as vice-chairman of the committee that worked for a year to plan Billy Graham's crusade in the Angel Stadium less than a mile from our church.

At the time of the crusade, Billy held a leadership seminar at our church. He said that he was impressed by the "movement" in our architectural setting—the fountains that leaped, the glass walls that slid open. "This would be a great setting for a moving picture. Have you thought of televising your church service?" Billy asked. "Let me show you how we're televising my crusades." He then introduced me to the television crew that was taping his rallies at Angel Stadium.

"But what would that cost?" I asked. The answer came from Billy's producer: "Probably four hundred thousand dollars a year for fifty-two weeks of programming, recorded and televised."

Billy added, "Gene Autry owns a strong station, and he might agree to sell you an hour on Sunday mornings."

"But four hundred thousand dollars is the size of our entire operating budget! We don't have that much extra to spend, and I wouldn't be able to borrow it. It's all . . ." How would I explain this concept to him? "It's . . . 'coal money'!"

Even after I'd told him about the loan I'd attempted to get for my coal in Ivanhoe, he was undeterred. "Let's let God make that decision," he insisted.

Then he shared his experience. "When I was challenged to go on radio after my Portland crusade, we put the fleece out," he said. "We asked God to make that decision by showing us pledges of support that would add up to fifty percent of the annual cost. Without advance PR, we simply asked our people—once, and only once—how much they would pledge to my radio ministry."

Billy continued, "We agreed in prayer that if the total one-time appeal added up to fifty percent of the annual cost, we'd take that as God's order to do it. One dollar short, and we'd take that as God's guidance to pass on the idea and forget it."

I was listening to a strategy I'd never heard before. I agreed to give it a try. First Billy's producer, Fred Deinert in Philadelphia, would join me and my business administrator in California in prayer. Then we'd take the issue to the people.

So on a Sunday in November, worshipers sitting in our morning service heard the following announcement:

"We're seeking God's guidance on whether we should televise our Sunday morning services. If we go ahead, we'll be the first and only weekly televised church service in California. We're asking you to write a number on the little white card in your program today. If the numbers add up to half of the annual cost, we'll take that as God's order to do it. If the grand total from this one-and-only appeal is so much as one dollar less, we'll take that as God's guidance to let the opportunity pass."

I closed with a prayer—and that was that!

On Monday morning Frank Bos, my business administrator, called. "We added the numbers, and they totaled one hundred and eighty-nine thousand dollars. That's eleven thousand dollars short of target."

I took a deep breath. It was a relief, actually; I wouldn't have to take on the burden of producing the show with only half the annual cost pledged!

But Frank had more to say. "I talked to Fred this morning and told him the outcome. He said you'll have to wait a few days for the final pledges to come in the mail. Some people typically go home to discuss giving with their spouse. You can't make another appeal, but you should wait for more data on this one."

"Let's wait two days," I answered.

By Tuesday the call came from Frank Bos. "Fred was right on, Bob," he said. "More cards came in, and they totaled two hundred and twelve thousand! I think that this is God's order to go on television."

I shivered. I trembled. But now I would have to go through with it! *Me? A preacher on television? Was that really what God wanted from me?*

Frank was waiting for my go-ahead, but I needed to think some more.

"Well, Bob?" he prompted.

All of us, including Billy, had been totally sincere. If this was indeed God leading us and answering our prayer for divine guidance, I would have to go for it. If I didn't, it would be disobedience.

"Call Gene Autry," I said. "Sign a contract to put our church on television."

Frank chuckled nervously. I tried to reassure him, saying, "The only way we can truly fail is . . . if we don't even try."

Reaching out to millions by way of television in no way lessened the importance of my reaching out to individuals in need.

During this period, social change and experimentation—hallmarks of the sixties and early seventies—were causing great pain and confusion in millions of families. I remember the day a couple came to visit me with their daughter, a young woman whom, only a few months earlier, they had sent off with high hopes to the

University of California at Berkeley. Instead, she had found her "home" among the "flower children" in the Haight-Ashbury District of San Francisco.

With long blond hair and sandals, Vicki sat sullenly across from me as if she were a prisoner, flanked by her two parents as guards. I chatted with her for just a moment, and then I asked her what she thought about God.

She looked up at me with glassy eyes and said, "I've found God in LSD, man. Every Friday night me and my friends conduct 'services.'" Then, with a dreamy smile, she said, "It's beautiful. You don't know what God is until you've seen Him in a tab of acid."

I smiled back at her and said, "I've found God in Jesus Christ; you claim to have found Him in LSD. Let's have a little contest."

She looked at me with suspicion.

"God is love," I said. "Would you agree?"

She nodded.

"Love is helping people. Would you agree with that as well?"

She screwed up her face, not sure where I was going with this, but finally she agreed.

Then I gave a challenge: "How much money have you and your friends collected for the poor during your 'services,' Vicki? How much have you given to the hungry? How much hope have you spread? How much comfort have you given?"

She was silent.

"I have to tell you, Vicki. I don't think that you've truly seen God's love as an active force through LSD."

I could tell that she was listening, that I was getting through. I asked her and her parents to stand. We joined hands and I invited them to pray with me.

"Jesus," I said. "I've personally experienced Your spirit of love. We don't need a chemical to create an experience with You. I pray that You'll come into the heart and life of this fine young woman."

When I opened my eyes, I noticed a tear trickling down her cheek. I reached my finger up to touch the drop.

"Look, Vicki," I said, holding the moistened finger up for her to see. "When this tear was forming and falling, didn't you feel beautiful inside?"

She nodded, and more tears began to fall.

"Vicki, this is the deepest and most joyous experience a human being can know. It's religious emotion. It's the movement of a Divine Spirit within you. Christ is coming into your life, Vicki. Let Him come in. This is God's love, Vicki. This is reality."

When she left that day, Vicki was changed—truly "born again"! She gave up drugs and went back to finish college. Now, years later, I still look forward to her annual Christmas letter, bringing me up to date on her bountiful life with her husband and children.

The ending of the old decade and the coming of the new was a watershed in many ways.

As I decided to go along with what seemed to be God's plan for the church—to go on television—I also had a few plans of my own. The year 1969 saw the old board going out and a new board coming in. My week for mad-dash landscaping had arrived!

On the first day of my five-day window of opportunity to plant those Italian cypress, bulldozers dug up and hauled away the asphalt. On days two and three, landscapers prepped the soil. And on the last two days, workers delivered and planted the trees.

As those young trees sat in their trough, freshly watered (and with their surroundings hosed down), I thought, *That six-hundred-foot-long hedge will reach a height of one hundred and twenty feet in the year 2050!*

I even planned and planted a "bank account" of Italian cypress that could be tapped and transplanted to replace any trees that might die from accident or infection.

When the new board came on one week later, I relished the compliments when several of them said, "Those new trees sure look pretty!"

Thirty years later, the cypress are nearly forty feet tall, standing proud, swaying gently to and fro—the prettiest green curtain I've ever seen.

It was now twelve years since our very first Christmas Eve service in Garden Grove. As 1969 drew to a close, our beautiful candlelit, Neutra-designed church was filled four times over: we seated one thousand persons at each of the four Christmas Eve services—standing room only.

The day after Christmas Arvella and I packed all five of our children into the car and left to spend a few days snug and warm in the beautiful mountain cabin I'd designed and built only two years earlier. It was high in the snow-covered San Bernardino Mountains overlooking Big Bear Lake—a two-hour drive from our home.

We had named the place Camelot because we all loved the music from the Broadway musical of that name. The title song's lyrics poured out from our phonograph in the small cabin perched high on the ridge. As we took in the view of the valley and the lake, we heard:

> In short there's simply not
> A more congenial spot
> For happy-ever-after-ing
> Than here in Camelot!

And for us this really was the Schullers' Camelot. I even had a wood sign carved and hung from the cabin's rafters announcing its name to the pine-covered valley beneath.

We had such fun in the fresh mountain snow that Christmas. I took my youngest, Gretchen—three years old that year—along with her six-year-old sister, Carol, down our steep, snow-covered drive-way on fast toboggan rides. Far from a television and with the tele-phone used for emergencies only, we engaged in numerous chess matches that the younger ones always seemed to win. We enjoyed family card games of Hearts and Rummy as we listened to the back-ground music of Nat King Cole. It was as close to heaven as we could get.

As I pondered the end of one decade and the beginning of another, I thought about three presidents—Kennedy, Johnson, and Nixon; three assassinations—JFK, Bobby Kennedy, and Martin Luther King, Jr.; and a ten-year-old Vietnam War that we couldn't win. It had been a bloody decade. Our many thousands of soldiers in battle would return—if they were among the lucky ones—defeated and assaulted in ways that most of us would never under-stand.

As this decade closed, I looked about me and saw that many of my clerical peers had disappeared from their pulpits and their parishes, victims of the war of politics. My wife had saved me from a course that could have been a disaster to my mission and my mes-sage. We had kept our focus and pressed on.

In my personal life, I had buried my father. I had seen the birth of the last of my five children. I had watched proudly as all three of my older children made their commitments to our faith, each now passionately focused, on his or her own goal.

In 1970 Arvella and I would celebrate our twentieth wedding anniversary (and, simultaneously, the twentieth anniversary of my ordination). The forty-year plan to build a great church that I had adopted on the day of my ordination was a dream that had been ful-filled in only half the expected time.

"So," I pondered introspectively, "What happens to a dreamer when his dreams come true—far ahead of schedule?" Then came the answer.

He dreams bigger dreams!

Thanks to Billy Graham, God had opened a wider vision: to televise the church service—and not just to a few overflow visitors watching on a TV screen in an adjoining hall. No, we would send the service—sight and sound and spirit—into the overflow space of people's houses, into hotels, and into hospitals in the greater Los Angeles metropolis. We would be the first church service televised every week in Southern California.

Fifteen years earlier I had started preaching from a snackbar rooftop at the Orange Drive-in Theater, preaching to people distanced from me in their automobiles.

Now, starting on February 8, 1970, I'd be reaching out again, to people listening and looking from the privacy and safety of their homes. They'd be not on the other side of a windshield, but on the other side of a TV screen. These fifteen years later I was, in many ways, right back where I'd started.

XXXI

Our mountaintop holiday was over too soon. Back in my office on the twelfth floor of the Tower of Hope, I was being briefed by Frank Bos, the church business administrator.

"So here's where we stand on the television project, Dr. Bob," he said. "From that one appeal we made last year, two hundred thousand dollars was pledged over a twelve-month period. No cash, but—not to worry—the cash will start coming in by the first week we're on the air. We've signed a contract to deliver our first taped program to Gene Autry's KTLA, to be aired on Sunday, February 8, 1970, at 10:00 A.M.—that's in three weeks.

"Weekly costs to buy that airtime will be four thousand dollars. In addition, we've signed a contract for Deinert [Billy Graham's producer] to come in with his crew and cameras, along with the TV truck that houses the recording equipment. That's the same truck, cameras, and equipment that Billy used and showed you three months ago. All of that will add up to an additional four thousand dollars per week."

"That adds up to costs of eight thousand dollars a week starting in less than a month," I said.

He nodded.

Double-checking, I asked, "And we have no cash paid in advance on any of these pledges?" I could hear nothing but the haunting taunts of doubt: *coal money, coal money, coal money!*

Frank laughed! "Not to worry. We don't need cash to pay bills until thirty days after we've incurred the costs! So what we spend in February, we need to be ready to pay in March. After we've been on the air, the mail with money should begin coming in just in time to pay those March bills!"

Frank's enthusiasm and abundant confidence overcame my terror. Optimism can be just as contagious as negative thinking!

I knew that Frank Bos was good at business and finances. He seemed to understand the concept of "coal money," so I felt that I could trust his calculations. Having set aside my fears, I began to grow more and more excited.

It was the same excitement I'd felt when I preached that first sermon from the snackbar roof on March 27, 1955. It was the same energy I'd felt when we held our first service in our temporary sanctuary, now our Fellowship Hall, on our new ten-acre land. It was the same jubilation we'd felt when we had our first service in our Neutra sanctuary on November 6, 1961, and when we had our groundbreaking for the Tower of Hope in 1967.

Energy flows from enthusiasm rooted in optimism. I felt it now as I stood on the edge of a new television venture!

Two days later, Wednesday, Frank Bos summoned me for what he called an emergency meeting.

"Fred Deinert just called," he began. "He was all ready to tape our first program. But the lighting guy says he can't record without installing extra lights. So Fred lined up the equipment, but he just learned this morning that bringing in all the extra power to feed these lights can't be done without installing another transformer onto our light pole."

"So?" I prompted.

He began to fidget, avoiding my eyes. "So . . . that transformer needs to be installed by this Friday to get all the lights ready for Sunday. If we don't record this Sunday, Fred says he can't have the show ready to air on the eighth. If we don't make that date, the contract is broken and we'll lose the timeslot. Other buyers are waiting in line."

I still couldn't figure out why Frank was so agitated. "Well, call the power company and tell them to get going," I suggested. "Have them install the transformer!"

"Bob," Frank pulled his chair closer and locked his eyes on mine. "It'll take them only one day to do the job. They can do it on Friday. But they want ten thousand dollars! And they won't install the transformer without being paid in advance. They need the whole ten thousand by tomorrow night!"

"How much cash do we have?"

"Just what I told you Monday: we have a stack of three-by-five cards with numbers written on them—promises, not cash. Not even ten dollars! Everything in the church accounts is designated for mortgage and salaries. We can't touch it, Bob. We're sitting here with nothing."

"You're wrong, Frank," I said. "We have God! And we have something else, Frank. We have tomorrow! Go home and have dinner. It's now God's responsibility to manage this problem."

I drove home and spent the evening with my family, feeling remarkably calm. Tomorrow would be a defining day, and I was at peace. Deep peace.

Why? Because I could see that God might be letting me off the hook—setting me free from a heavy responsibility I didn't need or particularly welcome. Financially, this TV business scared me; no two ways about it. In all the proposed four hundred thousand dollars of annual cost, none of it—not one dollar—would build equity! Land, buildings, even equipment built equity, but not television airtime.

Fifteen years earlier, after the purchase of our first organ, I had pegged our net worth at four hundred dollars. Those assets had grown until this day in 1970 to include land and buildings with a net worth of over two million dollars! By now I had learned a thing or two about investments, and I saw this television venture as extremely risky.

Yes, I battled an "ego thing." Little voices whispered, "This could make you famous!" But I would answer myself back, "Yeah, right! Famous enough for anyone who came along to attack my good name! Famous enough to make big news if we ever went bust!"

After all, there were over three hundred Protestant denominations in America, plus the larger Roman Catholic and Jewish communities, as well as all sorts of other new religions. If out of the two hundred million Americans alive in 1970 only two hundred thousand were members of the Reformed Church, I could expect the other hundred and ninety-nine-some million to fault me at any number of points.

And where would all the money come from? Not from my small denomination, that's for sure! This television ministry wasn't even an "official" denominational venture. The TV idea hadn't started in our national headquarters in New York City. I was free to "do my thing," but I could never go back and lay the bills on their table.

And already, so I was told, there was talk about me at denominational headquarters—and not of the positive kind either! My detractors said, "This Schuller with his drive-in church—he's been a maverick from the beginning, a strong follower of Dr. Peale and positive thinking." With Peale undergoing heavy criticism as well at this time, the association made me no points. "Schuller made negative comments about the politics of the National Council of Churches a few years back," the detractors continued, "and now he's going to go on television?!"

So, to be suddenly released from all the pressure of one more grandiose dream, one more venture that would thrust me further into unwelcome challenges and criticism . . . perhaps the Lord was setting me free. Perhaps this was simply my "lucky way out."

And so, on that Wednesday night, twenty-four hours before we needed ten thousand dollars to materialize out of nowhere to avoid cancellation—I slept like a babe!

Thursday—D day for me—came, and with it a full schedule of appointments and meetings lasting from eight to five. The last appointment, at four-thirty, was with Frank Bos.

We had to plan how we would announce the disappointments of the last week to our trusting congregants. I could handle that. I had often preached, "I'd rather attempt to do something great . . . and fail, than attempt to do nothing . . . and succeed!"

I enjoyed profound peace that Thursday morning and felt no guilt whatsoever. If I had to fold up the idea and walk away, I'd know that it wasn't because of my own negligence. I'd learned that when I face a genuine impossibility (and there are a *few* of those), I have a right—and a duty!—to refer it to the Boss! So I'd placed this project on God's desk. "I will build My church," he had promised. That was my mission statement every day.

My busy workday unfolded quickly, leaving me with no time to worry about the television dilemma. I had virtually forgotten about the ten thousand dollars when I cleared my desk for my four o'clock appointment. I didn't recognize the names penciled on my daily calendar in that timeslot, so I called in my secretary and asked for a briefing. "Can't tell you anything about them, Dr. Schuller," she said. "They said that they attended our church and needed to talk to you privately. Marriage problem, I suspect."

"Show them in, Lois—but hold them to thirty minutes. Buzz me when we've used up twenty-five. That's enough time to find out what's going on here and determine whether we need to schedule appointments down the road."

As I stood to greet them, I prepared myself for another take on the woes that marriage can produce. Did I have a box of Kleenex nearby?

Who should walk in but a stunningly handsome couple, radiating energy and joy. We shook hands, then sat down. I said, "Well, what brings you here today? Some problem, perhaps?"

"Oh, no, Dr. Schuller. We don't have a problem," the wife assured me. I couldn't recall ever hearing *that* as an opening line from what I assumed was a "counseling appointment."

She spoke again. "Dr. Schuller, we began attending this church in November, on a day when you preached on tithing. You shared how the Bible teaches that we should *earn* all we can, then *invest* all we can, then *share* all we can. You also explained that a biblical philanthropist begins by giving ten percent of what he or she earns back to God." They looked at one another, grinning like kids in a candy store.

Then she continued, "Well, when we both left church that morning we agreed that we would start tithing. We would begin in January when our accountant could tell us what the net profit was from our first year in our new business."

Then her husband picked up the story. "So last week our accountant gave us the numbers. Then we called for an appointment to see you and hand this over: it's our tithe."

I was still reeling from this sudden detour—marriage problem, to *no* marriage problem, to tithing. He handed me a check, then before I could read the numbers he said, "Dr. Schuller, our profit last year was one hundred thousand dollars. We made the check payable to Robert Schuller so that you could spend it for the ministry in any way that God might lead you."

The math was simple: one-tenth of one hundred thousand dollars is ten thousand dollars. But even as I did the calculation—even as I read the amount!—I struggled to comprehend. Finally, I looked up at them and said, "You have just launched a new television ministry!"

This stunning, unexpected, and truly historic gift was one of the largest contributions I'd ever received at any one time in my fifteen years in ministry! Suddenly the serenity and peace I'd felt over the previous twenty-four hours was gone. And in its place, joy—immense! And joy—indescribable! I now knew that this was truly God's idea.

With less than an hour left in the workday, Frank Bos called Edison Company. The next day, Friday, the transformer was installed!

Our move into television was now irreversible. I had delegated to Arvella the responsibility for selecting every detail to be included. She'd been choosing hymns and editing them for sexism; the words "Rise Up O Men of God" became, for example, "Rise Up O Church of God." She'd been working on scripture passages too, changing "Thou" and "Thy" to "You" and "Your" and passing over any that came across as negative. As Arvella would explain to her critics, "Most of our listeners can't and won't understand these texts. They'll throw out the whole Bible without giving it a chance!"

Arvella, with her intuitive sense for what people needed and wanted to hear with equal passion for a message, would retain control of all content for every program we would ever produce! And everything she knew about the business she learned through her own self-taught crash course in script-writing, stage management, and pre- and postproduction—all the while serving as a pastor's wife, with toddlers, school schedules, and maternal responsibilities abounding.

Did we really know what we were doing? How was this going to change the style of our living, our family, our church?

There's a January chill as I wake up Sunday morning to go over my sermon one last time. I wonder if the television cameras will make me nervous. Crowds don't rattle me ever, though I often feel uncertain *after* my appearances. I tend to drill Arvella and close friends after each sermon: "Was my message okay?" But while I'm talking to a crowd I find public speaking a joy; it's easy, and I feel right at home. But . . . television?

I won't be able to see the faces of those watching in homes across Southern California. I won't be able to see their responses, read their expressions, or feel their energy. But then again, I could never see the faces of those who sat in the Orange Drive-in Theater either. All I could see there were the glaring windshields of cars. This thought really helped! Preaching to television cameras will be just like preaching at the drive-in. And I'll still have a live audience as well. I'll still be able to feel *their* energy.

I'm so excited that, still wearing the running suit meant for knocking around the house, I jump in my car and drive to the church. I pull onto the property, quiet in the early morning. The sun is just beginning to rise behind me in the east. The sky is crisp and clear as only a Southern California winter morning can be. I drive toward the eastern glass wall of the Neutra sanctuary, now reflecting the orange and red and gold of the rising sun. The fountains are still slumbering in the pool that stretches one block long beside the glass wall of the church. I can see the eucalyptus trees reflecting their dark silhouettes. The trees and the sunrise appear on the glass like currents from the nearby Pacific, or heat waves that rise in the not-too-distant desert.

Parked in the drive-in section, I turn off the ignition and sit alone in my car, wondering how on earth I got where I am today. Fifteen years ago I drove across the Rockies, across the desert, all the way from the plains of the Midwest to this frontier of California. How in the world did this ministry grow to its present stature from one car carrying an unknown young couple with two children in tow? How, fifteen years later, do we now find ourselves standing on the edge of an incredible tomorrow—a tomorrow loaded with cameras, lights, and . . . possibilities beyond my wildest imagination.

I think about the Bible story of the loaves and fishes that I loved as a boy. Jesus needs to feed the crowd, but the only food available is the lunch of one little boy. The boy agonizes over giving up his precious meal, but once he decides he'll do it, Jesus uses that little lunch to feed five thousand people. How Jesus specializes in multiplying and maximizing slender resources!

I wasn't even five when I offered to God the one meager life of one little farmboy. But I gave God all I had to give: my future. Now here I am, thirty years later, amazed at what he's done with my tiny little offering.

My reverie is interrupted by the sound of a heavy engine rumbling up to me. It's the television truck! The same big TV truck I saw at the Billy Graham crusade. It's time to go home now and shower and dress, time to make sure that Arvella and the kids are awake.

A few hours later I'm back at the church, and for the first time in my life I'm wearing makeup! The producer insists that I wear this stuff so that my shiny face won't reflect the television lights and create a distracting glow. The unappealing goop is caked on my cheeks and my forehead, and I wonder why in the world women would want to do this to themselves every day!

The parking lot is filling now, and Arvella comes into my study. She hugs me and tells me how proud she is of me. She's so beautiful—more beautiful than I ever remember seeing her. I think about how hard she's worked all week, designing our service for this morning, and now she carries herself with such confidence! When the decision was on the table, I insisted, "I'll agree to televise, but under one condition: Arvella will produce the program; she'll be in charge." This, I knew, was our only hope of achieving excellence while retaining the integrity of our message.

Arvella stands erect and professional as she gives me a final grin. "You'll do *great*," she says. We have a short prayer. Then she leaves to attend to her duties as producer.

Moments later I'm summoned to the sanctuary. The service will begin shortly, and I'm filled with exhilaration. I remember the sensation I had growing up. I used to call it my "quiet, happy feeling." Now I call it God's presence.

I walk into the crowded church and up to the area behind the pulpit. I stand hidden from the congregation as a sound technician, serious and attentive, puts a bulky lavaliere microphone around my neck. He strategizes its placement as I watch curiously. He makes sure that my robe is just so, and then I'm left to myself again—but not for long.

Now Arvella comes to fix a few blotches of makeup that I've smudged off over the past half-hour. She turns me around and brushes off the back of my robe, fixes a few errant strands of hair, and tells me I'm all set.

I can see the big television truck sitting outside at the front entrance. I look down below at my congregation, the worshipers waiting expectantly as they observe three big television cameras and crew.

Arvella has gone into the television production truck, where the director and his assistants watch the screen. They wear earphones and are ready to tell the stage manager, who's standing near me in the pulpit, "Roll cameras!" The stage manager takes the call and demands "Silence!" from the live audience.

The countdown begins:

Ten . . . nine . . . eight . . .

Jets of water leap from the fountains outside!

Seven . . . six . . . five . . .

The grand sliding doors to the drive-in begin to open.

Four . . . three . . . two . . .

The red lights on top of the three cameras begin to glow! Now the stage manager raises his finger and points at me.

I'm on!

"This is the day the Lord has made!" I boom in introduction.

"Let us rejoice—"

I throw my arms up and walk toward the camera, but I look out beyond it.

"—and be glad—"

I thrust my head forward, pausing for an emphasis that would have made Miss Aeilts proud.

"—in it!"

The organ booms. For the first time since our earliest beginnings, the music is being played by an organist other than my wife. She sits in the production truck, professional and strong and proud as executive producer of the *Hour of Power*—program number *one!* And all I feel during the sixty minutes is wonder and joy and satisfaction.

I was forty-three years old when we first went on the air; Arvella was forty. I was proud that day. Together we had taken on the unknown.

At that moment I felt as if everything I'd ever done, every new thing I'd ever learned, every talent and gift ever released in me, every positive personality trait that surged in my veins—imagination, daydreaming, acting sense of the dramatic—had had its fulfillment. The clergyman in me, the communicator in me, the actor in me, the storyteller in me, the missionary in me—all these, at one culminating moment, had come together, propelling me full throttle into my lifelong destiny.

"It's a new day for your church," Fred Deinert told me afterward. "Now, when asked how many people attend your church, you'll have to add those sitting in their homes, in the hospitals, and in the hotels. Your Sunday audience has just increased, Bob, from a few thousand to tens of thousands.

"And via television those viewers will see you as their pastor. They'll seek your counsel and your prayers. They'll look to you in times of joy—like marriage. In times of sorrow—like funerals.

They'll seek your comfort—in times of sickness and suffering. Get ready, Bob: your congregation has just mushroomed. It now stretches all over Southern California, from Hollywood to San Diego!"

Fred was right. The first week after our first telecast we received seventy-five letters. Each one was read—and answered. And the offerings they included from the "television church congregation" were carefully receipted and recorded. With the passing of years we would see our weekly letters mount. One Sunday we received a response of over sixty thousand letters.

Then what I had suspected began to happen—superstars and celebrities "tuned in" to the show and, as a result, got "turned on." Now they could "come in, see, hear, feel, and find the faith" without worrying about an awestruck fan who might hound them for an autograph or photograph after the benediction.

The bulk of the listeners, though, were the same nonsectarian, secular people who'd come to us that first Sunday in the drive-in theater. The listening crowd—at our television church as at our drive-in church—were people from all walks of life searching for faith, hope, and love. And with the help of the God-inspired insight I'd found two years earlier found at the World Psychiatric Congress in Madrid, I was ready to be that voice of hope!

I thought about my role with this new television audience. I couldn't "preach" to this new group of people "coming" to my church. Many weren't committed to my faith, after all. It would be inappropriate if not unethical for me to admonish or rebuke people who hadn't yet decided they were ready to "play my game." Most of them weren't "seekers" as much as they were "sightseers" or "spectators," and the rules of the game don't apply to spectators in the stands.

The roles of teacher and evangelist weren't really appropriate for this broader audience either. So what was I? My calling was to deliver messages that would bring emotional, mental, and spiritual health to sin-sick souls that desperately needed hope. Given that calling, I was more *therapist* than preacher, teacher, or evangelist.

I came to define my role—a role unlike that of any other preacher I knew—as "a communicator of healing hope." I would be a "reporter" of "Good News," and that news would be therapeutic. I would attempt to bring a healing, healthy, biblical, Christ-honoring therapy to anyone willing to listen. And all listeners—believers and unbelievers alike—could be helped and lifted with this gospel of "Good News."

But sometimes even the therapist needs a shoulder to cry on.

Seven years before, I had become a homeowner, which was quite unusual for full-time pastors. We moved from our church-owned home to a home we purchased ourselves near the church. It was simple, but perfect. I'm in our small kitchen, usually vibrant and full of life with its garnet-red wall and pink-and-white candy-striped window shade. Just outside, the roses pick up the pinks and the reds, complementing Arvella's decorative touch. The date is October 27, 1970. I answer the phone to hear the voice of my sister Violet.

"Mom's dying, Harold. She's still conscious, but you'll have to hurry. She wants to see you before she goes."

I twist the long telephone cord around my body as I turn my back to my family and rest my face against the kitchen cabinet. Its embrace is hard and cold, but I need it nonetheless. I begin to cry.

Five-year-old Carol is playing nearby, and she stops to come comfort me.

"What's wrong, Daddy?" she asks.

Arvella, having heard enough to know what's happened, takes her away to explain.

Three hours later I'm in a plane high over the checkerboard landscape of Nebraska farmland.

Will I reach her for one last touch? Will I hear one final word? I want to see in her eyes, to hear in her voice, that I've become all that she ever dreamed for me to be—that I've done well. I want to tell her how much I'll miss her.

I think about sitting next to her on the piano bench. My head comes to just below her shoulder, and I like to rest my forehead on the back of her shoulder and peek beneath her arm for a glimpse of the ivory and ebony keys. Warmth washes over me as I bask in the reverie, listening to the keys respond to her firm but passionate touch. Hymns pour out and over me as I sit beside her in my imagination, oblivious to the other passengers and the aircraft I'm on.

Suddenly the reverie ends and I feel a knot in my stomach. *Please, God. Please let me get there on time.*

But I was too late. As I flew over those midwestern plains, my mother's aorta ruptured, and she was gone.

Mom's death was hard for me. I never did hear, outside of my hopeful imagining, the words that I had so longed to hear, though I learned to read her love in her face.

When I arrived at the hospital, attendants led me to her breathless frame, and I felt an aching grief pierce deeper than I'd known the soul could go. The only comfort I could find was in the words of her pastor: "I was with her during her final moments," he said, "and together we recited the first two verses of Isaiah 43."

This was Mom's favorite Bible passage. I knew that to have these words ringing in her heart as she breathed her last had given her more comfort than I could have brought her.

"Fear not," the verse began, "for I have redeemed you; I have called you by your name; you are mine. When you pass through the waters, I will be with you . . . for I am the Lord your God!"

In February 1971, as the *Hour of Power* celebrated its first anniversary, income matched output! Projections had been right on target. The annual operational costs had topped four hundred thousand dollars; the income of two hundred thousand dollars that had been pledged came in faithfully; and, to my astonishment and relief, the balance owed above and beyond the pledges came in through private donations sent by mail from Sunday morning television worshipers. In fact, we showed a small surplus after only twelve months on the air.

"You're feeding a broad spiritual hunger," Fred Deinert observed. "Let's try expanding. We can buy an hour in Philadelphia and an hour in Seattle and an hour in Chicago. After all, overhead and production costs are already covered in Los Angeles. I think that we can expect viewers in those cities to respond as well as the local folks, so the broadcasts should pay for themselves."

He was aggressive, yet sensibly conservative; as it turned out, he was also prophetic. In any case, I trusted his counsel. By 1972, our second anniversary, our television church was on the air and self-supporting in four U.S. cities: Los Angeles, Chicago, Philadelphia, and Seattle.

Following God's guidance, we discovered that the unchurched people whom God loved and wanted to encourage could be found in every city and state in America. This fact filled me with a passion for the potential of television. And I knew that the biggest untouched and unchurched mission field in America was New York City. There wasn't a single regularly scheduled Sunday morning church service on TV in that entire "world."

One day, thinking about the needs of New York and how they might be addressed, I discussed with Fred what our ministry had to offer. "Think about it," I said. "We're different than most religious groups: we're a 'mission' first, and then a church. What a difference that priority shift makes! Think about the letters that have come in during these two years. They don't say, 'You converted me to be a Reformed Church Christian.' They say, 'You saved my life!' We have the message of the Master, Jesus Christ, which brings mental health and emotional well-being to people! Fred, this is the gospel we're talking about. We really have Good News!"

Then I gave him a directive: "We have to get the *Hour of Power* on in New York City, Fred! We have the mission, the message, and the Master for that metropolis. We'll be nobody's competitor; we'll be the one and only church service delivered right into the homes of millions of people who are too prejudiced, or too afraid, or too spiritually unsophisticated to walk into a church service.

"I see the television audience as a whole new continent just discovered in the sea of space. We've got to use this new vehicle to go to New York City with the Good News the way my Uncle Henry got on a boat and went to China!"

Fred, the television expert, was shaking his head. "Sorry, Bob," he said. "There isn't a single station in that entire city owned by people who'd want to sell time to a Christian church service. You can forget it."

I was stunned. Wasn't enthusiasm supposed to be contagious? So why wasn't Fred supportive on this? I left his office subdued, but not totally convinced that he was right.

A few weeks later, a news story broke about a lawsuit filed against WOR, Channel 9, in New York City. The plaintiff was a small group of Jews who had converted to Christianity. Having put together a TV show called *Passover*, they had approached WOR to purchase airtime, and a contract had been signed.

But then the Jewish owners of the station had been confronted by leading rabbis in the city. "That show you plan to air is anti-Jewish!" they alleged.

As a result, WOR cancelled the contract before the show could be aired, and the Christian promoters and owners of *Passover* were now suing, claiming religious discrimination.

I called Fred Deinert and told him to send WOR a letter requesting the purchase of airtime for *Hour of Power*. I suspected that the lawsuit would make the station receptive. The strongest argument the owners could make for being nondiscriminatory would be to show a letter offering to sell time to a Christian group.

Within days Fred called back. "Good news, Bob: WOR offered to sell us an hour! Twelve noon on Sundays!"

But then his pessimism reemerged. "You're just breaking even in four cities you know," he reminded me, "and New York's a huge step. This could sink your whole ministry. This contract calls for your show to start on the morning of the fourth of July, the worst time of year to launch *anything*. Nobody's in town on the fourth of July weekend.

"To make matters worse, the price they're asking is way out of line. I don't think they really want us to take it. They just want a good defense in their lawsuit. Pray and check with your friends in New York; get some outside counsel before making this decision. It's just too risky!"

What Fred was saying made sense, but I still didn't want to let this opportunity go. I called a very close friend, a minister in New York. He answered on condition that his name would never be associated with what he was about to say. "If you've got four thousand dollars a week to throw away," he said, "fine; buy your time. But if you expect listeners in New York City to support your TV program, forget it. New York is made up of stubborn Jews, narrow-minded Catholics, and lukewarm Protestants!"

I gulped.

"And to be honest, Bob," he continued, "you and your showy church services are much too 'California' for East Coast taste."

I thanked him. I prayed, and as a final gauge for my decision, I asked myself three questions that had guided my decisions throughout my years of ministry:

1. *Would it be a great thing for God?* I listened and the answer came: yes.

2. *Would it help people who are hurting?* I listened and the answer came: yes.

3. *Is anybody else doing it?* I listened and the answer came: no.

I picked up the phone. "Send me the contract, Fred," I said. "I'll sign it."

Thirty years later I still remember the deep anxiety that shuddered through my body as I gave my signature on that line. The financial pressure had me terrified, and yet I felt—I *truly* felt—that this was another mandate from God.

Only a few weeks before we were to go on the air in New York City, Norman and Ruth Peale came out to visit us in California. They had lots of good things to say about our burgeoning ministry, so as I rode back to the airport with them, I shared my news about the proposed TV program in New York.

Suddenly I could sense a coolness in the mental climate of that car. Norman wasn't responding favorably. Was he threatened? Not by me, surely. Just in case, I said, "But Norman—no two people have done more for me than you and Ruth since I started this church. New York is *your* city; *your* church should be on television there. Take the airtime we've bought, Norman, and put Marble Collegiate on television."

He recoiled, "No, no, Bob—it's yours. You have to do it." But his tone was guarded and remote. Unfortunately, this distance between us was the beginning of a rift that would last for years.

Norman wasn't alone in his reservations. I began to receive word in roundabout ways that our national denominational board in New York was also cool about this aggressive "California" pastor who was "invading" New York. And not just once but every week! Coming into their territory without their consent or advice! None of the people or powers in New York that I thought of as friends sided with me on this risky move.

I was out on the edge, alone and scared. And I was worried about how the tough, sophisticated New Yorkers would receive this Iowa farmboy. But I couldn't relinquish my mission of love and hope.

Nowhere was it more desperately needed than on the streets of New York City.

The response to our program proved this assessment to be true. Our positive gospel message connected resoundingly with people at all social, economic, cultural, educational, and political levels. But an early review of names of persons on our mailing list showed that our largest audience was in the south Bronx, the most economically devastated borough in the city.

Months later I visited the area. What I saw was square block after square block of concrete jungle, home to horrific human disgrace, disease, and crime. "Hey, Dr. Schuller!" I heard in greeting from street folks, many of them young and eager for a better life.

I think of one young kid in particular who had to walk several flights of narrow stairs to reach his apartment in one of the poverty pockets of New York. I later learned that he waited for Sundays to turn on his TV and travel in his imagination to the land of palm trees, fountains, and gardens, much as I had done. And he heard his TV pastor tell him, "Believe in yourself! Believe in the God who made you! Believe in the God Jesus believed in! If you can dream it, you can do it!"

Years later, after he had made the big time only to die far too young and tragically, his mother came to visit me in Garden Grove to thank us for what we had done for her son: Freddie Prinze.

Similar expressions of gratitude came not only from poverty pockets of America, but from Beverly Hills and from the halls of political power in Washington.

I received my first "fan letter" from a superstar: Doris Day. That letter would lead to a warm and affectionate pastoral friendship. I learned a lot from Doris about how to communicate with the non-religious. "Don't ever use that word 'lost,' Bob; it comes to people's ears loaded with tons of emotional pain. Words are emotional bombs—or healing balm—so pick them carefully." She helped me more than she knew in my efforts to focus my skills on being a "therapist" in the name of Christ.

Glenn Ford was another big name—a name very well known to this Iowa farmboy—who became familiar to me. We got together often, and he would later invite me to officiate at his wedding in his home. There he gathered his buddies and me in his large bedroom to wait for the signal to mark the opening of the ceremony. In that one smoke-filled room were Glenn Ford; his best man, Bill Holden; and his good friends John Wayne and Frank Sinatra.

In Glenn's beautiful garden Bill Holden complimented me on the service, and I responded by saying, "Thanks! So how do you relate to this religion thing?"

"Let me tell you!" he said with a naughty twinkle. "Religion saved me! I was doing a film in the back country of Africa. We needed to use property the chief controlled, so he invited me to 'feast' with him. I did, and I was a happy guest until a course of eggs was served. The chief broke his open, and inside was a pink-skinned embryo of a chick. He pulled it out and plunked it into his mouth whole, chewing it as his face flushed with joy, juice oozing from the corners of his mouth! It was really terrible, Rev. But to him, it was obviously a delicacy! Then he handed an egg to me! He couldn't wait to see me share in this great treat."

Bill cringed and shuddered, then went on with his story.

"I knew that if I didn't eat it, the whole deal would be off. He'd be so offended that I'd have to pack up my bags and head back to Hollywood. But if I ate it, I knew I'd vomit it all up and then probably drop dead of a heart attack! I prayed, and out came the words, 'Oh, Chief, I'd love to, but I can't.' He was obviously shocked, Rev. Then I came up with, 'It's against my religion!' The chief bought the whole thing. A very courteous and respectful rejection. And he let us film whatever we needed. Yep, Rev., religion *saved* me, for sure!"

This wedding was the beginning of many pastoral connections with Hollywood.

I would pray with and for John Wayne as he fought his battle with cancer. Later, following "the Duke's" death, his daughter told me a story. Apparently, the Duke often watched our Sunday morning *Hour of Power* broadcast. Rarely on that show do I make an appeal to the viewers to accept Jesus, but one day, when I did, the Duke was watching. He got out of bed and dropped to his knees, accepting Jesus Christ as his Savior.

It also was the beginning of correspondence and serious conversations with Frank Sinatra. Arvella and I were invited to personal dinners and offered private seats in his Las Vegas shows. When his mother died in the crash of a private jet, he memorialized her with a window bearing her name in the Crystal Cathedral.

"Hey, Francis," I said to him once, "'I Did It My Way' is your trademark. Come sing it some Sunday in the Crystal Cathedral. Then we'll dissolve to the empty cross, and you'll change the last words to 'He did it—His way'!"

Francis loved the idea! "Yeah! Let's do it!" he said. But then some personal troubles erupted in his life, and the song never happened.

Lucille Ball came to be a friend as well. She sent me this letter, which I framed:

November 12, 1985

Dear Dr. Schuller:

I appreciated your letter so much. It certainly was the highlight of *my* day.

I go to your church every Sunday—no matter where I am I find you. The Crystal Cathedral is something I shall visit one of these days, I vow.

I recently watched you and Dr. Peale together and loved every minute of it. I haven't been able to see Norman and Ruth for several years, but I think of them constantly.

As you said to me, "Keep on keeping on"—I say to you, Keep on . . . God loves you, and so do I.

Lucy

I was honored to deliver her funeral sermon at her own Santa Monica Catholic Church.

Similar letters came from the Oval Office and from powerful and wealthy corporate chiefs. No less important, though, was the correspondence—letter after letter—that we received from the desperate and the destitute, saying, "You saved my life!"

Every individual, of every walk of life, shares one common need: *hope!* God was using me to meet that need in ways that only He could have sensed and seen. Little did I know just how deep and widespread the need for hope really was.

But in all that time I remained, by and large, a lonely dreamer. No letter ever came from my denominational leaders in New York. No letter during that entire decade came from the one man who had done more for me than anyone else, the one man who had remained my friend through all other times of separation from peers and colleagues: Dr. Norman Vincent Peale.

Then there was a crisis much closer to home!

Our street was earmarked for demolition to make way for a new freeway onramp.

The family was devastated. "We were going to live here the rest of our lives," Arvella protested. "This is our home! We *bought* it! We *own* it!"

Jeanne was equally upset, but for a different reason. "We don't want to move away from our friends!" she said.

Carol and Gretchen cried.

Being the optimist in the family, I said, "I think it's a good time to look for a better place anyway. After all, Arvella, you don't always feel safe here when I travel. We've had those few occasions when strangers have been a little too aggressive and insistent."

So our family prayer times began to center on this unexpected upheaval. Years before, I had seen a place in a country setting with a high hedge and a private fence that had a secured gate. I decided to take a drive and check it out. Now, just when we needed it, there was a FOR SALE sign on the large, tree-shaded lot. I drove to the corner gas station, called the real estate office, and asked to see the place.

The house had only two bedrooms, and it was run-down and pathetic, its grounds overgrown. But somehow I sensed that this was it. This place would be a safe, secure, and serene home for our family.

The property had almost two acres filled with trees that had been planted a hundred years earlier by the famous David Hewes—a wealthy Scottish lawyer. It had been landscaped by a world-famous architect from Edinburgh, Scotland, but during the last years both house and yard had fallen into serious disrepair and had become a drag on the market. That meant that the price was miraculously affordable, and we felt that God was answering our prayers.

Throughout the next year, with hammer and saw, young Bob and I built a lean-to for a horse and a pony. We put geese, ducks, and fish in the existing ponds, simulating a farm environment. Soon we found ourselves surrounded by raccoons, owls, possums, tree rats, and what Arvella called a "detestable" family of mice (which had invaded all areas of the house). For the next twenty-five years, we kept remodeling and enlarging the tiny home to make it practical for our large family. In time we would add a music room, a library, and eventually a dining room large enough to seat us all. (Today, including grandkids, we number thirty!)

Later, when our two youngest daughters married and were

unable to afford land in the inflated area of mid-eighties Orange County, they built their own homes on the same property, on either side of our house (where the lean-to corral and the driveway had been). We would find it a safe place for the grandchildren to run and play. They could simply knock at our door for a "treat" from Grandma or Grandpa. We would grow old with the joy of being surrounded by our children and grandchildren in this, our Schuller compound.

I felt truly blessed with this new move. Here I could delve into my hobby of gardening and landscaping. I could hear the warble of birds and the splash of fish in our fish ponds. I could have the solitude I needed to be creative and quiet. So, on weekends and evenings, I remained a daydreamer surrounded by the beauty of nature.

XXXII

The ministry that had begun on the tarpaper roof of a drive-in movie snackbar was now expanding far and wide.

By the 1970s our television broadcast was reaching homes all across America. I was now the author of several successful books. W. Clement Stone, the insurance magnate, was so taken by my *Self-Esteem: The New Reformation* that he purchased two hundred and fifty thousand copies of it and sent them to ministers across America. He also included me in a series of "success rallies" that he sponsored. At those rallies, I spoke in twenty-thousand-seat arenas on the same stage with Norman Vincent Peale and broadcaster Paul Harvey.

But for all this burgeoning influence, I was still surprised by the message I received one day from a visiting clergyman. This was in 1972, a time when the Cold War was still raging, not to mention our nation's heavy involvement in Vietnam and Cambodia.

"You must forget my name," this gentleman told me. "I have to remain anonymous, because I have been working with underground churches in Russia."

Suddenly he had my complete attention. It was as if I'd been drawn into a spy novel.

"Your world-famed skyscraper—the Tower of Hope—has made news in Moscow," he went on. "All architects in the USSR respect Richard Neutra as the greatest architect of the day. They cannot believe that in this scientific age such a revered man would build a huge church tower. Dr. Schuller, they are very upset with what the communists describe as 'a structure that robs the poor.' They're aghast at this 'monument to superstition.' However, a number of English-speaking Christians in the underground Russian church have been reading books and articles by you and have begged me to ask you to come and visit them. They need possibility thinking, Dr. Schuller. I would be honored to line up visits for you with one of these underground churches."

I was intrigued, excited, and cautiously optimistic. But my travels were now greatly limited, due to the television schedule. My summer schedule—the only time when I wasn't televising—was often booked with seminars, conferences, and church-growth meetings, as well as secular international engagements. Before I could agree to go to Russia, I first needed to check my present commitments. Then, if I were free, I'd have to plan a trip that was camouflaged so that Soviet officials wouldn't grow suspicious. My host, adamant about the need for secrecy, agreed.

An eagerness to see Russia now took hold of me. As it happened, only months after this intriguing invitation I was asked to be the professor of philosophy for Chapman University's campus afloat—a six-week summer-school cruise. It was 1972. The ship would depart from Long Beach, travel to Hawaii, then cruise through the South Pacific and on to the jungles of New Guinea. From there we would proceed to New Zealand and finally disembark in Hong Kong. In lieu of my receiving a salary, Arvella and our two college-aged children—Sheila and Robert—were invited to join me for this six-week trip. It would be an unforgettable learning experience for all of us and a perfect front for visiting underground churches in Russia.

Jeanne (now fifteen), Carol (eight), and Gretchen (five) would stay behind in Iowa. Arvella and I cherished our small-town roots and farm values and wanted our children to have them too. The kids enjoyed spending a part of each summer with their cousins, and the bond with their aunts and uncles was growing deep because of these visits. My brother, Henry, had long since married his beloved Alberta, but they had been unable to have children, so our children had become their "adopted" brood.

Arvella was torn at the prospect of the separation, but the children were too excited to take note of her almost tearful last-minute doting. So it was a day of mixed goodbyes as we sent them off to stay with their uncle.

The next day, assured that the three girls had arrived without a glitch, the four of us boarded the boat in Long Beach. During our six weeks on the high seas, we spent hours studying geology, philosophy (my class), and anthropology. This last subject was the perfect preparation for our visit with the primitive tribes in the jungles of New Guinea, where the men wore nothing more than a shell and a hollowed gourd, their dark bodies glistening with pig's grease.

While at sea, I even found a chance to do some work on a manuscript that I had promised the publisher by summer's end. Settled into a secluded upper deck area in the stern, I found that rare solitude essential to every writer. The view was liberating as I gazed at the long wake in a calm South Pacific waterway between small, uninhabited islands. I watched as we drifted past them in our smooth-sailing vessel, and creativity flowed.

When we at last reached Hong Kong, Ike Eichenberger, my chief aide and head of my Institute for Successfull Church Leadership, was waiting as the ship pulled in. We all enjoyed a few days touring the city together. Then it was time to say goodbye to Arvella and Sheila and Bob at the Hong Kong airport. It had been an invaluable trip for all of us and had strengthened the relationship between our own college teens and Arvella and me.

I handed Arvella my handwritten manuscript of what would be my next book, *You Can Be the Person You Want to Be*, and said, "Take good care of this, honey; it's the only copy." She gave me that look that says to us husbands, "Give me a little credit!" Then she kissed me deeply. For a moment I thought twice about going on, but excitement also bubbled up within me. I wanted desperately to see other worlds and lifestyles and catch a peek at God's workings around the globe.

Arvella sensed the conflict in me. "Honey, enjoy yourself," she said. "You deserve it. You've worked hard, and God has a plan for you on this trip. Don't worry about us. We'll be fine. Just be careful, and don't forget to bring an extra-special something home for the girls."

I promised, then begged her to kiss and hug them for me every night.

I hugged Sheila and Bob and said, "I'll see you in two weeks." I was planning to return just before they were to head back to my alma mater, Hope College.

As I watched them walk up the jetway to the awaiting plane, I felt very alone. It would be a long time before I'd see them again. Yet I was filled with anticipation for this leg of the trip. I thought of my Uncle Henry and his missionary work, and my excitement grew.

The side pocket of my bag was filled with traveler's checks. This was "mission" money to use when and where I sensed an urgent need. I wanted to bring encouragement and inspiration, but I also felt a need to bring "cash."

For a few weeks I wanted to be, as my friend Corrie ten Boom had put it, a "tramp for the Lord." I would avoid my own denominational "foreign" mission stations. I already knew about them. I wanted to see places, people, and projects that I knew nothing about.

"Start with David Wang in Hong Kong," I had been told. "He brings the most insight into the China scene." David was the head of Asian Outreach, an organization founded by the American evangelist Paul Kauffman, unsurpassed in experience and integrity in a lifetime of widely respected missionary work in Mainland China.

We took the ferry over from Kowloon, then a taxi to a very westernized commercial street. When we reached the office of Asia Outreach we found a young man sitting at a desk below a banner proclaiming HALLELUJAH ANYWAY! He introduced himself as David Wang.

I did a double-take and said, "I love that slogan, David! Tell me more."

"'Be thankful always' was Saint Paul's advice," he said. "My translation is 'Hallelujah anyway!'"

We had a good laugh. Then he handed me some beautiful four-color cards of flowers and gardens with Bible verses beautifully penned in Chinese. "You see, Dr. Schuller, my mission is to be a publisher. These texts are written in the new modern Chinese. Our ancient language had a thousand and more letters, so the common people never learned to read it. When Mao Tse-tung came to power, he knew that he couldn't control the huge country without improving literacy, so he created a new alphabet—simple and easy to learn. We've taken selected Bible verses and have been writing them by hand onto these cards, hoping to spread God's Word."

"But that's so slow," I said. "You need a printing press. You need the whole Bible."

"That's right! But you see, there have been no printing presses with the new letters outside Mao's control! But I had the new letters made for the first printing press outside of China! I had it made in Japan. And it's here—on the dock in Hong Kong. All I need is a thousand U.S. dollars and I can pick it up! And the first thing we'll print is the new Bible. Pray that God will find that money! I don't have it. If I don't pick the press up fast—like tomorrow—the Japanese factory will sell it to a secular Hong Kong publisher."

I reached in my pocket, pulled out a thousand dollars' worth of traveler's checks, and signed my name to them. A few months later, back home, I would receive the very first copy of the new Chinese Bible to come off the press.

I knew now that I was on a trip that would shape the rest of my life, a trip that would give new meaning to a phrase from Tennyson that had always guided me: "I am a part of all that I have met."

In India our visit took us first to Kashmir, then on to New Delhi, where I became acquainted with Mother Teresa's work for the first time.

I didn't meet her on this trip, but I was amazed as I watched the compassion of her dark-skinned nursing sisters as they ministered to the most hopeless of the human family. I didn't know how much she would personally affect my ministry and my relationship with Jesus Christ until we were able to spend time together some years later at a working session in Mexico. Then I would discover an intimate connection with her spirit. I would remain permanently influenced by her ministry and was honored to pay my last respects to her at her funeral.

Next, our mission trip took us to Iran—the city of Isfahan—where I met an inspiring Anglican churchman. In him I saw the same spirit that I had observed in David Wang, the same spirit that I had seen and felt at Mother Teresa's clinic in India. This same spirit—the Holy Spirit—I now saw flowing from the heart of this man as he excitedly built a chapel. His mission to the non-Christians (and even to the anti-Christians) in his country moved me.

While in downtown Isfahan one day, waiting for our car to pick us up, I saw an unusual ring displayed in the window of a small jewelry store. "What a pretty color blue!" I said to my new Anglican friend, waiting with me. "What kind of stone is that?"

"Let me inquire," he answered, stepping into the shop. The proprietor reached to retrieve it, then handed it to my new pastor friend. After some conversation between the two, he brought it out of the store to show me, saying, "It's lapis lazuli. It's an antique, with the emblem of a lion and the initials of the one-time owner. You press it into melted wax and seal your letters with it."

Before I could protest, he had lifted my right hand and slipped the ring on my finger, saying, "Here, this is for you." It fit perfectly.

He smiled. "It's yours! Remember the Christians here in Iran, Dr. Schuller. We need your prayers." He turned to the smiling proprietor in the window and laughed his farewell.

Six months later I sponsored his trip to California and we had private prayer time together. I prayed, "Someday Muslims and Christians must come to live together in the faith and the peace that both religions are exhorted to embrace." But when he returned home, he was assassinated, a victim of religious intolerance during the radical overthrow of the shah of Iran. The chapel he had built was burned to the ground. I still wear the ring in memory of him.

When it was time to board the plane for Russia, I didn't know the future fate of our Iranian friend, but similar intrigues were definitely on my mind.

While still on the plane, Ike and I went over the instructions I'd been given. There would be as many as six hundred people in a forest clearing outside Kiev, where I was scheduled to preach. We were to meet our host in a hotel in Kiev. I was to enter the lobby of the hotel at exactly six in the evening. He would approach me and ask, "Having a good trip?" If I hadn't yet had any encounters with Soviet authorities, I was to assume the coast was clear and say, "Yes, thank you." He'd then turn around, walk out, and head down the street to wait at the first corner. I'd let a few minutes go by, then walk out too. My host would proceed down the side street and wait for me in the shadows. If all was still clear and no one was tailing me, we'd step together into a waiting car and be off to the secret "gathering in the woods."

The danger, I knew, was that the Soviet secret police, the KGB, would be watching our every move. They'd probably have our hotel room bugged. Ike and I were most likely safe enough, but exposure could mean arrest and a lifetime of imprisonment for the leaders of this underground church. So if we were suspicious of any KGB eyes, when the host came to approach me I was to turn away and answer not a word, and the whole event would be off. He would then go to the Christians alone and explain.

When we landed in Moscow we were searched at customs, and the Bibles in our suitcases were confiscated. "Anti-Russian propaganda," we were told.

Then one of several grim-faced officers asked me, "What are you doing traveling the world?"

"I'm with Chapman University," I answered. I showed them the special letter, on university letterhead, that I'd been told to carry.

"Why did you come to Russia?" another asked.

I answered as I'd been briefed: "I study religion and wanted to visit your famous Museum of Atheism in Leningrad."

The officers smiled for the first time. They loved that answer and waved us through. An official "guide" was assigned to us, but of course she was really with the KGB. She would be with us every moment of our trip from Moscow to Leningrad.

Once in Leningrad we had a pleasant time at the usual tourist spots—the Hermitage art museum, the ballet, the opera house. But the museum wasn't part of our itinerary. On our last afternoon of sightseeing our guide announced, "This ends our tour. I'll take you back to the hotel to rest, for you leave early tomorrow for the airport. You'll fly to Lvov, change planes to Kiev, and the next day take the train from Kiev to Vienna.

"I'll say goodbye to you at the airport tomorrow. When you get off the plane at Kiev a new Intourist guide will meet you. She'll put you on the train to Vienna the next day. She'll depart once you're on the train. You'll be all right. You'll simply get off in Vienna."

I looked at my watch. It was one in the afternoon. "Thank you for everything," I said. "There's one more place I had hoped to see, but I note that it's not on the itinerary."

She looked at me, waiting.

"The Museum of Atheism," I said. "Have you been there? Could I see it?"

"Yes, I've heard of it. No, I've never been there. I'd like to see it too. It was once a huge Roman Catholic church. It's not far from here. We'll stop on the way back to the hotel."

Our tour car stopped in front of an imposing piece of architecture. Tall pillars dominated the enormous front of what had once been one of the most impressive Roman Catholic churches not only in Russia but in all of Europe. In the massive front entrance were sculpted apes, and then "ape men." The guide read the posters aloud: "Religion teaches that God created humans. We now know that we have evolved from apes."

I wanted to say, "But that awesome process of evolution was itself as much a miracle from God's hand as it would have been had He scooped us from clay and blown upon us!" But I said nothing. Our trip had gone well so far. It was important that I say and do nothing to make our guide suspicious. Tomorrow would be my trip to Kiev, my rendezvous with my nameless Christian guide, and my visit to the underground church. "Just keep quiet," I told myself.

The guide led us through the exhibits. We went down a set of steps following arrows, and there on the wall I saw large photographs of American planes dropping bombs in Vietnam. "Religion creates wars," said our guide, translating the banner. Then she continued, "Religious leaders promote war, racism, and oppression of the poor." And there on the wall, under a single banner, were photographs of the pope in Rome, Martin Luther King, Jr., Billy Graham, and . . . Robert Schuller!

Ike's mouth literally fell open. I nearly fainted. Our guide stared at me, then at my picture, but said nothing as she continued to read the description.

There was no point in dissembling; she clearly recognized my picture. "So what do they say about me?" I asked.

"They say that you built the biggest new church in America. They say that you steal money from the poor to pay for architectural monuments."

This certainly wasn't the time or place to contest that assessment, nor did I have the energy. "I'm really tired," I said. "May we go back to the hotel?"

It was a long, cold, silent ride back. I could see KGB spy wheels turning in our guide's head.

Once back in our hotel, I fell on my bed and prayed, and prayed, and prayed. "O God, what do I do about the meeting in Kiev tomorrow? Obviously I'll be watched. Do I go and visit the underground church that's been waiting for an encouraging message from this American? Or must I pass this by to spare them from detection and exposure?"

The next morning Ike and I were packed and ready to go on schedule. Our guide was even chillier than she'd been the previous afternoon; in fact, she was downright hostile, her words clipped and abrupt. She treated me like a powerful enemy to communism.

"I've called ahead," she said formally. "You will be met on your arrival in Kiev. Your escort will take care of you from there."

And with that we boarded our plane.

Now I was really afraid. Soviet authorities now knew that I wasn't simply a professor of philosophy at Chapman College in California.

In Kiev my fear became true anguish as our new guide guarded our every move. According to plan, I presented myself in the hotel lobby. Ike and I chatted and waited. In time, my friendly host, whom I hadn't seen for months, came in and walked casually by. I wanted desperately to greet him, but I couldn't. I turned my head away.

"Have a good trip?" I heard him ask. I ignored him; I turned away and continued my conversation with Ike. The minister caught the clue and walked on and out the front door, and my lips trembled. I hoped that no one noticed. This was the one and only time in my life that I *couldn't* push to the edge, because others might be exposed and imprisoned.

"We're free again!" I said to Ike as we boarded the train for Vienna. He nodded in silent and evident relief. We were in a small private compartment—just us and a man on the seat facing us. He introduced himself as an American, a professor at a U.S. university which he didn't identify. As we exchanged introductions, our door was opened quickly and noisily by a Russian in military uniform. He barked a command that I couldn't understand.

"He has to see your papers," the professor translated. We handed him our passports and tickets. He kept the tickets, handed the passports back, and left without a word.

After some time—I don't remember how much longer—the train came to a jolting stop. The officer was at the door again, barking orders to us. This time he'd brought a translator, who said, "We're at the border of Czechoslovakia. You do not have visas to enter Czechoslovakia." Then he demanded, "Passports!"

We handed our passports to the officer and he perused them, taking longer this time than the first. Through the translator he ordered, "One of you will go out to the border control with both passports and four U.S. dollar bills to buy your visas." He handed the passports to Ike. Miracle of miracles, between the two of us we had exactly and only four one-dollar bills!

The officer, commanding me to sit and wait, ushered Ike out of the compartment. Suddenly I recalled a rule of international travel that was never, under any circumstance, to be broken: "Never let go of your passport except to a government agent at immigration."

I felt ill at ease, but I knew that I could trust Ike. I waited . . . and waited. Then I heard a sound that sent shivers through my whole body: *hiss-ss-ss*—the sound of steam from a train starting to move! Again the hiss. Then I felt it: the train was moving—without Ike! And I was alone without a passport. The train picked up steam. We were now on our way, moving quickly.

The same military officer appeared at our compartment door, barking at me again. Without the translator, I couldn't understand.

The professor smiled at me and said, "He said your friend is on the train two cars ahead of us. He has the passports and visas. He can't come join you simply because the doors between the cars are locked."

What a relief!

In Vienna I telephoned home. It was three in the morning in California—not the best time to call—but Arvella answered quickly, and the warmth of her voice had never sounded more comforting to me.

A huge burden of anxiety was lifted, just by crossing a boundary into the West. But I still felt anguish for those Russian followers of Christ whom I'd been unable to help.

I never saw or heard from our would-be host again, the man who'd asked me to come. I never *wanted* to see Russia again—a country of vast and frightening repression. And yet, in time, that land would become a large and tremendously meaningful part of my tomorrow.

XXXIII

The flight from Vienna home to California was one of the longest plane rides of my life.

Questions tumbled through my mind, refusing to let me sleep. During those eleven hours suspended up in the sky, I found myself having a sort of midlife, midcareer identity crisis. Another way of looking at it, of course, was that God was redirecting me.

I was glad to be safely on my way home after a two-month around-the-world mission, but I was saddened that my ministry to the underground church had been aborted. And why had I been depicted in that Museum of Atheism?

I remembered our would-be host's telling me about the Russian translation of Neutra's book, *Survival Through Design.* He'd mentioned that it had been widely read in his country. Sure enough, in Leningrad's Museum of Atheism I'd seen a picture of the Tower of Hope from the pages of that book right next to my picture.

I recalled another Russian magazine article that had been sent to me by an associate. Pictures of our church accompanied an article about how money was spent on superstitious structures in America. I fended off the criticisms in my mind. *Someday the Russian people must be told the truth,* I thought. *These aren't monuments. They're instruments of hope! Russia needs freedom and faith!*

If, as Tennyson had said, "I am a part of all that I have ever met," then who am I now? After all this, what's my calling for the future? I prayed, "Lord, what mission do You have for the rest of my life?"

I had been called to build a church, and I had done that. But I was only forty-five years old and still had time and talent to give. I'd worn so many hats: missionary, land developer, architect, fundraiser, theologian, motivational lecturer, television broadcaster, senior executive administrative minister, minister to ministers, founder and overseer of the Institute for Successful Church Leadership.

Many ministers in America were looking for a new network of positive-thinking churches. One of my board members, Rich DeVos, had recommended that I take on the building of just such a network. But I couldn't handle that. I'd be accused of starting a new denomination!

Suddenly, as I thought about all of this on the plane home, it was all too much for me. My life back home had become a blur of obligations, while the trip I'd just been on had offered me more peace and joy in ministry and mission than I'd had in a long time (despite the harrowing experience in Russia).

Questions moved in my mind: Was God reguiding me? Should I turn our large, strong church over to the denomination for a replacement and retire from the life I'd lived for seventeen years?

In these early 1970s, our rising membership was about to make us the largest congregation in America's oldest denomination. The buildings on our twenty acres made us the largest church property in the Reformed Church. I had finished the job. I was now working on a systematic theology that could blend the positive insights of twentieth-century psychology with biblical and historical theology going back through Wesley, Calvin, and Saint Augustine. Ideally, I could publish it in just a few years. I hoped to work with the guidance of Viktor Frankl—the leading psychiatrist of our day. I also wanted to connect, consult, and work with Martin Marty—the most esteemed professor of religion (who was also a Schuller critic). Only when such a primer on a theology for the next century could pass the muster of Marty and Frankl—only then would I publish it.

No one else could do this particular job. Perhaps I should give it my full attention and allow it to consume me the way my seminary thesis had consumed me twenty-two years ago.

My mind was moving from one edge to the other.

As an author, I could live on the royalties, replenish my nonprofit foundation with income from commercial lecture fees, and spend the free months of every year being a tramp for the Lord. What a life! Free of fundraising for land and buildings, free to pursue philanthropy worldwide. The sky was the limit!

"Ladies and gentlemen, we're beginning our descent into Los Angeles," a flight attendant informed us. "Please fasten your seatbelts."

I would have to fasten my career seatbelt too.

Reentry after a long trip is always difficult, but this time it was excruciating! On the one hand, I was delighted to see my family. Having made it out of Russia, all I wanted was to hold on to Arvella and never let her go. But career-wise, I'd lost all enthusiasm.

The Tower of Hope—the tallest structure in Orange County—loomed high to welcome me home the first Sunday following my return. It was not only the tallest church tower on the Pacific coast, it was also the first and only "skyscraper" church facility in the world.

Yes. *Famous in Russia too,* I thought with a painful jolt as I looked up at the cross gleaming high atop that tower. It was the first structure in the area to catch the rising sun on this historic Sunday. The founding pastor was coming home from a visit to "enemy territory." The Cold War between the United States and the USSR was in full force. Both sides were boasting larger and ever-more powerful missiles, which they kept aimed at each other. The nuclear warheads lodged within those missiles could blast our largest cities off the map! The very existence of life on this planet was at stake.

I was coming home with a fresh world perspective, and all I could see were faces of spiritually hungry humans. I wanted passionately to preach a series of messages on peace to my congregation, now numbering hundreds of thousands every Sunday from New York to California. I had seen so much heartache on this trip. And our own country was still engaged in a war that would take the lives of over fifty thousand Americans.

Now I had an eighteen-year-old son facing the same question I had faced back at Hope College: fight in a war or pursue forward with his dream for the ministry. He would accept deferment while in college, but not before his mother and I had struggled with the worry that every parent faces when there's the possibility that a son might be lost in battle. I had close friends, and my son had close friends, who had already become victims and veterans of Vietnam.

This conflict that was killing our boys was also dividing and draining America's creative energies. All around the globe, it seemed, people were in terrible pain.

But preaching on peace was just too politicized in the early seventies. I couldn't afford to be drawn back into the political crossfire with a war still raging heatedly in Southeast Asia and the Cold War still being waged between the United States and the USSR. How could I return from Russia suddenly preaching peace? Wouldn't I appear to have been brainwashed? I was already a media target, simply because of my return from the USSR.

My first Sunday back we set an all-time record for attendance at the morning service. Rumors had mixed with reports regarding my round-the-world mission trip, and I found my congregation unusually excited as they gathered for worship.

Cars lined the streets leading to our church well before the service was to start, and traffic was bumper to bumper. The Neutra sanctuary recently had been enlarged to increase seating capacity from one thousand to fourteen hundred persons, but it still couldn't hold the bulging crowd. Five hundred lawn chairs had to be rented pronto and set up outside the sparkling glass east wall. From my high pulpit I would have face-to-face connection not only with the people inside the serene and stately sanctuary, but also with the hundreds sitting outside on the lawn and in their cars in the drive-in church. And then, of course, there were the television viewers.

But after two decades of phenomenal and virtually unexplainable growth, the fact of the matter was that the Garden Grove Community Church was literally bursting at the seams. Where were all the people coming from?

Sunday after Sunday, people who were already crowded together on the pews would, at my request, "do the Schuller shuffle," cramming even closer together to allow space for those standing in the back. But hundreds were generally still forced into the Fellowship Hall, where they'd view the service on closed-circuit television.

The winter before, we'd actually purchased three hundred blankets to distribute to those sitting on the grounds.

Where was this seventeen-year-old church headed? What was its future in California? In America? In the world? And could we afford to let seating capacity be the factor that strangled its growth?

Members of the board offered various opinions:

"Can't we knock out the west wall? That would enlarge the church by another thousand people."

"We've been on television only two years. In time, won't people just stay home and turn their living rooms into overflow rooms? Then we wouldn't have to add to our beautiful facility."

The debate and the discussion raged on, while I remained silent and depressed. In my mind, I was still on my world tour. Some part of me wanted to go back and spend the rest of my life being a world missionary.

Not one member of that board had any clue as to where I stood. With all they had to deal with, I didn't dare tell them I was struggling with a "career crisis" on top of it all.

But for seventeen years I'd been buying and building and building and buying! From the drive-in theater to the purchase of our first ten acres, to another ten acres, to the building of our first structure, then a larger sanctuary, then the Tower of Hope—I was *sick and tired* of wearing the cap of architect/developer/fundraiser. After all, my calling was to be a *preacher!*

On the inside I was screaming to escape, while on the outside I had to stay cool. The state of mind left me completely unprepared for the motion that was raised at our board meeting: "Mr. Chairman, I move that we engage an architect to research and recommend the best solution to accommodate our growing church."

Several voices quickly seconded the motion. Then a director spoke: "I call for the question." According to *Robert's Rules of Order,* I had no choice but to place the motion on the floor. And it passed—unanimously, I think, but only because, as chairman, I couldn't vote.

I drove home that night deeply troubled, feeling that I had no choice. I was bound by the church board's decision. I'd have to find an architect. Richard Neutra and I had been professional colleagues for fifteen years, and I had officiated at his funeral not long before. I couldn't imagine finding an architect who could match him. And even if I did, would his replacement and I connect as creatively as Richard and I had done? What if he became so ego-involved that he failed to respect the structures of his esteemed predecessor?

And where would the money come from? Surely it wasn't here in our middle-class congregation. Would the board be forced to accept the "cheapest" solution? Would our commitment to excellence in the art of architecture be reduced to mediocrity for reasons of cost?

Did I want to be a part of any of this? No way!

But I couldn't—under church law—refuse to carry out the consistory order. At that moment, if I could have turned the church over to a promising successor with a new architect already on board, I would have been ready to move on and out.

Yes—maybe it *was* time for me to resign. But first I would choose the architect, if for no other reason than to prevent our beautiful facility from being cheapened and downgraded.

The first candidate I interviewed was Benno Fisher, a past associate in Neutra's office. He had been in charge of enlarging the original Neutra church—knocking out the wall, adding a balcony, designing the largest vertical stone wall in architectural history. Benno and I considered all the options for enlarging the church without violating Neutra's original design. All options failed, for one reason or another.

I interviewed another architect. "You need to abandon your sanctuary as your church," he said. "Turn it into a large dining and conference hall. Replace it with a newer and larger building on your new ten acres. I can do it for you."

I recommended this plan to the board, and they hired him. He submitted a picture with a price, both ugly. Well, not really. The design just didn't work with Neutra's vision. "You don't wear attractive new tennis shoes with a tuxedo!" I said. But the others didn't see it that way.

"Look at the pricetag," I urged. "It would cost three million dollars!"

I was convinced that this architect was a mistake, as was his design. The board went ahead despite my protests and ordered a campaign to raise the cash. I remained anything but enthusiastic.

The financial committee of the consistory launched the capital funds drive with a lot of hoopla, but no matter how hard they tried, the building didn't attract the excitement necessary for financial success. I knew intuitively that something about it was wrong, and apparently the donors did too. Months of exasperation drained my energy as the board struggled to raise the money, but the congregation didn't buy it. The campaign failed, and inwardly I was relieved.

We abandoned the idea of building a larger sanctuary, and for two years I went into neutral gear—into denial. "We don't have to build a new sanctuary," I told myself. I was gravely mistaken, however. The television ministry was growing. Our congregation was growing. The Institute for Successful Church Leadership was growing.

It was at one of these Institute gatherings that I heard myself say, "Leadership is the force that sets growth goals." Several heads in the group nodded.

"Never surrender leadership to property," I challenged.

"Think big enough to let God's ideas fit into your church planning," I exhorted.

When Bill Hybels attended one of these seminars as a young minister from Illinois, we chatted during a seminar break and he asked my advice. "We're buying a large piece of land," he said. "But should we buy the whole piece—like about a hundred acres—when we could get by with a lot less?"

I didn't hesitate. "Buy the whole piece, Bill. As I told you, make your thinking big enough for God to fit in."

He did it. And some years later, he'd invite me to speak to his church in Chicago on that large site. But at the time, I—the proponent of positive thinking—didn't have the vision to solve my own church-growth obstacles.

Then came the Sunday when God yanked me back into the game.

I was called on to pastor a beautiful young couple faced with an incredible loss. Over the telephone a weeping young mother spoke through her sobs. "Are you the minister in that church with the big cross?" she asked.

I answered, "Yes, I am. How can I help you?"

"Our four-year-old drowned this week. We don't belong to any church. Can you do the funeral?"

To bury a child—how can a parent ever make it through such a tragedy? It was a deeply emotional service, even though I hadn't known the child. I came close to breaking down as I thought of my own young Gretchen, now seven years old. My arms were around the two of them as we left the cemetery on Friday.

"Come to church Sunday," I said. "You need a deeper power in your hearts that only faith can bring."

They nodded silently.

"I'll look for you Sunday. I'll scan the crowd until I see you, and when I lock eyes with you, you'll know that I'm sending prayers your way."

Sunday came. The Neutra church was jammed, so I called for "the Schuller shuffle." Ushers stood ready to escort those standing to newly created empty spaces at the ends of the pews. But I didn't see the mourning couple.

We had to keep the aisles and the entrance clear—fire department regulations. "There are seats in the overflow area in the garden," I announced, though there wouldn't be for long: cars were still arriving. Then, out of a car that was parked in a corner far away from the drive-in section, I saw the young mother and her husband being directed by an usher to empty chairs on the lawn—two empty ones on the front row where I could see their faces. They sat beneath a darkened sky that was layered with heavy clouds. My sermon was entitled "Powerful Faith for Problem Times," but before I could share my message, a cold, wind-driven rain began to fall. That day is so vivid in my memory.

I am standing in my pulpit, on the balcony that extends over the green California lawn. I'm protected from the downpour by a flat roof that acts as an umbrella. My eyes are locked on this young and handsome couple. I can't look away from the grieving mother—blond and delicate, not much older than thirty, with no umbrella for protection. I watch these two suffering, broken-hearted parents raise their small paper bulletins above their heads. They snuggle closer, and even at my distance I can see them shiver.

The young husband now holds his pullover sweater over her head to try to protect her. His arms look weak from days of bitter grief. The pain in his face looks to be approaching that of a nervous breakdown—not something I'm used to seeing on such a young face, its jaw cut sharp and handsome.

Finally he takes her hand and they lift their wet and aching bodies from the chairs, soon puddled again with fresh rain. And they leave—these people so desperately in need of God's loving care—they *leave!* Still holding hands as they walk away, they return to their car and drive off. They came for solace and left uncomforted.

The hurt still haunts me as I remember this scene—a scene that played in my mind over . . . and over . . . and over . . . and over during the next weeks and months.

I made a decision in my heart, right then and there, when I saw them leave. I would have to press through my impatience and frustration. I would have to find that world-class architect and build that larger church we so desperately needed. I felt the same immeasurable responsibility that a parent feels for a child in crisis. Though tired and worn, you can't abandon the one you birthed and love.

And so I would ask, once again, "What now, Lord?" But I had no idea how God would answer my plea.

XXXIV

Returning home from speaking at a church conference in Europe, I was nudged out of my state of reverie by my wife's loving elbow.

"Read this, Bob," Arvella said, handing me a glossy magazine with the headline "Ten Beautiful Places in America."

The article that had caught her attention with its photo described as "The Fort Worth Water Gardens, designed by Philip Johnson." Johnson? The name meant nothing to me. I'd never heard of him.

"He sounds like he's really a landscape architect," Arvella said. "Maybe you should start with him. You're so committed to Neutra's biorealism, bringing the environment into architecture. Maybe this guy is on your same wavelength, or can direct you to someone who is."

I was intrigued by the story. I had been struggling for two years to find someone to complete the setting that Richard Neutra had begun for us.

The following week *Time* magazine ran an article on architecture. The opening sentence declared, "Philip Johnson and I. M. Pei are the leading names in architecture today."

I called information in New York City, obtained Johnson's number, and got him on the line.

He'd never heard of me either, but when I mentioned my nearly ten years of work with the late Richard Neutra, he was willing to meet. I flew to New York in the fall of 1977. The city was gorgeous in its autumn colors.

I was welcomed into an office that reflected the kind of taste I was looking for. The high-rise structure had been designed by Philip Johnson and his partner, Mies van der Rohe. I was impressed.

Philip Johnson was warm but very professional as he took me to a small conversation area near a window overlooking the city. I explained the reason for my visit. Bald, with black-rimmed glasses and impeccable attire, he smiled and nodded at my mention of biorealism. At that moment—he would tell me later—he still thought I was an architect who had worked ten years with Richard Neutra, as a Neutra *associate!* He thought I was looking for a job!

"Mr. Johnson," I clarified, "I'm the pastor of a church, and we need a building to seat three thousand. The new structure has to blend with the existing environment, which is dominated by Neutra's tower, bell-frame, and sanctuary. This new sanctuary must enhance, not compete with, the other buildings on our campus. Can you make that happen?"

I had used this interviewing question with every architect I'd met with for the past two years.

Johnson smiled. "Absolutely," he said. "No problem."

He exuded self-assurance. I liked that—very, very much. He continued, "I respect and admire Mr. Neutra as one of the founders of 'the new international school of architecture.' I actually gave Mr. Neutra his first job in America when he arrived here from Austria. I named him to design a building for my father's business in Ohio. I'd love to integrate something with his work."

"There's one catch," I continued. "For six years I preached from the rooftop of the snackbar in a drive-in theater. I've now been preaching for over ten years in the huge glass Neutra sanctuary. It's beautiful, but the flat roof is solid wood. I miss the light from the sky! I want a building that seats three thousand—all glass—that's essentially married to nature's light!"

Johnson leaned back in his chair. Suddenly the smile was gone, and a serious, sober face reflected grave misgivings.

"A building seating three thousand made entirely of glass in an earthquake zone?" Then he uttered that naughty, foul, defamatory word:

"*Impossible!*"

I wanted to hand him my pocket dictionary. I wanted to say to him, "Look at this page—right here." And then I wanted him to see that the horrible word "impossible" had been cut out. I'd watch him blush. Then I'd tell him, "I cut that word out of my dictionary when I started my church nineteen years ago!"

But I didn't do any of this. Instead, I got straight to the point. "Mr. Johnson," I said, moving close and locking eyes with him, "*I don't believe it's impossible!*" Having said that naughty word, I then explained, "All you need to do is hire yourself some smarter engineers."

He tipped his head to the side as if weighing my conclusion. He must have come down on the side of possibility, because he said, "By the way, what kind of a budget do you have in mind?"

"We're not setting a budget, sir," I answered. "We can't afford one million, two million, three million, or more. We have *no* money. We'll borrow the money we need to retain you, and then you'll have to come up with a design that will inspire the congregation. It will have to be such a masterpiece that it will attract the money we need to build the structure! It will have to grab the imagination of sophisticated and successful people!"

Then I concluded, "Mr. Johnson, you can fail only if you don't try. I know that you'll succeed!"

Three weeks later he showed me his first drawings. When he unfolded them before me, he could read disappointment in my eyes.

"An all-glass ceiling?"

"That's what you asked for," he replied, exasperated.

"But the walls are all solid. Not glass!"

He defended his thinking. "I felt that the walls would give the congregation a sense of privacy—protection from uninvited visual intrusion from the outside." I could see that he was trying to be sensitive to the spiritual purpose of the building.

"But Mr. Johnson!" I said, "I want a church with a glass ceiling so that we can see the sky. A glass ceiling that will imply that there are no limits to our upward vision. But I also want glass walls. Worshipers need to be able to see the world outside and seek and sense emotional connections with other humans—even strangers! No fences, no ceilings—that's what my faith is all about!"

He looked disappointed at first. Then he caught the vision and his face began to sparkle. He and I were both hooked, at that very moment, on an "impossible" holy dream.

I would have to borrow two hundred thousand dollars to retain the architectural firm of Philip Johnson & Associates. And the next five years would be the most momentous and challenging time in my ministry, and in my family.

It's the spring of 1974. Robert Anthony is home, having completed his second year of pre-seminary work at Hope College. He's already registered for his third year there, but today he's excited as he asks to speak with Arvella and me.

As we gather in our small living room, Arvella and I exchange puzzled glances.

Bob sits in a chair opposite the loveseat that Arvella and I now share. "Dad?" he says tentatively.

I'm beginning to get nervous. What's he going to tell us?

"Dad? Mom? You know I've been dating a lot. Well, it's all been with the same girl, and . . . I really am in love with her, and, well— I asked her to marry me last night."

Oh, my goodness! Our first child getting married? Not yet!

"But Robert, you're only nineteen!" Arvella countered.

Then I jumped in. "How can you manage as a married college student? It's hard enough for us to make ends meet paying for your board and tuition. We can't afford added expenses. How will *you?*"

Then I reminded myself that our son was an adult. We'd always told our children that once they were eighteen, we'd acknowledge their entry into adulthood by allowing them to make their own decisions—even when we disagreed. How could I now renege on our promise? I'd have to let Bob make his own decision.

And so we did our best to make the wedding a beautiful experience, but we grieved when we said our goodbyes to the newlyweds as they headed back to Michigan and a new life far from home. Arvella and I reminded ourselves often that they weren't too different from ourselves, though we'd been nearly four years older and had had the stress of school behind us.

Now our traditional nightly ritual of praying for each family member by name took on a greater dimension. Our family was growing, and so as Arvella and I knelt by our bed—as we'd done every night since our wedding—we added extra prayers focused not only on Bob but also on his young wife.

In November 1975 I got a call from Philip Johnson.

"Dr. Schuller, I think I've got it. I mean an all-glass cathedral—roof and walls, everything! I'll fly to California and show you a little model I've built."

Not many days later, he walked into my office carrying a small aluminum briefcase. He opened it and I gasped. "Wow!" I said when I saw the star-shaped, diamond-sparkling model of an all-glass church. That's all I *could* say. He'd clearly caught the visual stimulus of what I was seeing and describing.

"It's four hundred and fourteen feet long, point to point," Philip said. "All roofs slope upward and meet at a crown, which opens to release all the heat. You're not allowed to air-condition a building such as this because of the new energy laws. Besides, it would bankrupt you. So we've designed it to be naturally wind-cooling, with a high ceiling of one hundred and twenty-six feet at its peak. That's twelve stories!

"The sanctuary will seat three thousand people. From the inside you'll look out to see sky and trees, but from the outside the windows will be black mirrors to deflect the hot sun, reflect the sky and trees, and give privacy to the worshipers from outside gawkers. It will be the largest space-frame structure in the world."

He waited for a moment. Then he said, "Well? What do you say, Dr. Schuller?"

With misty eyes, and with enthusiasm bursting in the depths of my soul, I answered, "Yes, it *must* be built. Planet earth must not be deprived of this treasure! If it takes ten years off of my life to give the leadership to this achievement, it's a price worth paying."

Little did I know how prophetic my assessment would be. In any case, though, any thought of a career change was now totally and completely gone!

I was trapped in a new dream, one that I could never abandon. I was responding in the same way at that moment as I had to the first dream of my life—that dream of ministry when I was only five years old. I was filled with a conviction that this goal must be reached, no matter what.

Four months later we celebrated the twentieth anniversary of the founding of our church. Seven thousand of our members and friends filled a huge banquet hall at the Anaheim Convention Center to see and hear what was promised to be a dramatic revelation of a fabulous new dream.

I held the model high. Then I surprised everybody by saying, "I believe that someone will give a million dollars to launch the financial campaign for the construction of this cathedral."

I told how, during a recent weekend retreat of the church board, I had shared my vision for the new church and had said, "No one will ever believe that the construction of this beautiful structure can happen. But they will if we have a gift of one million dollars. Let's pray for that." Then and there, for the first and only time in our history, all board members present fell to their knees and prayed specifically for God to find and lead us to the person who could make a million-dollar gift.

I heard gasps in the great crowd at the convention center. Then I shared with them where I had found the divine passion to pursue this "impossible" dream. I saw the face of that young couple again in my mind as if it had just happened. Then I said to them all at the close of my story, "You won't have to sit outdoors under winter covers when we build this new home for you! We don't know what it will cost—but I believe that God wants this. We'll trust Him and give Him a chance to work a miracle!"

In December of 1975 the architect reported a cost estimate of seven million dollars. I almost fainted! I read my own inspirational books to keep my positive thinking alive. I read my acrostic on the word STRIVE:

Start small.

Think possibilities.

Reach beyond your known abilities.

Invest all you have in your dream.

Visualize miracles.

Expect to experience success!

Then I began to wonder what heaps of criticism I might receive for "spending so much money." I made a covenant with God: "If You want it built, Lord, I'll take the heat if You'll provide the cash."

I had never been a materialist who worships money. To me the only value of money is that it gives people power to deliver good or evil. So the issue isn't, How much does it cost? The issue is, Does God want it?

A month later, in January of 1976, the architect delivered great news: "The structure is viable from an engineering point of view. The city's building department has okayed our preliminary request to build the cathedral."

But in February I felt overwhelmed. How would we be able to pay off our loan of two hundred thousand dollars? And where would we ever get another seven million dollars to build the cathedral?

The consistory was now faced with the issue of financing. Our bank—Farmers & Merchants—was at that time limited by law to a loan no larger than four million dollars. No other bank we talked with would touch the project. At a special consistory meeting one very successful deacon suggested that his broker could handle it by selling bonds to cover the entire cost.

"But what would the interest on something like that be?" I objected. "We can't afford that added expense in our operational budget."

He was confident that his approach would work, but I was wary and doubtful. He ended the standoff between the two of us by leaping from his seat in a burst of anger and storming out of the room, shouting, "Okay, then *you* go out and raise the cash, Schuller!"

The remaining board members sat in stunned silence. Not a voice was raised. The meeting was adjourned.

To this day I can still hear him slamming the door loudly as he made his angry exit. He resigned from the board and stopped coming to church, which was a great personal loss to me, because he was a close friend of our family.

And yet years later, when he became very ill, I made a hospital call on him and we were tearfully reunited as brothers in our faith.

I officiated at his funeral in the Crystal Cathedral—the object of our disagreement.

Meanwhile, I was left with the awesome assignment and responsibility of being the sole fundraiser for the next four years. No one offered to help me. And I had to live with the pressure.

In April 1976, four days before Easter Sunday, I called on a wealthy Orange County man named John Crean. I had read that he'd made a million-dollar lead-off gift to build a new YMCA in Anaheim. I'd never met him, but he agreed to see me. I showed him the plans.

"It'll never happen unless we get a big lead-off gift—like one million dollars," I said.

He answered, "I'd like to help, but I simply can't."

"May I pray before I leave?" I asked.

"Sure! I'm a good Lutheran," he said. "Go ahead."

Surprising myself (and I'm sure my host), I prayed, "O God, I'm so thankful that Mr. Crean would like to give a million dollars. Is it possible for You to figure out a way for him to do what he'd like to do but can't?"

The next day was Maundy Thursday. I received a telephone call at 11:06 A.M.; I'll never forget that time, down to the minute. It was John Crean on the line.

"Dr. Schuller," he began, "it's not a question of if; it's only a question of how and when. I'll get back to you, but you can count on a one-million-dollar lead-off gift! I'll be in touch!" And he hung up.

I whooped so loud that my secretary came running in to see if I was all right.

At that moment my faith soared. I now knew that God would create the resources to fulfill His dream for the building of the Crystal Cathedral.

I also knew that God would bring the right person . . . at the right time . . . for the right job.

God never answers our prayers in the negative, though He often answers, "Yes . . . if" or "Yes . . . when" or "Yes . . . but."

In May of 1976 John Crean and his wife, Donna, delivered fifty-five thousand shares of stock valued at just over eighteen dollars a share—a total value of one million dollars!

In June 1976 we decided to add to our plans a full basement—a one-acre construction beneath the ground floor of the cathedral—to accommodate the choirs, the music department, the orchestra and all concert and production requirements. This added forty-five thousand square feet of space, but it also bumped up the cost—from seven million dollars to ten million dollars!

That same month I flew to Chicago to ask W. Clement Stone, the insurance giant who had bought and distributed to ministers over two hundred and fifty thousand copies of one of my books, to give one million dollars toward our cathedral. We had a lovely dinner in his mansion, but his answer was negative. Pausing at the doorway before I left, we prayed, just the two of us, there in the shadows that fall where threshold light meets the darkness beyond.

The next morning, the phone rang in my hotel room. It was Clem Stone. "Schuller, tell you what I'll do: if you can collect the other nine million dollars in cash, I'll give the tenth million."

I was ecstatic! "Never believe in never," I said to myself.

In September 1976 I prayed for guidance. How could I possibly raise the rest of the nine million dollars? Suddenly I remembered seeing churches that had memorial names carved onto a plaque and mortared onto the brick façade.

I called Philip Johnson. "How many windows are in this cathedral, Philip?" I asked.

He laughed. "Oh, I think about ten thousand! Why?"

"Well, I have this idea. If we were to sell each window as a memorial for five hundred dollars, that would add up to five million dollars!"

I felt as if God were telling me, "Bob, the money will be raised only if thousands of small gifts are added to the few extraordinary gifts. The cathedral must be an inspiring monument to common people."

We launched the sale of memorial windows. To help people break down their thinking into manageable nuggets, I laid it out this way: "Five hundred dollars is only twenty dollars a month for twenty-five months."

By January 1977, all ten thousand windows had been sold! With one million dollars cash and four million in pledges to come in over twenty-four months, I was overjoyed. The project was now within range.

In the midst of our financial campaign for the Crystal Cathedral, I had a visit from a friend who worked with Missionary Aviation Fellowship.

"We have an opportunity to buy a helicopter for our medical mission in New Guinea," he told me. "You've traveled there and seen how these people live. They need access to medical help desperately, but we have no cash. You obviously have a gift for raising large sums of money. Can you help us?"

"How much do you need?" I asked.

He answered, "One hundred and eighty-nine thousand dollars."

"Let's pray together about this."

And as we did, it was as if I heard God say, "Buy it!"

"Let me get back to you," I said to my friend. "I think we can help."

I put the issue before the board. Enthusiastic about missions, they agreed that support for Missionary Aviation Fellowship was warranted. But when the question of money came up, they simply looked to me. So now, in the middle of building the Crystal Cathedral, I was going to buy a helicopter as well!

But owing to God's undying faithfulness, I succeeded. Three

months later, I was thrilled to present that gift to Missionary Aviation Fellowship.

In February of 1977 the news turned bad. I read a report that a new California environmental law was about to go into effect, prohibiting construction of any building if more than fifty percent of the exterior walls were glass. Our project was doomed! It was *one hundred percent glass!*

"Never believe in never!" I reminded myself.

Though I was strongly understanding of environmental awareness and responsibility, I couldn't abandon my dream of the Crystal Cathedral unless I was somehow divinely released from the challenge.

I called the mayor, then the head of the building department. "That's right," I was told. "That's the new law—but only for all building permits issued after this month."

Desperate, I called the architect. He and his associates rushed their work, and just days before the month's end we turned the first drawings in to City Hall. The project was approved only a few hours before the new regulation went into effect.

In March 1977 I received reports that the money from the sponsorship of windows was coming in. We were expecting to have another million by summer!

But then in April it was bad news again. My chief financial officer told me that the people who were sponsoring windows were diverting their normal contributions, the gifts that sustained our basic operations. That meant we were headed for trouble. I responded, "This is God's ministry. This is God's project. We simply must pray deeper prayers and work harder. Somehow, we'll survive."

During that summer, on my way to speak at a church conference in Australia, I spent a layover of a few nights on the Hawaiian island of Oahu to study and meditate. I found myself distracted by thoughts of home, and by the wild inflation that had begun to rage in America—at that time over thirty percent annually! A ten-million-dollar construction estimate, inflated at thirty percent, would suddenly leap to thirteen million dollars! A second year of such price changes would raise the thirteen-million-dollar estimate to seventeen million. I couldn't set my fears aside, so I decided to call Philip Johnson's partner, John Burgee.

"John, can you assure me that the building can still be built for ten million dollars?" I demanded.

"Absolutely. But inflation is taking its toll. You may have to leave the basement unfinished."

This is a painful compromise, but I'm relieved nonetheless.

"Then finish the drawings quickly," I urged. "Send them down to our builder, Clair Peck, and we'll let out the bids. I'll be back from my Australia assignment in three weeks. Let's hope we have a firm bid by then and can find the financing to start building."

On my way back from Australia, I stopped in Tahiti to rest and found an urgent phone message waiting for me. When I returned the call, I found my CFO brimming with enthusiasm. "Great news, Bob!" he exclaimed. "Crocker Bank in Los Angeles has offered a ten-million-dollar loan! This will complete the financing and relieve you of the pressure to raise the cash. The terms are ten years. The interest is two percent over prime. The interest will rise or fall as the prime rate changes. Isn't that great?"

I grew suddenly somber. I couldn't share his excitement. I felt that such a loan would be a mistake.

Then he proceeded to give me the rest of the story. "The board held a special session last night. We voted to accept the loan." I was stunned and silent for a moment.

"What's the prime rate today?" I finally asked, catching my breath.

"Nine and a half percent," he answered.

"So our interest rate would be eleven and a half percent?"

"Right."

"But interest rates are rising rapidly. We can't run that risk. I can't agree with taking on this loan. I have no choice but to exercise my right and veto the board's decision."

"But Bob, we'll be forced to abort our construction plans unless you raise that additional ten million dollars yourself!"

"So be it," I said.

Though I feared rising interest rates, I never could have guessed that the prime rate in September of 1980—the date of the opening of the cathedral—would be twenty-two percent! Our cost at two percent over prime would have been twenty-four percent! That would have bankrupted us! Only God knew, and only God controlled our leadership.

Having escaped impending disaster, I retreated with the family to Camelot. I had my fall sermon series to prepare, and the seclusion of the cabin would help me to quiet my thoughts. The time away would also allow Carol and Gretchen, who would be starting a new school year within the week, to make the most of their final days of summer.

It would be just the four of us at the cabin this time. Jeanne had already left for college in Illinois. Bob and his wife now lived near Fuller Seminary in Pasadena, California, where Bob was studying for his master's of divinity degree. Sheila had been hired as a children's supervisor for our church's burgeoning children's ministry, and she was now dating a wonderful man.

In the early mornings up at Camelot, I enjoyed taking the two girls water-skiing. During the day I'd hide away and get some work done, but we spent the evenings together as a family. Arvella would pack a picnic supper she'd made or we'd pick up Kentucky Fried Chicken, and we'd load it and us into the little motorboat we had docked at the lake. It would carry us across the glassy surface to some little inlet, where we could fish as the sun set with warm brilliance behind the mountain peaks that surrounded us. Boulder Bay, Papoose Bay—these inlets harbored our small boat while we picnicked and fished for tiny but feisty trout. Carol and

Gretchen would squeeze the worms onto the fishhooks like the little troupers they were (though sometimes Carol, our tomboy, had to help her little sister when a gushing worm made Gretchen grimace and scream). As the days went by, I gradually, finally, unwound from the stress that lay hidden in the cloud-covered valley below me.

Returning to the cabin, I would play card games with the girls as the music of Nat King Cole on the phonograph further relaxed us all.

But one evening the phone rang shortly after we returned from our fishing expedition. It was my dear friend and advisor Vic Andrews. "Sorry to disturb you, especially during the evening," he said. "I tried a little earlier, you must have been out. I wouldn't have called you, but it's urgent. The bids are in. We need a meeting. We'll come up there, if that's okay. It's too important to discuss over the phone."

The next day the contractor, Clair Peck, the architect, John Burgee (representing Philip Johnson), and Vic appear at our vacation retreat.

Clair tries to break it to me as gently as he can: "Dr. Schuller, the bids total a little *more* than ten million dollars." His tone isn't very convincing. "Actually, Dr. Schuller, they total . . . thirteen million, four hundred thousand."

I feel weak in my knees. Vic asks the obvious question: "Does that include everything?"

"Well, you'll have to put a ten percent contingency fee on top of that," he cautions. "A normal project runs into unforeseen expenses that average about ten percent more than the contract."

My blood begins to boil. I'm startled at how it rises in me. Before I can stop myself, I jump to my feet and boom in a loud voice, "That brings the price to over fourteen million, seven hundred thousand dollars!"

I'm trembling now, shaking like a leaf. Utterly stunned and bitterly disappointed, I stare at the man. He meets my gaze bravely, then looks down at the paper in his hand, which is also trembling.

"Only eight weeks ago you said that we could still build it for ten million dollars by 'not finishing off the basement.' This project is becoming *impossible!*"

There—I've said it! They stare at me, their mouths agape.

Impossible . . . IMPOSSIBLE . . . *IMPOSSIBLE!* I scream in my mind.

I ask to be excused and head quickly for the cabin's small bathroom. There I lean over the sink and close my eyes, trying desperately to calm myself. *How can this be happening?*

I'll have to abandon the Crystal Cathedral; that's what it comes down to. Even though I'll be letting down everybody who has contributed toward it, I'll *have* to give it up. That's the only answer, I decide.

It must seem an eternity to the men waiting outside the door, but in just a few minutes I manage to collect myself and reappear.

"Gentlemen," I announce calmly, "if that's all that you have to report, you're excused. We'll simply have to review the project when I get back to see if it's still viable."

The men gone, I sit with my head in my hands at the kitchen table. My youngest daughter, Gretchen, approaches me. She puts her arms around my bent shoulders and says, "Daddy, if you're very sad, I have lots of hugs to make you feel better. Do you need one?" At ten years old, she still has the ability to wrap me around her finger. I pick her up in a bear hug and for a few moments am lost in her small arms. Then, satisfied, she pulls back, smiles at me, and bounds back to the game she was playing with Carol.

I compose my thought and prepare a news release:

The Crystal Cathedral project will be abandoned. As the bids came in, the cost rose from ten million dollars to nearly fifteen million dollars. This exceeds our church's capabilities.

A vast weight seems to lift off my shoulders at the prospect of abandoning the project. It was accelerating too fast, moving at a rate that I simply couldn't manage. Then I rise from the table to do something that I dread.

I pick up the telephone and dial the number of John Crean, the first million-dollar donor. I have to tell him that the project is off.

John answers the phone in his usually friendly manner, and I say, "John, I'm sorry to report this, but I'm going to have to give you back your generous donation. Inflation has pushed up construction costs, and we have to abandon the project. The bids have all come in, and the Crystal Cathedral will cost nearly fifteen million dollars. We simply can't afford that. How would you like me to proceed in refunding your money?"

There. It's out, and I feel an even greater surge of relief. Then he says something that I'll never, ever forget.

"Schuller," he says, "dig a hole."

"Excuse me?"

"Dig a hole," he repeats. "Keep my donation and use it to dig a hole for the foundation. A hole shouldn't cost more than a million dollars. Will it?"

"Uh . . . no."

"Okay, then . . . dig a hole! Somehow, someway, the money will come."

With those words, the heavy pressure that lifted from me with the thought of abandoning the project crashes down. Still, I promise him that I'll do as he requests.

The stress stays with me, in fact mounts rapidly, as I head back down the winding mountain road with my family.

As I listen to Arvella and the girls singing nonsense songs, I meditate on the recent mandate of John Crean. Then I become aware of the towering boulders surrounding us and notice how precarious they appear. I'm struck by the realization that all of nature is made up of a delicate balance, a constant risk of living on the edge. So I conclude that it will be okay after all. The Crystal Cathedral is like that big mountain, the money problem is only a boulder—albeit a tottering one and faith provides the balance.

When I returned to my office I found a letter written by a Roman Catholic sister:

> Congratulations on the Crystal Cathedral!
>
> We wanted to build a new wing on the hospital and everyone said it was impossible with the inflating costs. But I said, "If Schuller can find money to build a Crystal Cathedral, don't you suppose we could find the money to build a new hospital?"
>
> That turned the decision-making meeting around, and I'm proud to tell you we are going to build that hospital.
>
> Thanks to the inspiration of your Crystal Cathedral project!

That letter made me realize that if I were to abandon this dream, I would negatively inspire others to abandon their dreams too! I couldn't do that. I had to move forward.

I went back to the contractor and asked him, "Can you build just the shell of the structure; and if so, what would that cost?"

He replied, "I can build that for nine million, two hundred thousand."

"Then that's what we'll build," I said decisively.

After all, I thought, *we have about two million dollars in the bank. The blueprints are almost paid for. I'll announce the groundbreaking ceremony, and we'll dig a hole!*

It's a chilly, overcast morning, December 4, 1977, as the congregation begins to arrive. The family stands near, looking handsome in their Sunday best. It's Carol's birthday, and she wears a new dress that was her present from us; it's red—always red, for our Christmas Carol. Her waist-length blond hair has been lopped off and is now swept away from her face in the latest "Farrah Fawcett" cut. Her legs have grown long and slender, making her look much older than thirteen, and I find myself relieved that she's into riding her horse and playing softball instead of being around boys.

Jeanne is now a lovely nineteen-year-old brunette, home for the groundbreaking from Wheaton College in Illinois. When she comes home to visit, the phone never stops ringing; guys are always trying one more time for that coveted date. Gretchen—still my "baby"—always has extra hugs and kisses for her daddy. She smiles at me proudly as we prepare. Bob, twenty-two, stands arm in arm nearby with his twenty-one-year-old wife—now pregnant with our first grandchild. Sheila, twenty-five, is giving herself to full-time ministry with the young people of our church. Blond and beautiful, she has moist eyes as she and her fiancé wave to me in anticipation.

A small group of advisors and friends cluster around me—including Glenn Ford, directly at my side—and thousands of people are gathered just beyond us. The crowd includes plenty of press representatives. The local press has followed us all along, but now national television cameras are whirring.

It's a memorable day for me, but my exuberance is tempered by the knowledge that tomorrow morning I'll have to face the terrible truth: we have only two million dollars in hand! We don't even have a financial plan to cover the cost of the structural shell that I've committed to. We have only enough for that hole in the ground.

And I never knew that a hole could cost *so* much!

The biggest bank commitment we could find (other than the Crocker Bank loan that had been linked to the rise and fall of the prime rate, which we had declined) was from Farmers & Merchants Bank in Garden Grove, promising the maximum of their legal loan capacity of four million dollars. We were still nearly six million dollars short of covering just the cost of the shell!

Meanwhile, *Time*, *Newsweek*, *Vogue*, and *Architectural Review* picked up the story; we appeared on *60 Minutes* with Dan Rather, the *Phil Donahue Show*, the *Mike Douglas Show*, and both *Today* and *Good Morning America*; and I was asked for interviews by journalists from Ireland, England, Australia, and South America!

But with the notoriety came criticism. In the weeks and months to follow, Christians—including many in my own denomination—would condemn the building of the Crystal Cathedral in their pulpits and journals, saying that the money should be spent helping the poor.

The secular press picked up the attack. In Russia, where people had condemned the Tower of Hope, they now added the Crystal Cathedral to their criticism, again claiming that we were "taking money from the poor."

My children began to hear it from their classmates, who would mimic their parents' criticisms. Carol and Gretchen came home from school crying and isolated on several occasions, not understanding why so many people thought that their dad was "bad." Jeanne struggled to defend me to her college classmates.

But not a single critic had a positive suggestion to offer on how to handle the problem of the overflow attendance we experienced week after week. Though we had started branch churches in the area and had been encouraging our people to go there, the crowds were still too large!

Nor did a single journalist or critic ever ask about the lifespan of the proposed building. I had learned in my work with Neutra that the only way to arrive at a true final cost was to divide the construction cost by lifespan. Many buildings have a short lifespan, but the lifespan of world-class architecture is in the hundreds of years!

And for all those who faulted the money we were spending, no one asked, "Where's the money going?" I knew that every penny would be going to laborers, truckers, welders, and cement workers, who would be making house payments with what they earned! And the Crystal Cathedral wasn't Disneyland: we weren't charging an admission fee and pocketing the money!

I was baffled, afraid, bewildered, helpless to defend my family, and very, very lonely as I wrestled with a wide assortment of adversaries.

In March 1978 the contractor called an urgent meeting. His legal department had advised him that he couldn't continue to sign contracts and proceed with the construction on the "hope and faith that the extra millions of dollars are going to come in over the next eighteen months from unpredictable offerings." He gave us an ultimatum: "Either have a firm bank commitment for the next three million dollars, or we'll close construction down."

"How soon do we need the next installment?" I asked.

He checked his notes and said, "We'll need six hundred thousand deposited in the bank in sixty days, another one million dollars by July, and then another one million four hundred thousand by the middle of October of this year."

Never believe in never, I kept telling myself. Day after day after day, midnight after midnight, I would recite my Possibility Thinker's Creed again and again, and I would draw strength from the words that God had given me over twenty years earlier: "I will build My church!"

I wrote an urgent letter to all my friends across America. They responded; and to my relief, in thirty days six hundred thousand dollars cash came in. But where would we get another one million dollars in cash by July?

It was at this time that Howard Kelley, a staff member of mine, and a minister by training, suggested that we pray for a "Million Dollar Sunday"—a day when the offerings in our church would total one million dollars.

I had never heard of such a thing. *Impossible!* I said to myself, secretly and shamefully. But Howard explained, "We'll ask all the people to plan and pray. We'll challenge the entire church to bring an offering of one million dollars in cash on one day in June so that you have the money in plenty of time for the July deadline."

After prayerful consideration, we decided to give the plan a try. *It will certainly give God a chance to work a miracle*, I thought.

I checked with the contractor to see whether he'd be willing to hold off at least until July on padlocking the wire fencing that now encircled the construction site. The challenge of our million-dollar collection would be held on June 18, and we asked him to wait for the outcome of that appeal. He agreed.

For weeks, classes, groups, organizations, and individuals planned, worked, prayed, and made decisions about what they would give. With this new enthusiasm from my parishioners, I no longer felt so alone. They were in this with me. It was a wonderful feeling.

Our goal was sharp and focused: *one million dollars on June 18!*

Arvella and I began examining our own personal assets to see what we would be able to give. As we did, I discovered that a study apartment I had purchased with an eight-thousand-dollar inheritance from my father's estate had inflated in value from thirty-six thousand dollars to just under two hundred thousand dollars! I arranged to get a new bank loan that would allow me to draw out one hundred and fifty thousand dollars of equity. I told the church board that on this one-million-dollar Sunday, I'd make the leadoff gift of one hundred and fifty thousand dollars.

Then I gave them a challenge: "I'm asking you, as a board, to match that with a collective pledge of an additional one hundred and fifty thousand dollars." They declined. Then, pouring salt on the wound, they told me, "You'll never collect a million dollars on a single Sunday!"

June 18, 1978, was a red-letter day in the history of our church. We had one of our largest crowds ever. Ushers wearing hard hats received the offering in wheelbarrows and large cement buckets suspended from derricks. That afternoon, when the gifts were counted, the news went out to all of Southern California that the congregation had committed not just one million dollars, but one million four hundred thousand dollars! Eight hundred and seventy thousand dollars had come in cash, the rest in pledges.

Not prompted by me — in fact, going totally against my advice — my daughter Carol had sold her horse for four hundred dollars so that she could participate. That Sunday she dropped four hundred one-dollar bills into the offering plate!

Hundreds of our members made similar and greater sacrifices. I think it's safe to say that this was the most moving Sunday in all my years of ministry.

With this huge success, construction could continue until September. But that was only three months away. Then we would need *another* one million dollars in cash! (And people wonder why my hair is so white!)

Shortly after that momentous Sunday, Arvella and I were off to Korea, where I would preach for my friend David Yonggi Cho and participate in a church-growth conference. His church was the largest congregation in the world, with seven hundred and fifty thousand members, and there, Arvella and I would be inspired to keep on building our church.

Once again, Carol and Gretchen would visit their "other home" in Iowa. Jeanne would join her college classmates in summer-school studies in the Holy Land.

When Arvella and I boarded the plane in Los Angeles, we were ecstatic and exhausted at the same time. We were *only* one million short of the demand made by the construction company, but we were a *whole* million short. That issue would be addressed upon our return.

We had until September, which at that moment felt a hundred years away. Arvella rested her head on my shoulder as the plane soared into the evening sky, taking us away from stress and responsibility and into renewal and rest. We'd just endured enough pressure to last a lifetime; now we deserved a little peace.

XXXV

As expected, our week in Seoul, South Korea, unfolded as a time of much-needed rejuvenation. At Sunday service, the Holy Spirit was tangibly present as the twenty thousand Asian Christians who thronged that day to Dr. Cho's church welcomed us. Their singing voices rose in alleluias that lifted and healed us.

The church-growth conference was also uplifting. Even though I was a leader and a keynote speaker, I found myself receiving more than I gave. The cathedral building program, its pressure, and the year's criticism back in the States, half a world away, could be forgotten for a time. My worn and battered spirit was soothed by the worship and fellowship.

Even more important, uninterrupted by our busy home and household, Arvella and I had a chance to regroup and really be with one another. How I'd needed to talk with her after the rush and roar and turmoil of recent months. Arvella was my love, and I felt both passion and deep contentment as I reconnected with her in Seoul.

It's Saturday, July 7, 1978. Arvella is at what Dr. Cho calls "Prayer Mountain," a rising landscape that harbors caves where Christians migrate daily to pray. So many worshipers come to pray that when you approach the mountain, a rumbling murmur of petitions sweeps like a wave down its side. Arvella won't be back for at least another hour or two, so I have time for a quick nap. It occurs to me that when I wake up, I'll go shopping and buy her a string of pearls.

In this delightful reverie, so far from the pain of home, I stretch out on the hotel bed and close my eyes.

Warmth rolls over me as sleep casts its delicious spell, and my mind takes flight to the land of dreams and downy highs. I have so much to be thankful for. Sheila has announced her plans to get married, and I think how happy she seems with her impressive young fiancé. Then I pass through this tingling half-awake, half-asleep state into a deep sleep, and my low, slow breathing settles into a quiet rhythm.

I jolt awake to the ringing of the telephone. I suspect it's Sheila again with more news—perhaps the exact date for her wedding. Or perhaps it's Dr. Cho.

I pick up the receiver, relaxed and groggy. "Hello?"

Silence.

"Hello?" I repeat. "This is Robert Schuller."

"Bob?" I know this voice. It's Mike, my public relations manager and close friend. I feel a sense of heaviness, because I fear he's going to tell me about some negative press on "Schuller's Crystal Cathedral project." The criticism feels so distant now. Can't I just keep it that way?

"Hi, Mike," I say, in a tone that reveals my reluctance. I don't mean it personally toward him, and I hope that he doesn't take offense. I'm too tired at the moment to explain myself, but he knows what a strain I've been under.

"I have some bad news," he says. "Are you sitting down?"

Oh, gee. Here it comes.

"Yeah, Mike," I say. In truth, though, I'm still lying on the bed, my eyes closed.

"Bob?" he says again, still tentative. For heaven's sake! Why can't he just tell me why he called so that I can go back to sleep?

"Bob . . . it's Carol."

I bolt up, fully awake now. Carol? Our daughter? Why would Mike call me about the girls? They're in Iowa. It's Friday night there. They're supposed to be flying home to California tomorrow. Maybe their flight has been rescheduled and we'll have to change the pickup for them.

"Yeah, Mike? What about the girls? Change in flight plans?"

"It's not that, Bob," he said. "I wish it were. Carol's been hurt."

I go lightheaded as the blood drains from me.

"She's been in an accident," he explains. "In Iowa."

My head is swirling now. I don't want to hear his next words. "Bob . . . she was on a motorcycle with her cousin, and they were hit head-on by a car."

I'm gagging, trying not to get sick.

"She was wearing a helmet, Bob . . . she's alive. The helmet saved her. But she's lost a lot of blood, Bob. And . . . her leg." Now he is stammering, "Bob, she may lose her leg. I . . ."

At the other end of the receiver I'm gasping for air.

"Bob . . . her life is still in danger. Right now she's in an ambulance en route to Sioux City."

O God, O God, I pray. Sioux City—only very critical injuries are sent to Sioux City. *O God, O God, O God.*

Then suddenly a peace settles upon me. My mind quiets.

"How about Gretchen?" I ask. "She's . . . ?" I think I hear Mike sniffle.

"Oh, yes. Gretchen is fine. Carol was riding with her cousin Mark. He was also hurt, but he'll be okay. It's Carol that everyone is worried about. I'm so sorry, Bob."

I have to think clearly now. I need to get us home. *Think, Bob, think!*

"Mike, I may have a hard time getting a flight back. Just pray and believe that we'll make it by tomorrow. But go ahead and book a plane for Arvella and me from L.A. to Sioux City for tomorrow night. And Mike—" My voice breaks now, and I begin to cry. "Thank you, Mike," I manage.

I place the phone back on the bedside table and lean forward, my elbows on my knees. My forehead falls onto my open palms, and I begin to tremble. From head to toe I shake and I quake and I sob. Finally I force my way past this terrifying moment and realize that I can't let what happened paralyze me; I have to get us home.

I pass a miserable hour alone in that hotel room. How long will Arvella be? I begin pacing, unable to sit still. Then there's a knock at the door. I rush to open it, and Arvella almost falls into me. She gives a slight gasp and then a giggle. "Oh, honey!" she says.

She sees immediately from my face that something bad has happened.

"What is it, Bob?" she asks.

My lip begins to tremble, but I can't find the words.

"Bob?" she presses.

"Arvella . . . no one has died. But . . ."

Her eyes are wide now.

"It's Carol," I say finally.

She gasps, throwing a pale hand over her mouth to hold in a little cry. "She's okay. I mean, it could be worse. She was on Mark's new motorcycle."

She closes her eyes, then puts her hands in front of her face and shakes her head back and forth.

Arvella hates motorcycles as much as I do, and the kids know it. But we both know our tomboy Carol—daredevilish, independent, thirteen-year-old Carol.

Arvella thrusts her face up toward mine. "Was she wearing a helmet?"

"Yes," I say. "Mike said it saved her life. But Arvella . . ." I have to tell her now. "Arvella, she's right now in an ambulance going to the hospital in Sioux City. She's still fighting to survive. The blood— she lost a lot, honey. And her leg; it's really bad. They might have to . . ."—I stumble over the word that's so foreign to me—"they might have to amputate."

All her strength falls away, and she drops her head to my chest but her tears last only for a moment.

The phone rings. It's Mike again, calling to say that they're doing the amputation right now.

Arvella walks over to the window. As she looks out over the foreign city, now gloomy with rain, a hush settles over her. Later, we would describe to each other the same overwhelming sense of peace that we felt enveloping our room.

"Alleluia, God is good." Pastor Cho repeats this over and over like a mantra on our way to the Seoul airport. As we wait for our departing flight, his beautiful Korean accent expresses the sentiment every pastor is supposed to convey in times such as this: "God will work this out for many blessings."

I remember the many times I've offered that same thought to grieving families. And I've been repeating snippets from my own sermons since Mike's phone call almost six hours earlier:

"It's not what happens to you that matters; it's how you react that matters."

"Trouble never leaves you where it finds you. Choose by an act of your will to accept positively what you can't change, and you'll find the strength and peace you need."

Arvella and I are lost in our own private pain as the plane bears us home. The night is almost past, but we're grateful to have found space on a horribly crowded ten-hour flight that will take us first to Honolulu. Then, after probably two hours at customs, and a lengthy layover, we will be on our way to Los Angeles—another five hours.

As the stewardess walks down the aisle, I catch a glimpse of two pretty legs and a pair of feet that fit nicely into high-heeled shoes. I think to myself, *She has two legs, two ankles, two feet. Carol has only one leg, one ankle, one foot.* Without warning, a rush of emotion wells up from within me, gathering and rising with volcanic force. The tears pour out, and I leap to my feet and rush to the lavatory.

I make it just in time, locking the door behind me before the sobs break free. I'm wailing in pain. I think about the pretty young stewardess in her high-heeled shoes. What will Carol do when she grows to this lovely age? What will it be like when she's supposed to meet a husband and fall in love and be swooned over and crooned over.

My wailing expresses all of the terror and anguish of my imagination. My little girl—her body thrown and torn and gashed, mutilated violently and mercilessly. I remember counting her ten little fingers and her ten little toes the day she was born.

My moans just keep coming and coming until suddenly, there in the lavatory, I see in my mind a picture of the twenty thousand worshipers at prayer in Korea. I see their faces radiating heaven's goodness. And I hear the rousing crescendo of their voices: "Alleluia! Alleluia!" Wonderful words—a stark contrast to the ugly sounds that are gushing from my mouth. Then I sense this message:

Schuller . . . if you have to bawl, then turn it into a ball.

I make a deliberate decision: *If I have to wail, then I'll turn it into praise.* By an act of sheer will, I force my mouth to transform my moans, turning each heart-wrenching sob into "Alleluia! Alleluia!" Gradually serenity begins to replace the sobs until I'm able to wash my face and return to my seat.

No sooner do I sit back down next to Arvella than I'm greeted by the slender, crossed ankles of the young woman across the aisle. I choke up again. "God, help me," I whisper.

Then I tell myself, "Carol has lost only a *leg*, Schuller! You're exaggerating this all out of proportion. She'll still be able to do all the things she really wants to do. She can play the violin, the piano, or the guitar. She can sit on the back of a horse. She's still tall and beautiful. Her face and head weren't damaged or injured."

Then this sentence floods into my mind:

Play it down and pray it up!

Arvella and I talk very little during these long, painful hours from Korea to Hawaii. We can't sleep. We cry a lot, and Arvella reads her Bible. Then God gives her some words from Psalm 57: "O God, my heart is quiet and confident. Let us greet the dawn with a song!"

Even as she reads these beautiful words, Arvella glances out the window and sees the tapestry of a Pacific sunrise from thirty-five thousand feet—the first of three sunrises on our trip from Korea to Iowa.

After we land in Hawaii, we phone the hospital to see what's happened to Carol during our ten-hour flight. Jeanne is there, as are Sheila and her fiancé, Jim. *Thank God!* "Carol's vital signs are stable," they report. "Her spirits are great."

With that reassurance we begin the next flight home. After a terribly long layover, we're airborne again, heading across the Pacific from Hawaii to Los Angeles.

Mike meets us at the L.A. airport and helps transfer our bags. To our surprise and gratitude, he's contacted Athalie Clarke, a dear friend and the heir to the Irvine estate in Southern California, and she's leased a private Lear jet that's waiting to take us on the last part of our journey to Iowa. Mike sees us off once more and we rise into the night sky.

The jet cuts through the blackness like a knife, and soon we're cruising at forty thousand feet. Over the Rocky Mountains, at that altitude, we emerge from the earth's shadow and the sky explodes into a riot of color. It's sunrise number two.

"Let us greet the dawn with a song!"

As the sleek aircraft descends for the approach to Sioux City, we're in the dark again, the Pacific sunrise that we just witnessed hidden by the earth's curviture. The lights on the landing strip shining brightly to greet us. They form a perfectly lighted cross shining in the darkness.

When we reach the terminal, Sheila and Jim are waiting for us. Sheila runs and hugs us, and I begin to cry.

"Oh, Dad," she says, "you'll be so proud of Carol! Her attitude is fantastic!"

Sheila drives us from the airport to the hospital. Outside the intensive care unit we try to gather our composure and our courage. "This is the Lord's day," I remind myself. Could even this be a day that God has made? Could I possibly rejoice in it? I begin to doubt myself.

As we enter Carol's room, the sky outside is lighting up with delicate pinks and blues. And so we witness, for the third time in what seems like one incredibly long day, sunrise—the promise of a new tomorrow. Again Psalm 57 whispers tenderly to me, "Let us greet the dawn with a song."

But when I see her I stop, cold and stricken. For a moment I can't move. Her face is so swollen! And . . . are those bruises? Is it the light? I look closer. The purple tinge is indeed bruising. I gulp and quake inside.

Arvella has already rushed to Carol's bedside, but I can't seem to move. Carol lies beneath a thin white sheet. Suspended in the air is the short, heavily bandaged stump of a leg. At the end of the bed her one remaining leg, all five toes visible, is poking out from under the sheet. Her blond hair is slicked back. Her bed is surrounded by machines and tubes and bottles and monitors and bandages—white bandages mostly, but soiled where the stump ends. Is it raw beneath that bandage? I feel nauseated.

"Dad?" Oh, my gosh. Her voice is so raspy, so weak! The words jolt me out of my near-disassociated state, and I realize that I'm still at the doorway.

"Dad?"

I'm silent. Speechless. Stunned at the sight of her.

Her face is still beautiful—but her whole body is black-and-blue and swollen out of shape.

I rush finally to hug her, but she shrieks with pain. We all learn to limit ourselves to stroking the foot and toes of her one leg, or touching her forehead, to impart a little love without hurting her.

Carol's eyes focus on me. What should my first words be to my darling Carol?

But she speaks again before I can say anything. "Dad, I think I know why this accident happened," she says.

She stops suddenly, wincing, her eyes closed, her brow contorted, her hand grasping mine. Gently I coo to her until the pain abates and her face relaxes.

"Tell me," I say.

"God has a special ministry for me," she says. She manages a smile. "He wants me to help people who've been hurt like I'm hurt."

Suddenly I realize that all I've sacrificed—reputation, social standing, the easy life—to bring my message of hope has been worth it, because I'm looking at this little girl who has discovered that God never leaves you where He finds you. He scoops you up into His big arms and carries you close. Carol has experienced something of the Divine; I can see it on her pretty face, despite the swelling and the bruises and the pain.

As I look at her now, nodding off into a morphine-induced slumber, I tell Arvella to go rest. I'll stay with Carol.

As I watch my daughter sleep, I imagine the scene as it was described to me. The motorcycle racing at seventy miles an hour. Then horns blaring, headlights swirling. Then the crunching and the pain and the blood and worse: they said she flew eighty-six feet! And then the bouncing and the sliding and the scraping and the spinning and the grating across the rough black asphalt. Is that why she's so raw? I imagine her landing, unable to move. Was she conscious? She doesn't remember the landing; she doesn't remember the scraping. She remembers the headlights and the flying, but not the landing; that's what they tell me.

Did God catch her? Did He catch her the way I would when she was little? I'd throw her into the air and catch her giggling, loving, toddling, soft body. Or did she land alone and then He came hovering and covering and holding and carrying as I'd done on the night of her birth? Did God hold her until she whispered of pleasant places and sweet surrender? She'd tell me later that He did. And if this would remain my only reward for my labor and relentless devotion to becoming a preacher of the Good News—if she were my only convert in this big world—for this night alone I would do it over and over and over again. And so my "Song of Joy" falls into a peaceful sleep and my soul is quiet, as together we "greet the dawn with a song."

Later, after Arvella returned, the doctor pulled us aside. "Your daughter was in terrible pain when she arrived," he told us. "She asked for medication to relieve it, but I couldn't give her any. It would have depressed her condition further. She accepted the pain patiently and quietly, even though it was very intense. You can be very proud of your daughter.

"Carol almost bled to death. We had to give her seventeen pints of blood, and at one point we lost her blood pressure and pulse altogether. I can't recall any patient ever being so strong. You're very fortunate to have her alive.

"Her leg has been amputated just below the knee, and the chances of saving the rest of the leg are slim at best. The knee and thigh were badly mangled. Unfortunately, she landed in a ditch with runoff from a slaughterhouse. Infection has already set in. I believe that we'll need to amputate more."

As we digested this information, we could feel the support of people around the world. Friends in Korea, the members of the Garden Grove Community Church, and people in churches all over America had already heard the news and were now praying for Carol. At that moment there was a tremendous outpouring of God's spirit over Arvella and I as we clung to one another.

When Carol could be moved, Athalie Clark again stepped in to help, this time providing a private ambulance plane to transfer our daughter to Children's Hospital in Orange County. It was a Monday night. Arvella, Sheila, Jim, Gretchen, and I stood by as an intensive care nurse eased the stretcher carrying Carol's bruised and broken body into the Lear jet. As it raced along for takeoff, it hit a bump that caused Carol to scream out with pain. But then we were airborne and heading for home.

As the jet streaked through the sky, our family sat numb and cramped in the small space. Making matters worse, we were tired and hungry. We stared out the window or watched Carol as she grimaced from the pain.

Soon I started singing—quietly at first, but then with more volume, until the others joined in.

Praise God from whom all blessings flow.
Praise Him, all creatures here below.
Praise Him above, ye heavenly hosts.
Praise Father, Son, and Holy Ghost.

The flight was difficult, especially for Arvella. Carol insisted that her mother hold her hand, and Gretchen slept with her head on Arvella's free shoulder. Gretchen's feet were propped up on Carol's two large canisters of oxygen. An incredible stench came from the infection in Carol's stump, strong and nauseating, and Arvella had to almost hypnotize herself to keep from vomiting.

At Children's Hospital in Orange County we were rushed into the intensive care unit, and Carol's aching body was eased gently into bed. "I'm glad to be home," she said with a sigh. As she was wheeled into surgery later, knowing that there was a good possibility she might wake up minus more of her leg, she gazed at us and spoke with determination. "I know one thing for sure. If I need more amputation, it won't change God's plan for my life."

We prayed fervently that Carol would be able to keep her knee. With that joint left, she might be able to maintain a normal walking gait someday. And for the time being, our prayers were answered. When the surgery was over, the knee remained.

But that was only the beginning of what would be months of highs and lows, intense pain and blessed relief, soul-shattering doubt and mind-boggling faith. The days faded into each other and turned into months as one infection after another raged within Carol's battle-worn body.

She would spend a total of seven months in that hospital and undergo over five surgeries before being released. The filth of that slaughterhouse ditch by an Iowa roadside was stubborn, containing bacteria that were resistant to all known antibiotics. Phantom pains assailed her day and night, plaguing her with the torment of a leg and foot that weren't even there. Arvella would rub Carol's remaining foot to relieve the pain of the toes that had been taken away months before. In ways we don't understand, this helped Carol. Somehow her mind must have processed the loving attention to one foot and communicated it to the nerves of the other, a form of almost mystical comfort.

I spent every moment I possibly could by her bedside. But I still had the Crystal Cathedral—that monumental responsibility—in the process of construction. I had to deal daily with decisions and pressures to keep the project on schedule. Almost every moment of that year I was torn. I would run to the site to handle a glitch in construction, then race to the hospital to give a quick word of encouragement to my daughter, whose condition was still critical and unpredictable from one hour to the next.

When I was tempted to exaggerate Carol's tragedy, I would remember the words God had given me on my trip home from Korea that first night: *Play it down and pray it up.* I was inspired by the courage that Carol herself displayed and amazed at the strength she found in my own corny little sayings: "There's no gain without pain." . . . "When the going gets tough, the tough get going." . . . "Look at what you have left, not at what you've lost." In times of her most excruciating pain, when such words were meaningless, she repeated the name of Jesus and was comforted.

Corrie ten Boom, the Holocaust survivor and spiritual leader, was a weekly visitor. She became a very special friend to Carol, soothing her with triumphant affirmation. Each word laced with a thick Dutch accent, Corrie would repeat, "Jesus is victor, Carol.

Jesus is victor!" She would say these words over and over again until Carol calmed beneath the lullaby.

Even though Carol often bordered on hysteria from the pain, she rarely felt sorry for herself or said, "I wish this had never happened." One day she did ask me one of the most difficult questions I've ever had to answer.

"Dad, what did they do with my leg?" she asked. "Did they throw it away in the trash?"

I shuddered. I cringed. But I didn't let her see my reaction. "No, honey," I answered. "They buried it, just like Grandma and Grandpa are buried."

I remember saying to her once, when things looked especially bad, "Watch out for self-pity, Carol."

"Don't worry about that, Dad," she said without hesitation. "I have enough problems without choosing *that* one."

Only once did she cry out, "I wish I'd died in the ditch!" It had been a hard day at the end of a hard week.

I gently rebuked her. "Those thoughts don't come from Jesus, honey," I told her. "Don't ever say or wish that things hadn't happened as they did. Futile regret is a negative spirit. Claim Jesus as the author of only inspiring and positive thoughts."

Another special friend that God gave her was the chaplain of the hospital, Father MacNamara. "Father Mac," as Carol called him, visited her every day; and later, when she was well enough to leave her isolation room, he took her in her wheelchair through the hospital's private convent gardens.

Father Mac gave Carol a photograph of Christ on the cross which he taped on the metal frame that held up her stump. "It reminds me that Jesus put up with a lot more hurt than I'm feeling," she said.

My Hollywood friends lavished Carol with attention. She received flowers from Frank Sinatra, an autographed photograph from John Wayne, with this handwritten message: "Carol—be happy—you are loved!" She had personal telephone calls from Tommy Lasorda and Steve Garvey (her favorite Dodger); they also paid her a personal visit. She received a telegram from President Jimmy Carter. I couldn't begin to tell these friends and countless others how much I appreciated their efforts to distract my daughter from the drudgery and pain of her days in isolation.

Once things looked fairly stable, the doctors did further surgery, hoping to release the muscles so that her leg would become more functional. The surgeon was pleased that he found no pockets of puss in her knee and thigh and felt optimistic about her progress. But three days later, the bacteria that had lain dormant for some time erupted with an unprecedented fury. Carol's temperature shot back up to a hundred and five and stayed in that range dangerously long. Her stump of a leg swelled, the infection raging like an out-of-control wildfire. Arvella and I were frantic. Carol lay stripped naked and packed in ice, shivering and begging for warmth, and there was nothing we could do to answer her cries.

We prayed passionately and urgently. We received word that Dr. Cho's church was praying for Carol around the clock on Prayer Mountain, where Arvella had been the day we'd heard of the accident. If this infection continued, the entire thigh and knee would have to be amputated. Her blood vessels were so weak that they were collapsing, which meant that staying hooked to her essential I.V. was difficult. Her surgeon and her infectious disease specialist worked night and day to help her.

The surgeon came to see us one day and said, "Listen, we're tampering with Carol's life now. This is dangerous. I have to take off the rest of that infectious limb or you'll lose her."

We scheduled the surgery for the next day.

But that very same day, the Federal Drug Administration released a new antibiotic, one that worked against the particular strain of bacteria that Carol had picked up in that ditch. She was the first person at Children's Hospital to receive it. Within hours her temperature began to drop, and we became convinced of the reality of healing prayer.

The surgeon was satisfied by that improvement; there would be no further amputation. Her thigh was left open, however, so that it could bleed and so that the staff could take cultures to check the progress of the disease. To our exhausted relief, the cultures began to show improvement. One day shortly before Christmas, the culture came back with no bacterial growth at all! The wound, however, would have to heal from the inside out.

The infection and the trauma of the past months had taken a terrible toll on Carol's young body. At a height of five feet seven inches, she now weighed only eighty-seven pounds. She would be confined to a wheelchair while she healed from her many surgeries. Once released from the hospital, she would face months of rehabilitation, during which she wouldn't even be able to bathe herself, and Arvella would have to give her round-the-clock care.

All that still laid ahead but for now we celebrated—the infection was gone!

The Saturday after this victorious report, Arvella left for the hospital first thing in the morning, as usual. "Stay home and wait for me, Bob," she said. "I'll come back with good news."

The morning hours stretched long before me, and I wished I'd gone along. What possible good news could she bring? I tried to study as I waited, but found it hard to concentrate. Finally I heard Arvella's car and ran to the front door.

"No, Bob," Arvella said when I appeared on the porch. "You have to go back in and wait. Wait by the Christmas tree."

I did as I'd been told, and soon the door opened again. "Close your eyes, Bob!"

I heard the grind of wheels bump over the threshold of our entry. When the sound ceased, I heard some metal clanking and exerted breathing.

"OK, Bob, open your eyes!"

There was Carol, standing on crutches in front of her wheelchair. And she had *two* legs! I choked with emotion. My little girl—my sweet, sweet darling little girl was going to be OK. She just stood there, now fourteen years old, with sandy curls framing her lovely face. My eyes traveled down to take in two ankles and two shoes, and I chuckled with joy. The surgeon had arranged a Christmas surprise for Carol—an artificial leg, or "prosthesis." It was for cosmetic purposes only. A walking prosthesis would have to wait until the swelling in her stump had gone down and the wounds completely healed.

But seeing Carol standing once again, tall and slender as a young fawn—that gave me the happiest Christmas of my whole life!

XXXVI

When you're the father of five, a crisis in the life of one of your children inevitably means less time and energy for the others, whom you love just as much.

I had cut out most of my outside speaking engagements in order to spend more time with Carol and Arvella. But Wheaton College in Illinois had been pressing me to speak there, and Wheaton, of course, was Jeanne Anne's college. She wanted me to come; it would mean a lot to her, she said. It would mean a lot to me too, because I hadn't really seen her much since Carol's accident. She'd had to return to her classes immediately after her summer Holy Land semester.

I agreed to fly out and speak at a morning chapel service. I'd get to town the night before, to have some private time with Jeannie. I'd speak the next morning and come straight back home to Carol and Arvella.

I wondered if this audience would understand all that I'd been doing, and my desire to see the cathedral built. After all, I was continuing to hear criticism from conservative evangelical Christians.

They were, more often than not, very blunt about their opinions—sometimes even brutal.

There had recently been a vicious attack against me and the Crystal Cathedral in *The Wittenberg Door*, a fundamentalist Christian magazine. One page of this particular issue—a page topped by a heading something like "What to do with fifteen million dollars"—had a line down the center. On one side of the midline was written, "Build a Crystal Cathedral"; on the other side was a long list of philanthropic endeavors. The article had hit the campus just days before I arrived.

Jeanne had always been proud of her dad; she loved me and believed in my work. The Garden Grove Community Church was her home. She was excited that I was coming to her school to share with her classmates my enthusiastic faith.

The morning I was to address the chapel, posters appeared in the college library protesting my appearance—signs that read, "Schuller doesn't preach the gospel"; "Schuller is building a monument to himself"; "Give the fifteen million dollars to the poor!"

We saw the signs on our way to the service. I glanced at Jeanne. Her large brown eyes were as big as saucers. Tears welled up and began to spill over her lower lids, trickling down her cheeks and smearing her mascara. She looked confused. *How could they?* her eyes seemed to say. There was nothing I could do but make my way into the chapel, give my message, and get out of there as soon as I could. Maybe with me gone, the students would calm down.

The next morning I was back in my office, hard at work. The phone rang, and it was Jeanne. Her classmates had been relentless in making cruel remarks to her about her father. She wanted to come home, she said. I tried to talk her out of it and eventually succeeded in convincing her to stay long enough to finish out the quarter. Then she could come home for Christmas; and if she still felt the same then, she could stay home. This solution seemed to pacify her, at least temporarily.

So Jeanne came home for Christmas, but she didn't go back for winter quarter. She needed time to be with us, time away from confrontations with her classmates. She did go back in the spring, however, and she did go on to graduate, making us proud.

Construction of the cathedral continued, but we would need another one million dollars this month or we would have to shut down. We had raised six hundred thousand dollars this past spring, and almost a million and a half on that "cash Sunday" in June of 1978; but we needed another one million soon. Out of the blue I received a letter from Chicago, Illinois, from a person I'd never met. "I've seen the picture of the Crystal Cathedral. It deserves to be built. Would a one-million-dollar gift from an elderly couple help you?"

Was it a crank letter? The stationery was embossed, in dark print, with the name Foster McGraw. We checked him out. He was the CEO of one of America's greatest corporations, America Hospital Supply, Inc.

This was clearly a miracle.

I flew to Chicago to meet the gentleman and his wife in their modest house. "When do you need my million-dollar check, Reverend?" Mr. Foster asked.

"Well," I said, reluctant to be pushy, "we need a million dollars in three weeks to prevent shutdown."

He looked at his wife and smiled. "That's no problem, is it dear?"

She smiled back. "Not at all," she said.

Within that week this letter came.

September 25, 1978

Dear Bob:

The enclosed check for $1,000,00.00, payable to the Garden Grove Community Church of the Reformed

Church in America, attests to our faith in you, your program, your staff and your faith in God's calling and our support of all the foregoing.

Our hope and prayers are that God will open hearts to provide the balance needed to complete your Crystal Cathedral, built to glorify God and help "bring His Kingdom on earth as it is in heaven."

Keep well, and God's special blessings on your daughter's great challenge. May God continue to love you and yours and bless your work in His name.

> Yours devotedly,
> Foster G. McGraw

And construction continued uninterrupted! Wow!

By December of 1978, another one million dollars had come in from window sales. For the first time, it actually had begun to look as if we were going to make it! This relief coupled with Carol's return home—what a December! The battle finally seemed to have waned.

Meanwhile, our oldest daughter, Sheila, was planning her wedding. In early February I drove her into Los Angeles to pick up her wedding gown. Her wedding day would be the most exciting day of her life, and she was happy to have her dad sharing this time of dreaming and preparing with her. And what a joy for me!

"My dress is expensive, Dad," she said, "and with Carol and the new cathedral and all—well, I guess I just wanted to thank you for buying it for me."

"Sheila," I said, "it gives me great pleasure to buy you this dress. I'm so happy to see your dreams come true. You waited all this time. Postponed your wedding because of Carol's accident. You've been greatly blessed with a wonderful man, and I want you to have a beautiful dress. Some people think a wedding dress is worn only once, but I think it's mentally worn more than any other dress a woman ever has."

Sheila looked at me with curiosity as I explained. "Girls tend to imagine wearing their wedding dress from the day they receive their first bride dress-up doll. And every time they dream of getting married, they put that dress on in fantasy. You'll be radiant in your gown on your wedding day, and you'll wear it every time you look at your wedding pictures for the rest of your life!"

The long-awaited event finally arrived on a crisp February day. I wasn't only going to walk the bride down the aisle and give her away, I was going to perform the ceremony too! It had been such a tumultuous year, so full of highs and lows, with so much emotion, that I was worried I'd start to cry during the service and spoil everything.

I knew that I had to think of something to help keep my emotions in check. Sharing this problem with our family doctor at church one day, he had offered, "No problem, Bob. I've got pills you can take that'll keep the tears back."

"But doctor, then I won't be able to really feel the joy either." So I thanked him and passed up the offer.

At last I came up with the perfect solution. Whenever I felt I was losing control, I'd just tell myself, "Remember, Dad, you're paying the bill!" That changed the mood pretty radically! It worked all too well as I walked the bride down the aisle to the altar. My problem now was how to keep from laughing!

Ever since the accident seven months before, Carol's one burning goal had been to walk down the aisle at her sister's wedding. And she did! She had a limp from the prosthesis that was hidden beneath the floor-length bridesmaid gown, and she was feeble on her forearm crutches—but she did it! My heart had never been more filled with celebration than when I saw Jeanne, Gretchen, and Carol as Sheila's attendants.

Less than a month after that beautiful family affair, disaster struck again. The steel framework of the cathedral was rising on schedule, etching a lacelike filigree against the skyline of a growing Orange County. Scaffolding reaching over a hundred feet up and covering an acre of ground had been erected on its floor. From this huge "structure within a rising structure" the workers stood to erect the framework in place. Then, on a stormy winter night—after the laborers had left for the day, thank God!—it all collapsed in a thundering crash heard throughout the neighborhood.

The next morning stunned construction workers and church staff looked upon something strangely resembling a giant's game of pick-up-sticks: large, heavy sections of steel were piled atop one another. It took weeks to remove and reconstruct (more solidly!) the scaffolding so that work could resume. Once the scaffolding was back in place, work picked up, with extra laborers assigned to the job to make up for lost time.

In March of 1979 I was invited to the eightieth birthday party of Foster McGraw, the elderly gentleman in Chicago who had given us the one-million-dollar gift. There were eight of us around a table at his country club.

"Sir," I greeted him, "if it hadn't been for your generosity, construction would have stalled—perhaps even permanently. Thank you so very much for your faith in me."

Then he slipped an envelope to me. "I like to give gifts on my birthday," he whispered. I opened it and out fell another one-million-dollar check. I was absolutely stunned! This would move the Crystal Cathedral beyond the shell stage toward the usable stage!

A month later, the Organ Committee reported that the pipe organ we had planned to move out of our existing sanctuary into the Crystal Cathedral was going to be inadequate. It would cost nearly a million dollars to supply all the parts, pipes, and console necessary to fill this huge cathedral with sound. Virgil Fox, the world-renowned organist, telephoned me and said, "Less than that would be a crime."

I agreed in principle. "But," I argued, "I don't have the money. Someday—maybe—but not now." Sometimes even dreams have to slow down a bit so the dreamer can catch up.

It's been almost one year to the day since Carol's accident. Arvella has been playing round-the-clock nursemaid to our slowly recovering daughter, and she's beginning to look weary and overburdened.

Then one day I get a call from Ralph Graham, our family doctor. "Can I come see you, Bob?" he asks. Dr. Graham has been a good and longtime friend, and he's always welcome in our home, but I don't like the sound of this. Arvella found a lump in her breast the week before and Dr. Graham did the biopsy. We've been waiting to hear the results. I've been assuming that everything will be okay. Arvella has found many such lumps in the years before, and they've always been benign, no problem. But why would Dr. Graham be coming to our home unless there's something wrong?

He and I sit in the music room that Arvella and I added to our tiny two-bedroom home just the year before. I'm drumming my fingers on the dark oak arms of my Grandpa John Henry Beltman's rocking chair. Arvella is in the bedroom, resting. The doctor leans close to me and speaks in hushed tones as I try to prepare myself for words I don't want to hear.

"Bob . . . that lump." He stops short, lowering his gaze. Then he collects himself and looks at me again. "I have bad news. It's malignant. We'll need to do a mastectomy."

I can't look at the man. After all, this is my wife's body that he's talking about. I've never imagined that I'd speak to another man about a thing so intimate. My wife and I have remained sexually active and happy since that first night on our honeymoon. I've taken her out on a weekly "date" all those years, protective insulation against the burnout that the ministry can inflict on marriages. She always dresses herself up, and we're every bit as romantic as we were during the days of our courtship. In fact, we've never ceased courting: emotionally, romantically, physically, she's remained my beautiful, sexy, darling Arvella. What will this mean for her sense of herself as a woman?

But this isn't just about her body-image. This is about her life! Women in our church have died from breast cancer. I've conducted more than one funeral brought about by this disease.

Ralph tries to subdue my creeping fear. "It looks good, though, Bob," he says reassuringly. "We think that with the mastectomy we can get it all."

I reluctantly look at him. I need to examine his eyes to see whether or not these are empty words. Ralph's eyes meet my probe. Then I feel a divine peace slowly coming into my spirit. I know that he is telling the truth. God is using him to bring perspective, and his manner comforts me. The terror fades.

"It will be okay," I tell myself. I breathe deeply. "We made it through many days with Carol; we can make it through this too."

Minutes go by in silence. Then I say, "Ralph, thank you for coming over to tell me yourself. You're a dear friend. I must go tell Arvella now." I see Ralph to the door and close it gently behind him.

I stand still, feeling icy and strange. I just need to think for a minute. I take a few deep breaths and then turn and walk reluctantly down the long hallway to the bedroom.

Arvella is no longer resting. She's standing looking out of the window into the garden, admiring the giant ficus tree. She doesn't turn to look at me. She's wrapped herself in her arms as if they were a warm shawl. Her long white fingers clutch her arms just below her shoulders. I walk up behind her and wrap my arms around her from behind. I bury my face in the back of her neck, smelling her sweet smell and feeling her soft auburn hair tickle my cheeks. I don't cry. I just breathe in her fragrance and personhood as if she might enter my senses and dwell within me forever.

After minutes in this silent embrace, she turns and looks at me. I finally speak, "Arvella—"

But she interrupts. "Honey, I know. I've known since I found that lump last week. It just didn't feel right. I knew when Dr. Graham first looked at it and said he thought it looked good. I knew he was wrong."

I begin to cry, but just a little. "Arvella, they have to take your breast," I said.

Her head drops. Then she mumbles, "I'm sorry."

This pierces me. Sorry? *Sorry?* I hold her away from me, turn her around, and look into her face, lifting it up to my gaze.

"Arvella—look at me. I didn't marry you for your breasts. I married you for your energy and your spirit and your brilliance. I married you for your excitement about life and for your tenacity. I married you for *who* you are, not *what* you are. That's what drives me to make love to you, and none of that will *ever* change."

I meant every single word I spoke, and she knew it. And so we held each other. And she spoke of the peace she felt. Together we talked of God's goodness and how we felt closer to one another, and closer to God, than we'd ever felt before.

XXXVII

Arvella's surgery was immediate and successful! She was fitted with a prosthesis only months after Carol was fitted for hers. Arvella and I would joke that if all else failed, we could go into the "spare parts" business.

Meanwhile, the cathedral was taking shape; the balconies stretching skyward were already changing the landscape of Orange County. With this increased visibility came both increased support and increased criticism. I had to deal with it all—fundraising, taking the heat, preaching, running the church, our *Hour of Power* productions, my wife, and my daughter—the latter two both still in a state of rehabilitation. It was a near-crushing load, and we all staggered under it.

To make matters worse, I knew that we wouldn't have cash for the pipe organ that Arvella wanted in the cathedral. This was a bitter disappointment to me, especially now. We had always, since day one, had an organ for our worship services.

Then one day a dear friend, Hazel Wright of Chicago, known for her philanthropy toward the arts and music, invited me to her home and offered one million dollars for the cathedral organ! Another miracle gift from heaven!

By December 1979 we had collected a total of twelve million dollars in cash. (This total included the solid, commitment of W. Clement Stone. We'd come a long way, but with the addition of the organ and added inflationary expenses, the cost was now above sixteen million dollars. We were still four million short.

The first batch of more than ten thousand windows was being installed, section by section, on the skeleton of the cathedral. We were now entering the final construction phase, and we were assured that the building could be dedicated in less than a year . . . *if* we could raise the millions more we still needed. But inflation that year was over thirty percent! Who could truly know the future?

I recalled my own words in a lecture that I'd just given to top corporate executives at the University of California, Irvine—words that had helped me years earlier: "Nobody has a money problem—only an idea problem." Now I prayed that God would give us an idea to raise the last four million dollars. I prayed that we would be able to open the doors of the Crystal Cathedral in September 1980, debt free! I prayed that we might be able to give the entire offering from the first Sunday services to help some great cause of hungry and hurting people around the world.

In February 1980, with Arvella and Carol fully rehabilitated, we announced the plan to raise the last four million dollars. I had learned that Beverly Sills, the world's most famous opera star, was about to retire, and so I decided to invite her to present her final gala recital as a spectacular benefit in and for the unfinished Crystal

Cathedral. We would try to sell each of the three thousand seats for fifteen hundred dollars each.

My wife came into my office one day waving a letter. "Beverly Sills is coming to help!" she exclaimed. Miss Sills had agreed to perform a benefit concert on May 13. For every donation of fifteen hundred dollars, we promised that we would affix a memorial plaque with the donor's name and city to the opera-style seats in the pews of the Crystal Cathedral.

I traveled to Vancouver, Canada, where friends had informed me there was a group who wanted to buy an entire balcony of three hundred seats for the Beverly Sills event! "Count on us for four hundred and fifty thousand dollars," the Canadian representative said. I returned home to find a letter from Frank and Barbara Sinatra with a check to reserve two seats. Then my friend Mickey Rooney called from New York. "My wife and I will be there," he said. The project was off to a great start.

On that gala spring evening the press was out in full force. The three major networks, the wire services, the big-name papers—it was a PR man's dream come true. I wore a tuxedo and Arvella a lovely formal gown. Cameras whirred and clicked and flashed. The house was sold out. The famous, the ultra-rich, and many perfectly ordinary people who had sacrificed to make their fifteen-hundred-dollar donation—all were packed into the rising edifice!

As the lights dimmed, Beverly Sills swept majestically onto the stage like a princess in a palace, her long satin gown floating across the salmon-colored marble. A moment later the orchestra began to play, and she burst into song.

Her soprano voice, usually rich and lovely, bounced from one glass wall to another. I was horrified. Shrill hollow sounds filled the cathedral. What's wrong? It can't be this celebrated artist! Is it the cathedral?

Arvella groaned and put a hand over her mouth. "Oh, my goodness," she said. "What's happened? Didn't they rehearse" She looked at me, aghast. I couldn't answer. I really didn't know; I assumed they had. I was sick.

It must be only a temporary sound-system dilemma, I rationalized. But that didn't help the many who sat and listened to a full hour of this madness. And poor Beverly Sills! I was appalled, embarrassed, and humiliated as the evening closed.

Arvella and I consoled each other on the way home, saying that the permanent sound system would be ever so much better with some simple fine-tuning. But I wasn't so sure. And we had to produce a television program from this seventeen-million-dollar echo chamber come September.

The next day the *Los Angeles Times* ran a scathing review. Martin Bernheimer said that the world-famous opera star had sounded like the lady singing "The Star-Spangled Banner" at a baseball game. Arvella got a handwritten letter that week from pianist Roger Williams, who offered his support: "Martin Bernheimer can go to hell!" he said.

The next night Beverly Sills was a guest on the *Johnny Carson Show*.

"Say," the ever-ebullient Johnny commented, "I hear you sang over at the Reverend Schuller's Crystal Cathedral the other night."

She smiled sweetly. "Yes," she quipped. "My voice is still there now, ricocheting from one glass wall to another, trying to find it's way out."

"I'm all for the Crystal Cathedral," Johnny said. "I've got stock in Windex!"

We had achieved our fundraising goal of four million dollars, but the formal dedication was only four months away, and that meant we all had a lot of work to do.

September 7, 1980, would see the last Sunday morning church service in the beautiful Neutra sanctuary. This landmark building held such high and holy memories for our church family that we decided to have the entire service there on this monumental day. We would sing our hymns. We would invoke God's presence. We would read from scripture. I would preach. Then, when it was time for the last word, we would all march into our new gathering place for the benediction—the first act of formal worship in the Crystal Cathedral.

So the hymns were sung, the sermon given—a beautiful service. Then, at the close, the organ boomed triumphantly and was answered back by the new organ in the cathedral. The congregation rose and began to file out. It was a solemn, beautiful procession— one that I was honored to lead alongside my son, the Reverend Robert Schuller (the second)! With the entire congregation of fifteen hundred people and the consistory following in a proud parade, we marched to our new home.

I carried the big old black pulpit Bible lovingly in my hands. Each minister and board member carried some article of worship, from the baptismal bowls to the communion cups.

Then, there in that shimmering, towering edifice of glass, I gave the benediction:

"May the Lord bless you and keep you. May the Lord cause His face to shine upon you and give you peace. In your going out and in your coming in, in your lying down and in your rising up, in your labor and in your leisure, in your laughter and in your tears, until you come to stand before Jesus, in that day in which there is no sunset and no dawning. Amen."

PART III

THE SUMMIT YEARS

Today's accomplishments are yesterday's impossibilities.
—Robert H. Schuller

XXXVIII

It's September 14, 1980. Twenty-six walkie-talkies hum in the hands of volunteers working to find places for the hundreds of cars entering our twenty-acre parking lot. The radios also connect the greeters at the three main entrances, the key ushers, and the sound and media personnel. Just last week we walked to the cathedral as a church family for the benediction. Today is the grand opening and dedication.

I'm so excited that I can't just sit and wait for a formal entry. I go up to the chancel and stand by the altar and watch as people are ushered to seats on the main floor and in the three balconies. A section of the south balcony has been reserved for the press. Dozens of cameras, still and moving, are positioned there, focused on my new pulpit.

Organ music fills the space, the world's largest all-glass auditorium. The glass that towers toward the heavens sparkles with sunny morning rays. The light striking the windowpanes sends shimmering sparkles of sun dancing on the clear and smooth surfaces, as on an early-morning ocean. A gentle breeze blows through the open doors and through some windows that have been opened, bringing with it a fresh and pleasant fragrance as well as a sense of openness.

I'm exhilarated by the wonder of the moment. I stride to the pulpit, and as I do, I throw my arms skyward and boom my now well-established signature greeting: "This is the day the Lord has made; let us rejoice and be glad in it!"

The majestic sounds of the organ boom out over the congregation. My voice cracks with emotion. We're finally here! Five years of
wrestling with struggle after struggle, both professional and personal, and we've finally crested the mountaintop. I'm deeply moved
as I consider the fact that, without the trust and generosity of thousands of humble and beautiful people, this great feat would never
have been accomplished.

Just a few minutes ago, a lone woman emerged from the massive
crowd. She reached out and touched me, glowing with excitement,
and said, "Dr. Schuller, my name is on a window in this cathedral.
I now feel as if I'm *somebody!* I now know that I made a difference!
I live on a small income, but my tithe paid off a window in two
years!" This morning's dedication has become her moment of glory,
shared with thousands of others.

The sun now falls upon my shoulders as it floods in through the
ninety-foot-high doors behind me. The birds chirp. The blue sky
gleams above my head as I begin to speak:

"Today we dedicate this cathedral to the glory of man for the
greater glory of God. Welcome to this service, which celebrates the
twenty-fifth anniversary of the founding of this ministry. Twenty-five
years ago we organized a new church with one hundred and fifty
members meeting in a rented drive-in theater. Now, today, all of
you are gathered with me in this glistening cathedral to dedicate our
new home and our renewed hearts to Jesus Christ. Thank you for
your trust. Thank you for coming to celebrate with me."

The audience rises to sing words to this hymn I wrote just a few
days earlier. I truly feel that I'm standing on the mountaintop as
their voices ring out:

People, people, everywhere.
Each a jewel fair and rare.
Wake up world! Lost in fear!
Jesus calls to hope and cheer.

People, people 'round this earth
Hunger for a deep self-worth.
See the cross! The holy sign!
Shape your life by this design.

People, people, will you dare
venture forth in noble prayer.
Claim your heritage divine,
Born to be a star to shine.

Christ, my Savior, help me see
This grand possibility.
Saved from sin's indignity,
saved to love eternally.

Be a window, let all see
Christ within you living free.
Be a mirror to reflect
Dignity and self-respect.

People, people, trust God's dream
That can feed your self-esteem,
Christ will build your life anew.
God loves you, and I do too.

News accounts the next day heralded the service as a "major religious event." We had all paid heavily, for many years, to create an instrument of inspiration that now was being described as "art in architecture."

I whooped for joy as I read the comments of the *New York Times*'s architecture critic, the famed Paul Goldberger. He wrote, "The architecture generates joy, which fits Dr. Schuller's theology very well."

He got it! The message had come through loud and clear!

The very next Sunday, to continue the high, I would have the honor of officiating at the ordination service of my only son, Robert Anthony. As a graduate of Hope College, with his degree in divinity from Fuller Theological Seminary in Pasadena, California, and now with a beautiful little baby girl (our first grandchild), he had what seemed a blessed life.

But back in Garden Grove we still weren't out of the woods. At our staff meeting the next morning, I asked, "What are the problems we need to correct?" They all answered in one spontaneous outburst:

"The sound system didn't work!"

My surprise must have showed in my face. "It's true, Dr. Schuller," said the team member next to me. "I couldn't hear in the section where I sat."

"And where was that?" I asked.

"In the middle of the main floor."

"Oh." That was all I could say. Not being able to hear in that central area wasn't a good sign.

"And where were *you* sitting?" I asked another.

"In the west balcony. I had trouble hearing too."

As I asked around, it became clear that it had been virtually impossible to hear well, no matter where a person was sitting. Words spoken from the altar and pulpit had been an echoed muddle, a secret message that each congregant had had to struggle to decipher.

From the earliest conception of this all-glass building, the architect had worried about the effect of sound reverberating against the smooth glass, though he hadn't shared the extent of his concern with us. The problem had become obvious during the fiasco of the Beverly Sills concert, and we had been trying to find a solution ever since.

The leading acoustic engineer in the country had been hired to analyze the venue and design a system that would work. He had come up with a plan that called for small speakers to be installed behind every pew, with elaborate computers controlling the speed at which the sound emerged. It had all been too complicated and sophisticated for me to comprehend, but the architect had said, "They use it very successfully in Saint Bart's church in New York—so let's go with it." And so we had—at a horrendous cost of hundreds of thousands of dollars. Now it had proved to be a bust!

"By next Sunday we'll fix it," I was told by our sound-system experts. They were at the controls all week to "iron out the problem." But after the next Sunday had come and gone, I would hear again a negative report.

"Could you hear me this morning?" I asked my staff.

They shook their heads in negative reply, and I groaned.

Now the third Sunday morning in the cathedral was only days away, and after spending hours on the phone, I still wasn't satisfied that the sound system would work. Promises had been made to me by good people brought in from New York, but there had been horrific disagreements between these experts.

I wanted to test the system out before Saturday. "Don't send me up there to experiment with a full house," I said. "Let's figure this out before Sunday comes."

"But an empty house is no test," they told me. "The system can be tested only in a full house, where bodies and clothes absorb the echo. Trust us!"

I had no choice but to trust them.

So on this third Sunday we tried again, and I received the ultimate negative review: the congregation began to stand up and walk out!

This had happened to me only once before, in the Orange Drive-in Theater during an Easter Sunday service! Right at the opening of my twenty-minute sermon, car engines had started; then vehicles had begun backing up and driving out. I hadn't known what was happening. Horns had honked. People had waved signals of frustration—arms flying out of open windows—as more cars had headed for the exit. I had paused, stared at the unreal scene, and called to anyone who would listen, "Can you hear me?"

Drivers of cars parked only thirty feet in front of me had shouted, "The sound system is off!" There'd been nothing I could do about it at that moment, there on the snackbar rooftop, so I'd simply reached over to a large bouquet of long-stemmed calla lilies on the altar behind me and pulled out one large bloom with a two-foot stem. Holding it high above my head, I'd stood there waving good-bye to the congregation of cars leaving for their Easter dinners.

All these years later, here I was, in my dream church, experiencing the same humiliation. People were getting up from their seats in all three balconies and on the main floor. And they were sending me the same message: the sound system doesn't work! Only this time I didn't have a calla lily to help me out.

I made my message brief, condensing what I'd planned to say. Then I walked down the stairs from the pulpit to my private room and waited at my desk for my wife—the one and only critic that I knew I could trust totally, completely. She didn't have to say a word; her look confirmed what I'd suspected. I put my head in my hands and moaned.

After eight years of praying and planning, and after an expenditure of millions of dollars, my dream had become a fiasco! What had we built? A huge white elephant? I would have welcomed a divine call to exit. But where could I go?

So I preached to myself. This sermon came out:

"Nobody has a problem; it's only a decision waiting to be made. If my so-called 'problem' is the result of a bad decision that I made yesterday, then all I have to do is make another decision—a *better* decision—today!"

So I went to my telephone and called national leaders in the specialized science of acoustics. I hired a new engineer, as reputable as the one hired by Johnson. He flew in from Texas.

His verdict? "Your system, Dr. Schuller, doesn't work!"

"I know that," I exclaimed in frustration. "What can we do about it?"

I wasn't ready for this expert's answer: "Take it all out. This system could never work in this all-glass building, no matter how you dolled it up. Take it all out and throw it in the dump! No one will buy it. Let me design a system that will work."

We groaned. Hundreds of thousands of dollars in the trash!? We had no choice, though; we did it. We bought his design and installed it at half the price of the first one—but still in the six figures (a few times over)!

Then came the test: a Sunday of preaching to a now-dwindling crowd of the faithful. No one walked out at least. That was encouraging.

"Well, how did it work?" I asked nervously after that service.

"We'll need to install carpets," the expert said. "Then it should be fine."

We called in the carpet company and they followed the expert's advice to the letter. But carpeting didn't solve the problem.

"You'll have to live with it, I guess. I'm sorry," the expert said, then flew back to Texas, never to be seen again.

I was completely disillusioned. The most difficult hardships are the ones with no end in sight. This one had gone on too long already, and I still had little hope that anyone could solve the problem. Here I was in a glass house, with my critics lining up outside to throw stones. And I probably wouldn't even hear them coming.

Some months later, a musical group on tour gave a concert in the cathedral. I was out of town and unable to attend, but Fred Southard, my CFO, heard it and came to see me immediately on my return. "I couldn't believe it, Bob," he said. "They brought in their own sound system, and it really worked!"

"Find out what they used and buy it," I said.

The job was done fast, and it worked! It also cost far less than either system put in by the experts. Now at last I could be heard. Our prayers had been answered. The Crystal Cathedral was, at last, the masterpiece I'd always envisioned.

One day shortly after we'd found our sound-system solution I looked down at the manuscript that I'd just finished and was ready to send to the publishers. I read the title, *Tough Times Never Last, But Tough People Do!* It would be my first book to make the *New York Times* bestseller list.

Most of the words in that manuscript had come from the internal struggles I had experienced through the past months. I reached down and placed my hand on the plastic binder that encased the pages, patted the manuscript, then spontaneously picked it up and hugged it. Then I took a deep breath and fell back exhausted into my chair. Finally . . . finally, I could rest—at least for a moment.

On the way home that afternoon, Arvella and I drove up to Los Angeles to visit Carol, who was back in the hospital. Three years had passed since the motorcycle accident. Now, at the age of sixteen, Carol had made a decision few teenagers ever have to face: she had elected to have more of her leg amputated. We had saved the knee—an answer to prayer, a miracle! But three years of physical therapy had failed to restore proper function to the knee joint. Carol had researched a new amputation technique in which that joint was separated in such a way that the cut was neither above nor below the knee. She, Arvella, and I had heard from professionals that this approach would give her less pain from the stump, and longer endurance on it, since the leg would be separated at a natural weight-bearing point.

Carol had been frustrated that her "frozen" knee caused her prosthesis to be stiff as a board. This had forced her to walk by swinging her hip wide in an unnatural gait, to stretch out on the back seat of a car if she wanted to go someplace, and to sit at the end of theater rows at the movies with her friends because her "fake leg" couldn't fit into tight places.

Carol had made her decision, but now, once again, she found herself in horrendous pain. When we stopped to see her that day, the surgeon was very optimistic that the surgery had been success-ful, so she was in good spirits.

When I walked into her room, relief swept over me. She didn't have that fragile, fighting-for-life appearance that I so vividly recalled. All the fear of losing her, the frustration at being unable to relieve her intense pain, the anxiety of walking into a hospital room not knowing what bad news would be awaiting me—all these could finally be let go. Three years ago the doctors had said that the bac-teria could lie dormant, causing an infection to flare at any given time. But this time . . . no infection!

Finally the door on this tragedy could be shut. After more therapy and specialized fittings, Carol would not only walk; she would be unstoppable! Full of energy, and with a new leg that could keep up with her, she found an active and fulfilling life again, including dat-ing up a storm! Now my worries as a father could center on the usual worries inherent in having a beautiful and vivacious teenage daughter.

Meanwhile, television stations in America were even more eager to get the *Hour of Power* account. We had become the first church ser-vice to be seen on the Armed Forces Network. Our ministry broad-cast moved fast up the religious rating charts, helped by one small but powerful addition to our programming. That was the introduc-tion of an interview guest every Sunday morning.

We had decided that the *Hour of Power* should be more than a "Schuller show." Every week we would introduce someone who had a great story to share. Many special people and positive causes deserved a platform that offered a national audience, and our burgeoning viewership offered such a national television platform. Our guests would entertain, yes, but they would also make powerful testaments to personal faith.

I was astounded by the list of people eager to share their stories—for free! Over the years we would have former President Gerald Ford as well as Vice-President Dan Quayle and Vice-President Al Gore. Movie stars included Mickey Rooney, Gregory Peck, Mary Martin, and Charlton Heston. Corporate chiefs included W. Clement Stone, Ray Kroc, and J. B. Fuqua. Military leaders included General Colin Powell and General Norman Schwarzkopf. Celebrities from the struggle against racism included Coretta Scott King and Rosa Parks. War heroes included Max Cleland and Scott O'Grady. Celebrated musician Yehudi Menuhin shared his faith. World-renowned religious leaders such as Norman Vincent Peale and Billy Graham joined us, as did Oral Roberts and Jesse Jackson. Prominent Roman Catholics Archbishop Fulton Sheen, Cardinal Roger Mahony, and Henri Nouwen were with us, as were leading psychiatrists William Glasser and Viktor Frankl.

But not *everybody* was famous. There were many powerful non-celebrities too, ordinary people with heart-stirring stories to tell. Among them was June Scobee Rogers, whose husband had commanded the *Challenger* space shuttle. With the rest of the world, she had watched the explosion that killed all seven astronauts.

The *Hour of Power* was the only televised weekly church service during which people of *all* races, ethnic origins, and political affiliations could look forward to hearing the weekly guests. There was no political bias to our program, just testimonials to the power of possibility thinking.

But just as the cathedral began to gain rave reviews for both televised and live performances, I would read the most damning article ever written about our ministry, before or since. And it appeared in my own denominational journal, *The Church Herald.*

I was deeply hurt when I read the parable written by the Reverend Wendell Karsen, a Reformed Church missionary in Hong Kong. In it, he imagined a time when millions of the earth's most wretched and starving people travel to Garden Grove to see the Crystal Cathedral. Coming closer, they see themselves reflected in the mirrored glass and recoil at the sight of their own misery. One of them picks up a rock and throws it at his own image. Others follow suit until the cathedral is reduced to rubble, then ransacked by the starving in search of food and raw materials to ease their suffering. (Didn't he realize that not one dollar went into the building? All the money went into checks that went into the pockets of laborers and truck drivers, and yes, even iron ore miners!)

My colleagues across America were as shocked as I was, but they weren't too surprised. After all, for years the editor of that journal had been unfriendly and unkind to me (to say the least). I was, in his opinion, *"only* a California preacher"—one who had been on the edge for years with a drive-in church, a television church, and now a glassed-in church seating three thousand people!

For whatever reason, critics such as Reverend Karsen failed to see the role played by great monuments to faith throughout the history of the church. The cathedrals at Chartres and Notre Dame, along with Westminster Abbey and St. Peter's in Rome, continue to inspire us centuries after the last workers set the last stone in place and inlaid the last stained-glass window.

And even if one sees the work of Jesus exclusively in terms of helping the poor, the ministry sustained and heartened by our Crystal Cathedral enables us to serve as the distribution center for as many as seventy-five hundred charity meals every week through World Opportunities International. It allows us to provide specific relief as needed for particular populations in particular regions—

such as the children in Chernobyl after the nuclear disaster there. It
sustains a prison ministry, a psychological counseling center, our
suicide prevention center, a Hispanic ministry, a Korean ministry, a
self-worth program called Confident Kids, and annual youth gatherings, the International Conference on Care and Kindness, etc.

We don't offer just a handout with any of these programs. We
offer life-altering uplift and hope.

How would criticism affect my children's world?—how might it
alienate my kids from others, causing them to wonder what motives
hid behind a simple "Hello" or "What's your name?"

We never knew who would collar us at a church function or a
school function or the grocery store or the mall to drill us with some
negative argument. Such mistrust and exposure had never been a
part of my own childhood in Sioux County. Having my family sub-
jected to it now made me very sad.

But outnumbering these criticisms, there were also wonderful
moments of support when we would be eating dinner out, shopping, or attending an event, and people would approach us in affirmation. The kind words of these beautiful and respectful people
would be a balm to soothe the ache of the cutting words of others.

And so we would see that occasional criticism couldn't dispel the
praise that many were voicing. And it couldn't rob us of the satisfaction and gratitude that we felt inside for all that God had done and
all that we'd been given as a family in one another.

We revered our family moments together even more now that I
was a face known to the public. We continued our trips to Big Bear,
where my children would, during the winter months, disguise me
with fuzzy winter caps and big sunglasses and overstuffed ski parkas
until only my nose would show, hoping that they could take me out
without having me recognized. They had great fun at this, but it
failed more often than not, and then I was left in public view in
these outrageous outfits! My family was my refuge, and after all that
we had faced together in the last years, there was a deep, deep satis-

faction in our unity. We had survived! We had encountered the unforeseeable and the monumental. We had refused to buckle beneath the challenges and the personal tragedies.

The early eighties saw Arvella healthy and strong again, and Carol, now a beautiful teenager, was devoting her life to church activities as well as skiing. She was working toward a new goal—to ski in the Disabled Olympics in 1984.

Gretchen, meanwhile, had become very involved with our youth group at church. She hadn't been spared her own trauma following Carol's accident. Arvella and I had practically moved to the hospital during those first months, leaving Gretchen to camp at her best friend's house. With Arvella nursing Carol back to health, driving her back and forth daily to rehabilitation, bathing her, dressing her, Gretchen had had to fend for herself for almost an entire year. The whole family system had been turned upside down. Carol had lost her leg, but Gretchen had lost part of her childhood.

As Carol became the "vulnerable" one, Gretchen had to become the "strong" one, and this reversal of the big-sister little-sister roles had taken its toll. Extracurricular activities had been near to impossible for Arvella and me to manage during Carol's recuperation, so Gretchen had been able to participate only occasionally. Furthermore, Carol and Gretchen had been close companions, so Gretchen had lost—for a time—far more than we dared to realize. Had it not been for the selfless care of a few dear church families, Gretchen probably would have suffered character-altering effects. Instead, these surrogate families had become God's provision for our youngest.

The Bible says that when we are weak, He is strong—and boy, had we needed His strength during those rough months! Arvella and I had had absolutely no ability to be all-in-all for all during that time. Now, as things were returning to normal, Gretchen was beginning to develop her own sense of identity. And she was growing into a lovely young teen who was diligent, serious, and sweet to all. She had done more than survive—she had *thrived!* To us, this was one more miracle.

Jeanne was now a lovely brunette in her mid-twenties, living in New York City and working for a highly respected public relations firm.

Sheila, in her early thirties, was happily married, the parent of a toddling boy, my first grandson, and pregnant with what would be another boy. Her husband worked full-time with the church, and Sheila assisted me with the development and editing of my books. After Arvella's cancer surgery, Sheila also became her mom's assistant in programming and editing the *Hour of Power*.

Bob, now in his late twenties, had grown into a fine young man. Married now for nearly ten years, he had a three-year-old girl, Angie Rae, and a one-year-old boy, Robert Anthony. He was pastoring a church that he'd started in the southern coastal town of San Juan Capistrano, doing all the hard work of building a congregation. Work that I knew so well.

In 1981, at the age of seventeen, Carol moved for three months to Winter Park, Colorado, to follow her dream of skiing in the 1984 Disabled Olympics. Specialized coaching could be found only in this little town, but letting her go proved one of the most difficult decisions that Arvella and I would face as parents. After much prayer and thought, we kissed her goodbye on a rainy Southern California morning, and she left for the Rocky Mountains to live with a family that we fully approved of.

In 1982 she went to train in New York with a young woman amputee, a number-one competitor who had specialized in the fastest of the alpine events—The Downhill. This was Carol's favored race. Carol's intense and individualized training advanced her to the Disabled Nationals in Squaw Valley, California, by the spring of 1983.

"Dad, you have to come watch me race!" she insisted.

And how could we refuse?

When we arrived in Squaw Valley it had been some months since we'd seen Carol, and she looked like a serious competitor now. She was so independent that she spent only limited moments with us, but her eyes shone with joy at our reunion. Jeanne had come for the occasion too, and Carol beamed with pride that her older sister, so sophisticated and "cool," had made the trip.

Whenever I'd pictured my daughter racing, I'd visualized her meandering gently from side to side down the slope. I certainly wasn't prepared for what I saw when I got to the race site: the competitors streaked straight down the mountain at lightning speed! I breathed a sigh of relief when Carol crossed the finish line safely. Only when I heard Jeanne scream, "Yeah, Carol!" and race toward her sister did I realize that Carol had taken first place in the junior division (for eighteen years and younger).

As a result of her success in that event, Carol was chosen to be an alternative to the Disabled Olympic team. She would return to Winter Park in that role the following year. Later that same year, she would be the only disabled U.S. skier to compete in a non-disabled speed-skiing series. Her fastest official speed on one leg would be sixty-nine miles per hour! To me this meant she had clearly overcome her tragedy and was now living a full and adjusted life.

Life was moving pretty fast for *all* of us. In 1983 I found myself with two books on the *New York Times* bestseller list: *Tough Times Never Last, But Tough People Do*, and *Tough-Minded Faith for Tender-Hearted People*. Fifty-five years after my birth in a flood, at the end of a dead-end road that had no name and no number, I was being called "famous."

But our lives weren't ours any longer. Even times of private pain were liable to become topics of conversation among people who knew nothing about us . . . as we were about to discover.

XXXIX

As so often in the past, the bad news begins with a phone call. It's a Saturday, just after Christmas, and I'm spending the day in my private study, where I often escape for meditation and preparation for my Sunday sermons. Here, I've discovered, I can still experience the solitude I grew to love as a boy by the banks of the Floyd.

Arvella and I are meeting in a little while for our weekly date. We're planning to share a quiet dinner in a place where I know I can find a private and inconspicuous corner. So I pick up the phone when it rings, expecting to hear my wife's lovely voice.

"Dad? It's Bob. I need to talk. Can I come see you?"

He doesn't speak in the tone of passion and conviction that I usually associate with my son. Instead, he sounds subdued, almost sorrowful. I feel a tightening in my belly.

"Of course, Bob," I assure him. "When would you like to come?"

"Now. I'm just down the street," he says, sounding apologetic.

"All right," I agree. "I'll expect you."

When my son arrives, what I see shakes me to my core. His six-foot-four frame is bowed and heavy. His face is tense, and his eyes won't meet my gaze. His brow is wrinkled and pain-ridden, and his eyes are red. He has a small suitcase in his hand. He stands silent and almost sheepish before me. I step aside to welcome him, because I find that I can't summon any words. The moment feels suddenly and dangerously fragile.

Bob walks past me and practically collapses onto a nearby sofa. Before I even have a chance to come to his side, he drops his head to his knees. He's sobbing uncontrollably.

I watch him. I wait, knowing that when the tears have emptied he will explain what's raging within him.

In time he looks up at me. He has collected himself enough to say, "Dad—I have to quit the ministry."

I'm silent at first. I know that this is just one of those bad moments that every minister encounters. He's exaggerating, and the best thing that I can do right now is to stay calm.

I offer what I hope is encouragement: "Bob, I'm sure that whatever has happened isn't that bad. I've made so many mistakes in my own life and ministry, but in the end things have worked out."

"No, Dad; you don't understand. Linda and I are getting a divorce."

Bam! I feel as if I've been kicked in the head. It isn't the words he's saying; it's the tone of finality.

"Dad, she's been telling me for the past nine and a half years she wants a divorce. In fact, she began saying it only two months after we got married."

Bob bites his lip, trying to quell the emotion.

"I kept telling her that divorce isn't an option. But Dad . . . in this situation possibility thinking just isn't working! Last month I talked her into agreeing to give it through the holidays. Christmas has come and gone now, and she's made her final decision. And Dad . . ."

Now he begins to sob once more, and the pain I see on this boy's face rips at my heart.

"Dad . . . I've put my children to bed every night and kissed their foreheads, and every single night since the day they were born I've had to wonder if they'd still be there in the morning. Then today I was sitting there, watching them play with their Christmas toys, and I knew that there's absolutely nothing else I can do!"

Bob presses his face into my shoulder and clutches me for strength. And so I hold him as if he were a little boy once again. I'm shocked that all this has been happening without my noticing. Arvella and I have sensed that things weren't right, but we've had no idea things were this bad. Bob has hidden his pain well, and now it's all coming out in one big, gushing flood.

He reins himself in again and continues his explanation. "She's made up her mind, Dad. Instead of making her leave and alarming

Angie and Bobby, I offered to move out of the house. She jumped at it, so here I am—alone. I can't go home tonight—not even to tuck my own children into bed!"

I hold back my tears and try to encourage him. "Robert, you're not alone," I say. "Know one thing: your wife may walk away from you, but God will *never* walk away from you! Divorce is serious business. It's a tragedy. In fact, you'll have to go through an examination by our denomination to retain your ordination and your license. But Bob, God has called you just as He called me when I was a young boy. You're ordained by God, and God is *not* divorcing you."

"But how can I be a minister when I can't even manage my own home?" he asks, his voice cracking. "There's no getting around it: I'll have to tell my congregation tomorrow morning."

"Bob, remember: 'In love's service, only broken hearts will do.'" I've quoted the line often, and Bob knows it well. But now it's taking on a deeper meaning for him.

I collect my thoughts for a moment before continuing: "Because of this unhappy experience, Bob, you'll no doubt be more compassionate and understanding—perhaps even more effective—than you have been. You didn't *invite* this, Bob; this wasn't your *choice*. But now it's time for you to let God either work a miracle by saving the marriage, or work a miracle by healing you after the marriage."

"Dad, can I stay here, in your study?" he asks, his voice part little boy, part man. "I don't have anywhere else to go. I can't even go to a hotel and sign my name—Robert Schuller."

And for the first time ever I hear a tinge of disdain for that name and what it brings with it. And I don't blame him, because I feel it too. But I hope, in due time, that he'll wear the name again with pride. In fact, I *know* that he will, because I know what he's made of; I know who he is and who he's called to be; and I know Who made him.

And so together we grieve. And I decide to believe in Bob even when he can't believe in himself. I look forward to the day when

God will resurrect that amputated part of him and make it whole again. For this I've come to know well: that God, in some way, in some fashion, does make the broken whole. Meanwhile, "in love's service, only broken hearts will do."

The next day I called Bob to see how the morning service had gone. He'd insisted on doing it on his own, and I had respected that, but I needed to know how his message had been received.

"Oh, Dad, I couldn't believe it," he said. His voice was hoarse, but within it was the sound of hope. "I didn't give scripture or prayer or anything. I just had to get it over with. I tried telling the people, but I could get only one line out, and that one line said it all. I was so humiliated that I couldn't look at them. I turned my back and began to sob.

"Dad, I felt so alone and so ashamed. That sanctuary was so quiet. I didn't know what would happen next. But then I felt a hand on my shoulder. It was so tender and so warm and so strong. I think it was one of my elders; I'm still not sure who. And then I felt another and another, and soon my congregation had left their seats, coming up on the stage. They just surrounded me with the strength of their bodies as I collapsed in their arms. It still hurts so bad, Dad, but I feel like I can do it now, because I'm not alone."

The worst was yet to come, as anyone who has gone through a divorce can attest. Arvella and I were forced to watch as another one of our children faced personal tragedy. Only this time it was a pain that went beyond the physical to the very soul and sense of self-esteem. My son was encountering what was deemed by many in the church to be unspeakable. And he would be watched with suspicious and critical eyes.

Of course, the press picked up the story, and denominational leaders and Christian observers had much to say.

It was one thing to have the nation observe a pain that could appear heroic, as in Carol's case. But here the suffering was neither unusual nor valiant; it was all too familiar to the average individual. In these circumstances, compassion can be like a shadow confronted by an army of clouds: it simply disappears. Perhaps we all subconsciously fear that the discovery of a righteous man's "failure" and "hardship" will jeopardize our own fragile immunity to the same fate. Is that why a wound to the soul is so much more devastating than one to the physical body? And if such a pain happens before a crowd of merciless witnesses, it delivers its jabs a thousandfold. Every gawking gaze empowers the growing and unquenchable remorse.

I never shared with my congregation — locally or on television — the private pain of my son, though the pain was woven into each message. I began a series on Job, and in that year we dedicated a life-size marble statue of this biblical hero. A text from the Book of Job was carved on the base of the statue:

"When He has tried me, I shall come forth as gold."

The press grilled my son, but though the coverage was cruel and unfair at times, we didn't allow outside criticism to stop any of us from embracing the tomorrows that would dawn. Eventually Bob would heal — though with scars, most assuredly. But the day would come, just as it had for Arvella and Carol, when Bob's scars would give way to a new day of promise. He would meet a woman far surpassing all his hopes and expectations. And once again he would go before his congregation — this time to say, "You wept with me in my grief; now rejoice with me in my joy." And so he would be wed to Donna in his own church, with his children, Angie and Bobbie, as attendants and the entire congregation as guests.

In January of 1984 Jeanne married archeological scholar Paul David Dunn, whom she had met while at her summer-school studies in the Holy Land. He had been living in Israel at the time and had been one of the Bible professors for her class.

In 1984 Carol competed once again in the Disabled Nationals, this time in Jackson Hole, Wyoming. She was now eighteen — her first year in the women's division—and she won second place in the downhill, third place in the slalom, and third place in the giant slalom. She received the silver medal for overall best woman racer at that national event. But then two weeks later she waved goodbye to the four girls who were headed off to the Olympics in Austria. They had been chosen the year before, when she had been less experienced. Faced with another four-year wait before the next Olympics, and following a spiritually rich time at home the following summer, Carol decided that it was time to trade in old dreams for new: she would not return to train with the team the following year.

Meanwhile, Gretchen was a senior in high school and planning her college studies. She was thinking seriously about going back to Sioux County, to our denominational college in Orange City, Iowa.

By 1985 the audience of the *Hour of Power* hit the two-million-viewer mark—not including hundreds of thousands who watched the cable system and thus weren't tabulated in the huge Arbitron numbers. Our power, I'm convinced, lay in the distinctiveness of our positive message, as reflected in our broad-based collection of positive listeners. Our income had climbed fast enough for us to expand to the strongest stations in all one hundred and seventy major markets in all fifty states. But success breeds envy.

One day I had a disturbing call. "Dr. Schuller, I've got to talk to you," my staffer in charge of negotiating the leases for airtime said. "We have a problem." *Now what?* I wondered.

"There are only so many quality spots on TV," he explained, "and there's another newcomer who wants some of them. He's contacted our most profitable stations and told them that, when our lease is up at the end of the year, he'll pay a huge increase if they'll let him buy our time."

"But that's unethical," I said.

"Sure it is, in the world of Christian ministry; but it's not *illegal*, and with the stations, money talks."

"Who is he?"

"You've never heard of him—but he's coming on strong and he won't go away!"

"So what's his affiliation?" I asked. "What's his name?"

"Assemblies of God. His name is Jimmy Swaggart."

I *had* heard of him, as it turned out. He'd commented publicly—and unfavorably—on our church and its ministry.

Not long after that conversation, I was watching the evening news when a horrific story appeared on CNN: "Television evangelist accused of sexual affairs." And on the screen was the face of Jim Bakker, the Pentecostal minister now embroiled in a sordid story of a sexual fling with his assistant, Jessica Hahn. He and his wife, Tammy Faye, were also accused of financial improprieties. He was being soundly condemned by religious leaders, starting with Jimmy Swaggart.

Then, only a week later, that selfsame Jimmy Swaggart was reported to be soliciting prostitutes! Swaggart—of all people! But he had been the first to attack Jim Bakker. He had condemned my ministry as being nonbiblical and as promoting false Christianity. He had even accused Mother Teresa of not measuring up to his own standard of faith and therefore "not going to heaven."

The secular press ate up the scandal, and suddenly all religious broadcasters were being smeared with the same brush. Ascribing guilt by association, television stations began to cancel our contracts. By 1987 our audience had dropped from a high of two million viewers a week to a low of less than one and a half million viewers.

On *Nightline,* Ted Koppel offered the opinion that all television evangelists should be investigated. Local newspapers picked up the challenge. The two largest—the *Los Angeles Times* and the *Orange County Register*—began to investigate me. They assigned reporters to explore the ministries and business dealings of Robert Schuller and the *Hour of Power*—anything tied to the Crystal Cathedral.

For thirty-three years the *Orange County Register* had supported our blue-ribbon reputation. Now, under the influence of one duplicitous, scandal-hunting reporter, negative stories began to appear, lining me up with Swaggart and Bakker.

One day I received a call from a close friend of thirty years, a corporate leader in the area and a prominent member of the church. He wanted to talk about the journalist who was fabricating these stories.

"Dr. Schuller," he said, sounding concerned, "this guy met with me privately. He told me that no one knew you and the inside story of your private life and ministry better than I do. He told me that he was going to do a major story on you—that he stood a chance of winning a Pulitzer Prize for "exposing" you. He told me to tell him anything I knew and that he would pay me. He told me that he was authorized to make sure I wouldn't be hurt; indeed, I would be financially compensated for whatever I might expose about you."

I had the sick feeling you get when you see highway patrol lights flashing behind your car, even when you know you haven't done anything wrong.

My friend tried to comfort me. "I told the guy I didn't have a clue what he was talking about. But I don't know who else he may contact. And he told me that he doesn't have to name his sources! He can publish innuendo from unfriendly people, calling what he's heard a 'reliable report from an unnamed source.' People could be tempted to play along with him to earn a buck!"

I checked with legal counsel. "Sorry, Dr. Schuller," my advisor reported, "but it's not against the law for a reporter to compensate his sources."

Stories began to appear that included distortions of some of our plans. What worried us most was not only the inaccuracies but the fact that the reporter obviously had access to descriptions of confidential reports. These papers weren't scandalous, by any means, but we began to feel very vulnerable. His source had to be someone with access to our private memos in upper management. We bought shredders; nothing was trusted to our office wastebaskets.

Outraged by this invasion of our privacy, I went to see the publisher of the *Orange County Register.* "Sit down, Dr. Schuller," he said with his usual warmth. After all, we'd been good friends for over thirty years.

"I will not sit down, sir," I answered. "For thirty years my life and work have been an open book. Your paper has always reported openly and fairly—until Jimmy Swaggart and Jim Bakker scandalized the world and cast all religious ministries in a bad light. Now you have a dangerously ambitious investigative reporter offering money to people who can accuse me of moral or financial impropriety. Bribery isn't *reporting;* it's *solicitation!*"

He listened quietly as I described what had been happening. "Let me handle it," he said. "I don't approve of reporters offering money for rumors." The negative stories stopped immediately. I later learned that the reporter had moved "upstairs" into some administrative role, and I never saw his byline again. As for the leak, it would remain a mystery. Rather than place our management personnel under suspicion, we chose to keep focused on ministry. "Though the wolf howls, the moon still shines."

But I had yet to read the story about us that the investigative reporters from the *Los Angeles Times* were preparing. I got wind that they'd been working for months and that the story would be coming out "any day." Meanwhile, the tabloids were merciless with Bakker and Swaggart, and none too kind to several others. Prominent ministers who escaped their wrath included Billy Graham and Robert Schuller.

Finally the *Los Angeles Times* alerted me they were ready to go with their story—a full-page article with a banner headline. Out of respect for me, they ran off a slick print of the page before the paper hit the streets, and the publisher sent it to me with a note:

Dear Dr. Schuller:

This story will appear in our paper tomorrow.
Congratulations!

Respectfully,

Tom Johnson

The headline was big, black, and bold:

CRYSTAL CATHEDRAL UNSCATHED!

The battle was over.

But the assault on television ministries had done its harm. Our audience was much smaller now than it had been, and the dynamic years of growth would never return. The total number of Americans watching all religious television ministries on Sunday mornings dropped from the pre-scandal high of six million viewers to four million. But our share of the market would climb to forty percent of all viewers—far and away the biggest share of the religious market—a position that we still hold as I write these lines.

In October of 1988 I was, for the last time, standing at the back of the Crystal Cathedral as a proud papa, not just as a pastor. Gretchen, my "baby," was gowned in beaded white. Her brunette hair and large brown eyes contrasted beautifully with her fair skin. This day I would walk her—my last daughter, Gretchen Joy Schuller—down the aisle and into the arms of our wonderful new son-in-law-to-be, James Penner.

Two years before, I'd had the honor of walking Carol down the aisle on her wedding day, giving her away to Tim Milner, a wonderful man she'd met through church. At that earlier wedding, Sheila (by then the mother of three boys), Donna (pregnant with Bob's third child), and Jeanne (pregnant with her first) had all been attendants; Gretchen had walked down the aisle as the maid of honor. A year later, Carol had given birth to her first baby, a girl, only two days before Sheila gave birth to her fourth son. Together in the same hospital, these two beautiful new moms cried in celebration of their little miracles.

But as Gretchen and I stood at the back of the church, I held her hand with her arm looped through mine and found myself reluctant to let her go.

"Gretchen," I said, my voice trembling, "you're my baby girl. How can I give you away?"

"Oh, Dad," she said, resting her head on my shoulder. She looked so much like Arvella.

"Mom and I will miss you," I added. "But of all the guys you dated—"

"Dad!" She recoiled in mock horror at my teasing. Then we giggled.

"Jim's the greatest, honey. I know he'll take good care of you. But he's a prize, so you'd better take good care of him too!"

The organ swelled then, and we began our procession.

All five of our children would be in the wedding photos, with their five spouses and a total of eleven grandchildren. Bobby and Angie, Bob's two oldest from his first marriage, were growing up as beautiful Christians. Our prayers had been answered, and the divorce hadn't negatively affected them in any way. (As I write these lines, both are called to ministry!)

And so, nearing the end of the 1980s, Arvella and I had emptied our nest. But our hearts were full, seeing all the blessings of God on each child.

This old married couple settled into a season of calm and pleasant days. But it was hardly time to ease into rocking chairs and gaze back into the past. More tomorrows lay ahead, with new adventures that would add a culmination of wonder to my whole life. This was one of those rare and beautiful times when everything seemed to come together into a harmonious and lovely blend.

The heralds of a new dawn for our ministry were two rather unlikely angels. The first was Rupert Murdoch, who welcomed me into his office in Beverly Hills with a firm handshake and a look of warmth and respect.

"I've heard a lot about you, sir," I opened. How could I not have? He owned newspapers and television stations around the world. "But I know nothing of your religious inclinations. Jewish? Catholic? Protestant? Atheist?"

"My grandfather was a Presbyterian pastor," he told me. "My wife is Catholic. We've attended your Crystal Cathedral, and we've seen your show. We have a mutual friend, Sir John Templeton, who told me about you in a letter."

Then he leaned forward, looking eager. "I'm about to turn on a new satellite that will be the first to footprint all of Europe. Its programs will be accessible for free on cable television, covering all of Europe. I'm going to call it the 'Sky Channel.'"

He let me consider all this for a moment. Then he went on. "I want one hour of religion every week on Sky. I've checked them all out, and I want your show, the *Hour of Power*."

"That's fantastic!" I exclaimed. Then I quickly tempered my response. "But I doubt that we can afford to buy your airtime. It's going to be expensive, and we have no surplus right now for expansion. We're still trying to survive the collateral damage we suffered from the scandals."

He smiled, paused, then came out with what would be a historic offer. "Dr. Schuller, there will be no charge for your airtime! To you — it's free!"

I have no idea what my face looked like as I listened, but I suppose "slack-jawed wonder" would have sized it up.

"Oh, there is one thing," he added. I braced for the catch. "We're turning the satellite on on Sunday morning, February 8, 1989. That's only a few weeks away. And I want the first program to be yours as we launch this new network. Your timeslot will be 7:00 A.M. Western European time, as long as I own the channel."

Both of us rose from our seats and shook hands enthusiastically. That relationship still continues today, over ten years later.

But miracles sometimes beget miracles. Our European broadcasts caught the attention of another powerful man: Armand Hammer, head of Occidental Petroleum and the heir to commercial ties with the Soviet Union going back to the days of Lenin.

"I've been one of your television parishioners for over ten years now, Bob," Hammer would say. "It's time for Russia to get the rich and rare religion that you preach. You've changed my life. If Murdoch can get you on television in Europe, I can get you on in the USSR!"

Russia? Me on Russian television? After my intrigue in that hotel lobby in Kiev, I'd vowed I'd never go back. The Cold War was still on, after all. Presumably my picture was still hanging in the Museum of Atheism in Leningrad. How could even Hammer get me on Soviet television?

But then I thought once again about my mission to "build bridges." And so I would decide to take another risk and follow Hammer to an edge that I'd never dreamed of, an edge that only God could access, where miracles would happen, and where I would see God as I'd never seen Him before.

XL

Armand Hammer was actually one of the most colorful and controversial figures of the twentieth century. The son of a fervid communist, he went on to build a worldwide capitalist empire.

The cornerstone of his fortune was a pharmaceutical business inherited from his father, but his father's more potent legacy was political contacts that gave the son access to the highest levels of power within the newly formed Soviet Union.

Those contacts had been initiated in the tumultuous days shortly after the Russian Revolution of 1917, an uprising during which the Russian people, inflamed by the hardships of World War I, had overthrown their out-of-touch ruler, Czar Nicholas. In the chaos that reigned in that vast country following the revolution, a fanatical wing of Russian socialism, the Bolshevik Party, seized power and threw the country into outright civil war, with factional armies—the Reds and the Whites—crisscrossing the land, and the constant threat of invasion from U.S. and British troops already mobilized to finish off the Kaiser's German army.

Soon after the Bolsheviks founded the Communist Party in 1918, the senior Hammer helped to found the Communist Party in the United States; his name and reputation was well known to Russian leaders.

During this period, in the early 1920s, the younger Hammer, just out of medical school, came up with the idea of exporting wheat to starving and war-ravaged Russia. This bit of enterprise brought him to the attention of Lenin, the Bolshevik leader. Here was a young man with business savvy and access to goods the Soviets needed, and with a political heritage—his father's communist affiliation— that Lenin admired.

So Armand Hammer became Lenin's main access point for trade with the West. Hammer took in grain and machinery and whatever else was needed, trading for money, priceless artwork, and the rights to exploit other business opportunities with the young government. He would retain that special role as a go-between and power-broker between the two worlds of East and West for as long as he lived. In the West he built up unbelievable wealth. And in the East he had the ear of every Soviet leader from Lenin to Gorbachev.

So that was the situation in February 1985, when I was resting in Hawaii and took a call from my son, Bob. "Dad, did you see that picture in *Life* magazine of Armand Hammer?" I had seen it, and I told him so. It was a huge photo showing the business leader in his bed looking up at three television sets, one for each of the three major television networks of the day—ABC, CBS, and NBC.

"Did you notice what was lying on his bedside table?" Bob asked.

"Nope."

"Check it out, Dad," he said mysteriously.

I went back to the magazine and opened it to the Hammer photo. I couldn't believe what I saw lying on the end-table in Hammer's bedroom: *Guidepost* magazine, the interfaith monthly inspirational publication from Norman Vincent Peale!

Recently Dr. Peale had agreed to preach in the Crystal Cathedral. He had made negative remarks about our building goals in the past, but our fifteen-year quiet and cool separation had finally ended in a warm reconciliation.

I shot off a letter to Armand Hammer. "I note that you read *Guidepost*. Dr. Norman Vincent Peale—the editor—is my friend. He'll be preaching in our Crystal Cathedral in three weeks. I'd be happy if you could join me. I'll reserve a place for you, and I invite you to be my guest at a private luncheon in my office immediately following the service." His acceptance was prompt and enthusiastic.

The eighty-six-year-old Hammer arrived in a large black limousine, and the three of us—Peale, Hammer, and I—had a wonderful meal. What I hadn't known until then was that Dr. Peale and Dr. Hammer had been longtime friends.

Privately Norman had briefed me on his view of the mysterious Armand Hammer. "He's pro-Russia, pro-America, pro-capitalism, anti-communism, anti-war, and anti-poverty. He's married to a Catholic and is very pro-positive thinking. I'm so glad that you'll finally meet. You two will do great things together."

The week following Peale's visit, on Sunday, March 3, 1985, Dr. Hammer agreed to be interviewed on the *Hour of Power*. Then a few more weeks passed, and on a rather drizzly day in late March of 1985 he called me.

"I've just returned from the USSR," he said. "I was there for the funeral of Chernenko and the installation of the new head of state, Mikhail Gorbachev. Big things are happening, Bob. We've got to talk."

I had no idea what he had on his mind, but I drove to his Occidental Petroleum office in Beverly Hills. The credenza behind his desk was lined with autographed photos of all of the U.S. presidents throughout my lifetime. Mixed in were pictures of other heads of state—including Lenin.

"I truly believe that we're going to see Russia change," he told me. "Let me tell you what happened on this last trip. I was at the front of the line in the reception for the new man, Gorbachev. He invited me into his private quarters. We spent an hour and a half together, and I was completely frank with him.

"'Mr. Gorbachev, I'm happy to meet you,' I said. 'I've known every leader of this country starting with Lenin. Now first just let me say that you're the first educated leader this country has had since Lenin. Second, you're the first young man to take the top job. Third, you have a smart wife. She's well educated and intelligent. Fourth, you have the freedom and the jet planes to travel all over the world and visit any free country and see how a free-market economy works.'"

Hammer stopped and looked at me intently for a moment, then continued. "I said to Gorbachev, 'Compare your system with ours, and you'll see that your system will never make it. Mr. Gorbachev, my father was a founding member of the Communist Party in America. He pleaded with me to reject capitalism and become a leader in the socialist world. I argued with my dad and finally told him that I couldn't—I *wouldn't*—for it would never work. It goes against human nature! Mr. Gorbachev, you're the man who could come to see this, could admit to this, could lead your people to freedom.'"

Then, Hammer told me, he'd hit the new leader of Russia with an aggressive challenge: "I said to him, 'Mr. Gorbachev—become the Abraham Lincoln of Russia!'"

But it wasn't until spring of 1989 that Dr. Hammer called to say, "I think now is the time for your message in Russia. You could help eliminate Russians' suspicion of America," he said persuasively. "Your message could help set the stage for ending the Cold War. We've got to get your positive message of peace-generating religion on television!"

"But I'm not sure that my message would be well received," I said doubtfully. I still hadn't recovered from my first exposure to the Soviet system years before.

"Bob, the Russian people will see your smile and be won over," he promised. "That's what attracted me to you. They'll feel love coming through that smile!"

"But Dr. Hammer, it could be hugely expensive—if they even agreed!"

Hammer laughed out loud. "I don't worry about money," he said. "Take a look at this check I just got! I looked, and my mouth dropped open. It was for one billion dollars. Then he looked at me squarely and seriously. "Think big!" he said. "Think positive! I'm going to take you and Arvella to Russia very soon. For me they'll let you air your show for free! I'll get back to you."

Dr. Hammer called me not too many days later to lay out his plan. It began with the following letter, which he instructed me to address to the head of the Soviet government.

May 25, 1989

Dear President Gorbachev:

I extend my congratulations and best wishes to you as you open up great possibilities for your countrymen.

I thank you for receiving this correspondence even as I thank our mutual dear friend, Dr. Armand Hammer, for his role in bringing this request to your attention.

I am tentatively planning a trip to Europe, Eastern Europe, and the Soviet Union. This, in part, is precipitated by the fact that my weekly television program is now the largest viewed program in the United States and is seen in twenty-two countries in Europe via the Sky Channel.

I'm humbly honored to be given an opportunity to speak every Sunday morning to the largest international organization afforded any politician or religious spokesperson. I hope to use my platform and position to advance the causes that are of mutual interest to all of us who seek peace and human brotherhood.

I would consider it a privilege to have the opportunity to meet you in person on my next trip through your beloved country. I would build my entire itinerary around your schedule.

Respectfully yours,
Robert H. Schuller

I sent the letter not to Russia, but to Hammer in Beverly Hills. He then sent it to his personal friend, the Russian ambassador to the United States, along with a letter of his own:

June 21, 1989

His Excellency Yuri Dubinin
Ambassador of the USSR
Embassy of the USSR
1125 16th Street, NW
Washington, D.C. 20036

Dear Yuri:

Recently I met in my office with Reverend Robert Schuller, the highly respected American clergyman with whom you may be familiar. Reverend Schuller, who hosts this country's most watched religious television program, is planning a trip to the Soviet Union and would very much like to meet President Gorbachev. He would schedule his trip at a time convenient to the President.

Reverend Schuller has been a friend of mine for many years and is a man of great and varied interests. He is quite influential in this country, and I believe that President Gorbachev would find meeting him to be very much worthwhile.

I enclose herewith a letter to President Gorbachev from Robert Schuller. I would appreciate it if you would forward this to his attention.

I hope that this letter finds you well. I have just returned myself from the Soviet Union, where I had the opportunity to observe a session of the Congress of People's Deputies. I had the feeling that history was being made, a feeling much the same to what I felt in Moscow in the 1920s. The eyes of all the world are trained on President Gorbachev as his bold leadership continues to transform your country and, indeed, the whole world.

With warmest regards,

Sincerely,
Armand

We waited. Then Hammer wrote a letter to the top government official in the USSR, to whom the manager of all radio and television reported:

November 27, 1989

His Excellency Mikhail F. Nenashev
Chairman
State Committee for Radio and Television
Moscow, USSR

Dear Chairman Nenaschev:

I will be in the Soviet Union next week, from 5 through 9 December, and would welcome the opportunity to meet with you to discuss several matters of mutual interest.

Specifically, I will be accompanied by my good friend, Rev. Robert Schuller, the highly regarded minister whose weekly television program is the most watched religious broadcast in the United States. Rev. Schuller has held preliminary discussions with your Deputy Chairman regarding the possibility of his asking for a Christmas Eve television broadcast to the people of the Soviet Union. Such a broadcast involving an American minister of Rev. Schuller's stature would be a significant event in relations between our countries and could lead to further cooperative television between our two countries.

I understand that Gosteleradio has indicated interest in this project. During my visit to Moscow, I would like to meet with you together with Dr. Schuller, to discuss this project and move forward in a mutually beneficial way. Dr. Schuller is "nonsectarian" and very aware of cultural considerations in any such broadcast. His is a message of universal hope for mankind.

You may respond through my office in Moscow.
With best wishes,

Sincerely,
Armand Hammer

It was a Monday in early December of 1989 when Hammer called to ask if Arvella and I could leave for Moscow that Thursday. He'd been granted an appointment with Valentin Lazutkin, the top man in Russian television.

I don't remember what plans were on my calendar. I never even looked; I said immediately, "Yes, sir!"

But then Mrs. Hammer—in the hospital recovering from a broken hip—took a turn for the worse.

I called to see what rearrangements we should make and was surprised to be told, "None!"

"But Armand, don't you think we should postpone the trip?" I urged. "You can't leave your wife in this condition. Please!"

He was adamant. Never had I heard him so determined. "My wife is in the best of care," he said. And then, before I could say another word, he added, "I've got to do this while I'm still alive. I'm ninety-one years old, Bob!"

So on December 5, 1989, Arvella and I arrived at the Los Angeles airport at ten in the morning. We were shown to a secluded area reserved for private jets and ushered into a private lobby, where we were told to wait until Dr. Hammer arrived.

Oxy One was the largest private jet I'd ever seen. It was a Boeing 727 specially outfitted as a flying condominium and traveling headquarters for what was one of the largest corporations in the world.

When he arrived, Dr. Hammer walked briskly, extending his hand first to Arvella, then to me, smiling broadly. He seemed as excited to be leaving as we were. He had just stopped off to see his wife at the hospital and brought a satisfactory report. To minister to his own health, his private physician traveled with us.

Once inside the aircraft he glanced at me with a hint of pride. "You know, this plane is the only private jet that has rights to fly into Moscow! I also have the one and only private telephone in Russia. You can pick it up and call anywhere in the world, anytime. I'll be able to keep in close touch with the hospital."

When our plane touched down in Moscow, we were welcomed as if we were heads of state. A luxurious private room, handshakes, hugs, and Russian kisses—a kiss on each cheek, and then a third on the first cheek.

"I can't believe this," I whispered to Arvella. "The first and last time I came to Russia they confiscated my Bibles in customs. At immigration I was treated like a spy."

On this trip we simply skipped immigration and customs altogether! A convoy of police cars escorted Hammer's black stretch Cadillac limousine, in which he and his aide, his doctor, Arvella, and I were seated. We were all bundled up for the cold Moscow weather. Hammer wore his distinctive full-length fur coat and classic Persian wool cap, and the rest of us had brought out our thickest winter gear. We drove immediately to the Occidental headquarters. Twenty minutes later, the elevator took us to the top floor.

Dr. Hammer headed straight for a desk that was clean and clear except for a telephone. We watched him dial and then speak into the receiver of the one and only private telephone in the USSR! After several minutes he put down the phone, turned to join us, and said, "Mrs. Hammer is the same. No improvement. Now let's sleep, and tomorrow we'll go to see Mr. Lazutkin at Gosteleradio."

The next day Dr. Hammer began the negotiations in fluent Russian, translating for Arvella and me. "Mr. Lazutkin, your government has been informed by their ambassador in Washington of this meeting," Hammer said, locking eyes with the head of Gosteleradio, "and your president, Mr. Gorbachev, knows about this meeting and has approved it." Lazutkin nodded his head in acknowledgment.

Then Dr. Hammer presented his case. "Probably no American knows Russia better than I do. And no American has worked as hard as I have for seventy years behind the scenes to keep peace between the two nations I love. And few people respect my guest, Dr. Schuller, more than I do. I was raised by a Russian Jew who didn't profess to believe in God, believing instead in communism. I inherited no faith.

"Some years ago I saw Dr. Schuller on TV. Something about him attracted me."

Lazutkin listened with cold eyes as Hammer continued. "I listened to Schuller week after week, and I found myself being moved positively and spiritually. He brought something refreshing and renewing to my mind. In one word, it's *hope*. And I believe that what he does for me he can do for my father's homeland. His message is religious in the best sense. I'm here to ask you to allow this country to hear him. In America, Christmas will be celebrated on December 25. Dr. Schuller and I want you and your people to see and hear a Christmas *Hour of Power* from Dr. Schuller."

A huge puff of smoke billowed out of Lazutkin's mouth. "May I pour you a drink?" our host asked. He spoke in Russian, interpreted by his aide. His eyes connected with Hammer, then with Arvella, Hammer's aide, and me. Without waiting for a response, he reached for a soft drink bottle, and his aide swiftly stood and assisted. We all joined in a lifted glass and a smile.

"Dr. Hammer," he said, "you have told me clearly where *you* are coming from. Now let me remind everyone at this table where *we* are coming from. Seventy years ago we broke from religious superstitions. We became the first state in history to adopt atheism. We have for all these years used all the human vehicles of education to eradicate religious beliefs from our scientifically educated populace." He blew another cloud of smoke as the translater passed his words along to Arvella and me. Lazutkin continued, "No society has ever been so well educated in atheism as you find in the USSR. How could I possibly allow a religious person to preach about God on our one television station?"

Without waiting for an answer, he then uttered the most surprising sentence I've ever heard. "However, we have observed that some positive developments can be seen in human personalities as an apparent result of religious roots. Without such roots we may be less than our potential. We are therefore taking a new look at religion."

Another cloud of smoke. Then he looked at me appraisingly and asked, "Dr. Schuller, are you a Baptist?"

"No, sir," I answered.

He gave a relieved smile. "Good!" he said. "Are you a Pentecostal?"

"No, sir."

"Good," he said. "Are you a Methodist?"

"No, sir."

Once again he answered, "Good."

Then, raising his voice and picking up the pace, he fired the bottom-line question. "Then what *is* your religion?" He glared at me as he waited for my answer, his head and shoulders jutting forward aggressively.

"I'm afraid you've never heard of it," I answered.

"Tell me anyway."

"I belong to a small denomination called the Reformed Church in America!"

Before I could elaborate, his face broke into a relieved smile.

"Reformed? They are in Hungary, Albania, and Holland!" I presumed he meant that the Reformed Church did not practice evangelism, which many interpreted as proselytizing.

"Dr. Schuller, I cannot televise your church service, but we have our *own* Barbara Walters every Sunday night at nine. I think you call that 'prime time.' She interviews professionals in the study of human personality. She interviews philosophers and psychologists, and she has even interviewed a Russian Orthodox priest.

"Here's what we could do. She could interview you. She would say, 'Dr. Armand Hammer'—everybody knows his name—'came to Moscow this week. He brought with him a most respected religious leader from America named Dr. Robert Schuller. Tonight we have a very unusual program never seen or heard in our nation's history. We are going to talk to Dr. Schuller.'

"Then she could ask a few safe opening questions such as, 'What do you do? Where do you live and work?' And you could answer, 'Well, I conduct church services.' And she could ask you, 'What happens in your church services?' And you could answer, 'Well, I preach a sermon.' Then she could ask you, 'What is a sermon? Can you give us an example?' Then the cameras could cut to you and you could give a fifteen- or twenty-minute sermon. How would that be?"

He smiled as if pleased with his proposal and then said, "That would be seen not as promoting religion but as giving insight into how some Americans think and practice religion."

I sensed that this had all been decided earlier, before this meeting. Did he have his orders handed to him from a higher authority?

"You must realize that you will be seen as our enemy," he went on. "We are still in a Cold War with your nation and with religion."

"I understand," I said. "But that would be a wonderful opportunity. Don't you agree, Dr. Hammer?"

Hammer smiled, then nodded.

"Then we'll tape it now!" Lazutkin announced. "Our Barbara Walters is in our studio now. Do you have your robe with you?"

"No," I said.

"But he's dressed fine as he is!" Hammer assured him.

"Then we will do it—now! And we will air it Sunday night, December 25," he said.

"At nine in the evening?" Hammer asked.

"Of course," Lazutkin responded. He stood up abruptly, walked briskly around the end of the table to give Hammer a most honored

Russian goodbye, then shook my hand. "Dr. Schuller," he said, "You can always know that you were the first foreigner in our history to be invited to talk to our whole country about God!"

Then he blew smoke in my face and said, "But I don't believe in God. I've never experienced Him."

I was startled by my immediate reaction. "Oh, you're wrong!" I said. "You *have* experienced Him. You just didn't recognize that it was God working in you. He's been working in your mind now, for example, causing you to make this offer to me! And there have been times in your life when you've experienced amazing mind shifts or when strongly positive moods have come over you. You've probably called such feelings 'hope' or 'love' or 'courage,' but they're the touch of God. Mr. Lazutkin, never forget what I'm going to tell you: God believes in you, even if you don't believe in Him!"

And then I saw it happen. In the eyes of this tough Russian bureaucrat, a sudden mist appeared.

The meeting was over. Lazutkin pointed to the aide who had been sitting at his side. "Boris here will interpret for you," he explained. "He'll lead you to the studio."

Hammer, having already said his Russian goodbyes, excused himself. "I'm going to my apartment to rest," he said. "Good luck with your broadcast!" The meeting, including all the preliminaries, had run to three draining hours. Hammer had been sharp and energetic throughout, so he was naturally tired. After all, he was ninety-one, had a pacemaker, and was under constant medical supervision. He whispered a bit of advice in my ear as he left.

My wife and I followed our escort to a private room, where we were told to wait until being called into the studio. I had never before—and have never since—been so totally overpowered by a sense of humility in the service of God.

I knew that this would be the most important speaking assignment in my earthly life, and yet I had no time to think or prepare for it. The history of the rise and spread of communism flashed before me.

Hopes for a peaceful resolution to this Cold War topped the concerns and prayers of all our leaders. Gorbachev certainly would be listening. All of the members of the Politburo would be tuned in. No American had ever been given such a platform from which to speak to all of the people in the entire USSR, along with all of the Eastern bloc nations! One TV network, with its one and only channel— "Channel One"—was piped into every TV-equipped home in every one of the seventeen republics that made up this Union of Soviet Socialist Republics. It was the world's largest mind-control television network. My audience would be in the hundreds of millions!

"O God, I need You as I've never before needed You in my life. God, help me!" I prayed.

My mind flashed back to my childhood. I pictured Uncle Henry putting his hand on my head and declaring that I would be a preacher; and I remembered how I'd prayed ever since that day—at the age of four years and eleven months—"Lord, make me a preacher when I grow up."

Now this? A preacher to the communist world?!

My memory flashed back again, this time to seeing my picture in the Museum of Atheism in Leningrad seventeen years earlier, and to our fearful exit from this "evil empire."

I thought, too, about how I had wanted to preach "peace" on my return from that trip but hadn't been able to, because communism had co-opted the word for its own propaganda purposes.

I pulled myself back to the present. I had to decide what to say. "Just smile and be yourself," Hammer had whispered before his exit. "You can leave your viewers with a powerful impression of peace and hope, and that impression will help influence everyone to move toward peace and trust. You're the right man in the right spot at the right time. The entire nation will see their American enemy with a new face! God bless you—just smile!"

But now I felt woefully inadequate. Having no prepared message with me, all I could do was pray with a passion.

Then into my mind flashed one Bible verse—Jeremiah 29:11. I knew that it had come to me in answer to my prayer. In that verse God speaks to his people through the prophet Jeremiah, "I have a plan for your life. It is a plan for good and not evil. It is a plan to give you a future with hope." I had repeated this verse over and over again to Carol in her hospital days.

As if she could read my thoughts, my wife offered her typically brilliant, typically God-inspired advice. "Tell them about Carol," she said. "I've heard that the Russians love children!"

With a quick knock at the door of our waiting room, my escort, Boris, appeared to usher me to a small studio in which their Barbara Walters was waiting. She was the most beautiful woman I'd seen in Russia, and I'll never forget her face—kind, respectful, and intelligent. I was suddenly relaxed and completely at peace. Gone was all of the anxiety that had overwhelmed me.

The interview went precisely as Lazutkin had outlined. In fact, he must have written her script for her. I was treated with all the respect I would have been due had my name been Dr. Armand Hammer.

"Give us an example of a sermon," she said.

And the camera cut from her to me alone.

I felt that this was God's chance to move into the Cold War standoff and tip the balance toward peace and reconciliation, and I was eager to be His servant. Feeling God's presence and guidance, I looked straight into the camera and began.

My sermon flowed out freely, not from my mind to their minds, but from my soul to theirs. It was a heart-to-heart sharing of my hope for the best for that country, because what was best for Russia would also be best for freedom and America.

I began with a "word from the God that the Bible writes about," quoting the text of Jeremiah 29:11. After talking about that text a bit, I said, "Be open to the positive possibility that faith can and will give you hope—in your darkest hour."

And then I let the life of our daughter Carol serve as the conclusion that I would leave with this nation. I told them what a beautiful and loving child she had been. How she had learned the Bible, including Psalm 23, whose words — "and though I walk through the valley of the shadow of death" — had come to her when she was lying alone in the ditch, bleeding and waiting for help. I told how her leg had had to be amputated, but how faith had given her hope.

I finished with a call for peace between Russia and America. "God has a plan for our countries," I said. "It is a plan for good and not evil. It is a plan to give you a future with hope." And then I smiled, long and fervently.

"Do you think they'll really translate it correctly?" Arvella asked as we were driven back to our hotel. "And do you think they'll really air it? Or will it go on a shelf?"

"I don't know," was all I could say. "I just don't know."

Back at the hotel we rested for a bit, knowing that we would have a big evening. We'd been invited by Dr. Hammer to join him for dinner at his condominium. "I've had a private residence in Moscow since Lenin," he had told us. "Lenin gave me a beautiful mansion. It was my home until Stalin took over. He took it from me. But I was able to buy this very modest but nice apartment to replace it."

Hammer had stressed the importance of the dinner to be held that evening. "Georgi Arbatov will be coming," he had said. "He's one of the most powerful and influential people in this country. I will ask him to assume responsibility to get the word out, starting with President Gorbachev, the Politburo, and the heads of the media, to tell everybody to listen to you on December 25. I will explain that your face and heart convey the true spirit of America. When Arbatov talks, the entire Politburo listens! They will all be tuned in to hear you! He listens to me. He'll do it."

We enjoyed the dinner very much. The meeting with Arbatov went well: from the outset he was respectful and kind — almost affectionate. He had seen my face on TV on his many trips to America and seemed sincerely enthusiastic about meeting me. He treated me as if I were a celebrity he liked! But where would this path lead?

The program was aired as promised, on December 25, 1989, at 9:00 P.M. Moscow time. The Russian authorities reported that it was the largest audience they'd ever had—over two hundred million people watching across the USSR and the Eastern bloc nations! And the viewers loved it! The producers had edited the sermon from twenty to fifteen minutes, but they had done so without altering the message. The entire sermon could be heard in my voice faintly, with the Russian translator's voice overriding mine. When I saw the tape, I knew why it had been so well received. The producers had picked a male voice that was perfect! His tone was gentle; his spirit was beautiful, conveyed in sounds of kindness, love, and peace!

Four months later, in early May 1990, I received word that Mikhail Gorbachev wanted me to bring a second "heart-to-heart talk" to his nation. He was planning a summit later that month with President George Bush in Washington, D.C., and wanted his anxious and worried people to be calmed.

His plan was that, on the eve of his departure, he would go into the television studio in Moscow to address his people on the upcoming summit. He would follow that with a brief taped message to Russia from President Bush. After a brief interval of quiet classical music, he would then introduce another message from "Robert Schuller, whom we heard bringing us a message of hope this past December 25."

I was told that I wouldn't need to go to Moscow; I could tape my message in California and send it to the station via express delivery. Valentin Lazutkin would handle the details there. "Yes, the same kind voice will translate you into Russian," I was told.

I was amazed! This invitation had come from Gorbachev without any prompting from me, and without any appeals or political maneuvering by Hammer (or any other person, to our knowledge).

In this staggering opportunity, I would serve not as a "preacher" or "teacher" or "evangelist" or "politician," but as a "therapist" setting the stage to shift the mass mood from fearful suspicion to emerging trust.

I recalled the World Psychiatric Congress in Madrid, Spain, and its closing plenary session on "human values in psychotherapy." The three lectures had been a turning point for me, exploring the concept that the basic principles for creating healthy relationships were faith, hope, and love, uniting Bible teaching and psychotherapeutic practice. I remembered that the congress had been attended by all of the leading psychiatrists in the USSR. I felt that the message of that congress—with its underlying focus on faith, hope, and love—was capable of creating a mass mindset that would allow a historic spiritual and emotional bridge to be built.

So I videotaped my message in Garden Grove, sending it from the Crystal Cathedral in America to Gosteleradio in Moscow. "My message is based on a Bible verse found in First Corinthians," I began. "The passage reads, 'Now abide faith, hope, and love. The greatest of these is love.'" In a calm voice I sent this second sermon to be heard by the same predictable audience of hundreds of millions of Russian citizens. It was aired as promised in primetime following Gorbachev's message and President Bush's remarks setting up the summit meeting that week in Washington.

Not many hours later the first reaction came in to us from Moscow. It was an invitation from Gorbachev to meet him and his wife later that week at a private reception and luncheon in the Russian Embassy in Washington. This would be the day before Gorbachev and Bush were to meet in their historic summit.

We accepted gladly and made arrangements to attend.

About forty other Americans were at the luncheon. A translator was assigned to each of us. As Gorbachev delivered his speech, my translator excitedly said to me, "He's talking about you. Listen carefully." Gorbachev smiled and pointed toward me, then said my name and asked me to stand up. As I rose to my feet, completely surprised, he said, "This man calmed our nation."

When asked to say a word in response, I told Mr. Gorbachev, in front of the group, "Tough times never last, but tough people do." I also told him, "God loves you, and so do I."

In covering the story, the *Los Angeles Times* would ask, "What about the long-standing conservative assessment that communists are 'godless'?"

My response was this: "I've come to understand now that many people who are communists, or were communists, are not godless people. To join those two words without qualification . . . has been a very irresponsible thing."

While in Washington I had a private meeting with Soviet broadcast officials, including Lazutkin. He opened by saying, "Dr. Schuller, you know that you have been well received in Russia. We cannot at this time air your entire church service every week, but we *can* offer a half-hour message from you once a month. Call it *Heart to Heart*," he said.

I loved that.

"We'll see after a few months where it leads," he said. Then he added the best news: "Of course, to a friend of Dr. Hammer— there's no cost to you!"

He smiled.

So did I.

In breaking the story, the *London Financial Times* called this development "one of the most extraordinary examples of changed attitudes in the Soviet Union."

The *Orange County Register*'s story, which appeared on May 30 and included the only interview Lazutkin ever offered, did a good job of summarizing the full context and rationale:

Schuller, Soviets Launch Program
Religious TV show to be aired monthly[1]

WASHINGTON—Saying his message would bring morality and hope to Soviets battered by economic upheavals, the Rev. Robert Schuller and Soviet television announced a venture Tuesday to put Schuller on the air monthly across the Soviet Union. . . .

With nationalistic strife and expected price increases tearing at the Soviet Union's already fragile political fabric, a Soviet official said Schuller's message is soothing to Soviet citizens living, as he put it, "in difficult times."

"People are very nervous. They need somebody to talk to and to listen to," said Valentin V. Lazutkin, vice chairman of the USSR State Committee for Television and Radio, or Gosteleradio. . . .

Soviet officials also were impressed by Schuller's ability to raise funds for children sickened by the 1986 nuclear disaster at Chernobyl, which Schuller promised to do in gratitude for airing him during the holiday season. . . .

Lazutkin illustrated Tuesday just how much the Soviet government's attitude toward organized religion has changed. Asked how the government could reconcile sponsorship of Schuller's programming when its official position endorsed atheism, Lazutkin said: "We don't count how many times he mentions God."

Meanwhile, I still had a church to run in Southern California! Back on our campus in Garden Grove, things continued to move forward. The decade had brought a maturing in the church. We

---

[1] *Orange County Register*, Wednesday, May 30, 1990 (by David Saltman, States News Service).

were gaining financial stability with our increasingly solid people-base. But one finishing touch was still needed.

September 14, 1990, would mark the tenth anniversary of the opening of the cathedral with the dedication of what some critics would come to call "one of the most beautiful bell-towers on planet earth."

The first ten years of operation had found all problems of this historic glass building finally resolved. But Philip Johnson had long planned this culminating brushstroke to our beautiful composition—a twenty-three-story bell-tower that would be the campanile of the cathedral.

"It won't be finished without it," Johnson had said. "Take away the crowning towers and steeples, and the great churches and cathedrals would look like big secular halls."

Johnson's design featured mirrored and faceted slender stainless steel columns, all free-standing in appearance, rising from ground level to a second smaller circumference level, then rising to a third, still smaller sparkling circumference. The total spire rose to two-hundred and thirty-six feet. The top matched (but didn't surpass) the height of the arms of the cross on the top of the Tower of Hope.

At the bell-tower's base was a small chapel—round, with a wall of thirty-three marble columns made from stone quarried around the world: one for every year of the life of Jesus. In this chapel the text "My house shall be called a house of prayer for all people" was displayed prominently. In the chapel's center was a faceted crystal cross designed by the Steuben glass company. It revolved slowly under lights, throwing rainbows on the multicolored marble walls to remind people of God's unending promise of eternal life!

The chapel was paid for in full by a million-dollar gift from Mary Hood—a dear friend from our *Hour of Power* congregation, while thousands of my friends from across America gave gifts of one thousand dollars to add to this glistening dream. Friends of my wife decided to honor her and surprise her by ordering a fifty-two-bell bronze carillon from Holland to ring their songs through our gardens. With a final two-million-dollar gift from the Creans, the campanile—an awesome piece of art—was now ready for dedication that September morning in 1990.

Then Carey Peck, son of the great movie actor and my dear friend Gregory Peck, made a most unusual offer.

"Dr. Schuller," he said, "I'm a skydiver. My group would like to dress in white and jump from a plane a couple of miles above the church. We'll join hands and form a cross," he offered. I nervously agreed.

Early on Sunday morning—at sunrise—I met Philip Johnson at the cathedral, and we looked at the glistening Crean Spire from below. He had flown in from New York for the dedication. He would see the finished work of his creation for the first time now, shimmering and sparkling in the rising morning sun. He stood alone with me, and I caught a glimpse of a Philip Johnson I'd never witnessed before.

"It's stunning!" he said, over and over. Then this world-famous architect, known for both his lack of humility and his atheism, said something astounding—first to me and then later that morning to a packed house, and to millions more watching on television. He said, "I thought I knew all about materials—light and space—but I look at this . . . and I realize that something bigger than I designed it."

It was his first public affirmation of a belief in God.

Then the crowd gathered outside. A reporter asked me, "Skydivers? Dr. Schuller, was this your idea?"

I answered, laughing, "Let's just wait till it's over. If they all live through it, then maybe I'll take some of the credit, but really . . . no. For once, this crazy idea didn't come from me!"

"Look—the plane," someone shouted. We all looked toward a small speck that appeared to be miles high. Could that be it?

"Look, look—look!" The cry grew louder and more widespread

as tiny white forms popped out of the belly of the craft. I heard a child ask, "Are they angels, Mommy?"

"Look—a cross! It's a flying cross!" The formation of ten divers, hands linked, descended silently, slowly, reverently, from more than a mile above us. The bells in the new carillon tower rang.

And then—so close to earth that the viewers gasped—the chutes opened and the cross disassembled as all of the skydivers landed softly and safely.

Now—at last—the final touch of the Crystal Cathedral was dedicated with these words: "For the glory of man; for the greater glory of God."

The trips to Russia would prove to be many and memorable as we entered the nineties. Our Christmas telecast from Moscow in 1989 had caused a rush of opportunities.

In February of 1990 the most renowned string instrumentalist of that country—Mstislav Rostropovich—was returning to Moscow for a grand solo concert after years of self-imposed exile. Armand Hammer obtained aisle seats for us in the very front row, right below the box seats where Raisa Gorbachev and the queen of Spain would be seated.

It was an awesome experience to see that hall packed with native Russians brimming over with love for their countryman. They rose to their feet—crying and applauding—and many rushed forward, their arms filled with flowers to be laid at the returning artist's feet. We were thrilled to witness a beautiful chapter in the historic conclusion to the half-century-old Cold War. The moment was made all the more special by the knowledge that the great freeze in East-West relations was thawing, and Hammer and I had been able to provide some of the warmth. We had much to celebrate.

On December 15, 1990, Dr. Hammer died at the age of ninety-two. This rare individual, my fellow crusader in a mission of peace and a man who demonstrated a vast faith in the powerful message of hope, had reached his last tomorrow. But I will remain forever indebted to him for giving me this new stage on which to be a "repairer of the breach" and a "restorer of paths to dwell in."

XLI

On September 2, 1991, with a global ministry to attend to, I'm in my all-too-familiar home away from home—the belly of a commercial aircraft. I no longer have my friend's winged condominium at my disposal. The trip seems odd now that Armand isn't with me. And neither is Arvella, this time.

My itinerary begins with meetings in Amsterdam, then moves on to Rome for an appointment with the pope, and then concludes in Moscow. I'm accompanied by my close friend Michael Nason and my son-in-law Paul Dunn, Jeanne Anne's husband. Paul, responsible for the oversight of our new television outreach in Europe, will go with me to meet with our Holland board of directors.

After endless hours in the air, we begin our descent into the land of my roots, and as we draw nearer to the earth I see windmills dotting the landscape. The lowland green has begun to pale a bit with autumn coming on. I think back to how my branch of the family began so many years before, with my Dutch grandpas and grandmas. What if they hadn't taken the risk of leaving their homeland? What if they hadn't been possibility thinkers, willing to become immigrant farmers? Would I now be en route to a meeting with Mikhail Gorbachev—leader of the USSR?

I ponder it all and decide:

You can go anywhere from nowhere!

The plane touches down in Amsterdam, and Mike, Paul, and I are met by our European correspondent, Joop Post. After collecting our luggage we follow Joop (pronounced "Yoop") to his small

European car. Paul helps Joop store the baggage in the trunk while Mike reviews the schedule for the evening. (It's his job to try to keep me on time and focused.) We have only a brief time for sightseeing before the rush of the night begins. There's to be a dinner cruise in a few hours.

Mike and I stand at the curb as he reads the itinerary, but I'm not really listening. I just want to get going. I head for the front passenger seat as always, because I'm the one with the long legs. I open the short door and swing low and fast into the front seat, and . . . THUNK!

I smash into the low roof of the car.

I grab the side of my head. *That hurt! Why do they make cars with such low roofs?*

I rub my temple as it begins to throb, expecting to feel a prominent knot. No knot, but, boy, that hurt!

Soon we're weaving down the highway at speeds way beyond what we drive at home. With each sudden move of the car, as we pass from one lane to the other, I feel jabbing pains in my head. Man, do I have a headache! I reach up again to hold my head.

"Bob, are you okay?" Mike says.

"Yeah, I'm fine. I just really knocked my head back there."

"Can we still meet with the *Hour of Power* officials, do you think?"

"Sure," I say; and we do, but we keep the meeting brief.

As we return to the car, Mike says, "Bob, do you still want Joop to take us by Corrie ten Boom's place?"

"Yes, please. I want to see the old clock shop again."

Corrie survived the death camps and lived to inspire others in books such as *The Hiding Place*; and her daily visits to Carol in the hospital inspired our whole family. It's been years since I saw where her family hid the Jews and where they were all discovered and taken captive by Hitler's troops, who hauled them to the German prison camps.

I decide that my headache will probably quiet down in a few minutes, so we continue on as planned. But it doesn't; it just grows worse as we stop to tour the tiny shop.

We shorten our visit and go directly to the hotel. Mike and Joop oversee the bellboy and our luggage, and . . . *Golly, my head hurts!*

I tell Paul, "I'm not hungry. You and Mike go to dinner without me. My headache's getting worse. I'd better rest or I'm going to be useless for tomorrow's travel to Rome. I can skip tonight's event."

Paul looks at me with concern. "Can I help you, Dad?"

"No, I'm fine," I assure him. "I just don't think I'd better push it tonight. Just plan to see me in the morning at breakfast, okay?"

"Well, do you want me to walk you to your room?" he offers.

"No, no. I'll get this other bellboy to take me. You and Mike go on."

Mike is also reluctant to go. "Bob, are you okay?" he presses.

"I have a terrible headache, Mike. I feel a little dizzy. It must be jet lag. I'm going to skip this dinner. I'll see you in the morning."

As I enter my hotel room, I notice that the tiny balcony, three stories up, offers a beautiful view of the city across the canal. I think of walking to the balcony for fresh air but instead simply tip the bellboy and, as soon as he leaves, fall onto the bed, still in my travel clothes.

But lying down doesn't help. I feel as if my head is ready to explode! I decide that a hot bath might relax my muscles and help this awful headache. I turn on the water and lean back against the sink.

Gosh . . . I need some aspirin. I turn the water off and leave the room to go to the concierge downstairs. He gives me a small packet of what I hope will conquer this pain. I don't wait to get to the room; I quickly open the packet and swallow the four small white pills. A heavy dose, but my head hurts mightily!

Back in the room I throw the aspirin wrapper into an ashtray and reenter the bathroom to turn the bath water back on.

I feel sick. Then all of a sudden I feel very dizzy and sleepy, and I *need help*, and my body feels heavy and achy, and . . .

That's all I remember. The next hours, even days, remain a black hole in time. I have no knowledge of the eight-hour emergency brain surgery. Even today I still remember nothing except dreamy stupors.

The next solid memory I have is of hearing words ringing, echoing, reverberating loudly in my mind. I try to open my eyes, but it isn't easy. I *must* open my eyes; I *must* write down these ringing words, this great line that I hear in my head. It will make a great sermon title or even a book title!

Such lines have become familiar friends over the years—words that I love. I feel again that familiar, quiet, happy feeling, and I doze again into a dreamy recollection of the day when Uncle Henry came back from China. It feels more real than ever as I hear the tires grind on the gravel and see Mom wiping her hands on her apron; *and I hear those words again, and I must write them down before I forget them!*

I'm awake now, desperately wanting a pen or pencil. Paper isn't so important; I'll write on anything—an envelope, a cardboard box, my hand!

Then I see a stranger approaching my bed. Tall and blond, she's dressed in white. I don't know or care where I am or what's happened. I call to her and she comes near.

"Please, do you have a pen?" I ask.

She looks at me, puzzled. She doesn't respond.

"Please, do you have a pen and paper? I have to write down some words."

Why won't she help me? I motion to her in frustration for a pen and paper, miming the act of writing. It seems an eternity before she figures out what I need and brings me a pen and paper. Finally!

I begin to write the words that are still sounding their call in my mind. I'm filled with that strange spiritual joy that's always near when I prepare my sermons. And so I write.

I'm proud of my new line. I can feel it radiating all through me. I hold the paper for a moment, treating it like a Tennyson original that I don't want to let go of. Then, as I look at the line on the paper again, I realize that the letters are just a garbled mess, just lines and scribbles.

That isn't what I wrote!

I try again. Still . . . squiggles and rough wavy lines.

No matter how I try, my hand won't do what I want it to do.

Finally, I give the paper back to the woman. She looks at it, puzzled again, and when she looks up I read pity in her eyes.

"Save that for me, please," I say.

She looks confused and turns away.

I'm so tired that I simply have to sleep some more. And so I fall asleep with my words repeating themselves in my mind:

How sweet it is to stand on the edge of tomorrow!
How sweet it is to stand on the edge of tomorrow!
How sweet it is to stand on the edge of tomorrow!

Some time later, through the haze of sleep, I hear a soft voice, like that of an angel. I smile, though I'm not awake. When I open my eyes, I see another lovely woman — *so* lovely. *Maybe she'll marry me,* I think.

"Bob?" she says.

I know this voice. It's as pretty as she is.

"Bob? It's Arvella, honey." I feel a sting coming into my eyes and something wet sliding down my cheek. I fall back to sleep with that pretty woman's face smiling at me and that soft voice calling my name.

———

The next thing I'm aware of is a rumbling beneath me, wheels rolling. I open my eyes. I see more white walls and more strangers. Then I see darkness. Am I outside? I feel chilly. I smell something funny . . . fumes? I fall back asleep.

Even now I remember little of the two weeks before I was transported home by plane—little about the accident, my surgeries, my son and my daughter and my wife coming to Amsterdam. Arvella, as she explained to me later, had asked the surgeon whether or not I'd ever speak or write again. He'd given her no promises. As I lay recovering from the first surgery, blood had pooled again, hemorrhaging in the recesses of my brain. The surgeon had had to operate again, drilling through the skull to allow the blood to drain out.

Prayer vigils had remained constant at home. Meanwhile, "Schuller dies in brain surgery" was only the first of many false reports in the press. My brother, Henry, heard the news and was filled with grief until he was able to reach my daughter Gretchen and get the true story.

On September 16 I arrived at the Los Angeles airport and was taken by ambulance to the University of California, Irvine (UCI) Medical Center, a half-mile from my church. It was my sixty-fifth birthday.

I hear the "Happy Birthday" song and see candles on a cake. But who are all these people around me? They seem familiar, these nice-looking people. I listen to their muted conversation.

"Does he know us, Mom?" a young voice says.

"I don't know, honey. The doctors said he may not know us for a while."

I turn to see who speaks so softly and authoritatively, because that voice makes me feel secure. It's that pretty woman—the one I want to marry. Then I remember: I *did* marry her! It's Arvella! She's my wife! I call her by name, and she smiles, a tear sliding down her cheek. She can't speak for a while because of the quiet tears. Why has my greeting brought out such emotion in her?

After a few minutes she says to me, "Bob, Carol has a special present for you. When you were having your surgery, she was getting her new leg. Remember how she had to go to Oklahoma to get it? She's back, and she can walk beautifully!"

I do think I remember this; it sounds vaguely familiar. My daughter—the one who . . . her leg?

I see a tall blond woman walking back and forth. She's walking better than I remember her walking before. A new leg? Hmmm. This *is* familiar. I ask her, "Did you get your new—pros . . . pros . . . thesis, Carol?" I get the words out, but they're slow and labored and slurred.

Clearly she understands me. "Yes, Daddy," she says. She sits at the head of my bed, her hand gently stroking my cheek. She tells me that I'm going to be fine and that she loves me. I hear her say, "Daddy, you spent a lot of hours by my bedside. I think it's time for me to return the favor." Her hand is warm and comforting, and I turn my face into that hand. She murmurs some words of prayer . . . and I cry.

"Dad?" It's another beautiful blond woman standing behind Carol. I recognize her: it's Sheila.

"Happy Birthday, Dad," she says, bending to kiss me.

Then everyone in the room begins singing to me. There's that "Happy Birthday" song again. I feel as though I am waking from a long dream and I sense that all around me is strangely familiar and yet so strangely fuzzy.

I look around at all the pretty faces, then focus in on one. That young brunette.

"Hi, Daddy," she says. "It's Gretchen." She bends to hug me, a familiar sensation.

Wow! What a tall and handsome dark-haired man standing

beside her! Is that my son? And what a pretty blond woman he has on his arm, her smile warm and comforting.

"Dad? It's Robert," he says. "They tell us you'll be able to see the cross on the Tower of Hope when they move you to your permanent room."

Another tall brunette comes to me. "Dad? It's Jeanne," she says, sensing my uncertainty. "Boy, you look cute! I never thought I'd see you go bald. And you're so skinny! Congratulations, Dad. You lost that weight you've been worrying about!"

Bald? I touch my head. Skinny? I look down at my belly, now flat and smooth. I look at these pretty people, and I smile and raise my eyebrows. I'm trying to say, "I look good, huh?" They're all giggling and crying—half and half—and their smiles make me smile. But where's my hair? Why am I home? Did I see the pope? Did I go to Russia?

I'm tired again, and I don't feel too well. My head hurts, so I curl into a ball. As I drift off into yet another sleep, I hear Arvella whisper to somebody, "He's afraid. He's afraid that no one will want him anymore."

I was released from the hospital on September 17, 1991, but I don't remember that either. I would spend the next days curled up in bed—sleeping, for the most part—except when I was prodded awake by my wife and encouraged to take a stroll or to engage in the physical therapy scheduled for me daily at UCI Medical Center.

"Dad? It's Carol"

I open my eyes and see my own bedroom nightstand. I see my lamp. I see my books and my blue leather Bible sitting on the nightstand. I see my easy chair near my bed. I see the big white-wood-bordered French window framing the view of a sun-splashed garden and the huge branches of our tall ficus tree. All of this is the backdrop behind my daughter.

"How are you, Daddy?" Carol asks.

"Fine," I say, optimistic on her behalf. "Where are the children?" Does she *have* children? Or is that Sheila? Oh, I get so confused.

"They're with Tim," she says. "I just wanted to come see you for a few minutes. I was praying for you, Daddy, and I was listening to a song, and I really thought you'd like to hear it. Close your eyes."

She puts her hand on my chest. My cotton pajamas rest warm against my skin beneath the heavy and comforting touch. I listen to her prayer, and then I hear the music from her CD player. First a guitar, the acoustic kind, resonating with a comforting sound that drapes serenity around me. Then I hear a mellow baritone voice sing:

"My hope is built on nothing less than Jesus' blood and righteousness; I dare not trust the sweetest frame, but wholly lean on Jesus' name."

Then the chorus:

"On Christ, the solid Rock, I stand. All other ground is sinking sand; all other ground is sinking sand."

Then comes the second stanza:

"When darkness veils His lovely face, I rest on His unchanging grace; in every high and stormy gale my anchor holds within the veil."

The words pierce me, and I can feel my face distort and my eyes pinch, the tears flowing, as I sing along with the chorus:

"On Christ, the solid Rock, I stand. All other ground is sinking sand; all other ground is sinking sand."

Then I fall toward a blissful sleep as I hear Carol rise, then hear the faint rustle of her clothing as she leaves.

These days of reverie and nostalgia had a dreamlike quality of their own. Drifting in and out of cozy sleep, I got back in touch with my childhood. I spent many hours reacquainting myself with the Floyd River and the old red barn and Mom and Dad—all in my dreams.

But soon I became restless, eager to get up and move around. After all, I hadn't reached my "somewhere" by dozing and napping.

"Bob! Get off that stool!" Arvella scolds.

What did I do? I just want to change that blasted light bulb! It bugs me that it doesn't work. Gee whiz—everyone is treating me as if I were a little kid.

"I'm a sixty-four-year-old man," I say, in what I think is a commanding tone. "Let me do what I want!"

She chides me again. "You're sixty-*five*, honey. You just had a birthday."

I leave the kitchen, perturbed, and go toward the music room. As I walk by a hall mirror, I see my bald pate and the ten-inch-long horseshoe-shaped scar that winds itself around the top of my head. I tell people that this is where they cut me open, as if with a can-opener, peeled back the skin to saw and drill the skullbone, then lifted the top off like a jack-o'-lantern. I let two fingers of my left hand find and traverse the two little hollows, gullied scars left from the surgeries. They've become my friends. Friends? Yes. Every time I feel these hollows, I remember that they gave me back the power to speak and write.

I enter the music room and fall sulking into Grandpa's rocker. The scar is proof enough that I experienced all that I've been told about, though I still have a hard time believing it.

Arvella finds me there.

"Honey, I didn't mean to scold you," she says apologetically. "It just scares me, Bob. The doctor says you shouldn't climb things. If you fall, you'll begin to bleed again, and we can't let that happen."

I look at her, here in this room, and I remember that this rocker where I'm sitting is the same one I sat in when Dr. Graham told me about her breast cancer. I begin to cry again. I cry a lot these days.

"What's wrong, Bob?" she asks.

"I just love you so much. You're so pretty, so kind. Will you marry me?"

She giggles. Then she gives me a kiss on my forehead.

"Can I get you anything, honey?"

"No, I'm fine. Thank you, though."

Then she heads back to finish her work in the kitchen.

On the coffee table, news clippings explaining the past weeks are spread about, mixed in with cards and pictures from my grand-kids. I pick up an article that displays the *Orange County Register*'s headline:

Schuller Recovering from Brain Surgery
Blow to His Head Burst Blood Vessel[*]

> The Rev. Robert H. Schuller, 64, pastor of Garden Grove's Crystal Cathedral, was alert and talking today in an Amster-dam hospital after undergoing emergency surgery for a burst blood vessel on his brain.
>
> "He's doing fine. I talked with him this afternoon," said Robert A. Schuller, his son, who kept a bedside vigil. "He said, 'When am I going home?'"

I did? I don't remember saying that! Bob was in Amsterdam? I don't remember his being there! I continue reading:

> The televangelist, host of the *Hour of Power* television ministry, apparently injured his head when he smacked it on the edge of a car roof outside his hotel in the Netherlands capital Sunday afternoon, said Michael Nason, an aide traveling with Schuller.

---

[*]*Orange County Register*, Tuesday, September 3, 1991.

I remember that! But it was when I was getting into the car at the *airport*, not outside the hotel! You got it wrong, buddy! I read on:

Found by Nason unconscious in his room, Schuller was rushed to the hospital for three hours of surgery . . .

Wrong again! It was eight hours!

. . . to remove blood on his brain. Schuller was in Amsterdam conferring with church leaders and preparing for a trip to Russia later this week.

Oh, yeah—Russia. My meetings—what about my meetings!
"Arvella?" I call her loudly, feeling somewhat frantic.
"Yes, honey?" she says, looking through the open door.
"Arvella, I never made it to Russia! Have Marjorie call and reschedule."
"Honey, Marjorie isn't your secretary anymore. Let's just wait a little while before we think about Russia. I hear Gorbachev is swamped, and he probably won't want to meet before next summer."
I'm not listening. I'm not even thinking about Russia anymore. I'm already back to reading.

"He hit his head just right. It was really a freak thing," Schuller's son said. "I think he's probably embarrassed by the whole thing."
Schuller has scrapped his plans to visit the Soviet Union and will return to Orange County as soon as physicians say he's fit to travel, his son said.

The Soviet Union!
"Arvella?" I call.

She walks in almost immediately, wiping her hands on her apron. "Yes, honey?"

"Call Marjorie and tell her to reschedule Russia."

"Honey, Marjorie isn't . . ."

I'm reading again:

After the operation, surgeons for Schuller told Nason that they were cautiously optimistic there was no brain damage or signs of future impairment.

Schuller had intended to stop in Amsterdam for a day and to meet with European *Hour of Power* officials before embarking on a trip to Rome for a private meeting with Pope John Paul II.

Schuller was then to go to Moscow for a special appearance on Soviet television. He also had planned to launch his show on commercial stations in Russia and the Ukraine.

Russia!

"Arvella?" I call.

She walks in folding a sheet. "Yes, honey?" she says, sighing heavily.

"Call Marjorie and tell her to reschedule Russia."

"Bob—" She sounds a little frustrated. Why is she frustrated?

She stands over me, watching as I read through the clipping, struggling with the details.

"Do you remember any of this, honey?" she asks.

"I remember hitting my head. I remember going to Corrie ten Boom's home—the clock shop. I remember getting the aspirin. I remember feeling really hot."

"Bob, when you arrived at the hospital, the surgeon told Paul that if you'd been twenty minutes later, you would have died. The aspirin made your blood so thin that it flooded for hours into your brain, and the blood had no way to drain out."

We're both silent for a long time. It's still so hard to comprehend everything that's happened, but something inside me knows that what Arvella tells me is true.

"Bob, you'd been out all night long on that balcony," she says, breaking the silence. "Do you know how cold it gets in Amsterdam in September?"

What balcony? I'm thinking. *I thought I passed out in the bathroom!*

I look down at the article in my hand. Sure enough, it says I was found "slumped unconscious on a chair on the balcony." Well!

Arvella, aware that I'm trying to piece things together, says, "Your body was blocking the outward-swinging French doors."

"In a chair?" I ask, testing my newfound knowledge from the article.

"No," she says, surprising me. "You were unconscious on the ground. The bellboy had to go to the room next to yours and put a ladder from that balcony railing to yours. Then he crawled across the ladder to your balcony so that he could move your body and open the door for rescuers."

Perhaps my face reveals a growing skepticism, because Arvella says, "Bob, you were in a *coma*. You almost *died*. What happened to you was *very serious*. Do you remember when Paul prayed for you?"

"No," I say, feeling a little queasy from the conversation.

"Paul said that he took your face in his hands and began to pray, and that when he did, you opened your eyes and smiled at him. You don't remember this?"

"No."

"What's the next thing you remember after feeling hot?"

"I remember waking up in a hospital, and I remember some words that I felt a burning need to write down."

Arvella reaches for a Bible on the coffee table and opens it. She pulls out a piece of paper and hands it to me. I see nothing but scribbles and scrawls—like a young toddler's efforts when he's first learning to draw.

It gives me a chill, though, because I recognize it. "I know this paper," I say, "and I know what it says."

Arvella's eyes light up as if I'm about to reveal the solution to some mystery she's long been trying to solve. She pays rapt attention as I hold up the paper and translate the illegible scribbling:

"*How sweet it is to stand on the edge of tomorrow.*"

Arvella draws her hand to her mouth, and her eyes brim with tears.

The doctors said that I would need more time—much more—before I would fully recover, if I *did* fully recover. There were no promises. But I had already regained most of my speech, and I had begun to regain my ability to write. Now it was my memory that I needed back—that and my hair! My memory would take the longest.

So much of what transpired between the time I filled the tub and the time I returned home was lost in details that I would simply never remember . . . and that Arvella would never forget.

She would never forget the sparrow that came and fluttered at the intensive care window on a day when she still didn't know whether I would live or die. That little bird, hovering in suspended flight outside a window six stories up—no ledge, no balcony—truly seemed heaven-sent. It hovered there as if to give her a message, a line from that gospel favorite, "His eye is on the sparrow."

Arvella would never forget the words of the surgeon telling her that even when a patient does recuperate following a brain trauma of this severity, that person's personality may be completely different than before. She would have to live with this uncertainty for some time, wondering whether I would return a different man. She could only trust the promise she'd received from that little bird—that God knew, and all would be well.

Arvella would never forget the courage of a young bellboy who risked his own life to crawl across a ladder stretched from one balcony to the next, three stories above the canal, to rescue a total stranger. She would never forget how easily I could have toppled over the railing on that balcony, to drown in the water below. Just as I might have slipped in that tub of hot water, my brain hemorrhaging from all the aspirin, and drowned.

Arvella would never forget the doctor telling her, once she'd arrived in Amsterdam, that I might not know who she was. How after all the years that we'd lived together, made love together, surmounted tragedies and difficulties together, raised babies together, she'd had to face the fact that I might suddenly not know her face or her name. And she would never forget the thrill of hearing me speak her name on my sixty-fifth birthday.

I returned to the pulpit on the Sunday morning of November 4, at the encouragement of a dear friend, J. B. Fuqua. He'd called a month and a half earlier from his home in Atlanta and had said, "Hi, Bob! How you doing?"

"Oh, fine, J. B. The doctors just took their can-opener, opened the top of my head, and vacuumed out all the negative thoughts!"

"That's a good opening line for when you're back in the pulpit," he said. "Now listen. Just as soon as you can, you need to get yourself back on that television screen. People need to see that you're alive. They want to hear your voice and know for themselves that you're okay—that you can still think and that you still have your famous smile."

"But I don't have any hair, J. B.!"

"I'm sure you'll find a way around that," he said dismissively. "Things like that never stopped you before!"

Six weeks later I had myself a wig and was back before my congregation, who gave me a standing ovation. The title of my sermon? "How Sweet It Is to Stand on the Edge of Tomorrow!"

XLII

In 1991 Russia suffered near-famine conditions. While still recuperating, I was able to encourage the formation of a coalition of major Protestant churches called Churches United in Global Mission (CUGM), and with their help we sent eleven thousand food packages to Moscow in care of the Orthodox Church. We sent a second shipment of food in March of 1992.

Meanwhile, negotiations resumed for the full *Hour of Power* to be telecast every Sunday from Moscow, replacing the brief half-hour *Heart to Heart* talks. This made it necessary for me to return to Moscow to sign the contract. I began to make plans for a trip.

I would need a translator, as well as someone to manage the Russian office of the *Hour of Power*. Through a woman who taught Russian at the nearby University of California, Irvine, we came to know (and hire) her son, Andrei Danilenko, a young Moscovite. His embrace of Christianity would change his life so dramatically during the next years that it would amaze even me.

In June of 1992, news of my arrival in Russia reached the head of that nation's army, a man who had been affected by my television ministry and was now a Christian. "You've helped me turn from atheism to Christianity, Dr. Schuller," he said. "You must come and speak to the seven hundred army officers under my command."

I did — but it didn't go over well, to say the least. Half of the officers protested that the meeting had been "forced upon them." Throughout my talk there was murmuring and grumbling from the audience.

I had a much better welcome from the parliament. Its representatives were impressed with not only our television ministry, but also our ministry to Chernobyl and our help during the food shortage.

I also met with the Russian agricultural committee, a subgroup from the full parliament. The committee chairman thanked me for our efforts to supply food, then said, "Dr. Schuller, we understand that you were raised on an Iowa farm. Your farms in the United States have always led the world in productivity. Our large collective farms are being broken up, and parliament has the job of deciding who will own the land.

"Dr. Schuller, I'm prepared to give you ownership of fifty thousand acres of prime agricultural land. Come and divide it into small farms like those you have in Iowa, and show us how we can produce enough food to feed our citizens."

"I can't take land from your people!" I exclaimed. "But what I can and will do is put together a team of world-class agricultural experts to come over here and advise you."

Upon my return to America I would travel to Minneapolis, Minnesota, for a meeting of Churches United in Global Mission. David Scoates, a Methodist minister, received the organizational assignment to oversee this project. He would pass it on to one of his parishioners, Ralph Hofstad. The recently retired CEO of Land o' Lakes, Inc., Hofstad would put together a committee that included the retired head of Iowa State University, Ames. This committee would create demonstration fields in Russia that won the attention of everyone involved in that nation's agriculture. Eight years later, Gorbachev would tell me that he saw this experiment in managing and marketing agricultural productivity as the single most successful and replicable example in the entire nation. To a farmboy from Iowa who never quite got the hang of farming himself, this was wonderful news.

But still in Russia, I had come specifically to sign a contract that had suddenly become snagged in red tape. We were supposed to begin airing the full *Hour of Power* weekly throughout Russia within days, but without Armand Hammer, I lacked the clout to make things move forward.

"Refinements need to be worked out," I was told. It wasn't until forty-five minutes before our plane was to lift off for America that we saw our friend Boris, again our escort, come running into the VIP waiting area of the airport waving a large piece of paper.

"Here it is, Dr. Schuller! They've signed it! You sign here, and you'll go on the air in only a few weeks!"

Our first telecast of the full *Hour of Power* aired on June 7, 1992. Three months later, I fulfilled my promise made to the parliament: we launched the Russian Farms Community Project.

In April of the following year, it was time for us to review the results of almost a year of the *Hour of Power* on Russian television. Was it really making a difference? Our message of possibility thinking was and is so strongly focused on the power of individualism. Without being confrontational, how could it penetrate a society steeped in collectivism, a people indoctrinated to believe in the wisdom of surrendering decision-making to authority figures?

We decided to check things out in person. On this 1993 trip our first meeting was with Gorbachev, now ousted from office. Andrei Danilenko, my translator, and I, met with the former leader in his official quarters.

"Dr. Schuller," he began, "I got you on television in Russia, and now I can't get on TV myself! No press will cover me! Yeltsin has all the power now."

Then, as if in confirmation of Mr. Gorbachev's assessment, Andrei slipped me a message. "Yeltsin's office called and wants us there for a meeting."

With the help of a police escort—lights flashing and sirens wailing—we rushed through the streets to the Kremlin walls, then through a great gate into the old power center of world communism.

We were escorted to what in America would be the Oval Office and cabinet meeting room, where the deputy chief of Yeltsin's administration, Mr. Vyacheslav Voklov, met us.

"Last Sunday," Voklov said, "May 25, 1993, was really the birthday of a new Russia. On that day we voted to adopt a constitution ending dictatorship and establishing democracy. Yeltsin's decision to throw open this decision to the people was widely criticized. Opponents said, 'What if they don't vote for it? Haven't the people all been indoctrinated to accept a paternalistic political system?'

"Dr. Schuller, we worked for weeks, day and night, to try to educate the people to vote for democracy. Just before the election I worked here all Saturday night. I slept only a few hours on that sofa! In the morning I turned on the TV. It was eight o'clock, and you came on. I've listened to you on your *Hour of Power* here in Russia for almost a year now—every Sunday! I know how large your audience is. With your smiling face, you said, 'This is the day the Lord has made; let us rejoice and be glad in it.'

"I knew then that seeing you and hearing you would, more than anything else, inspire the people to believe in themselves enough to go to the polls and vote for democracy! And your sermon—I swear—was as if planned just for Russia on this historic Sunday. You preached it as you have for the past fifty Sundays: 'Believe in Yourself!' I stood up in here and cried for joy and applauded and applauded. I knew that God had sent you here to inspire the people to believe in themselves and vote for a new country with freedom in the hands of the people."

Over the next years, the doors in Russia continued to open wider than ever to religion. It was good to know that I'd been allowed to help in that transition, but I certainly wasn't the only one who influenced Russia regarding religion. All different sorts of faiths and religions were suddenly being allowed in; and did they ever come in— in droves! Good ones and bad ones, including controversial cults from America and Japan.

Orthodox leaders were appalled. "What have we done?" they asked. They weren't any better pleased with evangelical Christians who came from America and began to tell people bluntly, "You may be a member of the Orthodox Church, but that won't save you."

As one can imagine, that wasn't a message welcomed by the thousand-year-old Russian church! Freedom to practice one's own religion? Yes, they agreed with that. But freedom to proselytize and try to convert Russian Orthodox believers to other faiths? That should *not* be allowed!

Parliament passed legislation limiting the freedom of all religious bodies in an effort to block proselytizing. Full freedom to minister required a certificate of accreditation, approved by parliament and the Orthodox Church. Any and all faiths that were seen as actual or potential proselytizers were refused certification. That included the Roman Catholic Church, Seventh Day Adventists, the Salvation Army, Billy Graham and the Baptists, the Pentecostals, and the Methodists.

They made one exception for their first American preacher in Russia: in 1999 they issued certificate number 001 to the Crystal Cathedral Ministries and to me, Robert Schuller.

A year later my young translator Andrei gave his personal testimony from the pulpit of the Crystal Cathedral. "I always thought of Christians as people who were constantly annoying you about Christianity," he said, "trying to make you born again. I never realized the beauty of Christianity until I met people like you, Dr. Schuller, who live the kind of lives that I want to be part of. And that's what changed my life. Not reading the Bible, and I'm sad to say, not watching your programs. What made me a Christian was meeting you and experiencing you and truly believing that you live out everything you say in your day-to-day life."

XLIII

Those closest to me tell me that a full recovery from my near death in Amsterdam, and the two brain surgeries that followed, took a full year.

Even though I was back in my Sunday morning pulpit after only a few months, it was difficult for me to prepare my messages and remain focused on what I wanted to say. But my congregation was so faithful and loving that they showed perfect patience when I couldn't find my place in the notes that Arvella had carefully written out for me. They prayed me through those long weeks of recovery as I stood before them in my flowing pulpit robe, the scars on my bald head hidden by an obvious wig.

It took still longer for me to seize fresh vision for my distant tomorrows. I couldn't tackle tomorrow until I had a clear assessment of today. Thus over the next couple of years I found myself searching for an honest answer to what I felt was the most important question I could address: "What power do I have in the position I occupy today?"

The question was important because overestimating my power—surrendering to ego, letting praise inflate my self-regard—would lead to irresponsible goal-setting. The fallout from such excess would be dangerous to my emotional well-being, my ministry, my staff, and my supporters. For that reason, I gave up for a time my life-long habit of moving with self-confidence to stand on the edge. After all, I was now sixty-six. My college and seminary classmates had their retirement landing gear down, aiming for a safe, sweet landing on the home airport, now within their sight. Sixty-eight was the retirement age long held by my denomination. In addition, my near brush with death had given me more than adequate reason to be cautious.

On the other hand, underestimating my power would be as destructive as overestimating it. I couldn't shake off the sermons I'd been preaching all of my life. How often I quote my friend, Fred Smith: "You know what hell would be for me? Hell would be to stand before God and have Him tell me what great things I could have done if I'd had more faith."

The questions before me reflected four stages of life:

1. Where have I come from?

2. Who am I?

3. What have I accomplished?

4. When is it time to hang it up?

Maybe the answer to the last question would be different for each role I'd played, and certainly there had been many:

AUTHOR

I had published thirty books now. As I noted earlier, two were on the *New York Times* bestseller list at the same time: *Tough Times Never Last, But Tough People Do*, and *Tough-Minded Faith for Tender-Hearted People*. I had no drive to add anything more to my oeuvre. I felt I had said all that I had to say. Publishers tried to tempt me to do an autobiography, but I reasoned, "If people are interested, they can see and judge for themselves. My work has been open to public review and criticism for forty years."

Then, one by one, my advisors and friends and confidants began to speak, and their message was the same: "Bob, you're innately a writer! You'd be miserable if you kept all of your feelings and ideas and observations bottled up! Besides, retirement and writing go beautifully hand in hand."

Okay, so maybe I'd do some writing.

MOTIVATOR

I was regularly invited to lecture at the largest motivational rallies held in America. It was common to count paid audiences of over twenty thousand people. And I'd get top billing with the best: W. Clement Stone, who sponsored as well as spoke at most of these energy-generating events, Norman Vincent Peale, and Paul Harvey. My fee for these commercial lectures was fifteen thousand dollars —

triple what Peale commanded. And my entire check was tax-exempt, because I'd chosen to donate all such extra income to my special fund for ministers.

My lectures, like my books and tapes, were distinctively tuned into psychology first, then theology. And I'd kept up-to-date in the field, attending international psychiatric and psychological conferences. But new faces and young voices were coming along. Could I, *should* I . . . exit gracefully and let them have the stage?

Again, friends and advisors began to speak: "Bob, you don't need to accept *every* motivational engagement that comes along. Just keep that door open."

MINISTER TO MINISTERS

How about the Robert Schuller Institute for Successful Church Leadership and the Fuqua School of Christian Communicaion, made possible by a generous gift from my spiritual friend, J.B. Fuqua, from Atlanta, Georgia? Should these ministries to ministers be abandoned? For over thirty years, more than two thousand church leaders annually had been coming to our workshops. When I'd founded the institute decades earlier—the first church-growth institute in America—I'd been on the cutting edge of leadership. Was I still on that edge?

"Leadership is the force that sets the goals," I'd lectured.

"Be a leader. Empower yourself with creative vision."

"Never surrender goal-setting to forces that limit your growth potential."

I loved to inspire ministers to catch a dream, size it up, and seize it. "What forces or faces or fears keep you from setting growth goals?" I would challenge them. "Use the power of possibility thinking to creatively conceive solutions to these barriers. Let your highest hopes—not your hurts or limitations—shape and set your dreams."

I was encouraged whenever I thought back on the students who had gone through my institute and then gone on to build better and bigger churches than I had:

- Bill Hybels: Willow Creek Community Church, Illinois

- Bishop Charles Blake: West Angeles Church of God in Christ, one of the largest black churches in the world

- Rick Warren: Saddleback Community Church, California

- Frank Harrington: Peachtree Presbyterian Church, Atlanta (now the largest Presbyterian church in America)

- Sundo Kim: First Methodist Church in Seoul, South Korea, the largest Methodist church in the world

Except for Frank Harrington, who came to the institute with a strong church, all of the others had come with nothing more than I had when I started.

Hundreds more came with nothing and picked up the dream of building a "mega-church." And many went back and shared the success principles in their own institutes. I experienced the pride of seeing students outrun their teacher. But did this mean that it was time for me to step down in this role?

Once again, I heard the voices of my peers tell me, "Bob, each minister has a unique voice. Sure, Hybels is excelling, as are Warren and Harrington and Kim and Blake and all the others. So what if there are now a ton of similar organizations? You have a unique voice and direction to give to ministers. Don't silence this!"

DEVELOPER

The role of developer was the first role that my contract with my denomination had demanded that I take on. In 1955 I had signed a contract to "build a church." That had meant that I would have to recruit the parishioners, find suitable land, hire an architect, come up with financing, and build a structure to house new programs for unchurched, nonreligious people.

From our beginnings in 1955 until 1990—a period of thirty-five years!—that had been the central mission for which I had been responsible and accountable.

In these pages I've told the story of how we built the sanctuary, then the Tower of Hope, with its counseling center and chapel. Those structures alone had more than fulfilled my assignment. I had been ready to set aside my developer's role once those tasks had been completed. But once I had realized the dire need for our expansion, I had felt that I couldn't with integrity check out until I had addressed that need. So I had made the additional commitment to the Crystal Cathedral and had stayed on simply to see it through.

The pressure and pain had been a high price for whatever pride of achievement followed. But we had finished the assignment, again without compromising excellence in the art of architecture. I had lived what I had preached: possibility thinking works wonders if you pay the price.

But then there had been *more*. We had needed comfortable and spacious classrooms for children, as well as office space for the expanding television ministry—growing worldwide. After several years of inner anguish I had made the decision to buy another nearly ten acres, and we had built a central Family Life Center and added more urgently needed parking space. This property had cost us six million dollars, and the structure—designed by architect Gin Wong—had cost another twenty million dollars.

Every night for three years I had awakened at three in the morning, painfully exercising possibility thinking. *Where would the money come from? Should I scale down my standards in architecture? After all, this building would house only classrooms, office space, and a gymnasium.* Night after night I had battled the temptation to meet with the architect and tell him to forget style and substance and just design the structure as inexpensively as possible, but I hadn't been able to bring myself to do that. Somehow we'd held to our goal of excellence, and I'd survived with the generosity of Athalie Clarke. She gifted her Hawaiian estate to the ministry and, when it was sold, her gift made the Family Life Center a very special place for children and families to find their dreams.

With the Family Life Center completed, we had felt called to add the crowning glory of the Crystal Cathedral: the bell-tower. As I described earlier, that process had resulted in the beautiful Crean Spire, its mirrored stainless steel facets rising over the Mary Hood Chapel. It hadn't been easy, but having read my own books, I'd known that "inch by inch, anything's a cinch."

Now there was nothing more this church needed. I could finally hang up my hard hat! Or so I thought.

Then a staffer, Howard Kelley, said, "We need a visitors' center to accommodate the hundreds of tourists and show them exhibits of how this church came to be."

My son egged me on. "You should buy the last ten acres, Dad," he said. "We need it for more parking."

"The last ten acres!?" I protested. "It's filled with thirty-one houses, plus streets and driveways! I'll let *you* handle this one." Sure enough, when a FOR SALE sign appeared, we bought the first house!

After that I lost track of how the project progressed. There's only so much *development* one man can take!

As I continued to contemplate my future roles in the ministry, I reviewed some of the ideas I had been preaching for forty years:

- Turn your scars into stars!

- There's no gain without pain!

- Every obstacle is an opportunity!

- Every problem hides a positive possibility!

- Frustrations can be fruitful!

- Turn your minus into a plus!

That last one really got me! The world's greatest plus sign is the cross. It was evidence that the most severe minus humanity faces— our sinful side and its negativity—had become a plus!

As a follower of Christ, I'm directed to "take up the cross and follow" Jesus—that is, learn from and model what Jesus taught and demonstrated in His living and in His dying.

Then I thought about this verse: "It is God at work in you giving you the will and the power to achieve His purpose" (Philippians 2:19).

Quitting on a God-given dream is never a God-approved option. "Go all the way to the end of your life; seek no escape." That's what Christ's cross tells me as I hear him say, "Follow me."

I had made my assessment: in order to determine what I should undertake in the future, I had reviewed the roles I had played and the challenges I had faced. Now I made what would be the single most challenging decision of my entire life: my message was my mission, and I couldn't abandon the dreams that my Lord still had for me.

After all, I was only sixty-six years old! I was still alive! My hair had grown back on my head, and now my hope was coming back into my heart!

"So God," I said, with renewed energy, "where will this resurrecting spirit lead me now?"

And I heard that small voice answer me with a question that I had thrown out to others so often: "What dreams would you have if you knew that you wouldn't fail?"

So I took a moment to free myself from the restrictions that limited thinking brings. I thought first about the possibility of buying the additional acres and taking on the project of another building. If we bought all thirty-one houses and cleared the streets and homes, we would finally have all of the original forty acres I had imagined forty years earlier. We would be able to add another four hundred parking spaces and gain an expanded lawn space that could hold an elegant visitors' center (to house a hospitality area, a gift shop, a theater, a food court, and archive space for the art and gifts we've received over the years and have been forced to store in a warehouse).

As I allowed my imagination to soar, I began to be inspired . . . again!

And so the decade of the nineties would see me once again in negotiations with a third gold-medal architect, this time Richard Meier, designer of the billion-dollar Getty Museum in Los Angeles. He would offer to design this last facility, saying to me one day, "I would be so proud to have one of my signature pieces between Richard Neutra's Tower of Hope and Philip Johnson's master-piece."

We purchased houses as they became available, talking with homeowners to encourage them to sell. Our goal was clear. But then one homeowner told us that yes, he would sell—but only for a price of one million dollars! That ended that.

Was God now answering our prayers in the negative? I couldn't believe that this could be!

I have often said, God doesn't say . . . "No." He says:

"Yes! If . . ."

Or He says:

"Yes! When . . ."

Or He says:

"Yes! But . . ."

I knew the answer. I had already heard the call again: "Build My church."

I had felt again that charge in my soul: "Deny yourself, take up your cross, and follow me."

Again I felt the exhortation: "You haven't finished building the church that I brought you here to build."

The message scared me. I knew now that I hadn't finally and fully succeeded. I hadn't followed to the end the big and beautiful dream that God had given me way back when I was preaching at the drive-in theater.

I couldn't use the challenges we now faced as excuses. Instead, I would once again have to wrestle with impossibilities. I would have to try to figure out if God was giving us an *if* or a *when* or a *but*.

Even as God had given me the power to build His church on a scale I had never imagined, even as He had lifted me up to the world stage, giving me the opportunity to influence the lives of millions, He now was reminding me that my work was unfinished. Somehow I'd have to buy all thirty-one houses and build that last building. I could not—must not—quit now!

It was just before Christmas, and I was buried under a full schedule. It didn't help that I wasn't feeling well.

My secretary buzzed me to say, "Dr. Schuller, Marie is here."

Oh, my, I thought to myself. *I really don't have time for her visit today.* But then I took a deep breath and told myself, "I guess I'll just have to make time."

I had been meeting with Marie Dorler for twenty-seven years now. She had been the first person to write to me when we launched our television ministry, and way back in 1970 she had requested the first of these annual visits. Back then, as a woman in her mid-fifties, she had been working as a nurse. Feeling sad and lonely, she had told me that she wanted to know more about the "positive" message she had stumbled upon when she turned her television to the *Hour of Power*. As we talked, she had made it clear that she wanted to become a Christian, but she asked one thing of me in return: she made me promise that, no matter how busy I got, I would meet with her once every year. Even if we shared only fifteen minutes together, she wanted a moment—face-to-face— with the pastor who had introduced her to Jesus Christ.

Over the years, Marie had contributed so very much to our ministry in that same personalized way. She was a priceless volunteer at our New Hope Counseling Center. Moreover, she took it upon herself to send a personal, handwritten note to every member of our church who became sick or simply needed a touch of personal warmth.

As she entered my twelfth-floor study that day, a woman now slowed by age, she said, "Bob, you don't look so good."

I tried to dismiss her assessment, but at her insistence I told her a little more about what was going on and how I was feeling. "Bob, that sounds like the early warnings of a heart attack. You've got all the classic symptoms. Promise me you'll make an appointment to see your doctor today."

I knew she had me. I couldn't break a promise to Marie. After she left I had to rush right away to a VIP luncheon, but there I only felt worse. I left the luncheon early to set up an appointment with my doctor for later in the day. When I saw him he confirmed Marie's "diagnosis." He put monitors on me right away, and within twelve hours he and his colleagues were doing angioplasty and inserting a stent into an artery, a procedure that very likely saved my life.

But I owe to Marie the sense of urgency that got me to the doctor. My taking time to serve Marie's life had in the end saved my own. It was like God was confirming, *"Schuller, had you decided to 'hang it all up' you would have missed meeting Marie."*

As I donned again my many hats, it seemed only fitting that Marie be used to remind me of my primary role as pastor and preacher—an identity I knew I could never "hang up." My boyhood calling would keep me focused not only on my *next* tomorrow but *every* tomorrow yet to come.

XLIV

It was January 18, 1997, inauguration weekend for the second term of President William Clinton, and I had been invited to a Saturday morning reception in the East Room of the White House. The President recognized and welcomed me as we shook hands. We had met in the Oval Office before, and just one year earlier he had asked me to be part of the U.S. delegation to the funeral of Israeli Prime Minister Yitzhak Rabin.

I've long had a habit of offering a blessing to people when I meet, and so at the reception I heard myself say quite impertinently, "Mr. President, I have a gift for you on this important weekend: the Bible verse that's been my special verse since I was ordained. It's Isaiah 58:12. Do you know it?"

"No, I don't think so," he said. "What is it?" His penetrating look told me that he was listening intently.

"You shall be called the repairer of the breach and the restorer of paths to dwell in," I quoted.

He blinked once or twice, obviously taken aback. Then he fumbled in his pocket, drew out a piece of paper, and asked me to write it down.

As I scribbled the text, the First Lady came up. "Tell Hillary what you said," he urged me. I repeated the text, and she, too, was visibly moved, inspired by this powerful thought from the prophet Isaiah.

In the next few days I heard rumors. An aide with Washington connections said, "The President has really claimed the Bible verse you gave him. I heard that he shared it with Bob Dole. He had Senator Dole ride with him in his limo from the White House up to the inauguration, and he told Dole that he was going to put his hand on that verse as he took his oath of office."

I couldn't believe it! In a note I wrote to the President, thanking him for including me in the inauguration-weekend reception, I said

I'd been pleased to hear such rumors and wondered whether they were true.

I received back the following note from President Clinton—handwritten:

Dear Dr. Schuller:

Thank you for your letter.

It is true that I shared the verse you gave me, and the story of your gift, with the Speaker and Senators Warner and Ford on the way to the Inauguration.

It is true that Hillary had the Bible open to Isaiah 58:12 [at the swearing-in].

I am sure the spirit of the passage has helped me in countless ways and may have helped me to see that I would give the Medal of Freedom to Senator Dole.

For all this and more I am in your debt.

February 3 is the day before the State of the Union, but I will make some time to see you if you can come.

Sincerely,
Bill Clinton

P.S. Please give my regards to our friend, J. B. Fuqua, a remarkable man!

Separately, I also received an invitation to sit in the seats reserved for the President's special guests in the gallery during his State of the Union Address to the joint houses of Congress. This would be my first participation in this historic occasion, at which all of the senators, congressional representatives, and members of the Supreme Court gather in one room at the same time.

On the evening of that address, I was directed to go to Hillary Clinton's office, where the guests would gather to be ushered into the gallery. I was then told to walk with the President's wife. As we entered the private seating area, I got my next surprise. Hillary smiled, nodded to me, and gestured to the empty chair next to her. "This is your seat, Dr. Schuller."

I've never felt quite so conspicuous as I did when I took my seat beside her on the first row of the balcony.

Then the announcement was made: "The President of the United States!"

Everyone stood and applauded appropriately as he made his entrance down the aisle and up to the podium. As I listened to his address, I was startled to hear him say my name, including me among "those whose lives reflect our shared values and the best of what we can become when we are one America." I felt very honored by that inclusion, but then my pleasure expanded tenfold: he quoted the Bible verse I had given him—"You shall be called the repairer of the breach. . . ."

Not many days later, he was kind enough to send me a deluxe printed copy of the address with his personal thanks.

Not all of the public reaction to my appearance would be positive, however. One letter went so far as to state, "Dr. Schuller, we saw you sitting next to Hillary. Are you now going to open a Hillary Clinton abortion clinic next to the Crystal Cathedral?"

But then came this invitation: "Dr. Schuller, President Lincoln's birthday is February 12. That falls on a Sunday, so the country will celebrate his birthday on Monday night, and President Clinton is inviting you to sleep in President Lincoln's bedroom on that night."

It was my first visit to this historic room. Late in the evening the President came in and welcomed me. I thanked him, and he asked for a prayer.

Afterward his eyes fell on one of my books that I had taken out of my briefcase. It was lying on a small table near where we were standing. He picked it up and read the title, *The Power of Being Debt Free*. I had written it with my son-in-law Paul David Dunn a few years earlier. In it I had made the case that no president and no Congress had ever dared to dream of wiping out the federal debt. The budget could be balanced, I had said, if it didn't have to carry that huge chunk of interest. I had called for possibility thinking by national leaders and had urged them to focus on the challenge of wiping out the debt. "Leadership is claimed and commanded by the mind that tackles a great idea that everyone believes is impossible," I had written, hoping that these words would inspire someone to take that risk. I had offered copies to all the senators and congressional representatives when it was published.

Holding the book, the President said, "Interesting. May I take it? I'm flying to Palm Springs tomorrow, and I can read it on the plane."

"I'm honored, sir," I answered. Then I offered, "Just imagine what good that interest money could do for causes that work to create a better country. We could use it for literacy, for education, for rebuilding inner cities!"

He smiled, and we said our goodnights.

I had no way of knowing at the time if the President would ever crack the cover of that book. It would be four years later before I learned just what influence it wound up having.

In September of that year I was asked to be a part of the President's delegation to the funeral for Mother Teresa.

In 1982 she had asked a favor of me. "Dr. Schuller, I would like a copy of the blessing that you wrote when you were building the Crystal Cathedral." I gladly wrote it out for her:

Lord, make my life a window for Your light to shine through, a mirror to reflect Your love to all I meet.

She took it, folded it, and tucked it in her tunic above her heart.

"Now," I said, "you owe me one, Sister." She wrote out this blessing, which I treasure still:

To Dr. Schuller: Be all and only for Jesus without him having to consult you first. —signed M. Teresa

So of course I accepted the President's invitation to her funeral. I made arrangements for what would be one of my longest air journeys. I was in Hawaii at the time, enjoying some time off with Arvella, so first we had to backtrack. Five hours from Honolulu to Los Angeles. Five hours from Los Angeles to Washington. Seven hours from Andrews Air Force Base, and then on to Ireland on one of the special President's planes. It was the plane that had carried President Kennedy's body from Texas to Washington, and where Johnson was sworn in as President. There we refueled, and then seven more hours from Ireland to Cairo. We refueled again, and then another seven hours from Cairo to Calcutta.

When we arrived, the city of Calcutta was solemn in its silent grief. On a main highway just outside the airport, I saw the first of many full-sized billboards—all white with the blue tunic of Mother Teresa on the left—declaring her farewell to the world: "Smile—it is the beginning of peace."

This was the sentiment she had shared with all new arrivals. I remembered how she had shared it with me as she held her two hands over mine some years earlier in Tijuana, Mexico. When she thanked me for my work, I had murmured, "I'm nothing next to you. You save the starving and the dying. I—my critics say—only smile and make people feel good."

Her eyes had twinkled. "I save people who are dying in body; you, Dr. Schuller, save people who are dying emotionally." Her face, just a few inches from mine, had radiated the love of Christ. Her hands, with their thick, broken nails, had felt like soft, warm gloves. Her lips had broken into the smile of Jesus as she said those words to me: "The smile is the beginning of peace."

Her funeral was, of course, packed with thousands from around the globe. World leaders, one at a time, walked to the casket to deliver large floral displays. But the focus in the long mass wasn't on the cardinals who filled the stage; nor was it on the casket, with its precious body of the queen of love and peace; nor was it on the sisters of her order, who were given seats of honor. No, the focus was on the cross, with the crucified Lord whom she had loved and served. All honor and glory was on Jesus Christ.

On the long ride home my seatmate was Doug Coe, who for nearly thirty years had put together the annual President's Prayer Breakfast in Washington, D.C. Each year Doug would invite as special guests not only the President of the United States, but all the members of Congress, as well as the diplomatic corps from all the countries of the world. Doug Coe knew all about witnessing to the non-Christian world. For the nearly twenty hours of our return trip I sat beside him and learned from his experience.

"As your ministry goes out to Asia and the Orient," he advised, "remember that so many of these countries have been, at one time or another in their history, invaded and controlled by European nations that have called themselves Christian. For that reason, be slow to use the words 'Christian' and 'Christianity.' Those two words have a lot of historical baggage. They can be an instant turn-off to Buddhists, Hindus, Muslims, and people who practice other ancient world religions."

"Then what do I call myself?" I asked.

"Call yourself a follower of Jesus Christ. And live Christ's life of love and peace.

"Remember, Jesus didn't come to start a new religion. He never coined or encouraged the use of the word 'Christianity.' He never told his disciples to call themselves 'Christians.' He did counsel them in these wise and wonderful words: 'I am the light of the world. He that follows me shall not walk in darkness, but in the light.' Our mission is not to convert people to a new religion, but rather to inspire them to be followers of Jesus Christ.

"I've seen hundreds of small groups made up of Buddhists and other world religions that meet regularly to study the life of Jesus. They read the Bible. They ask, 'How can we be followers of Christ?'

The world is open and hungry for Christ. Our mission is to share the life of Jesus with His Holy Spirit of God as the Good News it really is.

"I know of a small group of Buddhist priests in a small country best left unnamed. After several months studying the New Testament, these priests decided to go from house to house and simply ask, 'How can we help you?' They shocked the people. For always before when Buddhist priests approached people they had come asking for alms or food. Now they came with a revolutionary spirit: 'How can we help you?' And the bewildered populace asked them, 'Why are you doing this?' These monks in orange robes answered, 'We are followers of Jesus Christ. He wants to bring His love to you.'"

As our plane prepared to land in Washington, I was prepared to lift my ministry to a higher level of holy mission. My ministry of evangelism had been redesigned! My forces would shift from a mission of conversion to a mission of mercy. Instead of converting people from one affiliation to another, I would focus on connecting human hearts to the heart of my Savior, Jesus Christ. Then truly I could be assured of their salvation, for Jesus promised, "Those who come to Me, I shall not cast aside."

I was grateful to President Clinton for the warm hand of inclusion that he and his wife continued to extend to me, but like everyone else I was totally unprepared for the scandal that was about to overtake his presidency.

The President denied having "any sexual relations" with Monica Lewinsky, but the truth of his denial was soon called into question. As the ugly details of his actions in the Oval Office came out, the sordid scene erupted on the floor of the Senate. Clinton's close friend Senator Joseph Lieberman stood up among his colleagues and spoke with the voice of a prophet condemning what all Americans had experienced in their own disillusionment and depression.

I was being pressed from all sides to comment—my friendship with the President was no secret, after all—but I was reluctant to speak publicly about the matter. Pastor confidentiality was a mandate I had always taken very seriously. Then it was announced that the independent counsel would submit his report to all the newspapers for publication.

Two days before the release of that report I was contacted by the *New York Times.* "On the day of the release we have space on the editorial page for one op-ed piece," the reporter told me. "We want the piece to be written by a positive national and world religious leader. Will you, Dr. Schuller, oblige?"

Sensing my hesitancy to accept this weighty burden, he said, "Dr. Schuller, this will be by far the largest Saturday publication in our history. We're looking for a spiritual word. And we'll need it by Friday afternoon—that's twenty-four hours from now. Can we count on you?"

I prayed for guidance. Then, almost as if without my volition, I said, "Yes, sir; I'll submit a piece."

Had I done the right thing by agreeing to this? I wasn't sure. But on the other hand, my silence suggested that I condoned such flagrant immorality; and I certainly did not.

The Saturday *New York Times* printed my essay as I submitted it. I wasn't proud to write it, but I felt that something had to be said in the name of religion in America.

The President, Facing Isaiah's Challenge
by Robert H. Schuller*

Now that the report of Kenneth Starr, the independent counsel, has been delivered to Congress, the big question is,

---

*New York Times, Saturday, September 12, 1998.

What does the future hold for President Clinton? Will he finish his second term?

To shed light on that, let's go back to the beginning of this term. During a Saturday morning breakfast before the inauguration, I gave the President a Bible verse. He eagerly accepted it, and I could tell he was deeply and profoundly moved. The verse was from Isaiah 58:12: "You shall be called the repairer of the breach and the restorer of paths to dwell in."

The President used that verse as he put his hand on the Bible and took his oath of office on Capitol Hill, and he referred to it again in a prayer breakfast in Washington yesterday. The President has been drawn to this verse, despite failing to live up to its message.

Now nearly two years into his second term, we find our country deeply divided by a breach for which President Clinton himself, by his own admission, is responsible. It is not a breach between Democrats and Republicans, conservatives and liberals, but a breach between those committed to high and honorable morality and those who live on a sliding scale of immorality or amorality. The breach is evident in his own family and his own marriage.

I would like to call upon the President to take a fresh look at the verse in Isaiah and do everything he can to seriously and honestly live up to it. This is a challenge he has never faced up to before. I pray that he is up to it, because it is the most important decision in his entire presidency.

How will the President react and respond to the unfolding scandal now that Mr. Starr's report has been delivered? More damage control? More retrenching? More digging in, holding on, firing back, summoning the tears, in an effort to win back the support of enough people to keep himself in office? Will such actions repair the breach?

The question remains: Should Mr. Clinton remain in office? Fight it through? Wait for the vote to be taken in the Senate on impeachment? Might one vote from one senator prevent the two-thirds vote needed to remove him from office? In such an instance, the President would win, but would it be a noble and honorable victory, or would it be a Pyrrhic victory? Would it help heal the breach in our country, or would it make it deeper, bloodier?

I was most encouraged when the President stated at the prayer breakfast yesterday his willingness to seek wise counsel and professional help as he asks for our forgiveness. His determination to repair the breach that he has caused is likewise most heartening.

I pray that he remains true to his word, however painful and costly it may be for him to do so. I also ask the nation to pray for him. The President must make some hard decisions. These decisions will be painful. But even painful decisions are relatively easy to make if we know the right questions to ask.

The questions I think the President needs to ask himself are these:

1. Which course of action will be in the best interest of my family and my country?

2. Which course of action will begin to close the breach that I have caused by my behavior?

3. Which course of action will restore honor and dignity to me and to all others who have been hurt?

President Clinton must realize that today's decisions are tomorrow's realities. This means we should dedicate our lives to tomorrow, for we all have a responsibility to make tomorrow better than today. Today, we each have mountains to climb and crosses to bear, but none of us can do it alone. We need the love and support of family members and friends and, above all, a strong relationship with God.

The world is facing dangerous times, financially, politically, physically, spiritually and morally. The United States needs to be at its strongest now, more than ever. This country and the world demand honest, moral and humble leadership immediately. We can go no longer without it.

The nation awaits the President's answer.

The big question would not be answered for many tortured weeks. Did the President commit perjury? Did he lie under oath? Would the Senate call for an impeachment trial that could dig out the most sordid details? If so, what would our young people have to see and hear?

The answer to the impeachment inquiry would eventually come down from the congressional committee. It, too, would be released to the entire press. The newspapers of America were on edge.

Then a call came to me from the *Wall Street Journal:* "We're saving a central location on our editorial page for an op-ed piece. We're looking for a spiritual voice. Would you write it for us, please?"

I agreed, and on Monday, December 21, 1998, the *Wall Street Journal* carried the following piece:

Spare Us a Trial, Mr. President
by Robert H. Schuller*

After the independent counsel made his report, I prayed that the President would ask himself three questions: What course of action would be best, first for the country, second for his family and finally for himself? Which decision would

---

Wall Street Journal, Monday, December 21, 1998.

begin to close the breach instead of widening it further? Which response would hold the hope of restoring some honor and dignity to all who have been embarrassed by his behavior? In view of the crisis confronting us now, I ask that he reconsider those three questions again and pray for guidance.

I believe that President Clinton feels deeply the remorse that he has expressed for his immoral conduct and the pain it has caused his wife, his daughter and the nation. I believe that he has a deep love for his country. I believe that in the past, he has worked hard and well to resolve divisive problems, and to promote peace, progress and prosperity. How tragic that a president with such promise and ability has become a polarizing force.

I hope the Senate can find a constitutional way of avoiding a trial; I believe impeachment is punishment enough. But if there is no avoiding a trial in the Senate, then Mr. President, I ask that you look within your conscience and summon the will and strength to end this agony. By stepping aside, you can spare our nation weeks, perhaps months, of divisive debate and repulsive testimony. Your action can help restore public confidence in the moral fabric that sustains our form of government and the moral standards we have a right to demand in our leaders.

Mr. President, I suggest that the following prayer could be most wise and timely: "Lord, give me the guidance to know when to hold on and when to let go and the grace to make the right decision with dignity. Amen."

I had wondered how I would feel about speaking out so publicly about the President's behavior, especially when he had been gracious and kind to me. After all, I wasn't one to "preach" on "sin." But as I read my words in print, I knew that I had done what I should. I had no regrets.

The President and I have spoken and exchanged letters since that dark time, but we have never discussed the entire episode.

In May of 1999 I received the following letter from President Clinton. It was a response to the book I had given him four years earlier, *The Power of Being Debt Free*. I was sitting in my office on the twelfth floor when my secretary brought me the envelope with the presidential seal. I moved my finger along the folded edge carefully. *Why is he writing me?* I wondered. *What does he want?*

Penned in the President's own handwriting, the letter read:

5/6/99

Dear Rev. Schuller:

When I saw this article, I thought of you.

If Congress will adopt my Social Security plan, we'll pay the debt down to its lowest level since *before* World War I by 2015, and we can be debt free by 2018!

When you first mentioned this to me, I didn't think it could be done. As events at home and abroad unfolded, I became a "possibility thinker" on this issue!

I hope you're well.

               Sincerely,
               Bill Clinton

Despite my deep disappointment over his personal conduct, I now admired his courage in reconnecting with me and rewarding me with this letter of affirmation. He had understood the message and caught the vision of the book! In an attempt to regain moral leadership, he was now challenged to set our nation on a more positive course.

XLV

As the century, as well as the millennium, drew to a close, I was astounded to see how much my perspective had shifted. In my early years my world was Sioux County, Iowa, and the Dutch Reformed Church, but now I had a global awareness. Going "somewhere" from "nowhere" had begun to take on a whole new meaning. I was moving further and further into a mindset of religious inclusivity. This was another "edge," to be sure—but I had by now grown comfortable living on that edge. In fact, I liked it!

Early in 1999, preparations were well underway for a pilgrimage I was planning to make on Christmas Eve to an area above Bethlehem known as the Shepherds Hills. Unexpectedly, I received an invitation to pursue a mission of reconciliation amid the age-old religious conflicts of that land. I got the following letter on May 20, 1999:

His Honor Dr. Robert H. Schuller

Greetings and Peace,

I am grateful to God to have this opportunity to meet with you under the banner of faith and peace for humanity, and to serve the message of peace from both Jesus Christ and Muhammad. My desire is to achieve a better understanding between our two great nations and religions and to begin the new millennium with new bridges of love and fraternity between all Muslims and Christians for the benefit of all mankind.

I pray for your acceptance of my invitation and look forward to greeting you upon your arrival. I would love for you to join me addressing the Friday congregation Prayer at 11:00 A.M. on the 17th of December. If this is not possible, then I anticipate your arrival in Damascus from Jordan on the evening of December 20th, 1999. May God's peace and blessings be with you.

Sincerely,
Shaykh Ahmad Kuftaro
The Grand Mufti of Syria
Head of the Supreme Council
of Fatwa

In the world of Islam there are only six Grand Muftis. The pre-eminent Mufti of the six—Shaykh Ahmad Kuftaro—is the Grand Mufti of Syria. So this was quite an invitation.

What I didn't know at the time, of course, was that President Clinton's own efforts in the Middle East would converge with mine. Perhaps no other U.S. leader had put so much personal effort into trying to find a solution for this troubled region that both Jews and Palestinians call home, and where the three major religions of the world had been birthed. And now in December of 1999, at the same time that I would be speaking in Damascus, Mr. Clinton would be hosting the Washington peace talks with Israel's Prime Minister Barak and Syria's President Assad.

Surely this qualified as "repairing the breach"! President Clinton's brief was political, but whether he knew it or not, he was also working to fulfill a biblical mandate.

As my own time of departure for the Middle East drew near, and as news of the pending peace talks began to circulate, I listened with increased interest. Might we, after all of these years, witness this dance of instability resolving into harmony? Maybe it could happen! Maybe we could see the miracle of Christmas renewed: peace on earth, goodwill to all!

I would be the first Christian minister to preach a full-length sermon in one of the world's most influential mosques. It was enough that Grand Mufti Kuftaro wanted me to speak in Damascus during their sacred prayer time, as they began their holy week of Ramadan. But to speak in such a setting, at the same time that such political events were unfolding—that was awesome indeed!

Was I walking into a situation that could prove dangerous at this volatile moment, or could and would God use me to become an ambassador of peace, interacting with other faiths and communicating, respecting, and embracing religious leaders in peace?

Years ago I had written:

Make your dreams big enough for God to fit in.

I looked at this opportunity for service and realized that I never could have predicted nor measured God's definition of "big"—it so far outstretched my own!

It was dark as we touched down in Damascus on December 15, 1999. We had come from Tel Aviv, by way of Jordan.

"You can't fly directly to Syria from Israel," we'd been told. "But Jordan, being neutral, will allow the passage."

Everyone we met seemed both acutely aware of the talks then proceeding in Washington and energized by the prospect of peace. As we had toured the city of Jerusalem, for example, we had heard prayerful optimism from taxi drivers, hotel bellhops, and airport employees. I believed that I could see a divine strategy at work.

Yet there were still hurdles to overcome as all of us—Arvella and I, Carol, Mike Nason, and Vikki Vargas (Mike's wife)—progressed through our itinerary. Because of the heightened political tension between Israel and Syria, we'd had to be especially careful that the Israelis didn't stamp our passports in Tel Aviv. The government officials in Damascus could be given no hint that we'd been in their enemy's land. When the Israeli agents had moved to stamp our visas, we'd handed them blank pieces of paper instead. No problem—all five passports had been left untouched by the Tel Aviv authorities.

But then, as we were hosted by the minister of tourism while on a short layover in Jordan, one of his associates discovered an Israeli stamp in Arvella's passport from a trip four years earlier. Arvella wondered if she should stay in Jordan or return to Tel Aviv. The minister considered ripping out the page. Then we decided to open each passport to the Damascus visa and hold the preceding pages together with a paper clip. Our hope was that it would appear that we were simply well organized and had readied our documents for the convenience of border agents. If all went well, the authorities in Damascus would open each passport to the Syrian page, skipping (in Arvella's case) the page with the Israeli stamp. If it didn't go that way—well . . . we just hoped it would.

As soon as the plane taxied to the Damascus terminal and its door was opened, a man rushed on board and spoke to the stewardess. Then he proceeded down the aisle, questioning each passenger.

When he got to me he said, "Hello. Is your name Dr. Robert Schuller?"

I was a little nervous, but I responded calmly. "Yes, I'm Dr. Schuller."

"Please come with me," he said.

I looked at Arvella, and the official's eyes followed my glance.

"Is this . . ."—he looked at the paper in his hands—"Arvella?"

I nodded.

"Please, she comes too."

The Nasons and Carol jumped from their seats and followed. He looked at them, said nothing, and quickly escorted the five of us from the plane. We were taken into a private room, its walls, ceiling, and furniture covered in complex, arching patterns of lacy gold filigree.

There we were greeted by Bill Baker, our Muslim/Christian mediator, and our nerves calmed. Bill introduced us to a tall, good-looking young man and explained that he was the son of the Grand Mufti. (One day he will be successor to his now eighty-nine-year-old father.) Both men radiated a disarming warmth.

I pulled Bill aside and explained the problem with Arvella's visa stamp.

"Pray," was all he said.

For a long, anxious while we drank strong, spiced Arabic coffee, chatted desultorily, and waited.

I watched Bill go to some of the native men from our host group who greeted us in Damascus. They exchanged concerned words and he left again, this time with a few extra escorts.

Ten minutes later Bill returned with an exasperated expression. He raised his eyebrows at me but gave no further explanation.

After another period of waiting, an official appeared suddenly to escort us through the terminal and into several vehicles, which already had our luggage stowed neatly in the back. I assumed that this was a good sign.

Mike and Vikki were taken to one vehicle with Bill, Arvella, and I to a second with a native host who would be our translator, and Carol to a third with the Damascan hostess. I wondered if this was a good idea? Should I insist that Carol stay with us? But it was all moving too quickly.

Within minutes we were driving through a dark expanse of moonlit desert. Our Syrian driver began to speak excitedly to the translator.

"I cannot believe it! I cannot believe it! Praise be to Allah! I cannot believe it!"

Then the driver glanced at me in his rearview mirror. "Dr. Schuller," he said, "Allah took care of everything! Praise be to Allah!"

The translator explained the driver's enthusiasm. "We took the passports to the officials," he said. "Would you believe they picked up the first passport—Mike's—took off the paper clip, and went through the document page by page. Then they took Carol's passport and went through it page by page. They did the same with Vikki's. Then with yours. Then they took Arvella's, and we were nervous that we were in for real trouble. But Dr. Schuller, that soldier just opened it to the page where the clip was and stamped it! Her passport was the only one that wasn't scoured and studied page by page!"

I put my arm around Arvella's delicate shoulders and pulled her near.

By the time we arrived at the hotel it was late and we were all tired. After the stress of our welcome, I fell asleep with ease.

When I met the Grand Mufti the next morning—Thursday, December 16, 1999—I sensed the presence of God. It was the same feeling I'd had upon meeting Mother Teresa, David Yonggi Cho, Billy Graham, and many other great spiritual leaders. They all exuded an aura of overpowering love.

We were served an incredible meal as the children ran about in play and the Mufti sat as a grandfatherly model of kindness. I was moved as I thought of this place in the context of the apostle Paul's "Damascus road" experience. Damascus, the city of Paul's conversion.

I knew that the country's population of seventeen million was predominantly Muslim, but I wasn't sure what other religions were represented. "Sir, how many Christians are there in Syria?" I asked.

"Oh," he answered, "I would say that there are about seventeen million!"

"How could that be?"

Then he explained, "Muhammad brought the story of Jesus Christ and the Ten Commandments and belief in one God to the Arabs. Before, they had all been infidels—worshiping many, many 'pagan gods.'"

I remembered now how Bill had explained this to me. Muslims were thought to worship a different God named Allah, but really "Allah" was simply the Arabic word for "God," just as "God," in Spanish, is "Dios."

"Muhammad wrote a book called the Koran," the Grand Mufti continued, "in which he shared the faith that Jesus was born of the Virgin Mary and performed miracles and will some day come again to judge all people. He taught that peace was the great message of Jesus. 'Islam' means 'peace.' So in that sense we cannot be good and true Muslims if we are not also Christians."

The next morning, just before dawn, I awaken to the sound of a distant voice wailing in a minor key. It must be four o'clock or so. Yawning, I pull open the drapes and look out over a darkened city that's a haphazard blend of the ancient and modern, a mix of minarets and satellite dishes—white and visible in the lit urban landscape. Large round domes glimmer and shimmer, and tall, thin spires hold the loudspeakers that now blare out over the sleeping city, issuing the Muslim call to prayer. This is a world unlike any other. I can't say that I've seen any other Westerners, other than our party, since our arrival. The strangeness feels fresh and wonderful.

The religion of this land is foreign to me, and yet I feel a kinship, much as I feel connected to my close friends of the Jewish faith. And I think of what a religious environment this is, with a public voice that calls out over the city to remind everyone that there's a Supreme Being superior to and more important than day-to-day drudgery. I feel the call and so I pray, and on my knees I ask the Lord to do something marvelous this day.

Hours later we're racing in a car with such speed and so many near misses that I'm gasping for breath. *Look out!* I cry silently as an elderly woman almost steps in front of us. I'm a nervous wreck, though everyone seems to drive this way here. I make sure that I have my heart medicine along . . . just in case!

We pull up to a large, unpretentious building surrounded by mobs of people. The car behind us, bearing the women, follows close and stops at our bumper. We exit the cars and I glance back toward the other vehicle to catch a glimpse of Arvella, Vikki, and Carol emerging in their head-covering *hijabs*. Our hosts escort us, still segregated by gender, through the murmuring crowd of Syrians.

At the entrance to the mosque, we slip off our shoes and leave them. That act reminds me of the Lord's command to Moses: "Remove the thongs from your feet, for the ground on which you stand is holy." No one enters a mosque with shoes whose soles carry the filth of everyday life; such filth must not be allowed to profane this sacred place.

Mike and I are whisked one way while the women are taken off in some other direction. We're first given a tour of the college at the mosque. I'm shown from room to room, each full of young Muslim men who are busy studying. In some of the classrooms the students ask me questions. Their faces are warm and curious. I feel comfortable and honored in this place.

I see what appear to be Western faces—pale skin, red and blond and brown hair—mixed in with the darker shades. I also see the black skin of Africa, and I see Asians. I remember now the huge ethnic diversity in this religion, and I think of how, when they make their pilgrimage to Mecca, they wear white robes so that there will be no distinction in race or social standing.

In the next room I'm met by nearly three hundred young girls! With them I see Arvella, Carol, and Vikki, who are sitting with their hostesses at the front. I'm asked to say a few words. I look at these young faces, and I think of Carol at that same age in the hospital. I hadn't planned to speak, but with this sudden remembrance of my own daughter, I decide to share her story.

I point out Carol to the girls and tell them how when she was thirteen, right about their age, she was almost killed in a motorcycle accident. I tell the girls how she lost seventeen pints of blood and lived in the hospital for nearly eight months of her childhood. Their faces grow sober, and a few wipe away tears. They look back and forth from me to Carol. Carol smiles and shares glances with the young girls, and they smile at her shyly. I tell the girls how when Carol was lying in the ditch, she sensed the Lord come to her and speak to her a passage from Psalm 23: "Even though [you] walk through the valley of the shadow of death, [you] will fear no evil. [My] rod and [My] staff will comfort [you]."

Although this school visit is one of the highlights of my trip, the primary event is my scheduled appearance in the main sanctuary of the mosque. When the time for that prayer session comes, I look out onto a sea of men, crowded so close together that they're nearly on top of one another, each kneeling reverently on his own prayer rug. Only when I look up to a balcony separated by a long pane of glass can I see the familiar faces I'm searching for—Arvella and Carol and Vikki, crowded among a throng of women.

Bill Baker leans over to me and whispers, "There are seven floors in this mosque, two are underground, and everything is completely full! They say that there are about fifteen thousand people who've come to hear you. They had expected only five thousand. This is amazing, Dr. Schuller!"

I look up again and notice two mezzanines between the ground floor and the balcony holding the women. Faces, faces, and more faces everywhere I look.

Beside me is the kind old Grand Mufti Kuftaro. He begins his address to the people. He talks about the tense situation in the Middle East, and the responsibility of the true Muslim to love and live in absolute peace. Then he turns to me.

With love in my heart, I talk to the assembled gathering about the message of peace that Jesus Christ brought. The text is my north-star verse from Isaiah: "You shall be called the repairer of the breach and the restorer of paths to dwell in." I tell the crowd that they have the wonderful opportunity to participate in this prophecy.

Then I share with them one of the most beautiful statements I've ever heard. The day before, when we met in his home, the Grand Mufti said to me, "Religion is like rain from heaven. It falls to refresh the people. But extremism comes and pollutes the rain and makes it unhealthy for all." I confess that the Christian faith has been guilty of polluting this rain.

I go on to quote the rest of what the Mufti told me: "Extremism discolors the beautiful face of Islam, which is peace. Any Muslim who participates in violence is not a true Muslim and is not promoting Islam. We pray now for peace in the land."

In those moments, standing before a crowd of devout Muslims with the Grand Mufti, I know that we're all doing God's work together. Standing on the edge of a new millennium, we're laboring hand in hand to repair the breach.

Later in the day we visit face-to-face with Christian patriarchs in Damascus. Men with a lineage that could be traced all the way back to the apostle Paul's mission days. The Presbyterian patriarich, who had attended the gathering at the mosque, told me something that moved me deeply. "I was very impressed with what you said at the mosque—that you saw Jesus Christ in the eyes of the Mufti, in the Muslim," he said. "That gathering was a historic event. The peace of God will not be in the land until it's in our hearts.

"There are extremists in every religion: Christian, Muslim, Jew. If their voices are the loudest, the next century could be a century of religious wars. In the last one hundred years we have killed a hundred and fifty million people! The next century *must* be a century of peace, if we are to survive. I pray for the Mufti—that his spirit will sweep through the Muslim world—and I pray that we Christians will embrace those Muslims who, like us, are searching for peace. I believe that we're going to see real peace in Syria soon."

The day ended with a dinner that brought both Muslim and Christian leaders together, laughing and loving and sharing their thoughts and hopes. I was surprised that several Muslims thanked me for the *Hour of Power*. They had seen me on TV, with Arabic text translating my words.

I met once more with the Grand Mufti, truly one of the great Christ-honoring leaders of faith. He agreed to come and be my guest sometime in the near future during *our* holy time of worship in *our* holy gathering place—the Crystal Cathedral. Unfortunately, a heart problem prevented him from making the trip. However, we were truly honored to receive his forty-year-old son, the heir to the throne of the Grand Mufti, and a man who shares his father's beautiful spirit.

As I write these words, our *Hour of Power* is being broadcast every week from the Crystal Cathedral to a new audience—Indonesia, the world's largest Muslim nation. And I'm dreaming a bold impossible dream: that positive-thinking believers in God will rise above the illusions that our sectarian religions have imposed on the world, and that leaders of the major faiths will rise above doctrinal idiosyncrasies, choosing not to focus on disagreements, but rather to transcend divisive dogmas to work together to bring peace and prosperity and hope to the world.

Two days after our final get-together in Damascus, I join the group of travelers with whom I had originally planned my pilgrimage to the Holy Land. I stand on the balcony of a hotel overlooking the Sea of Galilee, where Christ had calmed the storm, walked on the waves, walked with and talked with and laughed with and cried with His disciples.

Beyond the sea, rising in silhouette, lay the hills of the Golan Heights—a major source of conflict between Syria and Israel, Arab and Jew. And as I look at these hills shadowed in the early-morning twilight, I see brilliant color first touch and then embrace them. Rays of gold split the sky, making an elaborate tapestry of purple and pink and red. Sunrise over the Sea of Galilee. A path of gold from those hills to me, across the Sea of Galilee, absorbs me in a vision of peace.

No matter what today brings, I ponder, *as long as there's tomorrow, there's hope.*

On Christmas Eve we stand on Shepherds Hills overlooking Bethlehem. Holding gleaming candles beneath a drizzling sky, and with the Bethlehem lights piercing through the clouds and rain, seven hundred of us who had traveled as a group to walk again through the land where our faith had been born two thousand years before gaze in quiet awe. Two of my children and two of my grandchildren are with me, as well as Arvella and many dear friends. It is a most poignant and holy time—the dawning of a new millennium and the realization of a dream come true.

XLVI

When I first met Victor Frankl, the famed psychiatrist and author of *Man's Search for Meaning,* I asked him, "Dr. Frankl, for you, what's the deepest truth of human existence?"

"Well, my friend," he told me, "for Freud it was the will to pleasure. For Adler it was the will to power. For me it's the will to meaning."

"But Dr. Frankl," I said, "why is that? What lies beneath that will to meaning?"

And he said, "I don't know."

Two years later we would spend three hours together in my Tower of Hope office. "Dr. Frankl, I have the answer to that question I asked you about why we all search for meaning. The answer is *human dignity.* An explanation is found in the Psalms. 'God has crowned me with glory and honor,' says Psalm 8:5. That means we've got royal blood in our veins, and I . . . you . . . the human race—we must have the respect of self and others. Healthy pride is every heart's hunger!"

This conversation runs through my head nearly twenty years later as I stand with the honored guests at the headquarters of the Russian Orthodox Church in Moscow. It's July 2000, and the occasion is the granting to me of an honorary doctorate in psychology and theology from the Orthodox University of Moscow. Knowing that I'm the first American to be so honored by that institution makes the occasion especially sweet, but it's already a glorious moment, the capstone of my lifelong attempt to minister with the healing power of faith, hope, and love.

That same theme of human dignity reappears six months later when Mikhail Gorbachev, the man who more than any other brought an end to the Cold War, is my special guest in the Crystal Cathedral. "Respect is the most important thing," he tells my *Hour of Power* audience. "There can be no freedom without spiritual freedom." That's why, he explains, one of the first and most important reforms of perestroika was the drafting of a law providing for freedom of faith and freedom of religion. "Human beings must be able to choose," he insists.

We talk about his own distinctive faith, how atheism had dominated his life as a member of the Communist Party, and yet how, at the moment of his daughter's birth, he found himself speaking of God. Mrs. Gorbachev had been told that she couldn't have children, and yet there was this beautiful baby girl! And as we talk, that beautiful daughter, now a medical doctor, sits before us with tears in her eyes, a firm believer in Jesus Christ.

I recall sitting in the private audience as Gorbachev himself ended a televised summit with George Bush and Margaret Thatcher and other world leaders, reviewing the end of the Cold War and looking ahead into the future, with these words: "And we must remember Jesus Christ."

Mr. Gorbachev's expressions of faith, as well as the upswelling of religious faith throughout the former communist world, fills me with hope.

"And you shall be a repairer of the breach," God has told me again and again, and I hear His voice echoing throughout this millennial year.

There have been many such experiences in the decades since I first followed God's command—exhilarating moments when I've marveled at the wonder of it all. The farmboy from Iowa, no longer daydreaming by the banks of the Floyd and preaching to cows, but serving God on a worldwide stage.

To have played some small part in healing the rift between East and West, to have worked to heal the rift between Muslim and Christian—these roles have been gifts from God. Looking back, I remember the first time in 1972 when I brought Bishop Fulton Sheen to preach in Garden Grove. We were attempting even then to heal the rift between Protestant and Catholic.

And yet there were rifts to be healed in my own life as well. I experienced a great healing moment in May 1997, when Western Theological Seminary chose me as the very first recipient of their Distinguished Alumni Award. There had been so many times over the years that I'd felt alone, so many times when the criticism had rained down on me. Schuller, that preacher in the drive-in movie theater, that preacher who talked about self-esteem rather than sin, that preacher who wrangled with the National Council of Churches and took the heat. And yet all along I had remained faithful under the discipline of my denomination, the Reformed Church in America. To me, this award from Western affirmed that I had kept that faith.

There were other times when God took me to the mountaintop, letting me play a role seemingly too significant for a boy from a road with no name. That's how I felt each time I visited with Pope John Paul II, when I presided at the funeral of Hubert Humphrey, and when I was part of President Clinton's party attending the funerals of Mother Teresa and Yitzhak Rabin. And yet I could feel the presence of God just as strongly when I conducted a funeral attended by only seventeen people, gathered to remember our beloved Marie Dorler, the woman who had asked to visit with me each year for twenty-seven years, and who may have saved my life; and whenever we offered the Crystal Cathedral for the funerals of local Orange County police officers and firefighters.

Our ministry had grown to encompass both grand adventures on foreign shores and the everyday business of helping everyday people get through the week. No matter how many "mountaintop experiences" God allowed me, there was still work to do down in the valley below.

"Build My church," God had told me. And it looked as if there was more building to do!

In seclusion at my writing refuge in Hawaii, I found myself unable to concentrate on anything but plans for the new Richard Meier visitors' center. I agonized over its slow progression. Never, with any of my other projects, had the waiting seemed so hard. *This is too much for me at my age*, I decided.

First, there was the issue of money—lots of it. Then there was that last remaining house—the holdout. One million dollars for a decades-old twelve-hundred-square-foot dwelling sitting on a piece of property not much bigger than an eighth of an acre?!

Trying to set my self-pity aside, I decided to pray. "What should I do about this?" I asked God. "It's just not responsible stewardship to pay one million dollars for a house that's worth only a fraction of that!"

Then a divine message came into my mind loud and clear. I truly believe that it was a response sent down to me from God. The response came in the form of a question: "Bob, why are you so materialistic?"

"Materialistic?" I exclaimed, shocked.

"Yes," God said. "You're hung up on money. That's being materialistic. Money is nothing; ministry is everything!"

"But I don't have the million dollars," I countered.

"I do," He replied. "Offer the seller of that home what he wants, and the money will come. Trust Me!"

I took God at His word. I went home and offered to buy the remaining house for one million dollars—after nearly ten years of haggling. Now I was *really* on the edge!

But once again, God came through. Within days of signing the deal for the house, I received a check for one million dollars from a total stranger.

No matter how many times I experience miracles, I'm always surprised.

We immediately ordered work to move forward. All thirty-one houses were removed in three months. Streets gone! Driveways gone! Telephone and power poles gone! A clean, clear, beautifully landscaped ten acres could now frame our beautiful open space *forty years* after we'd bought our original site. *Forty years* of dreaming and imagining and now we owned nearly the entire forty acres!

We would still need to find another twenty million to construct the elegant Richard Meier building itself.

Ken Walker is the president of Farmers & Merchants Bank in Garden Grove and Long Beach. He has been our church banker since the beginning of our ministry in 1955.

"You have a plan to finish one of the most beautiful church campuses built in this century," he said to me one day. "Your plan to add the last piece to complete the whole picture is perfect. I'll help you. I'll loan the full twenty million dollars at a half-point below prime."

Our banker clearly had faith!

But faith must be combined with work, and there was plenty of that to go around. Once again I crisscrossed America seeking pledges. Our congregation opened up their hearts and their pocketbooks and gave generously. With the help of donors large and small, the financing was secured and at last Richard Meier and I were able to launch the whole design.

"This campus—it's unbelievable how all the structures will form a finished picture that comes together perfectly," Meier said, adding, "I'm absolutely sure you had it all planned out forty years ago!"

"Not true at all," I answered him.

Surprised, Meier responded, "But the Tower of Hope is at the apex! And it's the tallest building, precisely where we would have placed it if we were designing all the buildings today as one composition." Meier elaborated, "It's as if you had originally planned first the Tower of Hope then the Crystal Cathedral, leaving just a perfect vacant space between these two large-scale structures for one last piece—my grand hospitality center." Meier added, and concluded, "You must have had it all in your mind these last four decades."

"No way!" I insisted, "But Philip Johnson told me something years ago. He said, 'There's another Master Designer who's been in charge of this project.' That's my explanation, Richard. It's too flawless to have happened otherwise—four architects in four decades producing a single collective development in such an inspirational skyline of art in architecture!"

Two months before the groundbreaking I stand on this vacant lot looking to the east—where the sun rises, where tomorrows come from. I walk these grounds early in the morning when only a few maintenance workers and security personnel are here and there doing their work.

The sun lies hidden below the east horizon, and I feel that familiar stirring just before something is about to be birthed. The Tower of Hope is on my right, south of where I stand. The original Neutra sanctuary, now our large fellowship hall, is to my right, slightly east of the tower. The Crystal Cathedral is a little to the left of me, on the north, with the bell-tower—that incredible crystal spire—rising dramatically in the background. Directly on my left is the Memorial Gardens Cemetery, and beyond that is the Family Life Center.

I recall the many times in my childhood I'd stand at the barn, looking at what I thought was such a nice cluster of buildings, arranged to compose one balanced picture of our family farmyard. I hear Dad say to me again, "Harold, someday our dusty dirt road won't be a 'nowhere' road; it will be a 'somewhere' road. That's where dreams are born." And here I am seeing the first rays of sun strike the top of the cross on the Tower of Hope, skim across the high edge of the Crystal Cathedral, flash from the pinnacle of the spire . . . here is my "somewhere" where over the past forty years my dreams were born and all have come true. Then suddenly, I see in my imagination the final piece of art in architecture that will, one day soon—very soon—rise in this space where I now stand. Visitors will come from around the world to be welcomed into this International Center for Possibility Thinking—welcomed by a message that this building proudly proclaims, "*If you can dream it, you can do it!*"

Then into my imagination there enters a little boy standing in almost-new overalls, cuffed up carefully, trying to be neat, his black Sunday shoes looking out of place with the denim. He stands at the dead-end of a long dusty road—the sun rising behind him. He is looking out into a "somewhere" that he knows must exist—a "somewhere" that he will find someday.

Is he looking at me?

Now I see him bounding up and down as he comes toward me, saying, "I'm going to be a preacher when I grow up!"

Then just as suddenly—this is a daydream, after all—he stands beside me at the entrance of the soon-to-be center. His parents follow behind, slowly, pensively, cautiously. I have never met this lad, but I feel as if I have.

His eyes sparkle from a private sun shining within his heart as he asks me:

"Can my dream really come true, too, like yours? Can I really do it?"

I answer, "Listen—I was born at the dead-end of a dirt road that had no name and no number—in a flood. You can go anywhere from nowhere!"

"How?" he asks.

"By living on the edge," I answer.

And then I repeat for him lines I've quoted so often:

"Come to the edge!" God said.
"It's dangerous there," I answer.
"Come to the edge!" God said.
"But I might fall!"
"Come to the edge!" God said.
So I did.
And He *pushed* me!
And I flew!

I imagine all this as the sun suddenly breaks full and bright over the horizon. I lift my arms joyously as I did that first Sunday when I stood in the drive-in and said, "This is the day the Lord has made; let us rejoice and be glad in it." I don't say anything in this perfect moment. Instead, I just close my eyes and lift my face, greeting the dawning of today's promises. Then I hear the Little Dreamer whisper in awe beside me: "How sweet it is to stand on the edge of tomorrow."

EPILOGUE

It's Sunday, March 11, 2001. The weather is typical for Orange County this time of year, a little brisk, the desert air softened by a bit of mist off the Pacific. In fact, the threat of rain prompts me to end my sermon early and move everyone outside to the site just west of the Crystal Cathedral. It's time for the groundbreaking ceremony for our visitors' center, the International Center for Possibility Thinking.

The United States Naval Academy glee club stands tall in their white uniforms singing "Anchors Aweigh" and "America the Beautiful" as the congregation regroups at the building site, led by me and my son, Robert A. Schuller. We're joined by Richard Meier, the architect who designed the building and John Anderson, President of the American Institute of Architects.

Cameras flash as we turn over the first spades of earth. We laugh and shake hands, and everyone cheers. Balloons break free and rise into the sky as we're showered in confetti.

It's a moment of pure joy. This groundbreaking is the final brushstroke in this great scenic picture I've been creating for over forty years.

I know that my dreams could not have come true without the generosity of tens of thousands of individuals, including forty people who made gifts on the million-dollar level. I know that I cannot, I must not forget the thousands of people who have helped make my journey a joy.

To honor these generous friends we will have, in the grand lobby of the visitors' center, an exquisite wall of bricks. But it won't be constructed with just any ordinary brick. No, the wall will be made of twenty thousand bricks of optical glass. Each brick an inch by eight inches in size, and each will bear the name of an individual to be remembered. This entryway will become the wall of dreamers of great dreams.

I recall key individuals who helped make my lifetime dream come true. I will donate bricks with these names who deserve the credit for much of the best in my journey.

The first is Miss Aeilts, who helped make me what I am. A simple teacher of music and drama in my obscure high school in Iowa, she had no idea how she affected me, changed me, helped me discover my talents. She put me in dramatics, made me go on stage. She put me in a quartet, which led to a later college quartet, which led me to California, an American state where the culture—for good or ill—allows persons to dream beyond traditional boundaries. California—the place that gave my dreams freedom to breathe.

Then there is Bud Hinga; he was my history professor at Hope College, the one who said, "Beginning is half done." And Lars Granberg, my psychology professor.

The fourth name is Henry Poppen, another childhood missionary hero. He suffered as a private prisoner of Mao Tse-tung and now is buried in our Cathedral Memorial Gardens.

And there's the name of my Uncle Henry, who by his brave example inspired a young boy from nowhere to dream of somewhere, and to believe that "if you can dream it, you can do it."

I go on with my list, thinking now of all the places my journey has led me. And I realize how all the paths I've taken are being affirmed. My path toward a marriage of psychology and theology has been affirmed by my honorary degree from Moscow Orthodox University. My path toward theological and denominational acceptance had been affirmed when I became the first graduate from Western Theological Seminary in one hundred years to receive the distinguished alumni award.

And now, in this context of dreams and dreamers, John Anderson, president of the American Institute of Architects, steps forward to present to me his organization's inaugural "Lifetime Achievement in Excellence Award." It's an honor that moves me to private tears; all my life I've been addicted to excellence, never yielding to mediocrity, no matter the cost. I will be the very first recipient of this new architectural award, crowning fifty years of effort.

My head spins with the pleasure of the moment, as well as the incongruity. Robert Schuller, whose California ministry began on the tarpaper roof of a drive-in theater's snackbar. Robert Schuller, who came from a road with no name in the middle of nowhere. And yet I'm being honored for my contribution to architecture—an art form that I value so highly. This distinguished body of professionals, the American Institute of Architects, is affirming that in answering God's call to build His church, I have been a good and faithful servant. Building this campus has been at the core of my life's work for forty-six years. That phase of my life's work is coming to final fulfillment, and yet the work will live on, because great architecture "says something." It's not just elegant but *eloquent*. It calls people to strive for excellence. Like a sermon in glass and steel, it uplifts the collective human spirit, and thus it is timeless.

As John Anderson reads the proclamation, tears come to my eyes again. He says that I have "ventured forth where others feared to tread." He calls me "an impassioned advocate . . . of the power of architecture to enrich and elevate the human experience." He speaks of my "unshakable faith" and "unerring instinct." And then he concludes with words that still ring in my soul: he says that I have built "upon this rock a city whose streets are paved with music and whose message is a light unto the world."

Returning for one final moment to my list of dreamers of great dreams, I must single out the name of Arvella DeHaan Schuller. She has been a part of me since the beginning, so I want her with me, as she has always been, as I bring this book to a close.

We were married in the middle of the century, in the middle of the year, in the middle of the month—June 15, 1950. We have lived in love and work together for the last half of the last century of the second millennium. The most exciting time in our lives has been, and continues to be, without a doubt these so-called Golden Years.

If any affirmation is needed for this most important path in my life, our marriage, it can be found in the five remarkable children we have been blessed with, who have chosen equally remarkable mates. Even more remarkable, each of them with their spouses generously and professionally contributes so much to the ministry in his or her own unique way.

With this talented, dedicated, generous, trustworthy, trained family team woven into the fabric of our ministry, I can rest assured that the Crystal Cathedral will continue its influence well beyond my own lifetime. A dream fulfilled!

It is certain that our family has always been my circle of emotional strength. I never could have done it and I could not continue to do it without them.

It's also been our dream that all of our eighteen grandchildren, like our five children, will marry positive believers in Jesus Christ. And now today I imagine our eighteen grandchildren beginning eighteen new families in which Christ is honored, the Ten Commandments are followed, the Bible is read, and prayers are faithfully offered by all in love, every day!

That will be the most meaningful of dreams fulfilled. And I live on the edge of seeing this dream come true.

This journey is my true story. Some of the bruises and blessings, most of the honors, and many of the hurts are not mentioned; they have already been told.

I think of my life as having four quarters, as in a football game. Each quarter is twenty-five years long. As this book comes out, I've finished the third quarter. Now I'm heading into the fourth. Will the Coach let me play the full game? Will I live to be a hundred? I don't know, but no matter what the number, I plan to spend every year dreaming dreams that still lead me to the edge.

So, here I go—pride behind me, love around me, and hope ahead of me, into the rest of my tomorrows!

INDEX